The Concordance Database Manual

M. Alan Haley

Apress®

The Concordance Database Manual

Copyright © 2006 by M. Alan Haley

ISBN-13: 978-1-59059-603-6

ISBN-10: 1-59059-603-X

Printed and bound in the United States of America 9 8 7 6 5 4 3 2 1

Trademarked names may appear in this book. Rather than use a trademark symbol with every occurrence of a trademarked name, we use the names only in an editorial fashion and to the benefit of the trademark owner, with no intention of infringement of the trademark.

Lead Editor: Jim Sumser
Technical Reviewer: Sean King
Editorial Board: Steve Anglin, Ewan Buckingham, Gary Cornell, Jason Gilmore, Jonathan Gennick, Jonathan Hassell, James Huddleston, Chris Mills, Matthew Moodie, Dominic Shakeshaft, Jim Sumser, Keir Thomas, Matt Wade
Project Manager: Sofia Marchant
Copy Edit Manager: Nicole LeClerc
Copy Editor: Susannah Pfalzer
Assistant Production Director: Kari Brooks-Copony
Production Editor: Katie Stence
Compositor: Linda Weidemann, Wolf Creek Press
Proofreader: Elizabeth Berry
Indexer: Valerie Perry
Artist: April Milne
Cover Designer: Kurt Krames
Manufacturing Director: Tom Debolski

Distributed to the book trade worldwide by Springer-Verlag New York, Inc., 233 Spring Street, 6th Floor, New York, NY 10013. Phone 1-800-SPRINGER, fax 201-348-4505, e-mail `orders-ny@springer-sbm.com`, or visit `http://www.springeronline.com`.

For information on translations, please contact Apress directly at 2560 Ninth Street, Suite 219, Berkeley, CA 94710. Phone 510-549-5930, fax 510-549-5939, e-mail `info@apress.com`, or visit `http://www.apress.com`.

The information in this book is distributed on an "as is" basis, without warranty. Although every precaution has been taken in the preparation of this work, neither the author(s) nor Apress shall have any liability to any person or entity with respect to any loss or damage caused or alleged to be caused directly or indirectly by the information contained in this work.

The source code for this book is available to readers at `http://www.apress.com` in the Source Code section. You will need to answer questions pertaining to this book in order to successfully download the code.

I dedicate this, my first published book, to my good friend James McAlister, who had nothing whatsoever to do with the actual publication of this manual, but who so desperately wanted to see his name in print, I couldn't help but take pity on him.

Leave me alone now, James.

Contents at a Glance

Contents

About the Author

M. ALAN HALEY has worked in the fields of information technology and litigation support for approximately ten years. Prior to working at a law firm, he was senior software and database developer for an insurance company in Northern California. His first exposure to the use of databases in support of litigation was to design and create plaintiff-tracking databases for a law firm based in San Francisco. Alan relocated to the East Coast in 2003, and has worked for the law firm Ropes & Gray, LLP since August 2004.

About the Technical Reviewer

SEAN KING has been in the litigation technology support industry for six years. He's a graduate, magna cum laude, of Manhattan College, Bronx, NY, with a degree in philosophy and history. Following his time at Manhattan College, he worked for more than four years at Kaye Scholer, LLP, in the litigation support department. His main responsibilities included providing consultation to clients and attorneys on how best to manage product liability litigation information and documents. He oversaw the design and use of a variety of databases tracking product liability case information, and maintained document review and production databases such as Concordance.

In May 2005, Sean King joined Ropes & Gray, LLP in New York, and is the litigation technology specialist there. He oversees the use of various litigation technology software used in the firm's New York offices, including the use of Concordance as a document review and production tool. He provides consultation to clients, attorneys, and paralegals on document collection, review, and management methods and solutions for each litigation. During his time at Ropes & Gray, LLP, Sean has used a variety of document review applications—both in-house and ASP solution applications.

Sean King is a member of the International Legal Technology Association (ILTA) and the East Coast Association of Litigation Support Managers (ECALSM).

Acknowledgments

Many thanks to Sean King, without whom this book would not be possible. Also, many thanks to the litigation support department at Ropes & Gray—a top-notch group of dedicated and talented professionals.

Introduction

I set about to write this book because, to my surprise, I realized through some basic research that there are no formal source materials to document the use and maintenance of Concordance databases. In fact, this dearth applies to the state of litigation support as an industry and as a whole. This is an issue that must be addressed by the industry itself, one book at a time.

I'm happy (and relieved) to submit to you this initial offering. Given Concordance's permeation of the market, I believe it to be long overdue.

The Concordance software has existed since 1984, originating as a project initiated by Dataflight Software to create a powerful full-text information retrieval system that could be deployed on personal computers. Now, more than 20 years later, Concordance is widely recognized as one of the most useful and fundamental litigation support software packages available.

The ease with which Concordance can be installed and databases created and deployed is a testament to the success of the original aim of the project. A side effect of that ease is that nearly anyone can publish a Concordance database to end users, and in many litigation support departments, *anyone* will. Because of this, databases are often not created efficiently, and Concordance isn't exploited to its full effect.

The end result of the publication of this book will be, I hope, to address the specific needs of Concordance administrators, and also to contribute to the sparse literature of litigation support in general.

CHAPTER 1

Introducing Concordance

Concordance is software that's used for document management and retrieval. It's in a class of software that's used to manage sets of data that have individual objects containing large amounts of text: transcripts, books and bibliographic citations, or other files. This type of software is often referred to as a *full-text information retrieval system*. Document retrieval is facilitated by quick and accurate searches that identify data (text) that matches a user's search criteria. The system then presents to the user only the resulting database objects. If you've used a search engine such as Google or Yahoo! to locate information on the Web, you've used a full-text information retrieval system.

Before discussing how Concordance works in depth, I'll first talk about what *documents* are and how they can be gathered. Documents, which include physical paper and electronic files, can be repackaged from their original format in most circumstances, and loaded into Concordance as individual *document records*. If the original material represented by Concordance, either paper or electronic, contains text, it can be converted into a format that can be retrieved. In this way, Concordance can facilitate the organization, management, and mining of otherwise unwieldy amounts of text.

After collection, administrators of a full-text information retrieval system are often required to create digital representations of the harvested documents. These images are linked to the retrieval system, and are presented to end users in *image viewers*. Because image viewers can be an integral part of the administration of a full-text information retrieval system, I'll briefly discuss what the images are and how they're viewed.

The following brief treatment will present you with some concerns when collecting information that will eventually be loaded into a full-text information retrieval system such as Concordance. The considerations you must take into account when gathering data, particularly pursuant to a legal matter, are too numerous to cover in a single chapter, and individuals who are responsible for collecting documents are advised to research the issue thoroughly. To assist with this, some resources available to the litigation support professional are outlined at the end of the chapter.

Types of Data That Can Be Collected

During the course of a legal matter, legal staff collects various materials for review. Historically, the most common items collected were paper documents. Since the advent of the desktop workstation and computer networks, a new dimension has been added to document collection: files of a digital nature. In the past, before technology in the workplace became common, the amount of data accessible to a single employee might have consisted of documents stored in a few filing cabinets. Collection of material relevant to a legal matter involved making copies of all the pages in the litigant's filing cabinets and carting them off for review. The process might have been demanding in terms of human resources, but the overall strategy of document collection was straightforward.

In the 21st century, with computer technology becoming more efficient in terms of performance and cost, a litigant might have those same filing cabinets, but might also have gigabytes of electronic material—the virtual equivalent of dozens of filing cabinets packed into the space of a desktop workstation. Furthermore, if the litigant is just one of several litigants, and if they have access to a file-sharing network where work-related files are stored on powerful, high capacity servers, the material to be collected might be in the terabytes.

During the lifespan of a legal matter, a legal team might expect to collect all the types of material shown in Figure 1-1, in various stages. Although it's highly irregular that technology support staff will actually do the document collection itself, a litigation support professional can be expected to act as a consultant to legal staff, guiding them when necessary to ensure that material is harvested appropriately. Ultimately, this material can be loaded into Concordance, which can act as a central repository for all data collected during the evolution of a litigation.

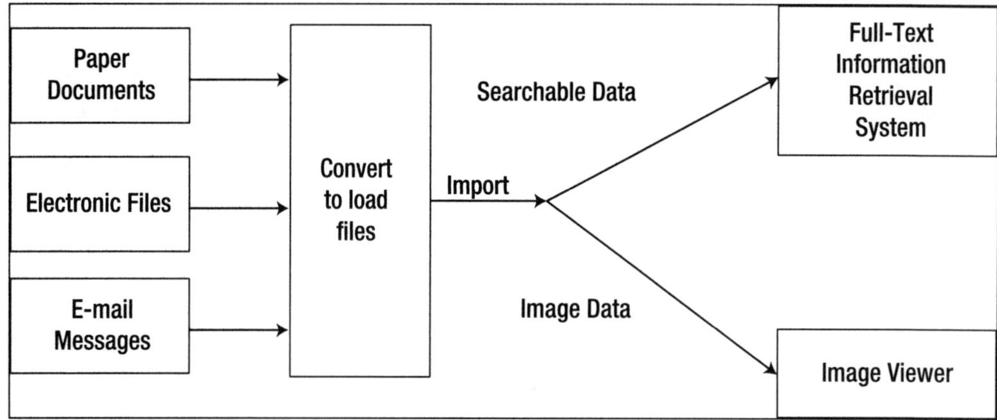

Figure 1-1. *Document collection gathers documents (paper or electronic) that are converted into a format that can be loaded into a full-text information retrieval system. You can use an optional image viewer to view associated images that represent the documents stored in the system.*

Paper

A common type of evidentiary material is paper: letters, contracts, reference guides, notes of meetings, and so on. In this context, the term *document* refers to a collection of pages of paper. For example, a handwritten note on the back of a napkin is a *document* that has a single *page*. On the other hand, a reference manual is also a single document, but might have hundreds or thousands of pages.

The terms *light litigation* and *heavy litigation* are often used to describe the natural state of documents prior to collection. These terms have been created because they help a harvesting team estimate the cost and effort required to organize and manage documents. An ideal set of documents is free of blemishes, consists of typewritten text, is well ordered (perhaps organized by date), and has well-defined document boundaries (each document is terminated by a separator page, or each document is stored in a separate folder). Documents of this type are known as *light litigation* and are relatively easy to manage. Conversely, documents that are jumbled together in no logical order; that consist mainly of handwritten text, or that have handwritten notes in the margins of pages (known as *marginalia*); or that have been bound by heavy staples or blinder clips are known as *heavy litigation.*

If the collected paper is destined for a full-text information retrieval system, it must be scanned by a software program. This process creates digital representations of the source material. In many circumstances, the scanning also attempts to recognize text displayed on the paper using a process known as *Optical Character Recognition* (OCR). The accuracy of this process ultimately determines the accuracy of retrieval: a botched OCR procedure can result in malformed results that are dissimilar from the source material. Even if the OCR procedure is flawless, the source material itself might contain flaws—perhaps there are stains or the paper is ragged—so the converted OCR text will be inaccurate. In general, light litigation comes through OCR with accuracy and heavy litigation doesn't. The better the input, the better the output.

Electronic Files

Now that work environments make common use of desktop workstations, a document collection team is faced with the extra task of determining the relevance of electronic files. This collection might be as simple as harvesting all word processing documents on an employee's computer, or it might be as technologically advanced as making an exact copy of a computer's hard drive that can be restored at a later date on a different computer. In some circumstances, it might even be necessary to obtain a company's full set of backup tapes, which amounts to collecting *all* the data accessible to the involved litigants. Document collection and analysis of electronic files is often referred to as *electronic data discovery* (EDD).

Some initial considerations for a harvesting team include the following questions:

- Is it sufficient just to copy all word processing and spreadsheet documents, or are there other files, such as text files or database programs, that must be collected as well?

- Does the nature of the legal matter require the collection of additional file types created by Computer-Aided Design (CAD) software or tax preparation programs?

- How does a team determine which files are relevant? Is it preferable to take all *potentially* useful documents (this could amount to hundreds of thousands of files) for later review? Or, if possible, should there by an initial analysis, on site, to cull files that are clearly of no value?

- How does one identify files that are potential duplicates, and what methods should be used to remove or otherwise flag these duplicates?

A harvesting team faces these types of questions when collecting paper documents as well. However, the team doesn't have to worry about altering the actual documents themselves when the team makes copies for later review: a clean photocopy of a document is generally accepted as an exact representation of the original material. However, just the act of copying digital files from one medium (perhaps a hard drive) to another (perhaps a DVD) can alter file properties, such as the date a file was created, or the date a file was last modified. If date ranges are important, the harvesting team must ensure that when files are copied, the new files retain the same file properties as the originals.

When using a full-text information retrieval system, staff will find that some of the electronic files gathered by a collection team, although potentially relevant to the legal matter overall, cannot be reasonably imported into a full-text information retrieval system. A file that has a .ZIP extension, for example, could well be an archive file created by the program WinZip (http://www.winzip.com/). The archive file itself might contain other files that have been compressed to minimize the amount of space they collectively occupy on the user's hard drive. The individual files might be word processing documents, and *can* be loaded into a full-text information retrieval system, but must be extracted from the compressed file first. In fact, the compressed file might contain other compressed files, so that several levels of extraction might be required. The archive in Figure 1-2 illustrates this. The harvesting team must decide in advance how to identify and handle files of this type.

■Note   When creating compressed archives using WinZip, the properties of files included in the archive, such as the date a file was created, and the date a file was last modified, are retained.

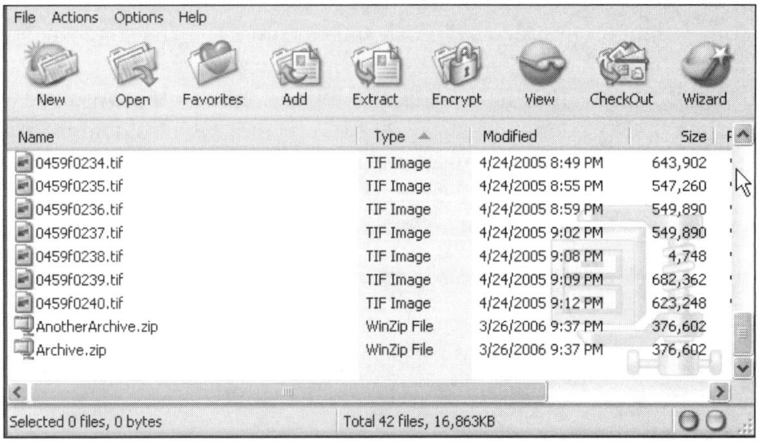

Figure 1-2. *This WinZip archive contains several files, some of which might or might not contain text that can be extracted via an OCR process (the TIF images), and some that are themselves archives (AnotherArchive.zip and Archive.zip).*

Other file types that may be relevant to a legal matter might present other challenges as well. For example, Microsoft Access databases are single files that commonly have an .MDB extension, but when opened, contain a variety of objects that are unique to the program, such as tables, queries, and reports. The database in Figure 1-3 contains two tables. These individual objects might contain important information, but cannot be imported into most full-text information retrieval systems separately without some additional step that breaks the single file apart. The team might wish to examine such a database file in the application in which it was designed (often referred to as the *native* application), and it might wish to import a document record into its full-text information retrieval system to record the existence of the file for reference purposes. Unless specific steps are taken to break the file apart, though, the team won't be able to load and search the database file without that extra step.

Figure 1-3. *This Access database is a single file that contains other objects, such as the two tables that are displayed in the illustration: billrate and covstat. If the file were imported into a full-text information retrieval system without additional processing, the information in these tables might be lost to the system's search facility.*

Some file types cannot have plain text in them converted into a searchable format because they have no plain text. Many files on a workstation are *compiled* (a process in which a series of instructions written by a programmer is translated into machine language) in a *binary* format (a numbering system that uses the values of 0 and 1) that represents data that can be easily processed by a computer. The program Notepad.exe, for example, which is used to launch the Microsoft Windows program Notepad (a simple text editor) is intended to be opened and activated by a user, and is then used to view and edit other files that themselves contain plain text. A harvesting team might want the program file, Notepad.exe, to have a document record in its text retrieval system for reference purposes, but the record itself representing the file Notepad.exe contains no searchable text. Figure 1-4 illustrates the characters in Notepad.exe that appear when opened with a text editor.

Because of these additional considerations, a harvesting team will want to assess the file types it expects to gather, and to define which file types are to be excluded, or which require special treatment.

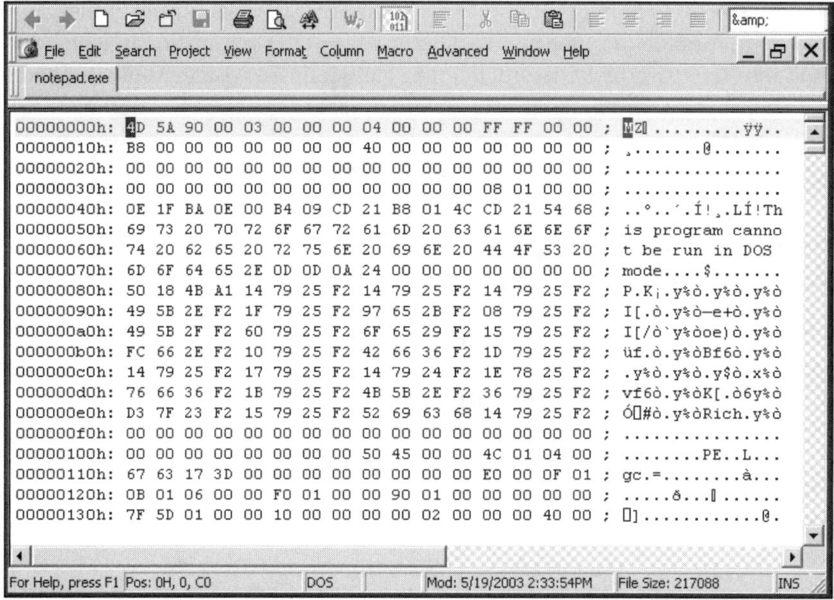

Figure 1-4. *This is how the file Notepad.exe looks when opened with a text editor—in this example, UltraEdit. Little of the contents of this program file is capable of being extracted by an OCR process, as the program has been compiled into machine language.*

E-Mail

E-mail messages are electronic files that, because of their omnipresence in society, have become vital during legal discovery. Because of the peculiarities of their format, they require additional care during collection.

There are numerous types of e-mail clients. A *client* is software that's used to send, retrieve, and display e-mail messages. E-mail clients also grant the user the ability to send and access *attachments*, which are separate files that are associated with an e-mail message. Examples of e-mail clients include Microsoft Outlook, Microsoft Outlook Express, IBM's Lotus Notes, and QUALCOMM's Eudora. There are also Web mail services (http://www.hotmail.com, http://www.gmail.com, http://mail.yahoo.com) that enable a Web browser such as Netscape Browser or Microsoft Internet Explorer to act as an e-mail client. Furthermore, some Web mail can be accessed (and exported) from standalone e-mail clients.

Although it's possible for many e-mail clients to operate autonomously on a user desktop workstation (assuming they have a valid connection to the Internet), the most common deployment of e-mail solutions in an office environment is to use a centralized e-mail server. Outgoing and incoming messages are routed through the server, which may store the messages in distinct files or directories that represent separate e-mail users, and are commonly referred to as a user's *inbox*. The e-mail server may retain a user's messages for a time and up to a certain limit, or messages can be routed through the server and down to the user's client permanently, and no copy of the message is stored on the server after delivery. The way that an e-mail client is configured determines where a harvesting team will gather e-mail data, either on a litigant's desktop workstation, or on a network server.

Although an e-mail message may be presented using plain text, the data in a message can also be formatted to display various font styles. A common way to introduce advanced formatting options is for a message to contain *rich text*. Rich text is a set of instructions that a compatible e-mail client can use to modify font size, font face, and font weight. If the client isn't compatible, formatting considerations are abandoned, and the message is viewed as plain text. The term *render* is often used to describe the process in which a client interprets formatting instructions, and applies them to data.

E-mail messages, particularly those that are routed by Web mail hosts, can also contain *tags* used in the HyperText Markup Language (HTML), which is similar to rich text in that it's used to alter the presentation of e-mail messages. (HTML is also the standard in which Web pages are coded for proper rendering in a Web browser.)

Note Concordance is capable of displaying rich text so that the original format of an e-mail is retained. It cannot render HTML tags in the same way that a Web mail client does.

The type of e-mail client also determines how e-mails are stored as digital files. Depending on the configuration, Microsoft Outlook can store e-mail messages in files that have a .PST extension. Microsoft Outlook Express stores e-mail messages in a file with a .DBX extension. IBM's Lotus Notes uses a file with an .NSF extension. What's common to the formats is that all e-mail messages for the user are stored in a single file that can be regarded as an e-mail message database. To access individual messages, a user must open the file with the appropriate e-mail client.

Other formats are possible. For example, Microsoft Outlook can export individual e-mail messages as separate files with .MSG extensions, where each file corresponds to a separate e-mail message. In fact, almost all e-mail clients feature a way to export some or all e-mail messages to a separate export file or files, which can then be imported into a full-text information retrieval system. When harvesting e-mail messages, the collection team must confer with knowledgeable technical staff to determine the most effective method to gather data.

Note Concordance is configured to import Microsoft Outlook .PST files and to treat each e-mail message as a separate document record. During this process, separate attachments are extracted and associated with the document record. Concordance can also import separate .MSG files as individual document records. Other e-mail file formats, such as .DBX and .NSF, cannot be imported into Concordance in their native form, and require conversion to a format acceptable to Concordance prior to importation.

Transcripts and Depositions

In addition to standard features that manage document types and data associated with them, Concordance also has the ability to import and manage specific instances of document records known as *transcripts* and *depositions*. Although not normally part of data harvesting, transcripts and depositions are an important part of the lifecycle of a legal matter. Having ready access to them in a searchable form can be useful to a legal team.

A transcript is a typewritten record. In the legal industry, transcripts are drafted by court reporters during a legal proceeding. Outside a court of law, legal staff may record witness testimony in a similar manner, and these written records are known as depositions.

Transcripts and depositions are well-defined and highly structured documents. Page size is usually 8.5″ × 11″; individual pages are numbered; individual lines of text are double-spaced, and are also numbered. Although there's some variation, each line usually contains no more than 60 characters, and each page usually contains no more than 25 lines per page. Often, each line contains a timestamp. Transcripts and depositions may contain *Q&A pairs* that represent questions and answers. An example of a transcript is displayed in Figure 1-5.

```
 1    UNITED STATES DISTRICT COURT

 2    FOR THE DISTRICT OF DELAWARE

 3    Case No. xx-xxx-xxxx

 4
      ACME, INC.,
 5
                    Plaintiff,
 6
      vs.
 7
      YOYODYNE INDUSTRIES, INC.,
 8
                    Defendants.
 9
                         John Bigboote
10                       4335 Patann St.
                         Jackson, MS
11
                         April 1, 2000
12                       11:30 a.m.

13         Deposition of BUCKAROO BANZAI, II, pursuant
      to Agreement, before Emilio Lizardo, Registered
14    Diplomate Reporter and Notary of the State of
      Colorado.
15
```

Figure 1-5. *An example of a transcript*

If a transcript or deposition is in an electronic format, and if that format is acceptable to Concordance, the program can import the file as a document record, as in Figure 1-6. Procedures for importing and searching transcripts and depositions are described in greater detail in Chapter 6.

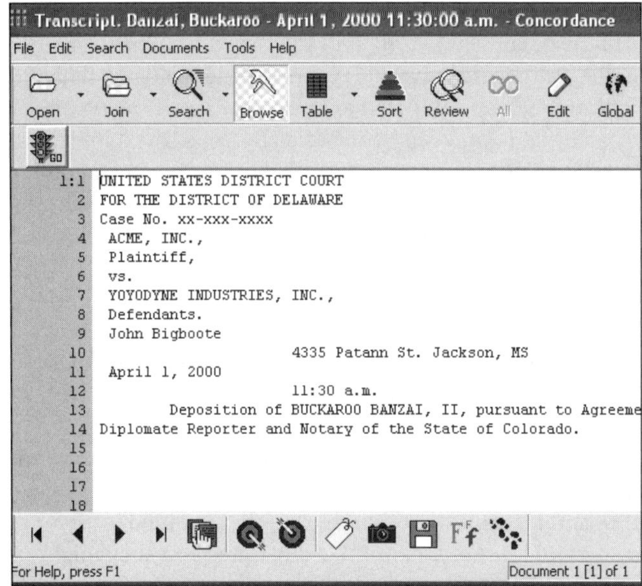

Figure 1-6. *The same transcript that's displayed in Figure 1-5, imported into Concordance. The contents of the transcript can now be searched.*

Image Data

Some full-text information retrieval systems are integrated with an image viewer that displays a graphic image representing what a document looks like. The image viewer might be built into the software program itself, or it might be separate software that synchronizes with the search and retrieval system.

Note The company that manufactures Concordance—Dataflight Software, Inc.—also manufactures a separate image viewer, Opticon, that can synchronize with Concordance. It isn't a requirement; Concordance can operate independently of any image viewer.

Regardless of how an image viewer is integrated with a full-text information retrieval system, the purpose of the viewer is to display an exact representation of a document record. If the document record originated as a digital file, the image viewer can act to launch the file's native application, thereby displaying the file in its original form. In other circumstances, however, document records that originated as digital files are converted to graphical images, and those images are displayed instead. If the document record originated as a paper document, the image viewer can open a graphical image that's a picture of the original document.

The advantage of granting the user the ability to view the original document is that the user can see an exact representation of the document record, and view aspects of the record that have no digital representation in the search and retrieval system. Consider a typed letter that has handwritten marginalia, and that has been subjected to an OCR process. The typed portions of the text are easily recognized by OCR, and can be searched by the full-text information retrieval system. The marginalia, however, written by hand in what might be questionable penmanship, might not have been extracted by OCR and are therefore not retrievable. Users can see this additional text in the document if they have access to a photo-quality rendition of the original document record.

Another example of how an image viewer can expand the usefulness of a full-text information retrieval system is if document records represent drawings, such as schematics or blueprints. Other than a document title or document author, these documents might have little text that can be extracted by OCR. The drawings would be inaccessible to the user without an image viewer.

Giving users access to images instead of the original files grants them the ability to record comments on the images without defacing the original. This is particularly useful if the document records originated as digital files, and it's important that they not be modified in any way. These comments are often known as *annotations*. Figure 1-7 illustrates how they might appear on an image. There might be times when a review team wishes to exclude, or *redact*, sections of an image so that other parties can't view sensitive information when document records and images are shared with other companies or firms.

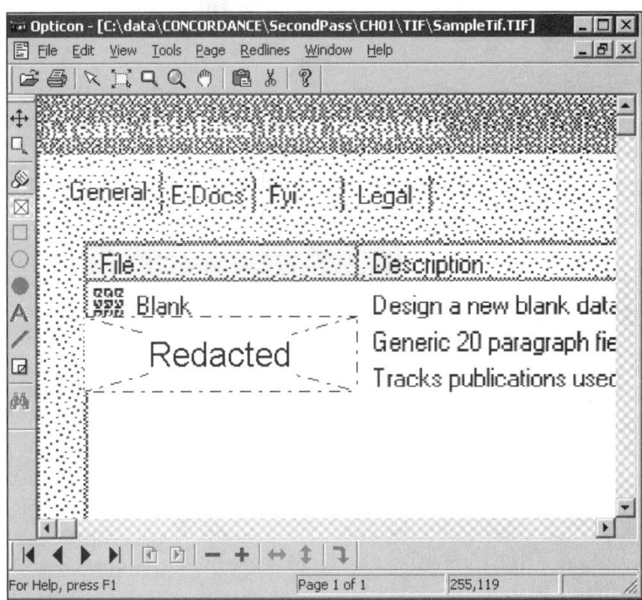

Figure 1-7. *An example of a graphical image displayed in an image viewer (Opticon) that has annotations and redactions. The label E-Docs has been highlighted by the use of an empty rectangle; the label File has been highlighted by a transparent yellow rectangle; a section of text has been hidden entirely by a rectangle labeled with the word REDACTED.*

Graphical images use *data compression algorithms* that translate colors and hues into digital information. Different types of compression exist. *Lossy data compression* is an efficient method to digitize images. However, it involves some loss of detail, so the resulting graphical image, although an accurate representation of the original, isn't an exact rendition. The *Joint Photographic Experts Group* (JPEG) method of lossy compression is a common form of digitizing images so that the resulting file size is small. Images created using the JPEG standard are ideal for transmission over the Internet, when bandwidth is a concern. *Lossless data compression* allows a more precise rendition of the original: the digital image is more detailed, but the overall file size of the image is larger when compared to the same image created using lossy compression. The *Tagged Image File Format* (TIFF) algorithm is a popular lossless compression technique that has become a standard in document imaging. Although TIFF images can display color, many administrators responsible for the maintenance of document management systems that use an image viewer prefer TIFF images that are monochrome (black and white) to minimize file size. This is particularly desirable when a full-text information retrieval system contains hundreds of thousands of document records that link to millions of images.

■**Note** Opticon can open both JPEG and TIFF images. It can also open bitmap files (.BMP), GIF files (.GIF), PCX files (.PCX), and CALS files (.CAL or .MIL).

Additional Resources

Litigation support is an industry in flux. Technological evolutions have broadened the responsibilities of litigation support professionals so that they must have expertise, not just about legal procedures, but also about the effect of technology on those legal procedures.

Resources do exist, though the dynamic nature of the industry means that sometimes those resources are difficult to locate for the uninitiated. A summary of some of those resources follows, with associated Web sites, when applicable.

Litigation Support Department

Litigation Support Department (Ad Litem Consulting, 2006) is a 297 page book written by Mark Lieb, a professional in the litigation support field. Mr. Lieb is cofounder of the Litigation Support Vendors Association (LSVA), a nonprofit organization dedicated to the industry.

Lieb's book covers a broad array of topics of interest to the litigation support professional, ranging from the standard corporate hierarchy of a company that might contain a litigation support department, to assigned roles and expected responsibilities of litigation support employees, budgets, and common software tools. The book contains sections devoted to paper and electronic document collection during the life of a legal matter, and is an excellent reference.

Sarbanes-Oxley

On July 30, 2002, the Sarbanes-Oxley Act was signed into law, updating financial reporting requirements for companies that do business in the United States. Named after its sponsors, Senator Paul Sarbanes and Representative Michael G. Oxley, the law set guidelines for accounting oversight and corporate financial disclosure, among other things. In response to the act, the U.S. Securities and Exchange Commission (SEC) itself issued a series of regulations that cover corporate accountability.

The Sarbanes-Oxley Act set guidelines for the treatment and retention of electronic data to which companies must conform to be considered compliant. For example, courts treat e-mail messages as legitimate business records, and those files must be retained. Although most companies already have some sort of backup policy that governs the retention of e-mail messages, those policies might rely on the recycling of backup tapes, where older data is overwritten with a newer backup. In some circumstances, Sarbanes-Oxley regards this as a conscious decision to destroy data that's potentially relevant to any future investigation.

The complete text of the law is accessible from the Government Printing Office (GPO) Web site in a PDF format: `http://frwebgate.access.gpo.gov/cgi-bin/getdoc.cgi?dbname=107_cong_bills&docid=f:h3763enr.tst.pdf`. A document-collection team tasked with harvesting electronic data from a client should have a good understanding of the rules and guidelines set forth in the act to avoid any potential liabilities during the collection.

Professional Organizations

There are many regional societies for litigation support professionals. Membership usually involves a small fee. However, the ability to meet with other professionals in the litigation support field can be invaluable in terms of exposure to the problems (and solutions) faced by others in the industry, particularly as they relate to managing a successful document collection.

- *Atlanta Association of Litigation Support Managers*: `http://www.aalsm.com/`

- *The Chicago Association of Litigation Support Managers (CALSM)*: `http://www.calsm.org/calsm/calsm.asp`

- *East Coast Association of Litigation Support Managers (ECALSM)*: `http://www.ecalsm.com/`

- *International High Technology Crime Investigation Association (IHTCIA)*: `http://www.htcia.org/`

- *Minnesota Association of Litigation Support Managers (MALSM)*: `http://www.malsm.org/`

Online Resources

Given the ease of sharing information on the Internet, the Web has become an ideal medium for litigation support professionals, and other personnel who use full-text information retrieval systems, to share information.

- *Litigation Support Vendors Association (LSVA)*: `http://www.lsva.com`

  The LSVA operates a Web site that includes a forum moderated by professionals working at companies that specialize in litigation support services, and also moderated by software companies that produce programs used by litigation support professionals. Individual forums include Electronic Discovery, Paper Discovery, and Computer Forensics.

- *Yahoo! Groups*: http://groups.yahoo.com/

  Yahoo! offers a series of industry-related groups dedicated to litigation support. One of them, the Litigation Support List (http://finance.groups.yahoo.com/group/litsupport/), has more than 5,000 members and is a listserv (a mailing program for communicating with people who have subscribed to the same list) that allows members to post questions and offer solutions and opinions. Some of the groups, such as litigation_support (http://groups.yahoo.com/group/litigation_support/), are affiliated with a professional society; litigation_support is the official online forum of the LSVA.

- *Law.com*: http://www.law.com/

  Law.com is a Web site run by ALM (http://www.alm.com/), a media company that serves a variety of professions, including law, real estate, and finance. The Law.com Web site itself is a clearinghouse of information of interest to legal professionals. The Web site's Legal Technology section (http://www.law.com/jsp/ltn/index.jsp) offers information and articles about software, hardware, and EDD.

Summary

This chapter has introduced the concept of a full-text information retrieval system, of which Concordance is a specific example. Document collection, both of paper documents and electronic files, is an integral, albeit preliminary, aspect to administering a full-text information retrieval system. This is especially true when the application is used to manage information pursuant to a legal matter.

After documents have been collected, litigation support staff might be called upon to oversee the creation of digital images that represent document records. These images are accessible to end users by means of a companion image viewer. The image viewer acts in conjunction with the full-text information retrieval system so that images are synchronized with documents that the system has retrieved. Concordance's companion viewer is called Opticon, though other viewers exist, and can be used in lieu of this program.

The rest of this book is devoted to these general topics as they relate to Concordance itself, and expands upon them, so that you'll obtain a thorough knowledge of the administration of Concordance databases.

CHAPTER 2

Using and Installing Concordance

In the preceding chapter, I introduced the concept of a full-text information retrieval system. In this chapter, the discussion is more specific to Concordance itself. Prior to a detailed treatment of administrative concerns in future chapters, you'll benefit from a generalized discussion of how the software is used and some of the considerations that go into deploying it.

You no doubt have a series of preliminary questions, which this chapter will address. Just what is a Concordance database? How can it be used? How do users interact with a database? How does data get into a Concordance database? Are there limitations to how much data Concordance can manage? Are there hardware requirements? Once you understand the scope of the software—the topic of this chapter—you'll easily be able to follow an expanded discussion of these topics in later chapters.

Finally, I'll take you step by step through installing the software, with screenshots of each Windows dialog encountered during the procedure.

Note Throughout this book, the term *Windows dialog* is used to describe interactive screens that request information from a user. Dialogs include message boxes and other windows that prompt a user to provide input required for the continued operation of a program, such as choosing a file to open.

What Concordance Does

Concordance is, literally, a base for data, and although the software can accurately be classified as a full-text information retrieval system, it can also be referred to as a *database management system* (DBMS). A DBMS is software used to formally structure a collection of related data. In more general terms, it can be any system designed to organize information. You're already familiar with several types of database management systems. A desk drawer in which important papers have been alphabetized and stored for quick retrieval is an example of an analog (nondigital) DBMS. So, too, is an Excel workbook, with several worksheets, each containing well-ordered columns and rows. Each column represents a definition of data (the column header or label), and each row contains specific values shared across columns and common to a single object: a record.

Like a desk drawer, Concordance is used to centralize information. And like Excel, Concordance stores elements of data in well-defined digital units. In Excel, these structures are referred to as *cells*. In the more general context of a digital database system, such units of data are referred to as *fields*. A collection of fields (analogous to columns of data in Excel) across a row is used to describe a single object. This object can be anything: a bibliographic citation (common fields might be named PUB_YEAR or PRIMARY_AUTHOR); a recipe (common fields might be named INGREDIENTS or RECOMMENDED_SERVINGS); or an employee (common fields might be named FIRST_NAME or SSN). In the legal industry, rows of data in a Concordance database frequently represent evidence that has been collected pursuant to a legal matter: the paper documents or electronic files described in the previous chapter. Common fields might be named SOURCE, DOC_DATE, or DOCUMENT_TEXT.

Beyond simply storing data, Concordance has features that allow for the quick and efficient retrieval of textual information stored in records. Although there are many types of data in Concordance, two fundamentally important types are *coded data* (sometimes referred to as *fielded data*) and *full-text data*. In a Concordance database, full text refers to the words, sentences, and paragraphs contained on the pages of documents. Coded data refers to other elements that pertain to document records that might or might not be contained in full text, but that have been placed in unique fields to streamline the organization (and eventual retrieval) of document data.

To facilitate retrieval, Concordance adds an extra dimension to the storage of data in fields: it requires the administrator to define what type of data is to be contained in a field, and is an important part of database design. This is called *data typing*, and assists Concordance in storing information efficiently. Thus, if a field is named CREATE_DATE, and describes the date on which a document record was created, an administrator can and should assign to the field the data type of DATE. There are four types of data in Concordance: DATE, NUMERIC, TEXT, and PARAGRAPH. As will be demonstrated in later chapters, the type of data in a field defines the method in which data in that field can be retrieved most efficiently.

A collection of many rows of data, where each row contains one or more fields, and where all rows combine to describe a universe of related objects, is known as a *database*. In the same way that you can use the Microsoft application, Word, to create and manage a potentially unlimited number of word processing files, you can use Concordance to create and manage an unlimited number of databases. And, like Word for Windows, where some documents may be common to a single subject matter, you can use Concordance to create multiple databases that describe various aspects of a more generalized matter. In a law firm, all documents collected for a client might be stored in one database, while all documents provided by opposing counsel might be stored in a separate Concordance database. A program like Word is used to administer word processing documents; a program like Concordance is used to administer entire databases.

■**Note** Although a program like Word can create a word processing document in a single electronic file (usually with a .DOC extension), a Concordance database is comprised of a series of related files (each with a different file extension) that work together to define a database. Concordance creates these files automatically, so that an administrator need not be concerned with their interoperability.

A Closer Look at Concordance Database Structure

To give an overview of how Concordance manages data, I'll briefly discuss the hypothetical structure of a Concordance database to illustrate by example. Recall that you can use a database management system to describe just about any type of object: bibliographic information, recipes, or employee data. The same is true of Concordance. However, one of the most common applications of a Concordance database is to store information relating to a set of documents. The following discussion relates primarily to how Concordance manages document data, where a separate record in a Concordance database represents a separate document. The following design choices aren't requirements; different Concordance databases used for other applications may be structured in a fundamentally different manner. In fact, one of the most important aspects of administering a Concordance database begins before a database exists, and involves the definition of which types of fields will be in the database, how they will be named, and what type of data will go in them. Database design is a crucial and preliminary aspect of database administration.

A Sample Concordance Database

When used to manage documents, a Concordance database is normally designed to track them by means of a *document control number*. These values define *boundaries* (beginning and ending pages) of each document. To that end, you need to assign the pages in documents an alphanumeric identifier. This numbering system can be as simple as a different number for each page (1, 2, 3, . . . *n*). Alternatively, it may use an alphabetic prefix or suffix to identify some common characteristic shared by a set of documents: A00001, A00002, . . . , A*n* to describe pages collected from one source, and B00001, B00002, . . . , B*n* to describe pages collected from another source. This consideration is most relevant when documents from different collection sources are stored in a single Concordance database. Although there are exceptions, the numbering system must be unique so that no two pages in a document database share the same control number.

■**Note** If control numbers aren't unique, a Concordance database can be said to contain duplicates; that is, two or more documents share the same control number. In some circumstances—perhaps when tracking different iterations of the same document—this might be desirable. However, even when duplicates are allowed in a database, you should add an additional field to a document record that contains a unique identifier per record.

During the processing of documents, while converting them into an electronic format that's acceptable to Concordance, the *beginning control number* and *ending control number* of each document must be known, because these values define where a document—and therefore a database record—begins and ends. In this type of application, there should be at least two fields, which you can name BEGDOC and ENDDOC, respectively.

■Note An administrator assigns names of fields during the design of a Concordance database. Field names used throughout this book are suggestions, not requirements. In general, field names are alphanumeric, are descriptive of the data contained in a field, and—specific to Concordance—can be no more than 12 characters long.

In addition to document boundary fields, other fields might be desirable. For example, the type of a document might be stored in a separate field named DOC_TYPE, and might contain discrete values such as *memo, letter,* or *invoice.* For an application that manages document data, such fields aren't a requirement, but may assist users with grouping sets of documents together.

Ultimately, users of a document management database might wish to locate document records by searching for certain words and phrases contained in the text of documents. Another desirable field is one that contains this text. Unlike a BEG_DOC, END_DOC, or DOC_TYPE field, which contains chunks of data of finite length, full-text data for a document might contain tens or hundreds of thousands of characters (see Table 2-1). (If given the TEXT data type during initial database design, Concordance mandates that data in fields is allowed up to 60 characters.) Fields that contain the entire textual contents of a document are given a special data type, PARAGRAPH. An appropriate name for this field might be OCR.

Our database now has four fields (see Table 2-1).

Table 2-1. *Four Database Fields for Managing Document Data*

Field Name	Data Type	Sample Data
BEG_DOC	TEXT	0000001
END_DOC	TEXT	0000010
DOC_TYPE	TEXT	Memo
OCR	PARAGRAPH	When in the Course of human events it becomes necessary for one people to dissolve the political bands which have connected them with another and to assume among the powers of the earth, the separate and equal station to which the Laws of Nature and of Nature's God entitle them, a decent respect to the opinions of mankind requires that they should declare the causes which impel them to the separation . . .

Interacting with the Sample Database

When you open a database in Concordance, you're given three primary methods of interacting with and viewing data. You use Concordance's *Browse view* to view the entire contents of a single record. You use Concordance's *Table view* to view a series of records, where the abbreviated contents of each record are displayed as a single line. These views may be combined in a split screen so that you can select a record in *Table view* by clicking it, which causes the entire contents of that record to appear in *Browse view* (see Figure 2-1).

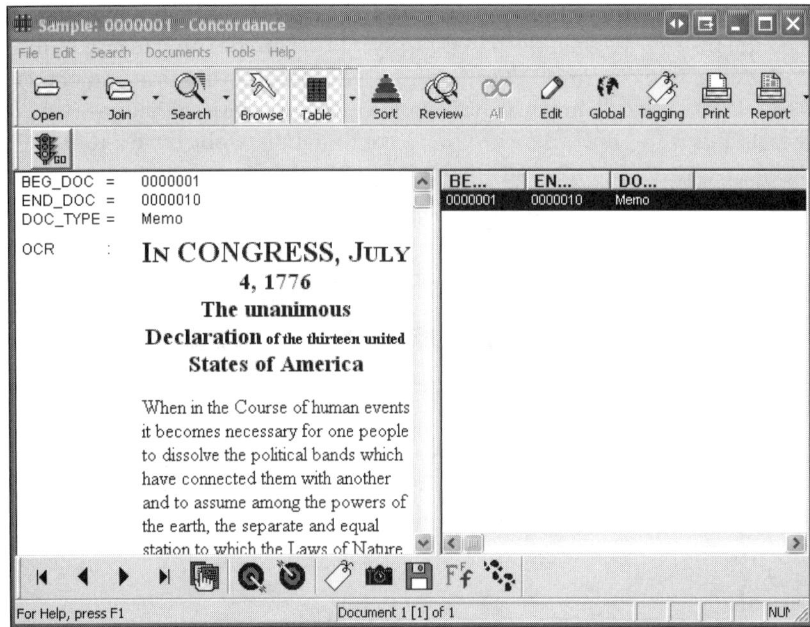

Figure 2-1. *Split screen with Browse view in the left pane and Table view in the right pane. Browse view enables you to view the entire contents of a document record. Table view enables you to see several records listed in a series of rows. In this example, just one record is highlighted.*

Concordance allows you to add your own data to documents. You can create a document-level *tag*, name it accordingly, and then use that tag to designate specific sets of documents. You can create multiple tags and then apply combinations of them to several records, as in Figure 2-2. Groups of documents tagged in this way can be easily retrieved as subsets of all records contained in the database.

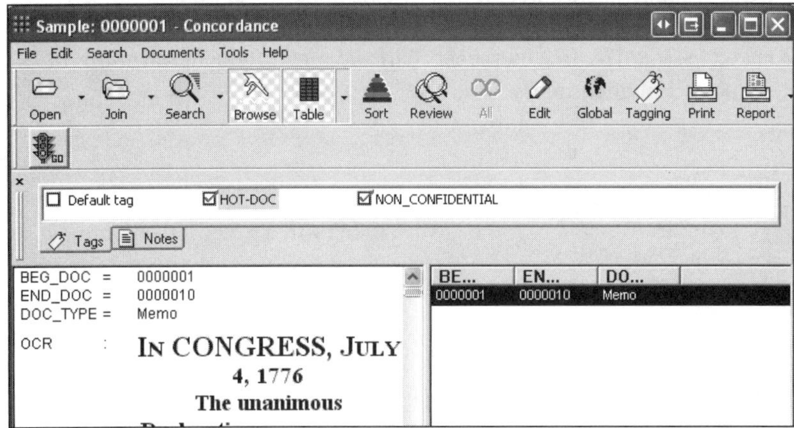

Figure 2-2. *Document-level tags. This document has been tagged with both the HOT-DOC and NON_CONFIDENTIAL tags.*

You can also use tags to designate sentences or phrases in the body of a document, in a manner similar to document-level tagging. Used in this way, the tag applies only to a section of text, and is known as *Issues* (see Figure 2-3). Furthermore, you can add your own subjective comments to selected sections of text, known as *Notes*, and you can retrieve this subjective data through searches. In this way, Concordance allows a combination of objective and subjective searches to keep a team continuously advancing in its research. No work need be duplicated or wasted.

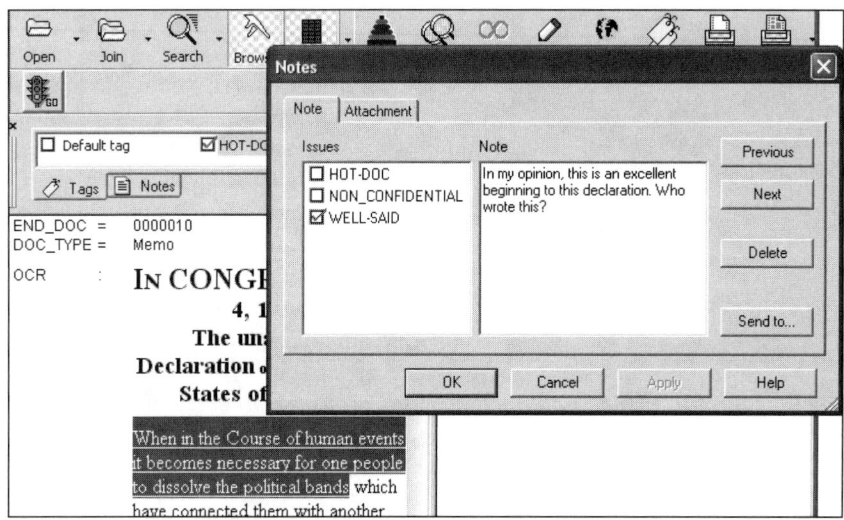

Figure 2-3. *A tag used as an issue: the section of text "When in the Course of human events…" has been given the WELL-SAID issue tag. A user has also added a comment, known as a Note. This annotation applies only to the highlighted section of text.*

Concordance allows an administrator to add specific fields that lay outside the objective data fields common to documents. Users can edit these fields directly, via Concordance's *Edit* view, which is the third primary method of interacting with data (see Figure 2-4). An administrator can add a field called USER_NOTES, in which users can add meaningful descriptions of how they interpret the meaning of documents.

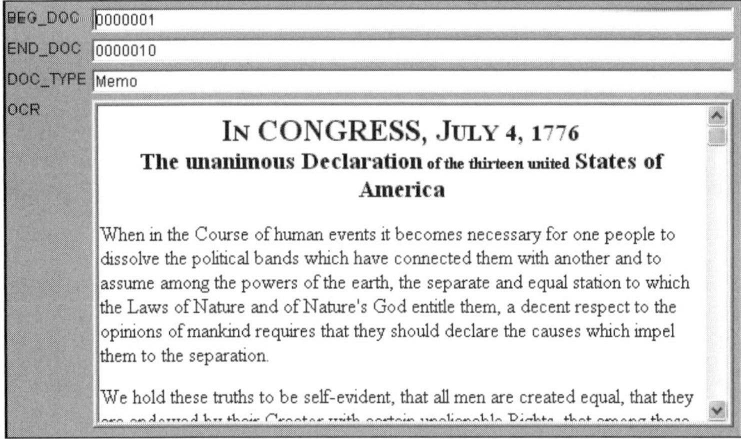

Figure 2-4. *Concordance's Edit view. The user can modify the contents of the displayed fields.*

Searching

Searching for records and retrieving them is, of course, an integral part of a full-text information and retrieval system. Concordance features a variety of interactive screens that allow a user to search for words or phrases in the full text of documents, or to search for values contained in coded fields, or to combine both types of searches.

Many users prefer to use Concordance's Query by Example tool, a search tool that displays fields in Concordance, and that offers options of how to search for information (see Figure 2-5).

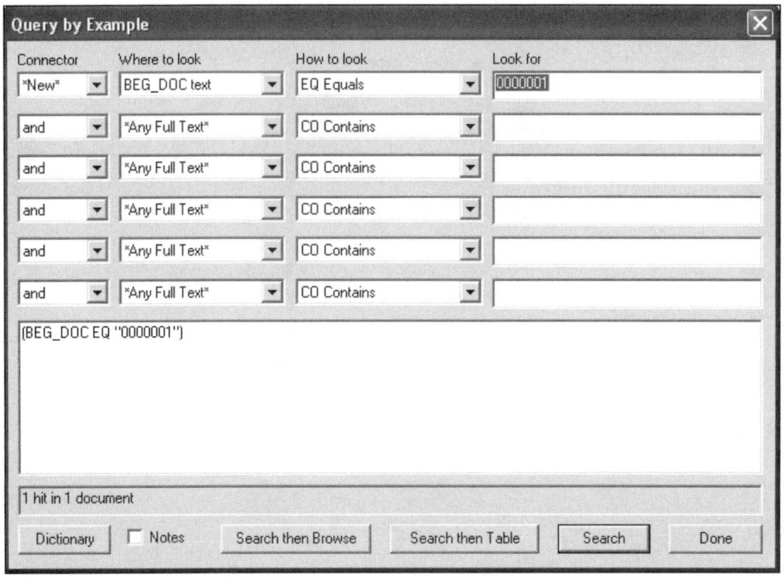

Figure 2-5. *Concordance's Form search*

Another way to search Concordance is via the <Quick Search> text field located under Concordance's menu items (see Figure 2-6). This method isn't as structured as the Query by Example tool, but is quite flexible.

Figure 2-6. *The <Quick Search> search bar. Users can enter search criteria here directly.*

Other methods of retrieving records exist, and are described in more detail in Chapter 9. Regardless of the method a user prefers, search accuracy in Concordance is facilitated by a well-designed database, a well-known set of data (that is, users understand what fields are and what they mean), and a basic understanding of Concordance's search syntax. Later chapters also contain a thorough discussion of this syntax.

Full Text

To search for a word or phrase using the <Quick Search> text field, you enter the desired word or phrase into the text field, then press the Enter key or click the traffic light icon. Concordance locates relevant documents and then displays them to the user.

A full-text search locates document records in which a user's search criteria exists anywhere in fields that have been given a PARAGRAPH data type. (Coded fields can be treated in this manner as well, according to database design.) A successful search results in *hits* that are highlighted in Browse view (see Figure 2-7).

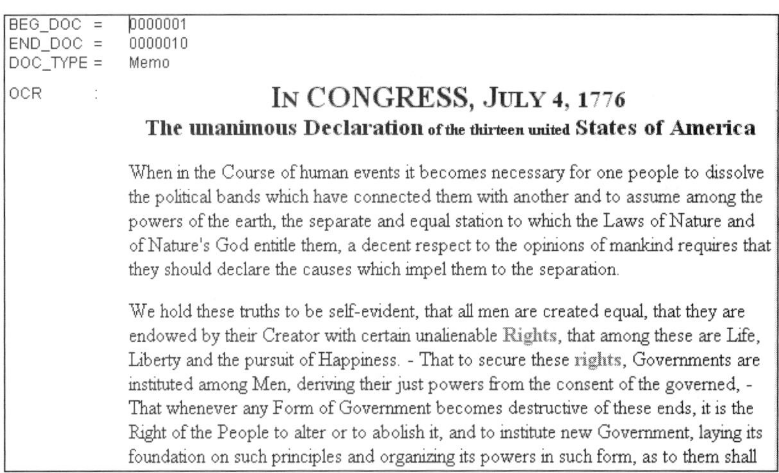

Figure 2-7. *The search term "RIGHTS" has been highlighted in this document record.*

Coded Fields

Recall that coded fields have data types that are TEXT, DATE, or NUMERIC. By default, these fields aren't accessible via full-text searches, and specific search syntax is required. In general, that syntax takes the following form:

```
FIELD_NAME  OPERATOR  VALUE_TO_BE_SEARCHED
```

- `FIELD_NAME` is the name of the field to be searched.

- `OPERATOR` is a comparison, such as *greater than* (GT) or *equals* (=).

- `VALUE_TO_BE_SEARCHED` is the desired criteria.

Figure 2-8 illustrates how this search syntax appears in Concordance's <Quick Search> text field.

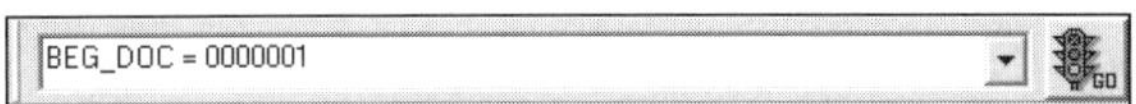

Figure 2-8. *An example of a coded field search*

Relational Operators

As with popular Web search engines, you can use basic operators such as *and, or,* and *not* to perform more complex searches. Entering **Smith not Brown** in the <Quick Search> text field locates those records that contain the name Smith, but that don't also contain the name Brown.

A more complete family of operators exists, and is discussed in greater detail in Chapter 9. Some of these operators are appropriate for full text, while others are appropriate with coded fields, specifically comparison operators. A `DATE_CREATED` field, designated with a *date* data type, supports the search `DATE_CREATED >= "1/1/2002"`, so that only records created on or after that date are retrieved.

Concordance Database Limitations

The manufacturers of Concordance have designed the software so that a single Concordance database can house up to 33,554,431 individual documents, where the full text of each individual document (collection of pages) can contain up to three billion individual characters. These are the *maximum* limits of a Concordance database, and are not feasible in practice. To ensure speedy search and retrieval, a Concordance database should be capped off at roughly 18 million documents. This doesn't mean that Concordance ceases being a viable alternative for a situation that calls for more than 18 million documents. Concordance includes methods to join separate databases together so that they appear as one virtual database, a method known as *concatenation.* There are also administrative methods to keep the full text of documents intact, but to minimize the size of the individual data files that comprise a Concordance database.

Loading Data

Loading data into Concordance is an important administrative task. Users can create new, blank records, and can hand-key data into fields directly via Concordance's Edit view. There are instances in which this method of entering data into Concordance is perfectly acceptable.

It's also possible to import some types of electronic files into Concordance directly. For example, Concordance can import individual e-mails from a Microsoft Outlook .PST e-mail database file. Each e-mail message is treated as a separate document record.

A common practice is for a Concordance administrator to rely on the services of a third-party vendor to oversee the conversion of paper and electronic files of a disparate nature into a format that's acceptable to Concordance. This alternative is appropriate when the document universe is large, and the procedures to convert files into a Concordance-ready format exceed a department's resources.

Vendors might provide data as raw text files, or they might provide actual Concordance databases. The Concordance software provides methods to import both from the Documents ➤ Import menu.

The Import submenu offers the following choices:

- *Concordance Database*: This is the simplest type of import. If data has been provided in a Concordance format, and if the fields and data types in the import database are exactly the same as the destination database, importation can be accomplished by means of just a few mouse clicks.

- *Delimited Text*: Delimited text refers to text files in which individual fields (including the full text of a document) are separated by an agreed-upon delimiter and are bracketed by an agreed-upon qualifier.

- *E-Documents*: If no vendor is used, and a Concordance administrator has a folder filled with electronic artifacts, this option allows the administrator to point Concordance at a specific directory containing these files, and import each file as a separate document record into a Concordance database.

- *Transcripts*: You can import transcripts and depositions if the Concordance database has been created as a *transcript* database from the "Create database from template" dialog that's opened from the File ➤ New menu. You can select a *transcript* template.

- *E-mail*: You can import individual e-mails into Concordance from Microsoft's messaging systems, Microsoft Outlook and Microsoft Exchange. This option is only enabled if these products are installed on the client PC or a network server.

Coordinating with Vendors

Concordance administrators depend heavily on the quality of data that's provided to them by third-party vendors that specialize in receiving large sets of paper and electronic documents, converting them, and transforming the results into output files that the Concordance administrator can load into a database.

In fact, the Concordance administrator is in many ways at the mercy of third-party vendors. A Concordance database only delivers accurate search results if the data that's loaded into it is, itself, accurate. Managing and converting large sets of documents is a challenging process, and a trivial error introduced at the beginning of a batch process can cascade into unpredictable results.

Often, the link between the Concordance administrator and the third-party vendor can break the chain of a research team's workflow, if expectations aren't clearly communicated and deliverables clearly understood. To that end, Concordance administrators are advised to draft, in advance, clearly defined standards that define how data is to be delivered.

Installation and Requirements

When a firm or company purchases Concordance from the software manufacturer, Dataflight, a decision is made about the number of users allowed to use the software. Concordance licensing uses a per seat model, so that a concurrent number of users are allowed to activate the program at any given time. The Concordance executable, Concordance.exe, contains licensing information embedded within its source code. The program tracks the number of users actively using the program, and denies access to additional users when the limit of allowed users is reached. This fact can affect how the program is likely to be installed.

During most installations, you must decide if the program will be installed locally on a workstation, or onto a networked server. This decision will determine where database files and the Concordance executable are stored.

For example, if a firm has a ten seat license, a common installation method would be to install both the database files and the executable on a network server. In this paradigm, you won't install the program on individual workstations, but rather, on a networked server. You'll eventually run a workstation setup file, provided with Concordance's installation disks, on each client PC. This setup file informs the client of the network location of Concordance data files.

If an individual has a single license copy, he or she may install the program on a network, or on his or her own workstation. If Concordance is installed on a network, this architecture is similar to the preceding situation, with an end user base of just a single user. If installed on the individual's workstation, all program and database files are stored on the client computer: the workstation acts as both a server and a client.

If, instead, a firm has purchased an *Enterprise* license, a scheme appropriate for large organizations, the administrator is at liberty to install the program on as many workstations and servers as needed, and in whatever configuration desired. You can and should consult with Dataflight regarding the optimal method of installation that ensures the maximum number of users are allowed to access databases within the appropriate licensing model.

Before Concordance can be installed, you should ensure that end users have the appropriate permissions to read and write to files stored in folders designated for Concordance databases. You'll also want to confirm that the hardware on the server or workstation that will use Concordance conforms to minimum standards, outlined in the following section.

Hardware Requirements

A networked server that will contain Concordance's database files should have the following attributes:

- A PC with a Pentium processor with a clock speed of at least 100MHz

- 128MB of RAM

- A CD-ROM drive

- A hard disk drive

These are minimum standards, and apply to a network server on which Concordance will be installed. As of this writing, clock speeds of PCs sold by leading manufacturers can exceed 3.0GHz, and servers can be configured to have several gigabytes of RAM. With regard to hard drive space, more is better. In terms of budgeting, a database administrator should set aside at least $3,000 for a simple network server to store Concordance data files. More expensive network servers exist. Consultation with a qualified member of a firm's IT staff is recommended.

The hardware requirements per client are similar to those of the minimum standards of the networked server; that is, a Pentium 100MHz or better CPU, and a minimum of 128MB of RAM, although 256MB of RAM is recommended. In practice, the more RAM an administrator can install in a client PC, the better. The reason for this is the way in which Concordance clients communicate with the networked server. When a user asks a question of a Concordance database, it is the *client*—not the *server*—that does the filtering and sorting. This means that all records are transferred across a network from the server to the client, and then the client PC does the work of selecting records. For mid- to large-sized databases, with hundreds of thousands or millions of rows, 256MB of RAM is inadequate.

Concordance Server Installation: Step by Step

Installation itself is easy: you insert the CD provided by the manufacturer into a computer's CD-ROM drive, and follow the on-screen prompts (detailed in Figures 2-9 through 2-15).

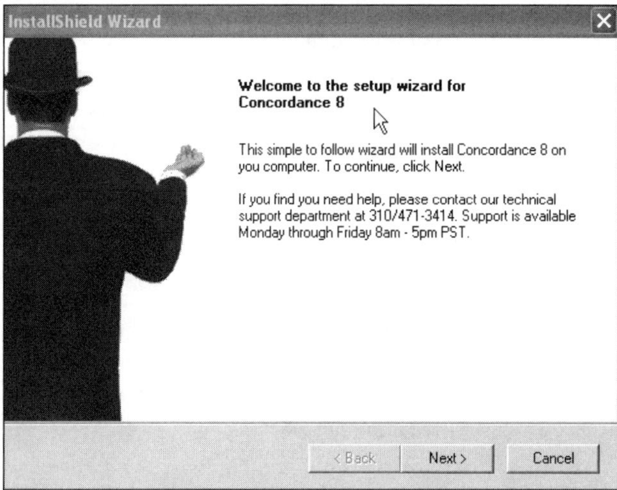

Figure 2-9. *After inserting the installation CD, you're prompted with a splash screen.*

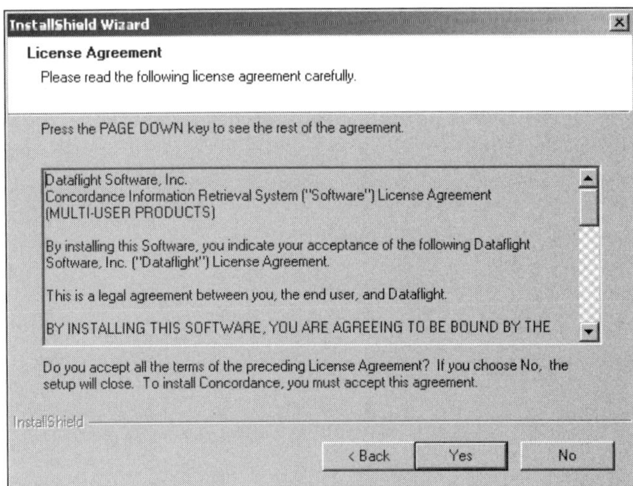

Figure 2-10. *The first dialog of the installation wizard (after the initial splash screen) displays the End User License Agreement (EULA).*

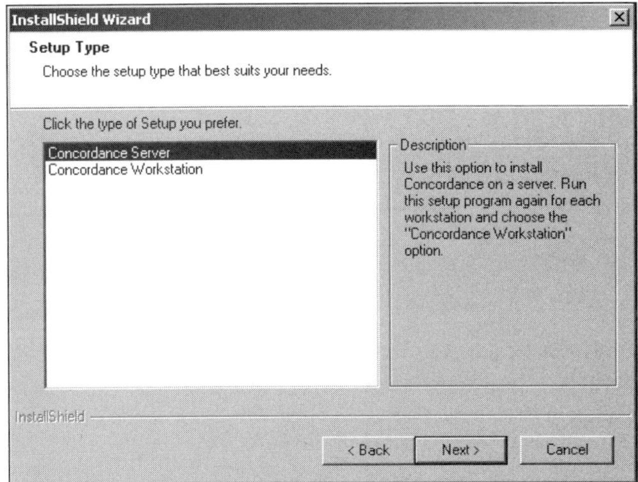

Figure 2-11. *To install Concordance on a server, you should highlight the Concordance Server option. You use the Concordance Workstation option to configure client workstations to interact with a server-side installation.*

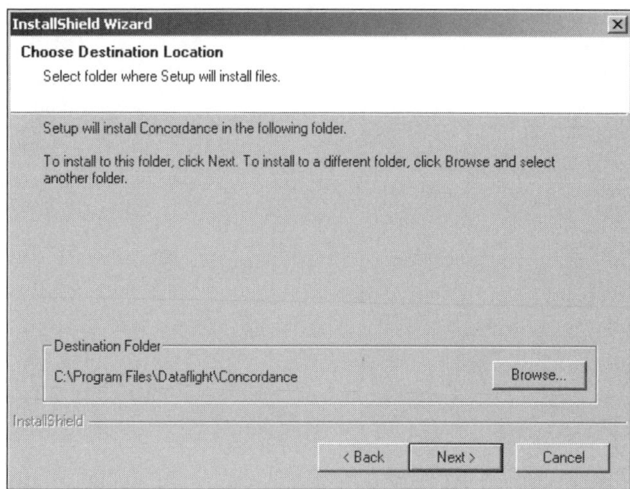

Figure 2-12. *You select the destination folder where Concordance is installed from this dialog. The default is C:\Program Files\Dataflight\Concordance. If you desire another location, click the Browse button.*

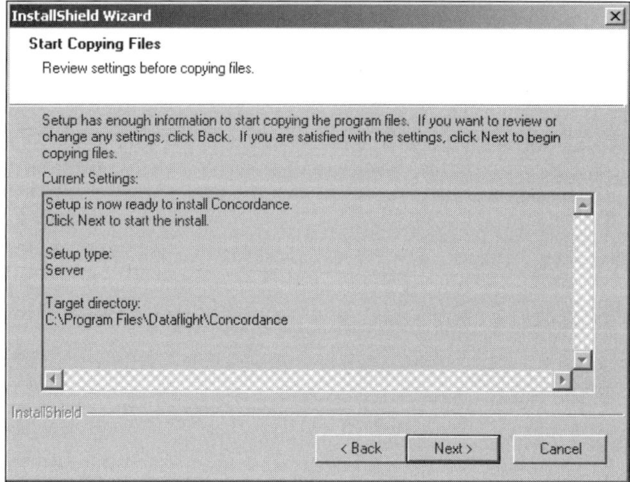

Figure 2-13. *This is a confirmation screen. If any of the parameters are incorrect, you can click the Back button and update the location of installation files, or change the type of installation (server or workstation).*

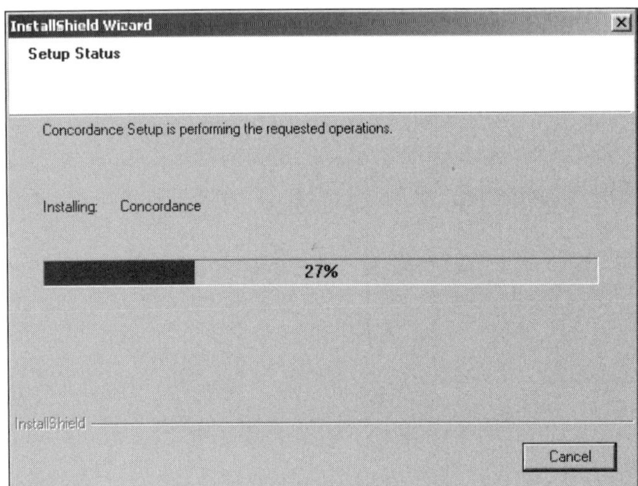

Figure 2-14. *A progress bar displays the status of the installation.*

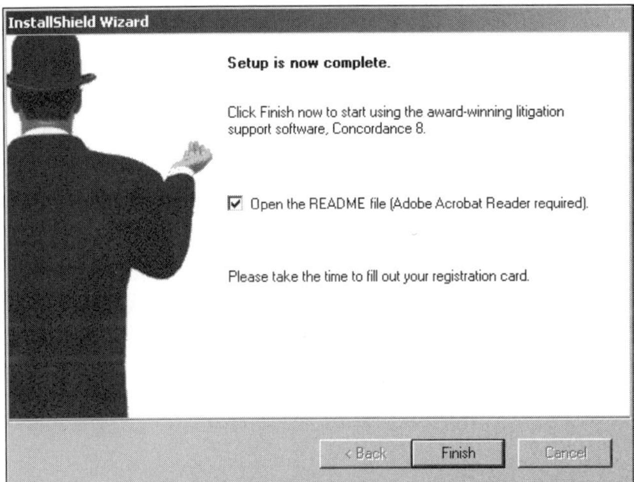

Figure 2-15. *The final dialog of the installation wizard. If you select the "Open the README file" checkbox, then click the Finish button, and if the intallation computer has Adobe Reader installed, a .PDF document opens that details upgrades and enhancements made to Concordance since its last version.*

Concordance Workstation Installation: Step by Step

The workstation installation routine is run on each client workstation that connects to a networked installation of Concordance. The workstation setup doesn't install the Concordance program on the client PC. Instead, it configures the client to connect to the server installation.

The Splash, EULA, and Setup Type dialogs that open during the Workstation Installation Wizard are the same as those detailed in the preceding section outlining a networked installation. You want to highlight the Concordance Workstation entry on the Setup Type dialog. The remaining dialogs are described in Figures 2-16 through 2-19.

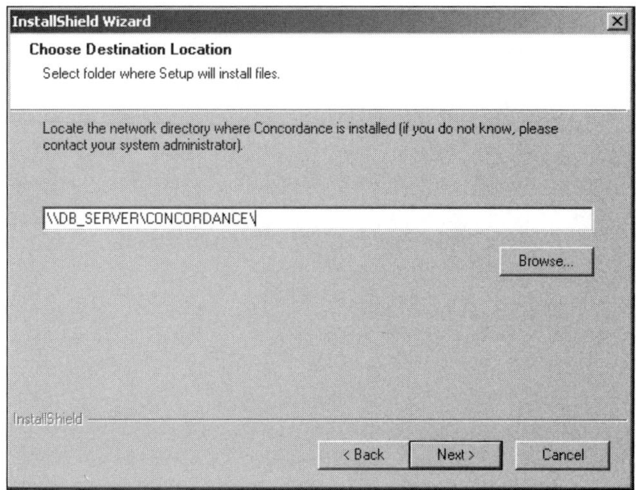

Figure 2-16. *You must inform the Workstation Installation Wizard of the location of Concordance files installed on a networked server.*

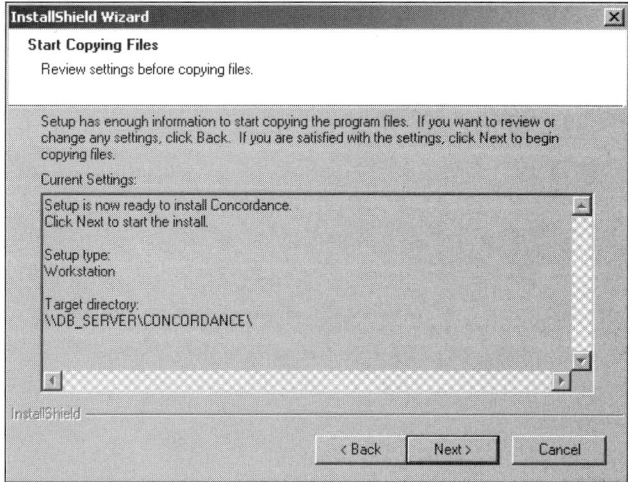

Figure 2-17. *A confirmation dialog. You can click the Back button and update information provided in previous dialogs.*

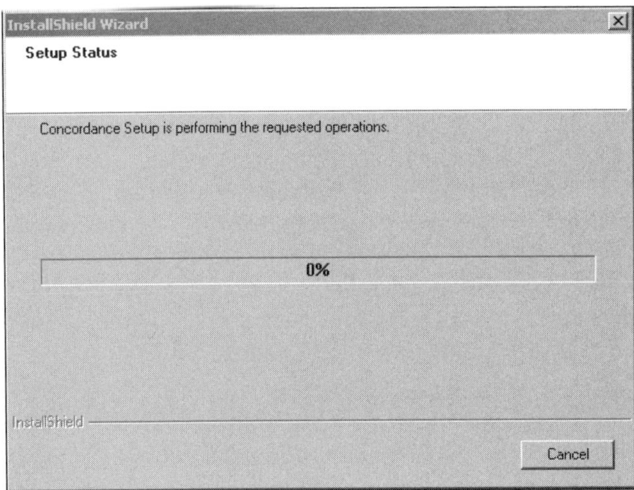

Figure 2-18. *A progress bar displays the status of the installation.*

Figure 2-19. *The final dialog of the Workstation Installation Wizard*

When the Workstation Installation Wizard is completed, the client PC will have a new folder accessible by clicking the Windows Start button and the All Programs option. The new folder is labeled Dataflight, and it contains a Concordance icon that maps to the networked executable used to launch Concordance.

Summary

Concordance is both a database management system and a full-text information retrieval system, because it organizes and stores data about objects in a collection of data typed fields, and it features advanced searching tools that can locate and retrieve records that conform to a user's search criteria. Rows of data in Concordance combine to form a database, and a single Concordance database is a collection of related file types that operate together.

You can interact with a Concordance database through one of three views: Browse, which displays the entire contents of a single record; Table, which displays the abbreviated contents of several records in a list; and Edit, which allows a user to modify data in a database. Further modifications of record data include document-level and issue-level tagging, and the addition of comments to selections of text.

You can retrieve records in a variety of ways. One of the simplest methods is to use Concordance's <Quick Search> text field. A user enters search criteria, presses the Enter key (or clicks the traffic light icon), and if there are successful matches, the results will be presented to the user. Although the mechanics of searching are simple, in practical use the accuracy of searches is greatly improved by a well-trained user base, as Concordance's search tools do require some knowledge of the software's search syntax.

There are several methods of entering data into a Concordance database, from allowing users to hand-key data directly, to calling on an outside company—a third-party vendor—to prepare special load files. Coordinating with vendors is an important part of Concordance administration.

All these topics warrant further discussion, and later chapters will expand upon them. The next chapter will address an important and often overlooked aspect of Concordance administration: database design.

CHAPTER 3

Managing Data

The two preceding chapters have defined what Concordance is, what it does, and how it's installed. Although the remainder of this book will be more specific to the actual administration of Concordance, this chapter will outline more empirical concerns. In general, a Concordance administrator can be said to manage data. However, the phrase *data management* refers to more than just the processing of digital files. The Concordance administrator must be familiar with a variety of data formats, certainly. But he or she must also be familiar with some basic computing standards, with concerns that result from document collection, and with the capabilities of other professionals in the field of data processing with whom he or she will likely coordinate.

The first half of this chapter is devoted to some of the more common data formats the administrator will encounter. The last half outlines the capabilities of data processing companies that can assist the administrator after document collection, but before a database is loaded.

Data Formats

You can use Concordance to manage a variety of data. Some data can be imported into Concordance directly, but other kinds require conversion. In the sections on Concordance and delimited data formats, conversion is assumed to be complete, and files are ready to be imported. However, in the section that describes electronic source material, you can't make this assumption. Although Concordance can import some electronic files directly, there's usually some preprocessing phase. The discussion will thus identify common data formats and, when applicable, will highlight issues raised during preprocessing.

Concordance Data

No discussion of data formats accessible to Concordance would be complete without briefly noting that you can import and export data to and from a Concordance database in a Concordance format. Managing database records in this way is common when a firm or company shares data with another corporate entity that also uses Concordance, or when sets of records—although valuable as a reference—are no longer needed in an active database and can be archived.

Recall that Concordance uses a suite of files that act together to define a single database. When data is exported from Concordance, these files are automatically created. The administrator selects the records to export (this might be a subset of the entire database), then selects the fields that should be exported (not all fields need be exported), and then selects the output destination, preferably an empty folder. The program itself manages the creation of the requisite files that define the new, exported database.

When data is imported from another Concordance database, the application will assume that the source database is fully functioning and that all requisite files exist. In general, it's preferable that the source database's structure mirrors that of the destination database: field names and data types are the same.

ASCII Text

Every character on a standard computer keyboard, and additional characters that aren't normally visible to users, are given a numerical designation as defined by the American Standard Code for Information Interchange (ASCII). These numerical designations are a universal standard, and are understood by all computer software operating systems (Windows, Macintosh, and Linux), regardless of hardware architecture. Many programs—Concordance included—are designed specifically to recognize ASCII (pronounced *AS-KEY*) data. Because of the universality of ASCII formats, many organizations use ASCII as a method for transmitting data. Characters in these files are often referred to as *plain* or *clear text*, because a human can interpret data in the files when rendered by software. An easy way to create a clear text file is to use the simple Notepad.exe program that ships with Microsoft Windows operating systems. Create a new Notepad document, type a sentence, save it—and the resulting file is an ASCII text file.

In addition to letters (upper and lowercase), numbers, and common punctuation, ASCII codifies a variety of "characters" that are nonprintable. Rather than display text, these characters affect how text is processed. For example, the Tab key on a keyboard can be represented by an ASCII code. Another example is a line break, which forces following text to start on a new line.

Basic ASCII maps 128 numerical values to 128 letters, numbers, punctuation marks (collectively referred to as *glyphs*), and nonprintable characters. To illustrate this, a partial chart of the first few letters of the English alphabet is shown in Table 3-1.

Table 3-1. *A Partial List of Capital Letters and Their ASCII Code Designations*

Decimal Value	Glyph
65	A
66	B
67	C
68	D

A software program reads a value and understands that it represents the corresponding glyph.

Extended ASCII

When the ASCII standard was first published in 1967, the number of accessible glyphs was sufficient. As technology improved, it was found that the original character set was limited and more glyphs were needed. Extensions of ASCII emerged. The term *extended ASCII* refers to additional characters that augment the original 128 values. There are several variants of extended ASCII. To be precise, when evaluating an ASCII file that uses an extended character set, you should be informed in advance of just which variant has been used to prepare the file. In practice, however, this is usually not necessary. Because of the saturation of Microsoft software in today's computing environment, the extended ASCII character set adopted by Microsoft and used by most Microsoft products, *ISO 8859-1*, can be assumed.

Note The name ISO 8859-1 derives from the International Organization for Standardization (ISO), a multi-national body that produces global standards for governments and businesses.

Table 3-2 shows a partial list of the ISO 8859-1 variant of extended ASCII.

Table 3-2. *A Partial List of the ISO 8859-1 Extended Character Set*

Decimal Value	Glyph
252	ü
253	ý
254	þ
255	ÿ

Assuming that the precise ASCII coding standard is known, both the entity providing the data and the entity receiving the data must agree in advance on the *data structure*. In this context, the structure of a file doesn't refer to the method used to encode it (ASCII). Instead, it refers to how data is organized in the file. For example, in a data file used by a company's Human Resources department, the first nine characters of each line of the file might be reserved for each employee's Social Security number.

A popular method of defining a data structure is to use a *delimited format*. In this paradigm, sets of related data are bracketed by a common character, called a *text qualifier*. Between each set of related data, a *delimiter* is used to clearly designate the distinction between data elements. Finally, groups of data that combine to describe an object are sometimes referred to as *rows* (even if their contents comprise many lines of text). The end of each row is designated by a *line separator*. A delimited ASCII text file should have a *text qualifier*, a *delimiter*, and a *line separator* to structure data uniformly.

The following five lines of data represent a delimited text file in which the text qualifier is a single quote, the delimiter is a comma, and the line separator is a line break (new line). Note that the first line doesn't pertain to a specific employee. It's used to record the names of related groups of characters on other rows.

```
"SSN","NAME","POSITION"
"123456789","SMITH", "1"
"987654321","JONES", "2"
"555666888","CHU", "3"
"876345918","O'Grady","2"
```

When delimited data is imported, each delimited set of data (for example, the NAME data in the preceding example) has a corresponding field in a Concordance database, and each row of data is imported as a separate database record. Delimited files are often used to transfer data to and from Concordance databases, as you can also export database records from Concordance to a delimited format.

Electronic Files

A Concordance administrator can expect to oversee the management of large amounts of electronic data that originated in other software. Concordance has the ability to import some types of computer files directly, without any additional preprocessing that might create delimited files, as described in the preceding section. Depending on the nature of a research matter, it's possible for you to process many millions of electronic files, and load them into one or more Concordance databases. In general, each electronic file is represented as a single database record in Concordance.

In the discussion that follows, electronic files are assumed to be in their *native format*, where this term refers to the original nature of the files prior to any transformation. A file's *native application* is the software program that initially created the file. The term *file type* refers to the class of the file, and can usually be determined from a *file extension*, a two to four character designation that's appended to the file name. For example, the file 2003Budget.xls is known to be a Microsoft Excel workbook by the .XLS suffix. The native application is Excel, and the file extension is .XLS.

Prior to loading native files into Concordance, you'll want to evaluate them, to determine if they should be loaded at all. The research team that will eventually use Concordance can help. Are there file types that can be ignored? If incoming native files are derived from multiple sources, are some of those sources not relevant to the matter? Perhaps the nature of the intended research means that some file types, although theoretically valid for importation into Concordance, are known to be without merit. Some time spent away from a keyboard in deliberation with the end users of Concordance can greatly reduce the amount of data that will be processed, and the eventual impact on a review team.

Beyond empirical valuations, you'll find that, of the electronic material deemed relevant, some files and some file types cannot be imported. They're either inappropriate for loading by their very nature, or they might be unneeded duplicates.

File Exclusions

In Chapter 1, the program Notepad.exe was shown to lack clear text. Notepad is an example of an *executable* file; that is, a program intended to be run by a user, as opposed to a file that a user interprets or modifies. The file extension .EXE is often used to identify a program of this type.

When viewed with a text editor, the characters in Notepad, although comprehensible to a computer, are generally indecipherable to a human. In a Concordance database, there might be some value in assigning a database record to denote the existence of the program, but there's no apparent value to importing Notepad's machine code.

There are other examples of files that won't import into Concordance. An obvious example might be an audio file that contains no searchable text. Other files might not be so readily recognized. Files with an extension .SYS are often computer *system* files that an operating system uses, and are never accessible to a user directly. Again, it might be desirable to record the existence of such files by creating records for them in a Concordance database, but if no such requirement exists, you can ignore them.

A partial list of file types that are of no practical use to Concordance is shown in Table 3-3. This list contains some of the more common file types a Concordance administrator can encounter. It isn't complete.

Table 3-3. *Partial List of Files That Don't Contain Clear Text*

File Extension	File Type	Description
.DLL	Dynamic Link Library	A support file used by other programs
.TTF	TrueType Font	An outline font format used for displaying fonts on a computer monitor and for printing
.WAV	Waveform Audio	A digital audio file
.SWF	Shockwave Flash	Displays animations created using Macromedia's Flash
.ICO	Windows icon	A small graphic that represents a file or application

Note You can find a more thorough listing of file extensions at `http://filext.com/`.

A summary index of file types, perhaps displaying file extensions represented in source material, is clearly desirable. There are a variety of methods to obtain one, as discussed in the following sections.

Software Designed to Create Lists of Files

There are shareware and freeware utilities, usually available for download from the Web, that scan the contents of a directory and store the results in a text file. Two examples are SuperDox (`http://www.litigationtech.com/superdox/`) and FileLister (`http://www.tawbaware.com/filelist.htm`). You can see an example of FileLister in Figure 3-1. These two particular programs both provide additional options that allow a user to exclude certain file types, or to specify how deeply into a directory the scan should go.

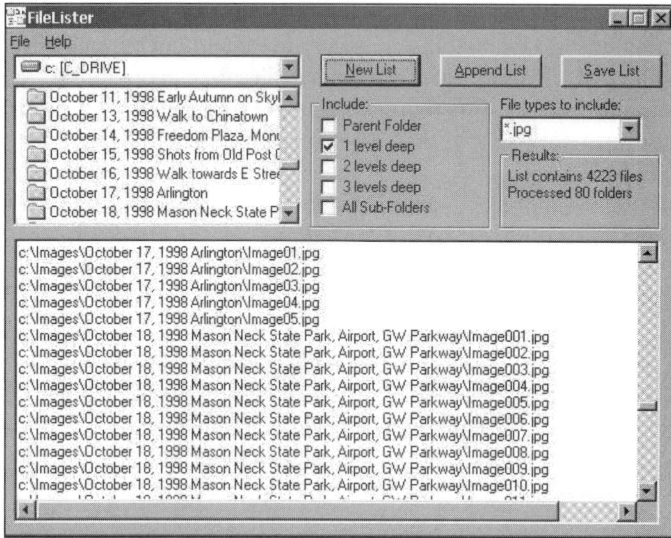

Figure 3-1. *The shareware program FileLister, a program that can be used to create a digital index of files*

The dir Command

Windows operating systems allow a user to open a *command line interface*, a screen that accepts user input in the form of typed commands (see Figure 3-2). You can activate it by typing the word **cmd** in the Run dialog, which you open from the Windows Start button and the Run menu item. You can also activate it by clicking the Command Prompt icon ▣ that appears on the Accessories menu, from the All Programs option.

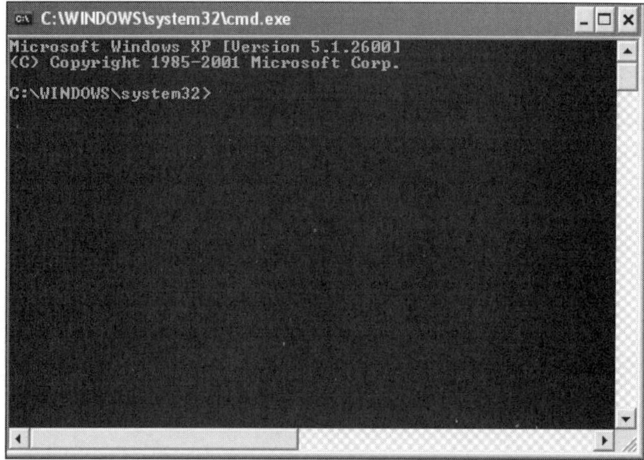

Figure 3-2. *A Windows command line interface*

You use the command `dir` to list directories and their contents. You can redirect this output to an electronic file, using the `dir` command's *switches*. Switches are options added to a command that specify how the command is to be executed. The switch `/b` uses a "bare format" that excludes any additional summary information. The switch `/s` forces the `dir` command to scan all subdirectories under the current directory. The switch `> FileList.txt` redirects output to a new file named FileList.txt. The user chooses the actual name of the file; FileList.txt is merely a suggestion. The new file is stored in the parent directory that is to be scanned.

The command `dir > FileList.txt /b /s` creates a FileList.txt text file that contains all directory names and file names of the current directory (see Figure 3-3).

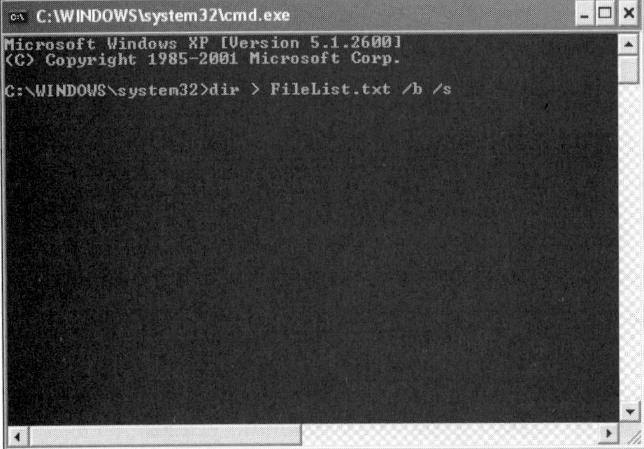

Figure 3-3. *The command dir > FileList.txt /b /s is used to create a file, FileList.txt, that contains an index of all files and folders in the current directory, C:\WINDOWS\system32.*

You can view the resulting text file using any text editor (see Figure 3-4).

■Note You can access a full listing of switches and the syntax of how the `dir` command is used by typing **help dir** and pressing the Enter key from a command line interface. For a broader explanation of how a command line interface is used on a Windows operating system, refer to Windows' own help files.

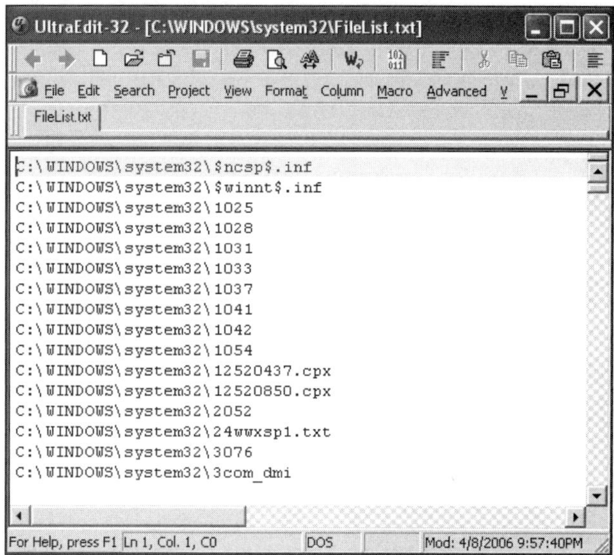

Figure 3-4. *The index, FileList.txt, when viewed using a text editor*

Assistance from an Outside Company

As will be discussed later in this chapter, it's often customary for a Concordance administrator to outsource the preprocessing of large amounts of data to a company that specializes in this type of service. One service a qualified company can provide is a summary index that lists files and their types, in a format that the administrator and research staff can review prior to any additional preprocessing.

Deduplication

Concordance administrators will find that, when analyzing electronic documents, many files are exactly the same. This is a common scenario when it relates to e-mail messages. For example, if e-mail is harvested from multiple sources within a company, that same message might exist in several locations. The original message will be in a sender's outbox, while copies of it might exist in one or more recipient inboxes, if the message was sent to the sender's coworkers, and if their e-mails were part of the collection. If the sender has created backup copies of his or her e-mail, the original message may be contained in other files as well. The contents of the message might be more important than tracking its copies, and a preliminary step of *deduplication* might be desired. Deduplication refers to identifying identical files for the purpose of selecting just a single instance for eventual review. This reduces the amount of data that an administrator will load into a Concordance database, and will eventually relieve the workload on a review team, as the team will be required to evaluate fewer records.

Although Concordance has a feature that allows an administrator to identify duplicate records already in a database, the deduplication procedure described in this section is part of a preprocessing phase that occurs prior to database loading. Concordance has no native ability to deduplicate external files. In most circumstances, a Concordance administrator relies on an external company for this service. Qualified companies have specialized software that's designed for this purpose.

A common method employed during deduplication is to assign each electronic file a unique value that can be compared to the values of other files. The actual value depends on the data contained in the file, and can be considered an alias. When values for two or more files match, the files in question are potential duplicates. These *hash values* are a way of codifying documents, and are used in lieu of comparing every character of an electronic file with every character in all other files in a document universe. This latter method, although simple in theory, is far too resource intensive, and in most circumstances, could not be completed in a timely manner. Codifying documents by means of a hash value greatly expedites the procedure (see Figure 3-5).

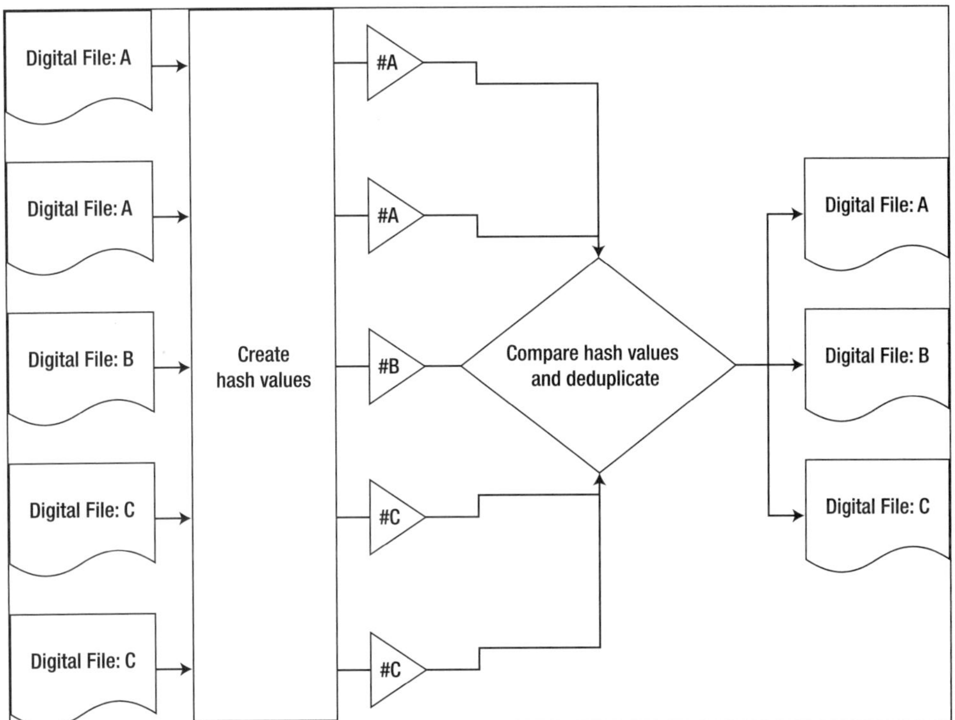

Figure 3-5. *A functional diagram of deduplicating files by assigning hash values. Digital File A is represented twice, Digital File B represented once, and Digital File C represented twice. A# is a string of characters that corresponds to Digital File A, B# corresponds to Digital File B, and C# corresponds to Digital File C. When hash values are compared, duplicates are identified and removed, resulting in just the single instances of Digital File A, Digital File B, and Digital File C.*

Although a hash value is derived from data in a file, creating the value from the entire contents of the file might be too precise a method of identifying duplicates. Consider again the example of multiple instances of the same e-mail delivered to several sources. These e-mail messages contain identical data in the message body, but other data is associated with them that might be unique per message, such as the timestamp assigned to each message upon delivery by each recipient's workstation. An application of hash values that includes the timestamp might not successfully identify duplicates. In practice, it's often preferable to apply the hash value to a subset of data in each message. In this context, some subsets of a document's data are referred to as *metadata*. For an e-mail message, the SUBJECT line is an example of metadata. A less precise, though more accurate, method of identifying duplicates might take into account the SUBJECT, TO, and ATTACHMENT COUNT metadata fields of e-mail messages. Note that electronic documents that aren't e-mail messages also contain metadata. For example, a Microsoft Word document has CREATED, MODIFIED, and ACCESSED properties that can be important to a deduplication. The metadata that should be used for the process of deduplication depends on the collection itself, and how stringent the administrator and review team wishes the procedure to be.

There are several ways to assign a hash value to an electronic file. As of this writing, the most popular method uses a mathematical algorithm known as *Message Digest 5* (MD5), originally designed in 1991 by Professor Ronald Rivest, and employed in a variety of security applications. A thorough discussion of how this algorithm creates a hash value exceeds the scope of this book, and from a practical perspective isn't necessary.

Using Vendors to Assist with Processing Data

In most applications of a Concordance database, the administrator inherits a body of paper or electronic documents that, in their native format, cannot be loaded into Concordance. Additional preprocessing is required to convert the source material into a Concordance-compatible electronic format. Although some large corporations or law firms have the internal resources to convert paper or electronic documents into Concordance-ready load files, many companies rely on a separate corporate entity, a *vendor*, which specializes in document and data preprocessing.

The challenge for a Concordance database administrator is to locate vendors that are capable of producing quality load files, in a timely manner, and at an affordable rate. In recent years, corporations and law firms have come to rely more heavily on full-text information retrieval systems, and the number of vendors that have the ability to preprocess documents has increased. Many of these vendors originated as "copy shops" and have a local presence within a city. There are also many established and national companies that have regional offices and can service a wide geographic area.

Why Is a Vendor Necessary?

A vendor is often used if a document collection inherited by a Concordance database administrator is so large that the manpower required to scan and transform the documents is prohibitive. Furthermore, some aspects of preprocessing, such as deduplication, require specialized software and the employment of skilled technicians.

Scanning Documents

The Concordance software doesn't contain the necessary components to scan and OCR paper documents. This means that when a Concordance administrator inherits a box of paper, he or she cannot load documents using Concordance itself. A separate suite of software must be used.

The term *scanning* refers to the method used to convert paper documents to electronic files. Individual sheets of paper are run through hardware capable of high-speed collation. Software is then used to scan each sheet and identify individual characters (OCR). The characters are then formatted in a format acceptable to Concordance.

If just one sheet of paper represents an entire document, the process is complete and the next document is collated and scanned. If the sheet is the first of several sheets that define a document, each sheet is scanned and converted until the program reaches the last page—the end point. Document boundaries identifying the first and last sheets are digitally signed, and the next document processed.

Coding

In the preceding discussion, it was assumed that the only aspect of a document that's converted into a Concordance-ready load file is the text of a document itself. However, other fields can be used in a Concordance database record. Some are required. Beginning and ending document numbers are necessary to determine where one database record ends and another begins. Other fields, although not essential to the correct structure of a Concordance database, might nevertheless be considered as essential to a review team. An example of such a field might be an AUTHOR field. Although the text of a document might contain the name of the individual who authored the document, it might also contain that individual's initials, the individual's nickname, an employee ID, or perhaps some other permutation—*J. Public, John Q. Public, JQPublic,* or *JQP*. For the purposes of review, staff might wish to identify every document authored by a specific individual, regardless of how that individual might be referenced throughout the universe of document records. One method to accomplish this might be to designate a specific AUTHOR field during the design phase of a Concordance database. This type of field cannot be populated during document scanning, a process that is automatic. In fact, no automated procedure exists that can be trained to intuit and standardize permutations of a name. A scanning vendor is often asked to examine each document during preprocessing, visually identify the name of the author, and key this information into an output load file. Human intervention is required, and this process is referred to as *coding*.

Vendor Costs

Every interaction with a vendor about a particular project starts with costs. Owing to the potentially large size of document conversions (a million pages isn't unusual), a Concordance administrator might wish to obtain multiple, competing quotes from several vendors. An administrator should obtain, in writing, a list of expected deliverables and an expected cost estimate, with a plan of how to proceed if the costs exceed a certain threshold level.

Per Page Costs, Heavy vs. Light Litigation

In Chapter 1, the terms heavy and light litigation were used to describe the overall quality of source documents. The terms refer to the legibility of the text, the material quality of the paper, and the method used to bind documents. Heavy litigation is much more difficult to process than light litigation, and is therefore more expensive per page.

Table 3-4 offers examples of document quality, with a brief description of how the state of the material can affect preprocessing.

Table 3-4. *Examples and Considerations of Light and Heavy Litigation*

Document	Type	Comments
A LaserJet printout of a Word document with no residual ink artifacts	Light litigation	Document can be easily scanned.
A LaserJet printout of a ten-page Word document that has been stapled ten times along the document's left-hand edge	Heavy litigation	Staples must be removed prior to processing.
A single photocopy of a one-page typed memo that's skewed (that is, the original wasn't set in the photocopier correctly)	Heavy litigation	Skewing of documents can severely impair the accuracy of OCR scanning processes. Even a slight skewing of .5 degree can degrade OCR accuracy to a point where full text is too inaccurate to be useful.
Collections of typed pages that are fastened by paper clips	Light litigation	Staples must be removed prior to processing.
A book	Heavy litigation	The spine must be broken and each sheet separated and removed prior to scanning.
A handwritten note	Heavy litigation	Might yield no OCR data, depending on the quality of the handwriting.

As of this writing, you can expect light litigation to cost between 10 and 15 cents per page, and heavy litigation to cost as much as 25 cents per page. A vendor's time and effort can be minimized, and costs reduced, if support staff takes the time to unitize documents in advance (removing staples and paper clips, defining document boundaries with Post-Its or sticky tags), and to separate light litigation from heavy litigation.

Coding Costs

Recall that a coded field is a field that contains data about a document, such as AUTHOR. Coding requires human intervention, and the costs associated with preprocessing will increase. As of this writing, coding costs can add at least 75 cents per document. However, the price increase can vary. For example, coding might require scanning personnel to read through an entire document to determine its author. This additional time and effort results in increased costs.

Because of the higher prices associated with coding, a review team might decide to perform coding on its own, after a Concordance database has been populated.

Electronic Data Conversion

Pricing for electronic media is a difficult issue. Sight unseen, there's no way to estimate how many files a 20 gigabyte hard drive might actually contain, and no way for a vendor to estimate how much it will cost to preprocess files. The hard drive might contain four video files that are 5GB each, it might contain 200,000 individual text files, or (more likely) it might contain tens of thousands of diverse files of varying file types and varying sizes.

As part of a contract with a vendor, it's not uncommon for the vendor to accept source data and compile a full listing of all files as an aid to ensuing negotiations regarding cost. If the vendor's bid is chosen, it usually absorbs the cost of this preliminary analysis. If the vendor isn't chosen, the cost of the preliminary analysis will usually be negligible to the overall cost of processing the documents in total. Regardless, the administrator should obtain an exact cost for any preliminary analysis.

Vendors often offer bids for processing native files per gigabyte instead of per page. Pricing can vary widely, from $2,500 and up.

Setting Standards

Allowing a vendor to guess what the structure of a data deliverable should be is a mistake. It should be understood that if the vendor is faced with an aspect of the project that hasn't already been discussed, the Concordance administrator should be consulted. It's better for workflow to be halted for an hour, than for a digital delivery to be badly malformed.

You'll want to maintain a reference document that outlines, in general terms, the preferred format of data structure and delivery. These specifications will be fluid, as requirements for new projects and new databases evolve. The document can be circulated to vendors as part of a pricing negotiation so that vendors know minimum requirements in advance.

General specifications include, but should not be limited to, the following:

- Methods of delivery of data, either by CD, DVD, or external hard drive.

- How delivery media should be labeled. At a minimum, the media should have a label that includes the name or accounting number of the issue or matter; the full contact information of the vendor, including the name and phone number of a point of contact at the vendor; the name of the support staff at a corporation or firm who requested the data; the number of Concordance records and the number of associated image files; and the date of actual delivery. CD or DVD labels should also provide enough blank or white space to allow a Concordance administrator to record notes on the media label itself.

- The method in which a vendor will inform the Concordance administrator that new media will be delivered, before it's actually delivered.

- What files should be contained on delivery media, and how those files should be named and foldered.

- What delimiters, text qualifiers, and record terminators should be used in delimited files.

- Whether or not field names should be included in the first row of any load file.

- The format of date fields; for example, MM/DD/YY, MM/DD/YYYY, DD/MM/YYYY, and so on.

Summary

The Concordance administrator will come into contact with several data formats: Concordance data itself, ASCII data, delimited data, and no end of various native file types. At first, the amount of data that results from a collection can seem overwhelming. However, through advance planning and consultation with end users, and through electronic deduplication processes, the administrator can reject documents that have no relevance to a matter, and bring the final document universe to a manageable level.

Electronic deduplication processes are normally overseen by a company outside of a firm that specializes in assisting administrators with electronic conversions. Duplication is just one service that these vendors can perform; in many companies, all preprocessing of document records, both paper and electronic, is outsourced. When vendors are involved, the administrator will want to provide clear explanations of expected deliverables. For high-volume departments, these standards can be memorialized in a single document that can be circulated to vendors during initial bidding.

The next chapter will carry you through the entire life cycle of a database, from initial creation, to field modification, to applying security, to loading data. The rest of this book will deal with Concordance-specific administrative tasks.

CHAPTER 4

Creating and Deploying a Concordance Database

This chapter will convey to you, through a series of illustrated steps, the procedures required for creating, deploying, and loading a Concordance database. The concepts discussed in this chapter are covered in much greater detail in other parts of this book; they're presented here in brief so that you can gain a basic understanding of the development and deployment cycle of a Concordance database. To summarize the steps: the administrator creates a blank database, specifies the location of database files, defines database fields (and data types), then loads the Concordance database from external data files. After a Concordance database has been loaded, it's usually necessary for the administrator to index the database to fully enable Concordance's full-text capabilities. *Indexing* refers to a process in which Concordance builds special files that facilitate searches.

Security can be applied to a Concordance database through Concordance's own software architecture. It's the administrator's responsibility to create user accounts and to define field-level permissions. These procedures are also discussed in this chapter.

Creating a New Concordance Database

A single Concordance database is defined by a series of separate files that work together. For example, the primary database file that a user activates to open a Concordance database has a .DCB (data control block) extension. ▓ For a database named DOCUMENT_REVIEW.DCB, there might be in excess of a dozen separate files, with separate file extensions, that Concordance creates automatically during a database's lifespan. For example, the *dictionary file* (created during indexing) associated with the database DOCUMENT_REVIEW.DCB is named DOCUMENT_REVIEW.DCT. When you create a new Concordance database, Concordance requires you to select a folder in which to store database files before the database is created. Concordance creates all files that define a database in this folder. Multiple database files for two or more databases can be stored in the same folder, if—and only if—no two databases have the same name. In general, you might wish to create one folder per database, to avoid confusion. All files that define the database DOCUMENT_REVIEW can be contained in a folder devoted to the database, perhaps with the name DOCUMENT_REVIEW. If you're responsible for ten separate Concordance databases, there can be ten separate folders, one per database.

To create a new Concordance database, use the File ➤ New menu item. A "Create database from template" dialog box opens (see Figure 4-1).

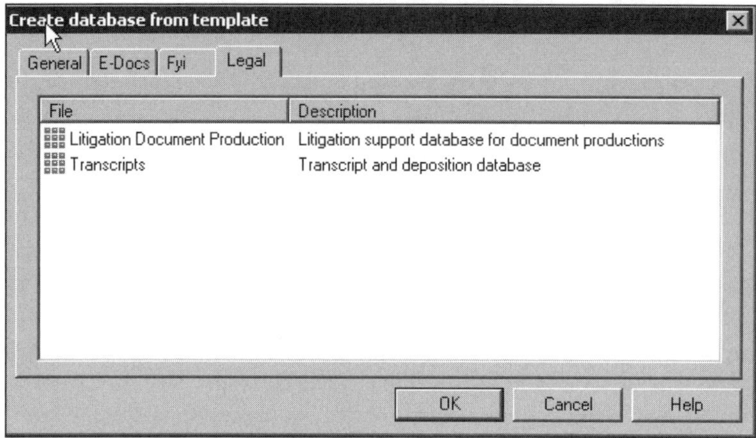

Figure 4-1. *The "Create database from template" dialog box*

You might choose to create a database shell from an existing template in which data fields are already defined, or to create a generic, blank database with no field definitions.

The Legal tab of the "Create database from template" dialog has two items that correspond to a Litigation Document Production database shell, and to a Transcripts shell. For the purposes of a discovery process relating to a legal matter, the Litigation Document Production shell contains many useful fields. These fields may be modified as research progresses and needs evolve. Highlighting the Litigation Document Production item and then clicking the OK button opens a Save As dialog, prompting you to specify a folder that contains the Concordance database files. In this example, the chosen database name is EX01.DCB. You enter the desired database name in the "File name" text field (see Figure 4-2).

Clicking the Save button creates an empty Concordance database with a series of useful predefined fields. To view these fields, use the File ➤ Modify menu item to open a Modify dialog box that displays all fields in the database (see Figure 4-3).

This is a viable, albeit empty, Concordance database. It must be loaded from an external data file. Although Concordance is compatible with a variety of data formats, for the purposes of this example, a delimited text file will be used.

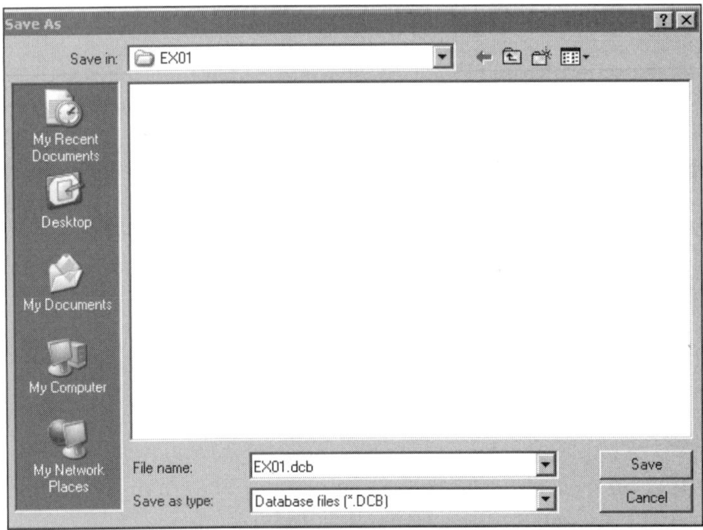

Figure 4-2. *The folder has been created in advance of the database, and named EX01 for easy recognition.*

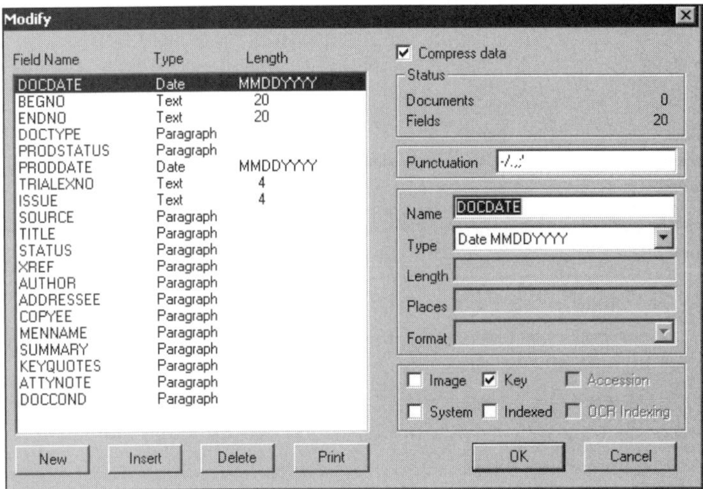

Figure 4-3. *Fields that are created when creating a Concordance database from the Litigation Document Production template*

Loading Delimited Data into Concordance

Concordance can import several different types of data. In the example covered in this section, import data is in a delimited format. A more extensive discussion of import techniques that apply to all types of compatible data formats appears in Chapter 6.

The number of delimited fields in a load file should match the type and sequence of fields in the database to be loaded. If the type of data contained in the delimited fields doesn't match the data type of the fields to which they correspond, data will be corrupted. Preliminary analysis of data files is essential to ensuring that load files are clean. Reviewing data files might be as simple as opening the files in a text editor and scanning rows for egregious errors, or it might be as advanced as loading the data into a staging database first, then reviewing the results.

To load a delimited data file into the EX01.DCB database created using the procedures described in the preceding section, use the Documents ➤ Import ➤ Delimited Text menu item. This opens the Import dialog box shown in Figure 4-4. You have the option to use a wizard to guide you through the load process. Here, a *wizard* refers to a series of helpful, interactive Windows dialogs that prompt a user for input. Concordance has many wizards that are designed to simplify otherwise involved administrative procedures.

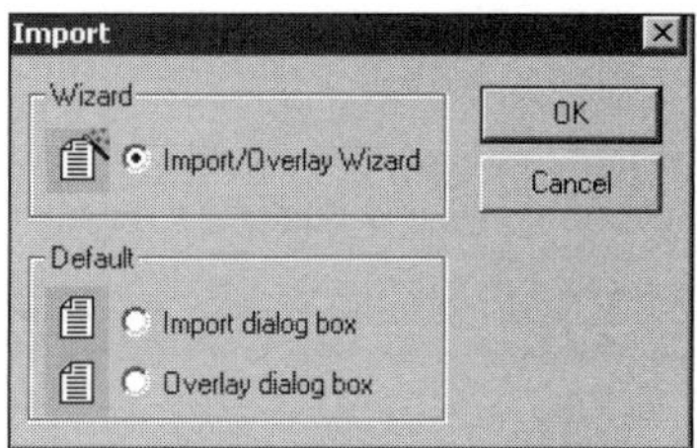

Figure 4-4. *The Import/Overlay Wizard guides you through the load process.*

After selecting the Import/Overlay Wizard option and clicking the OK button, the Import Wizard activates (see Figure 4-5). The first screen opened by the wizard allows you either to append records to the database (to load new records) or to overlay records (to update existing records).

Next, the wizard asks you to specify the type of delimiters used in the load file. Unlike the text qualifiers, delimiters, and record separators used in the simple delimited example in Chapter 3, Concordance has default characters that perform the same function, displayed in Figure 4-6. These default characters have been selected because it's highly unlikely that they'll occur in the data itself, thereby throwing off field counts. Most vendors can provide data files using these delimiters. However, there are other types of delimiters. Comma-delimited files, such as the example in Chapter 3, are quite common. It might also be true that the administrator and a vendor have previously agreed upon a set of delimiter characters that are unique. You can select these characters from the Format dialog.

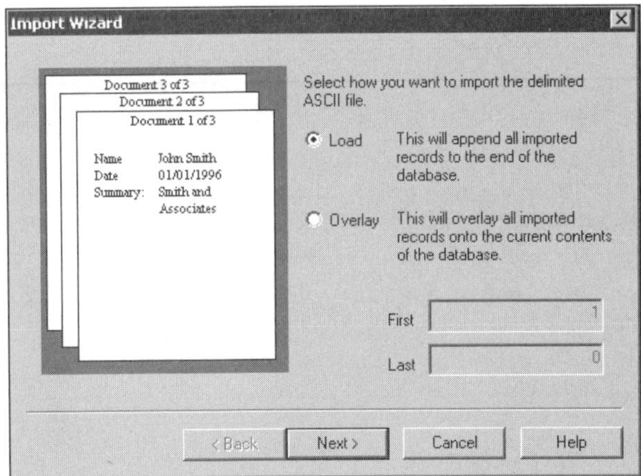

Figure 4-5. *To load new records, select the Load radio button.*

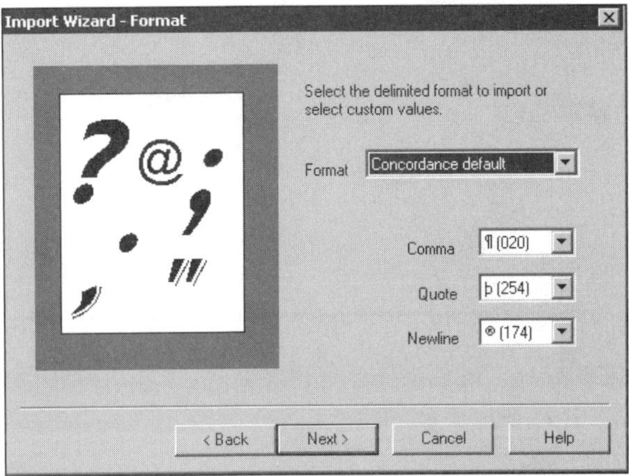

Figure 4-6. *Specifying the type of delimiters used in the load file*

If there are dates in the load file, you must inform Concordance how they're formatted. This also means the vendor that provides the load file must be instructed in advance how the dates are to be formatted. Date formats used throughout a load file must be consistent, as the format selected from the screen shown in Figure 4-7 applies to *all* date fields throughout the file.

The next dialog allows you to specify which fields are to be included in the load (see Figure 4-8). The left-hand list box displays all fields that are in the database, while the right-hand list box displays fields that have been selected as part of the load. Use the "Skip first line" check box if the load file lists the names of fields in the first row.

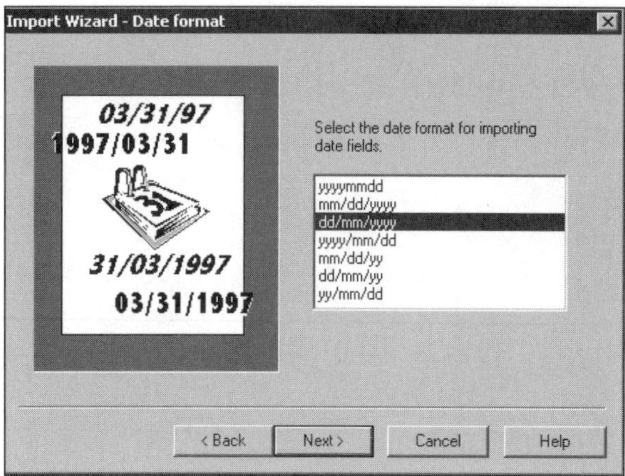

Figure 4-7. *Specifying the date format*

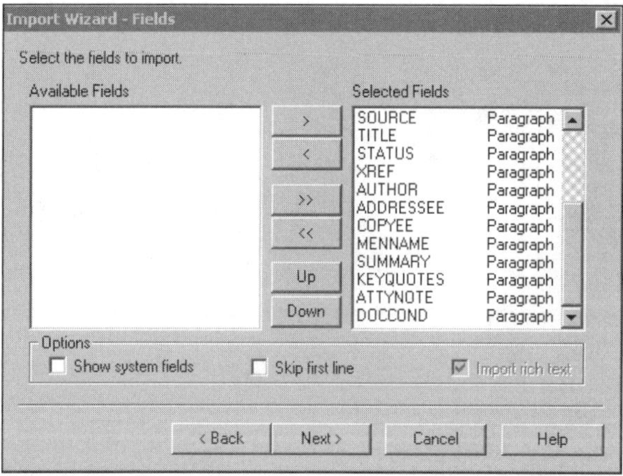

Figure 4-8. *Selecting fields as part of the data load*

The next dialog allows you to select the actual load file itself, using the Browse button (see Figure 4-9).

The final dialog box summarizes the progress of the load (see Figure 4-10). Clicking the Finish button starts the load. Note that Concordance doesn't report errors when importing data, with one exception: the wizard informs you if a field has an *overflow*, which means that a value loaded into a field is larger than the field allows, as defined by its data type. Otherwise, if dates are malformed or a field isn't filled in for whatever reason, you won't see the error from the wizard. You'll want to analyze data files prior to loading to correct errors in advance.

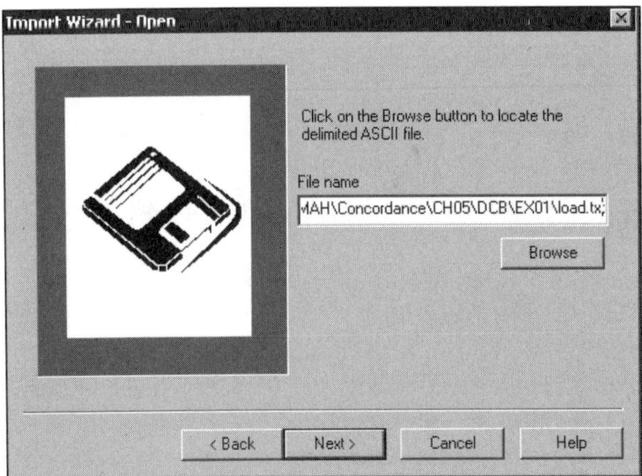

Figure 4-9. *Selecting the load file*

Figure 4-10. *The final dialog in the Import Wizard, which summarizes the status of a load*

Indexing Data

Depending on how a Concordance database is designed, once data is loaded, it might not be immediately available to Concordance's search facilities. Usually, a process known as *indexing* is required. Indexing is applied to two types of fields in a Concordance database: fields that have been designated with a PARAGRAPH data type, or fields of other data types for which the indexed attribute has been set to True. Any field that has a PARAGRAPH data type is indexed by default, although fields that have other data types are indexed only if you specify that the field should be indexed.

■Note You can toggle the Index attribute for a field using the Modify dialog, which you can access from the File menu, Modify submenu item.

Concordance fully automates the indexing procedure, though you must initially trigger it from the File ➤ Index menu item. When an index is triggered, Concordance builds lists of all words contained in paragraph fields (and other fields with their index attribute set to True). These lists enable Concordance's full-text searching capabilities.

Reindexing is the same as indexing, though it's invoked when data in a Concordance database is updated or when new records have been loaded. When data in a Concordance database changes, you must update the files that enable full-text searching, the dictionary file (which contains a list of all unique words), and the inverted text file (which contains the placement and frequency of words in the dictionary file) via reindexing. You must knowingly trigger reindexing. The File menu provides a visual cue. If the Reindex submenu item has a check mark next to it, the database requires reindexing.

Applying Security

In addition to any folder- or file-level permissions enforced on a network, a secondary layer of security is available in Concordance's own security model. This security model allows you to create users and define roles for them. It isn't applied by default. You must actively enforce it after the database is created.

Security in a Concordance database is twofold: restricting users from modifying, viewing, or searching specific fields, and restricting access to menu items.

Security is specific to each instance of a Concordance database, so that user security modified in one database doesn't cascade to other databases. You must modify user permissions for each database, in each database.

Creating an Administrator Account

All modifications to user accounts are accomplished from the Security dialog box opened from the File ➤ Administration ➤ Security menu item. Even if security hasn't been applied to a Concordance database, you'll be prompted for a login and password when this menu item is selected. If no security has been applied to the Concordance database, leave the User and Password fields blank. The Security dialog box opens (see Figure 4-11).

For each database, it's good practice to remove any default account created by Concordance and to create a dedicated *administrator* account, with full permissions, to modify and otherwise supervise a database. This means granting the administrator account "Full access" and allowing the administrator account access to every menu item from the "Menu access" tab. To grant permissions for a field, select each field and click the "Full access" check box. To select every field—this is recommended for the administrator account—highlight the first field, then use the Shift key in conjunction with the End key to highlight every field. To apply security formally after the administrator account has been created, click the "Enable security" check box and the "Logon required" check box on the "Field rights" tab.

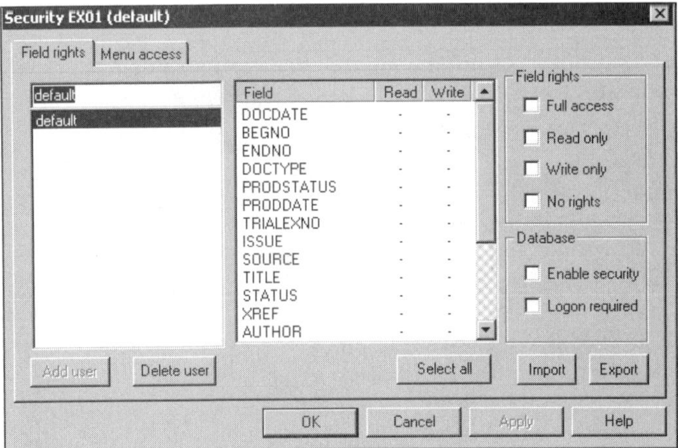

Figure 4-11. *Security dialog box. No users have been created yet.*

Note If "Enable security" alone is checked, this will enforce security, but not prompt a user with a login when he or she activates a database. In this paradigm, Concordance will capture the user's network login and compare that to the list of user names in Concordance's own security model.

To create an account, enter the desired login (for example, admin), and then click the Add User button. The user name is created and added to the list.

Once you've created the administrator account and given it full control over the database, and once you've checked the "Enable security" and "Logon required" check boxes, click OK to return to Concordance. At this point, two things are true about user accounts:

- The admin account has no password.

- The default account still exists as a valid account. The default account is used when a user attempts to log on with an account ID that isn't in Concordance's list of users.

To secure the database completely, reactivate the Security dialog from the File ➤ Administration ➤ Security menu item. When prompted for a logon, entering the desired password this first time sets it. When choosing a password for the first time, Concordance requires a confirmation by forcing a user to type the password again. Once confirmed, the Security dialog is activated and the password for the administrator account set.

There's no method to recover a password in Concordance. If the administrator password is lost or forgotten, the account is effectively locked out of the database. Be sure to write the administrator password down for each database, and keep the passwords in a safe, secure place.

Setting Field Permissions

The admin account created using the procedures outlined in the preceding section has rights to create other user accounts. The method is the same as creating the admin account itself: add the desired login in the text field located in the upper left-hand corner of the Security dialog, then click the Add User button.

Once you've added a user, you must set field rights for each field by highlighting (or multi-selecting) fields and clicking the desired level of permission: "Full access," "Read only," "Write only," and "No rights" (see Figure 4-12).

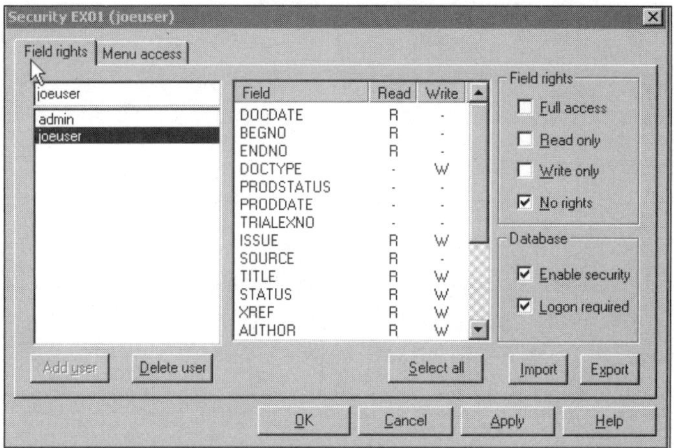

Figure 4-12. *The account joeuser has read permissions for the fields DOCDATE, BEGNO, and ENDNO; write permissions for the field DOCTYPE; and no access to the PRODSTATUS, PRODDATE, and TRIALEXNO fields. Note that a combination of read and write access (denoted by the letters R and W) implies full access.*

Setting Menu Access Permissions

In addition to field-level permissions, you have the ability to restrict which parent menu items and which options from each menu tree are accessible to users. It's strongly recommended that you take time out to configure menu trees as appropriate for regular users. The alternative—to allow all users full access to all menu items—can be disastrous. For example, a user could completely empty a database of all records by means of the Zap menu item on the File menu.

It's possible for you to customize menus completely. However, the Security dialog contains a "Menu access" tab with several useful presets: Supervisor, Administrator, Editor, Researcher, and No access. Each preset automatically enables or disables menus and menu items as appropriate for a user role. If joeuser is to perform basic research, you can highlight the name, joeuser, then click the Researcher button (see Figure 4-13). This disables the File, Edit, Documents, and Tools menus, leaving only the Search and Help menus active.

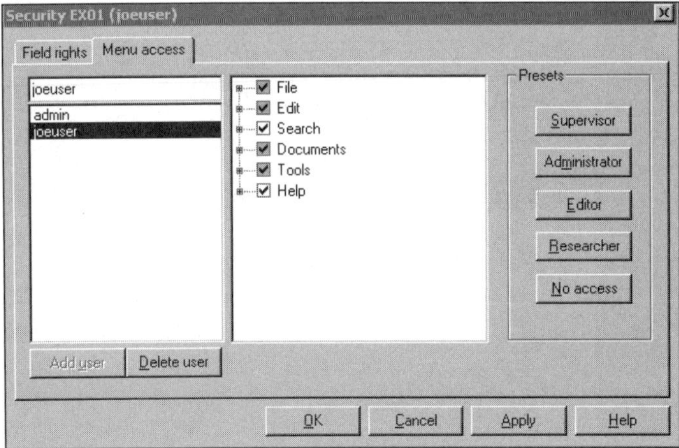

Figure 4-13. *joeuser has been given the role of Researcher. Note the menu items that have been grayed out and disabled.*

Summary

This chapter covered the basic steps of creating a new Concordance database, loading it, and securing it. In practice, more time would be devoted to planning the structure of the database before any data files were created. Furthermore, additional time would be spent on validating the load file, to ensure data isn't malformed. However, many of the steps outlined in this chapter are common to every development cycle: the database must be created as an empty shell and data must be loaded into it. Securing the database, although highly recommended, isn't a requirement.

In future chapters, topics touched on briefly here will be expanded and clarified. The next chapter will focus specifically on database creation, and setting field-level properties.

CHAPTER 5

Designing Databases and Defining Field Properties

From initial database conception to final deployment, a Concordance administrator can be responsible for seemingly unrelated decisions, from determining how much network space is needed for a database, to determining the specific behavior of a field when a user presses the Enter key. A common thread, however, is that all the decisions an administrator makes are affected by design, and by the way that design is defined in an instance of a Concordance database.

The first half of this chapter is devoted to general best practices. Although no single database structure is appropriate to all deployments, general design suggestions can be applied to most applications, and can greatly simplify administration.

The actual mechanics of database design from within the Concordance software involve creating a database, then creating fields, naming them, assigning data types, and setting attributes that control the behavior of the fields. The last half of the chapter describes how a database is created, and then moves on to the various field-level settings that can be applied via Concordance, and what these settings do.

Planning

Concordance databases that are deployed without reference to a set standard of database design are difficult to maintain. These standards should be shared with vendors as well. Administrators may come to rely on vendors to provide Concordance load files that are error free and uniform across several separate loads. Without clear specifications, even a reliable vendor might produce varying results.

In software development, it's a common rule of thumb that each hour of actual work at a keyboard should be preceded by three hours of design and planning. This might not be possible in your specific work environment, owing to time and budget constraints. Still, you should regard preplanning as an investment that will yield results over time as databases are deployed more smoothly.

Clear lines of communication between you and end users are a further investment of time that can also save money. You'll often be in a position of managing expectations as well as managing databases. Once you fully understand the needs of a research team, you can translate those needs into the design of an actual database.

You can create a basic *specification sheet* that applies to any database, because many aspects of Concordance database design are common. The specifications can be tailored to meet the needs of each unique matter, as necessary. A spec sheet standardizes deployments, and is useful during negotiations with a prospective vendor. A vendor should be informed, from the outset, of the level of detail and quality that's expected in deliverables.

End users can provide valuable input regarding desired database features. For example, are there fields users want, such as COMMENTS, that you might not think to include in a database's design by default? Or perhaps some fields can be prepopulated with data, reducing the burden on data entry personnel?

However, some of the first considerations that can go into a spec sheet are independent of database functionality: naming conventions for files and fields, data formats, and the method of data delivery.

File Naming Conventions

If a vendor is to supply data in a Concordance format, the actual names of the files should only use alphanumeric data. No white space or nonalphanumeric characters should be used. A database for the matter *John Q. Public vs. The Acme & White Corporation* shouldn't be named John Q. Public vs. The Acme & White Corporation.dcb. This name is somewhat unwieldy, and the use of white space, the period, and the & symbol might confuse other software tools that technical staff might use for scanning network files to provide administrative summary reports about network usage.

Most firms or corporations use some sort of internal accounting number to identify a project. Perhaps an accounting department has assigned the matter *John Q. Public vs. The Acme & White Corporation* the abbreviation JQPvAcmeWhite. Some accounting departments will assign a matter a purely arbitrary designation, such as a combination of letters and numbers: JQP00010. These accounting designations are ideal names for databases, with the addition of a date. For example, JQPvAcmeWhite_LOAD_071004.dcb represents a database provided by a vendor on July 10, 2004.

If a vendor supplies data in a different format, these same types of naming conventions should be applied. JQPvAcmeWhite_LOAD_071004.txt is a viable name for a delimited load file. The key is that names should be concise and, if possible, should describe the purpose of the file.

Field Naming Conventions

Field names also should be concise and, if possible, self-explanatory. Concordance has a limit of 12 characters per field name. For example, the field name FILEEXTENSION must be trimmed to FILEEXTENSIO to fit into the allowed space provided by Concordance. The type of data that the field named FILEEXTENSION contains is clear; FILEEXTENSIO is somewhat less self-explanatory. If data is to be supplied in delimited text files, the vendor should be directed to include field names as the first line of each file.

Field names should be uniform across all data loads. Without a specific designation of field names, a vendor might provide subsequent sets of data with inconsistent names. For a database that contains a document date field, one data load might use the field name DOCDATE, while another might use the field name CREATE_DATE. This is more than a matter of cosmetics, but also of efficiency: you might be required to load dozens of separate data sets into the same database. If field names aren't uniform and if load files are provided in a Concordance format, personnel must consciously make a mapping *from* the fields in the vendor-supplied data *to* the destination database on their network. This requirement is less stringent when load data is provided as delimited files, because you can specify that Concordance should skip the first line of a file if it contains field names. Nevertheless, uniformity should be a goal.

To avoid any confusion, a vendor should be supplied with a complete list of field names, what each field means, the respective data type, and any additional data requirements for each field (see Table 5-1).

Table 5-1. *Sample Chart of Field Names and Data Types*

Name	Description	Data Type	Notes	Example
BEGDOC	Beginning document number	TEXT(6)	Zero filled	0000001
ENDDOC	Ending document number	TEXT(6)	Zero filled	0000010
DOCDATE	Document date	DATE (MM/DD/YYYY)		01/01/2004
OCR1	Full text	PARAGRAPH		Now is the time for all good men to come to the aid of their country . . .

Note that the format of DATE fields can cause some confusion when load files are delimited. Although it's possible to view dates in different formats in Concordance (MMDDYYYY, YYYYMMDD, DDMMYYYY), the actual date data in delimited load files must be uniform across the entire file, even if several fields contain date data. In other words, when data is in a database, you're free to modify how it's displayed, but when dates are initially loaded, their format must be consistent. To simplify administrative procedures, that format should be consistent across separate load files.

Useful Administrative Fields

Often overlooked in database design, administrative fields can be of considerable use to the maintenance of Concordance databases. You can configure the following fields so that they autopopulate during loading:

Creation date: This is the date when a record is loaded. It's useful for isolating batches of records from a specific date. During database design, a field that has been given a DATE data type can be set to autopopulate with the current system data from Concordance's Edit ➤ Validation menu (see Figure 5-1). CDATE is an appropriate name for this type of field.

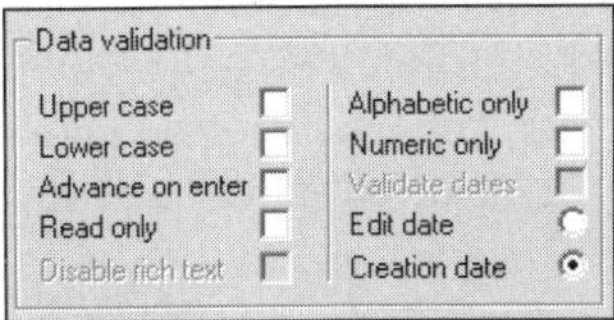

Figure 5-1. *The "Creation date" radio button modifies a field so that it records the date a record is loaded.*

Edit date: This is the date when a record is edited. It's useful for tracking changes made by a specific user on a specific date. Each time a user makes an edit to a record, the date, the user's login, and an alphanumeric identifier assigned to the edit are recorded in this field. Multiple edits are entered as separate lines in the field:

```
20060319 201956 Eas [IMYM2B-1] BCampbell;
20060319 201159 Eas [ZAVHA8-1] BCampbell;
20060319 191854 Eas [BMRRXD-1] JJones;
```

Because the data is alphanumeric (not just a date value), you should set the data type for this field to PARAGRAPH. Subsequent edits to the same record will be written as separate line items in this field. Like the CDATE field described earlier, you can set this field to auto-populate from Concordance's Edit ➤ Validation menu. When an edit field is configured in this way, one line will be inserted into the field at the time of loading, as appending new records to a database is considered to be a valid edit (see Figure 5-2). EDATE is an appropriate name for this type of field.

Note "Creation date" and "Edit date" values are written into the fields at the time that data is imported or edited. These fields should be created, and their attributes set, before data is loaded or modified in a database. You can create these fields after a database has been populated with data, though the "Create date" field will contain the Concordance equivalent to a null date, 00/00/0000, for records already loaded in this field.

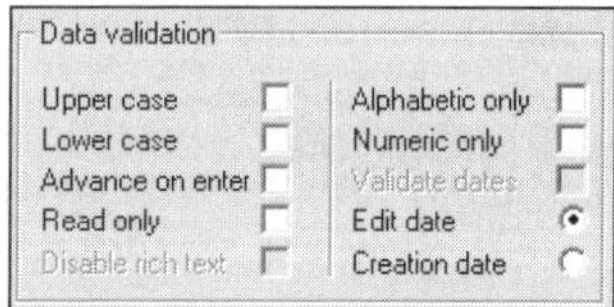

Figure 5-2. *The "Edit date" radio button modifies a field so that it records information about when a record was last edited, and the user who performed the edit.*

Accession ID (autonumber): Although individual records may be assigned separate document ID values during the scanning and OCR process, it's useful to have an additional numeric identifier for each record that's both arbitrary and unique to the database itself. In general, it's a good practice for a database to have its own identifier, independent of any identifier supplied by an outside agency. The reasons for this might not be immediately obvious. For example, missing numbers indicate that records have been deleted, a determination that might not be possible from any other test. Also, you can facilitate isolating otherwise unrelated records through a search of an accession ID field, such as AUTOID <=100, which locates the first 100 records in a database.

You set the accession attribute during the design of a database, from the File ➤ Modify menu (see Figure 5-3).

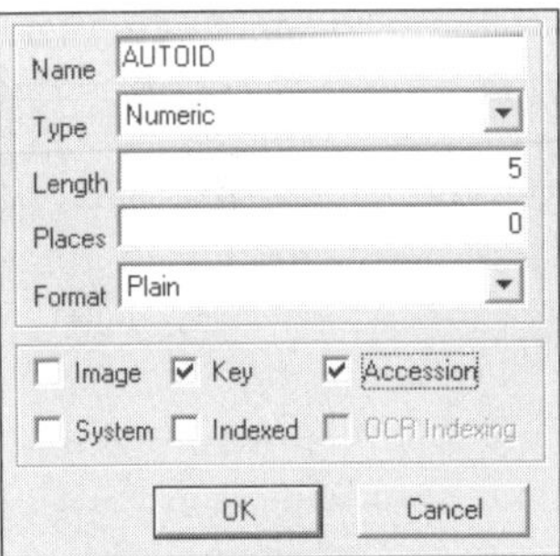

Figure 5-3. *The Accession property, accessible from the Modify dialog, sets a field so that it acts as an autonumber field.*

Volume: It's a common practice among scanning and coding vendors to identify specific data loads by means of a VOLUME field (see Figure 5-4). This is especially useful when data is provided on separate media, perhaps on a dozen separate DVDs. Each DVD should be clearly labeled with a unique volume value (DVD001, DVD002, DVD003), *and* that value should be included as a separate field in the data itself. It isn't uncommon that a set of data must be reprocessed, either because of a technical error during scanning and coding, or because of changing needs from a research team. Being able to identify sets of data for each media type is essential for deleting records that will be reloaded from updated media. VOLUME is an appropriate name for this type of field.

Figure 5-4. *You can use a VOLUME field to associate records in a database with a specific load. In the preceding example, the search VOLUME = DVD001 has retrieved a record that was loaded from a DVD that was identified as 001.*

In practice, you'll find it useful to have a vendor supply a VOLUME field prepopulated with volume data. However, the CDATE, EDATE, and AUTOID values are more accurately set at the time when you load data, not when a vendor supplies it. For this reason, the vendor could be directed not to supply these fields. If they already exist in the destination database, they'll populate automatically when new records are added. It's a matter of preference.

Data Formats for Load Files

In much of the previous discussion, it was assumed that a vendor will supply data in a Concordance format. This is a most convenient method of transmitting data. Loading data from a Concordance database to another Concordance database is straightforward, assuming that the names of the fields in both databases are the same (hence the importance of uniformity).

As of this writing, vendors may still provide data in a Concordance 7.0 format, which is incompatible with the latest release of Concordance, version 8.0. If data is supplied in a version 7.0 format and is destined for a Concordance 8.0 database, support staff must first open the load data in version 8.0 and then convert it from 7.0 to 8.0. This can be accomplished from the Tools ➤ Convert to V8 menu.

Note In most circumstances, CDs and DVDs cannot be updated. To convert a version 7.0 Concordance database, you should copy database files to your network, set the read only attribute to False, then attempt to upgrade the database.

A vendor might opt to provide data in a delimited format instead. This is perfectly acceptable, though litigation support staff must clearly identify to the vendor which characters should be used as field and record delimiters, the order in which fields should be laid out, and if the first line should list field names.

Method of Delivery

A vendor might deliver data in a manner that isn't conducive to efficient loading. For example, loading data from a dozen separate CDs is much more time consuming than loading data that has been stored on a 100GB external hard drive, for the simple reason that loading each CD requires staff to insert it, load data, then eject each CD. A complete spec sheet should explicitly outline the preferred manner of data delivery, identifying the preferred media (CD, DVD, or external hard drive), and how the media should be labeled. Too often, support staff might inherit hundreds of CDs and DVDs that don't indicate the matter to which they belong, the date of delivery, the point of contact at the vendor responsible for the media, and who is knowledgeable about how the data was processed.

If data is to be provided on fixed media, the vendor might choose to label the media in such a way that makes it difficult for support staff to record—on the media itself—what action was taken. Colorful vendor logos covering the face of a CD allow no space for markup.

At a minimum, each CD or DVD should list the following:

- The legal matter name

- The matter's accounting designation

- The data volume

- The date of delivery

- Complete vendor name and address

- Vendor point of contact, with phone number and e-mail address

- Name of person to whom the media is delivered

An alternate method of tracking this information is to request that a vendor include it in a small text file, perhaps named ReadMe.txt, on the media.

In addition to writing on the face of a CD or DVD when it was processed, support staff might find it useful to keep a tracking chart, perhaps in a spreadsheet program, to record the date of delivery, the date when the media was loaded, the individual who loaded it, and any additional comments regarding the load itself.

An alternate method of data delivery is purely electronic. Although the size of load files usually precludes transmission via e-mail, some vendors can serve files from a *File Transfer Protocol* (FTP) server. FTP is a way for a user to connect to a server, via the Internet, for the purpose of uploading or downloading files. This is a valid method of transferring data, but there are risks involved. Unless the FTP server has been preconfigured to be secure, *anonymous access* grants any user the ability to access data. FTP transfers also have the disadvantage of breaking midstream if Internet connectivity of either the user or the host is lost, though methods do exist in which a download may be resumed from the breakpoint. From an administrative perspective, many Concordance technicians prefer to receive physical media for the purposes of cataloguing and disaster recovery.

Assessing the Size of a Project

It's helpful for you to be on hand for consultation while research staff assess the size of a project, not only to provide cost estimates for processing, but also to ensure that the firm's network resources are sufficient to support the technical needs of the research team. Ultimately, the size of a Concordance database is proportional to the amount of text stored in fields in database records (excluding images linked via an optional image viewer). You might wish to approximate quantitative relationships between the number and types of documents collected, and how much space a database will occupy on a network.

Document collections can consist of paper documents, electronic files, or both. A precise document count cannot be known until post-processing, after a vendor has provided load files. However, correlations between storage methods (boxes and filing cabinets for paper documents; CDs and DVDs for electronic files) can yield approximate document and page counts, and those counts can be loosely translated into database size.

Before discussing approximation methods, it's necessary to review what's meant by a *document* and a *page* in the context of a Concordance database. In most applications, pages are the smallest unit that can be tracked in Concordance. Pages combine to form documents, and documents are represented by database records. For this reason, "database records" are sometimes referred to as "document records."

For physical documents, this is easy to illustrate. A letter that's comprised of two sheets of paper is usually represented by a single record in Concordance (see Figure 5-5), where a PAGECOUNT field might contain a numerical value representing the number of pages. Although there are exceptions, standard-sized physical pages that contain written text will contain roughly the same amount of data, for each page, with fluctuations depending on font style and font size.

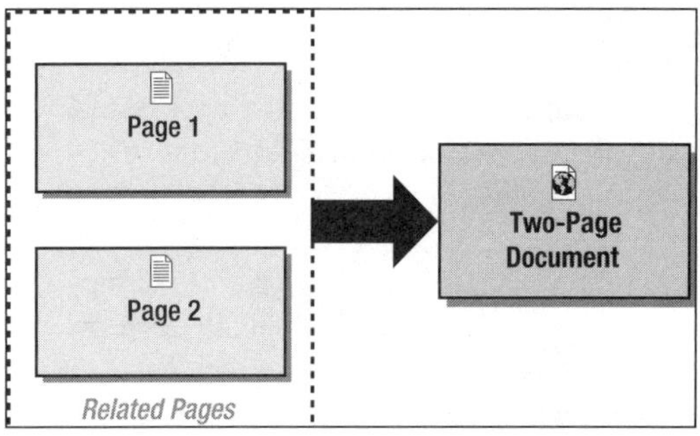

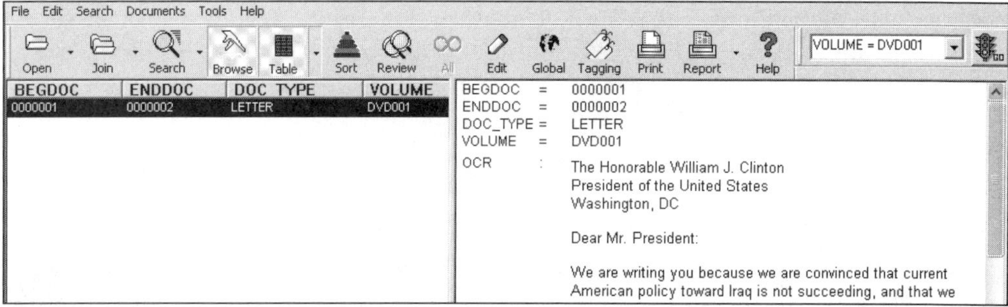

Figure 5-5. *An example of a document record that has two pages. The diagram on top demonstrates how two individual sheets of paper combine to form a single document. The screen below demonstrates how this record appears in Concordance. The BEGDOC and ENDDOC fields show that the single document record represents two individual pages of paper.*

When a collection consists of paper documents, you can estimate the number of pages using the values in Table 5-2 as a guide.

Table 5-2. *Approximate Page Counts Corresponding to Storage of Physical Documents*

Container	Approximate Page Count	Comments
Stack of paper, per inch	120–125 pages	Unbound paper
Storage box (10″×12″×15″)	2,000–2,500 pages	Small box, common to office environments
Transfer file box (10″×12″×24″)	4,500–5,000 pages	Larger box, common to office environments
Vertical file drawer	3,500–4,000 pages	Drawer in a filing cabinet
Lateral file drawer	4,500–5,000 pages	Drawer in a filing cabinet

The relationship between an electronic file and a database record in Concordance is just as well defined as that of paper documents. An electronic file is usually represented as a single database record. However, it can be more difficult to create a correlation between electronic files and pages in Concordance. For example, a Microsoft Word document might have well-defined page breaks, and that correlation is clear. However, an Excel workbook might have multiple worksheets, and no defined breaks within those sheets. Columns might or might not be expanded so that all data is visible, and they might even be hidden. How many "pages" (and therefore how much data) comprise the workbook? This is difficult to guess. When handling electronic data, it might be possible to estimate the number of database records by counting files, but it's much more difficult to estimate the database's final size.

When a collection consists of electronic files, you can estimate the number of pages using the values in Table 5-3 as a guide.

Table 5-3. *Approximate Page Counts Corresponding to Storage of Electronic Documents*

Type	Approximate Page Count	Comments
3.5″ floppy disk	1,000–1,400 pages	Assumes approximately 1.4MB capacity
CD-ROM	50,000–70,000 pages	Assumes approximately 650MB storage capacity
DVD	400,000–470,000 pages	Assumes 4.7GB storage capacity
Hard drive (internal or external)	10,000–40,000,000 pages	Assumes .1–400GB storage capacity

How do document records contribute to the amount of space consumed by a database on a network? This relationship can only be approximated, and with less precision than the document collection approximations described in Table 5-3. Given that you'll always want to have free space available on a network, it's preferable to overestimate the size of a database. Although real-world Concordance databases of 50,000 document records exist that are less than 0.1GB, it's possible to have fewer records translate into a much larger database. As a rule of thumb, you'll want to allocate 1GB of network space to every 75,000 records.

■Note This discussion refers only to the files that combine to define a Concordance database, and not to any image data that an optional image viewer might use.

Examples of Database Structure

The simplest Concordance database has a field that refers to the beginning page number of each document that each record represents. If the text of documents is to be captured and available to searches, there must be at least one field designated to store that text, and the data type of that field set to PARAGRAPH. It's customary to name the field in some way to indicate its use, such as OCR or FULLTEXT. Because there's an upper limit to the number of characters that a single PARAGRAPH field can store, some administrators prefer to designate two fields for full text, and to name them OCR1 and OCR2 (or FULLTEXT1 and FULLTEXT2). During the loading of the database, data that won't fit in the first full-text field will spill over into the next full-text field if—and only if—the field names are the same and are numbered sequentially.

Note Depending on the application, it might be useful to provide a full-text field for a research team to record comments, called TEAMNOTES.

Referring to the section "Useful Administrative Fields," a simple Concordance database can have the fields shown in Table 5-4 (field names are suggestions).

Table 5-4. *Field Names, Definitions, and Data Types for a Simple Concordance Database*

Name	Description	Data Type
BEGDOC	Beginning document number	TEXT
ENDDOC	Ending document number	TEXT
OCR1	Full-text field for data extracted through an OCR process	PARAGRAPH
OCR2	Spillover full-text field	PARAGRAPH
TEAMNOTES	Research team comments	PARAGRAPH
VOLUME	Media volume	TEXT
AUTOID	Accession field	NUMERIC
CDATE	Date record was created	DATE
EDATE	Date record was last edited	PARAGRAPH

Other database applications might use a completely different set of fields. For example, Concordance ships with a database template for use in a hypothetical research project, which serves to track individual publications. Table 5-5 lists the fields in this database. Note that there are no document ID fields or any of the administrative fields discussed earlier in this section. You'd have to create these fields using the File ➤ Modify submenu after the database has been created.

Table 5-5. *Field, Definitions, and Data Types for a Template Bibliographic Database*

Name	Description	Data Type
DOCTYPE	Document type; for example, memo, letter, manual, and so on	PARAGRAPH
PUBLISHED	Date paper was published	DATE (MMDDYYYY)
AUTHOR	Authors of paper	PARAGRAPH
TITLE	Title of paper	PARAGRAPH
ABSTRACT	Abstract of paper	PARAGRAPH
CITATION	Additional research notes	PARAGRAPH
COMMENT	Additional research notes	PARAGRAPH
SOURCE	Origin of paper	PARAGRAPH
NOTES	Additional research notes	PARAGRAPH
FULLTEXT	Full text of paper	PARAGRAPH

Determining Required Roles for Users

An important part of planning for the design and deployment of a Concordance database is to determine the roles of users. Although it's possible to deploy a Concordance database without using Concordance's own, internal security model, this practice isn't recommended. In an unsecured Concordance database, all users have access to all menu items, even those that allow administrators to delete every record from a database (the File ➤ Zap menu item). There's also the issue of confidentiality. In an unsecured Concordance database, all users have access to all data stored in every field. Furthermore, if a Concordance database isn't secured, any network user can access the database.

Concordance's security model allows you to determine which menu items a user can access. Purely administrative features, such as packing a database (to remove deleted records), should be disabled for any user who isn't an administrator. You might also wish to prevent a user from editing a record by disabling the Edit ➤ Edit menu.

Concordance has the following user groups, which have preset menu access: Supervisor, Administrator, Editor, Researcher, and No access. You might, instead, opt to set menu access for each user, rather than assign each user to one of these preset groups.

Concordance's security model allows you to control which fields a user can see. This can be helpful if a Concordance database is to be shared with guest researchers who shouldn't have access to the confidential comments made by the rest of a research team in a TEAMNOTES field.

To determine menu-level and field-level access, you must think out the respective role of each user in advance of deploying the database, and set permissions accordingly.

Creating Concordance Databases

Eventually, after an appropriate planning phase, you'll create a blank Concordance database. This process can be quite involved, depending on the scope of the application. However, templates can simplify and streamline this process. Regardless of whether a template is used, or if you prefer to create an empty database shell, and then create and define each field separately, you start with the File ➤ New menu (see Figure 5-6).

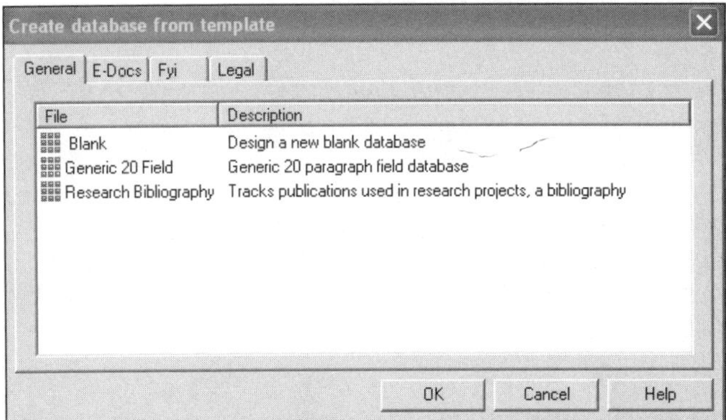

Figure 5-6. *The "Create database from template" popup dialog that appears when selecting the File menu, New submenu item*

Creating Databases from Templates

A template is an empty database model. It has predefined field names and data types that you can use to create new instances of a database. An experienced administrator who has overseen many database deployments will find some characteristics of his or her databases to be common, and therefore appropriate for inclusion into a template. Although Concordance ships with a handful of templates already, you're free to create new templates as needed.

Templates are meant to be the most generic instance of a database project, and you'll most likely have to modify fields in a template during a deployment. Modifying fields in an instance of a database built from a template doesn't modify the original template itself.

Database template files are stored in the Dataflight\Concordance\Templates folder. Any subfolder created under the Dataflight\Concordance\Templates folder will create a new tab on the "Create database from template" popup dialog, allowing you to add further organization to similar templates.

Compare the folder structure in Figure 5-7 to the tabs in the dialog shown in Figure 5-8.

Name ▲	Size	Type	Date Modified
E-Docs		File Folder	4/17/2005 9:39 PM
FYI		File Folder	4/17/2005 9:39 PM
Legal		File Folder	4/17/2005 9:39 PM
Generic 20 Field.Dcb	12 KB	Concordance Database	7/23/2004 12:42 PM
Generic 20 Field.Ini	1 KB	Configuration Settings	7/23/2004 12:42 PM
Generic 20 Field.Key	4 KB	Registration Entries	2/25/2004 10:17 AM
Research Bibliography.Dcb	12 KB	Concordance Database	9/25/2005 8:24 PM
Research Bibliography.Ini	1 KB	Configuration Settings	9/25/2005 8:24 PM
Research Bibliography.Key	4 KB	Registration Entries	1/30/2004 10:00 AM

Figure 5-7. *Folder structure where database template files are located*

File	Description
Blank	Design a new blank database
Generic 20 Field	Generic 20 paragraph field database
Research Bibliography	Tracks publications used in research projects, a bibliography

General | E-Docs | Fyi | Legal

Figure 5-8. *Tabs on the "Create database from template" popup dialog are produced from the folders that have been created under the Concordance\Templates directory.*

To create a custom template, you can export the structure of a database from the Documents ➤ Export ➤ Structure menu item. You *must* export the structure to the Dataflight\Concordance\Templates folder or one of its subfolders.

Note Field-level attributes such as data type, read only, image key, and so on are exported with the database structure and will carry over into new databases created from the template. However, security settings for individual Concordance users won't carry over.

Creating Databases from Scratch

If you don't use a template, you can create an empty database using the Blank option from the General tab on the "Create database from template" popup dialog. No fields are generated by default, and it's incumbent on you to name, assign data types, set field-level attributes, and set field-level validation for every field. You accomplish all this from the Modify dialog that opens from the File ➤ Modify menu item. You can create and delete fields, and configure most attributes from this screen (see Figure 5-9).

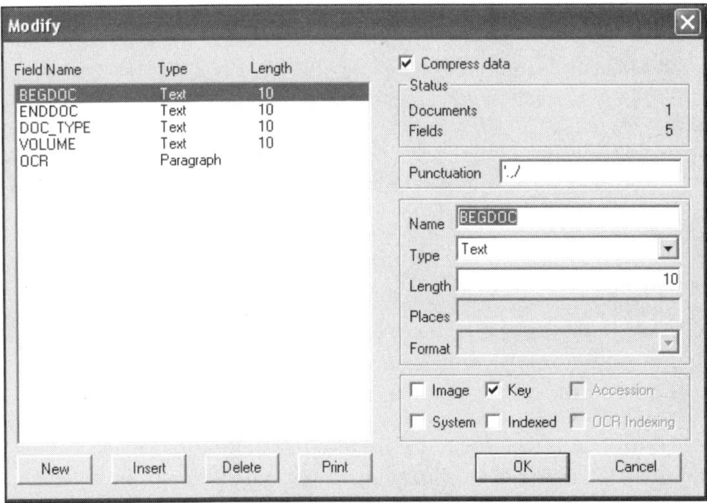

Figure 5-9. *You use the Modifiy dialog to create, modify, and define individual fields in a Concordance database. You can access it from the File ➤ Modify menu.*

Field Data Types

You must give every field in Concordance a data type. The data type of a field governs what type of data is allowed in the field. For example, the field DOCDATE, which contains the date a document was created, cannot contain nonnumeric characters. Data typing fields aids you in ensuring that the data contained in a database is accurate.

The following data types are available for fields in a Concordance database:

- *TEXT*: Appropriate for alphanumeric values that don't exceed 60 characters in length.

- *NUMERIC*: Appropriate for number values. The length attribute governs how many characters are allowed for the number. A length of 4 allows values from 0000 to 9999 to be entered in the field. The places attribute sets the position of a decimal place. For a numeric field with a length of 4 and a position of 2, the allowed values are 00.00 to 99.99. The format attribute governs how the numeric values appear to users, and can be one of the following settings: Plain, Comma, Currency, and Zero filled. The Plain setting is the default format attribute for a NUMERIC field.

- *DATE MMDDYYYY, DATE YYYYMMDD, DATE DDMMYYYY*: Appropriate for dates. The three options conform to the formats of the dates when viewed by users, where MMDDYYYY means two digits that represent a month, two digits that represent a day, and four digits that represent a year.

  Dates in external delimited load files are allowed to have separating hyphens or slashes. Given the format MMDDYYYY, the dates 09/01/2005 and 09012005 are both valid values.

- *PARAGRAPH*: Appropriate for text values that exceed 60 characters. This is the data type for fields that contain the full text of documents. The length attribute, available for the TEXT data type, cannot be set for PARAGRAPH fields.

  The most common method of searching for values in a PARAGRAPH field is to use Concordance's free-form search syntax. However, you can apply relational operators such as <, >, and = to PARAGRAPH fields.

  When Concordance sorts values in a PARAGRAPH field, it only uses the first 60 characters of the field to accomplish the sort.

Field Attributes from the Modify Dialog

In addition to field data types, you can set other attributes for individual fields. When modifying the structure of a database from the File ➤ Modify menu, available attributes appear as a series of check boxes just under the Name and Type text fields.

- *Image*: You must set only one field as the *image key* for a Concordance database, if the database is linked with an optional image viewer, such as Opticon. When the viewer is opened (by means of the camera button ![camera], which appears on the bottom of the screen in Concordance's Table or Browse view), the image key value is passed to the viewer, which uses that data to identify the file paths of the corresponding set of images that are associated with the document record. Because Concordance stores records at a document level, and each document is associated with a series of individual images, there should be two fields per record that define the beginning and end of each document, such as BEGDOC and ENDDOC. In this example, the BEGDOC field would be defined as the image key, not the ENDDOC field.

- *System*: System fields are created by Concordance itself, and aren't normally visible to users by default. Under normal circumstances, you won't be called upon to create or modify system fields.

- *Key*: To understand what this attribute means, you need a basic understanding of how Concordance's retrieval works. Concordance uses a method called *indexing* to facilitate speedy searches. When a database is indexed, fields that have a PARAGRAPH data type are processed through a text parser. This procedure identifies textual units, and builds an efficient "map" of where those textual units occur throughout document records. This map is stored as optimized files that act to support the database. In this way, when a user passes a keyword to the Concordance search engine, hits are located and retrieved for the user efficiently and quickly.

Although fields that have a PARAGRAPH data type are treated to this indexing process by default, fields that have a TEXT, NUMERIC, or DATE data type are not. These fields, sometimes referred to as *fixed fields*, require the user to specify a field's name, a comparison criteria (often referred to as a *relational operator*), and the data being evaluated.

However, using a relational operator requires Concordance to perform a comparison of every value in every record in the database, and to make a determination if a given record fits the desired search criteria. The following search requires Concordance to move to the first record in the database, examine the DOCDATE value in that record, compare it to "1/1/2004", determine if the value there fits the desired search criteria, then move to the next record in the database and complete a similar evaluation:

```
DOCDATE >= "1/1/2004"
```

For a database that stores tens or hundreds of thousands of records, this process might take many minutes to complete.

To speed searches that rely on nonindexed fields, Concordance allows you to set a useful field as a *key* field. Values in a field that has been designated as key are indexed in a manner similar to that of PARAGRAPH fields. In other words, Concordance builds an index of the contents of the key field—a guide that stores metadata about the field in a format that's optimized so that searches are completed efficiently. The indices that result from key fields are stored in Concordance files that have a .KEY extension, and are separate from the master index files built by the regular index process.

■Note In general, any nonindexed fields that users rely on in many of their searches are likely candidates as key fields. For example, many users will initially locate documents by a document ID, if known. For that reason, you can set BEGDOC and ENDDOC fields as key fields to expedite users' searches.

- *Indexed*: PARAGRAPH fields are indexed by default. Fields that have other data types are not. Setting this attribute for a TEXT, NUMERIC, or DATE field forces Concordance to treat the values in those fields in the same way that PARAGRAPH fields are treated when the database is indexed. This process speeds searches for values in NUMERIC, TEXT, or DATE fields, but indexing these fields doesn't replace the need to use relational operators when comparing values in these fields against criteria. Unlike a key field, textual units identified in indexed fields are stored in master index files.

- *Accession*: An accession field is an autonumber field. It's only available to those fields that have been given a numeric data type. Each record in the database is assigned a unique number, starting at 1. As new records are added, the accession field is advanced by a value of 1 with each new record. Accession numbers for records that have been deleted aren't reused. Gaps in accession fields can therefore indicate to the user or administrator that records have been deleted from a database.

- *OCR Indexing:* This attribute refines the methods of indexing for a field. Because of errors that result from OCR processes, many of the textual units identified during indexing might be gross misspellings or random associations of characters that result from blemishes on a printed page. OCR Indexing attempts to remove these useless textual units from the final index.

Field Attributes from the Data Entry Attributes Dialog

In addition to specific attributes that can be set for fields, you can apply additional rules of validation. These rules are accessible from the Edit ➤ Validation menu. Specific validation is applied on a field level. You must select the field to validate from the list box on the left-hand side of the Data Entry Attributes dialog, then set the appropriate validation (see Figure 5-10).

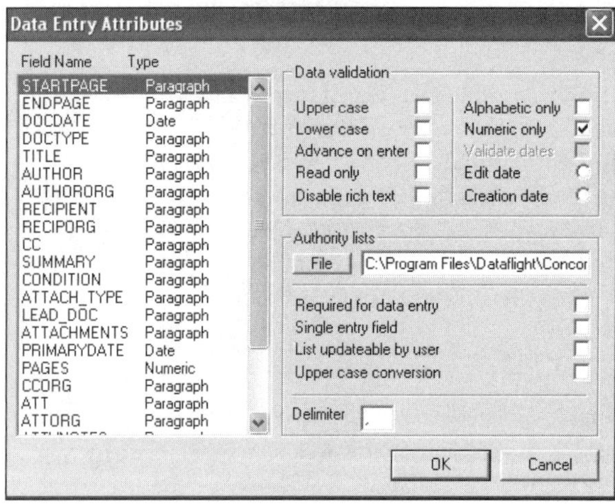

Figure 5-10. *Field-level attributes accessible from the Edit ➤ Validate item*

- *Upper case:* Forces data to convert to upper case when data is stored in the database. Because searches in Concordance aren't case sensitive, this setting affects how data appears, not how it's searched.

- *Lower case:* Forces data to convert to lower case when data is stored in the database. Because searches in Concordance aren't case sensitive, this setting affects how data appears, not how it's searched.

- *Advance on enter:* Pressing the Enter key during Concordance's edit mode (Edit ➤ Edit menu) produces different results, depending on a field's data type. If the field is a PARAGRAPH field, the cursor will remain in the field, but it will advance to the next line in the field. If the field is a TEXT, NUMERIC, or DATE field, the cursor will advance to the next field that's editable.

  Checking the "Advance on enter" attribute for a PARAGRAPH field overrides this behavior, forcing the cursor to advance to the next field.

- *Read only:* Setting this attribute for a field prevents a user from editing data in the field while in Concordance's edit mode (Edit ➤ Edit menu). Fields that are read only appear with a gray background. Fields that can be edited appear with a white background.

Note The "Read only" attribute doesn't affect a user's ability to tag documents or to add annotations.

- *Disable rich text:* Rich text, a standard formalized by Microsoft, refers to a series of formatting codes that enable, among other things, font type and font weight to be modified. Disabling rich text strips away underlying formatting code so that text appears with no embellishment in Concordance's Browse view.

- *Alphabetic only:* Only letters of the alphabet (including punctuation) are allowed in the field. The effect of this attribute is for Concordance not to respond if a user presses a numeric key.

- *Numeric only:* Only numbers (including punctuation) are allowed in the field. The effect of this attribute is for Concordance not to respond if a user presses a letter key.

- *Validate dates:* Forces Concordance to evaluate data in a date field and determine if the data stored there is in a valid date format.

- *Edit date:* "Edit date" fields record the login, date, and time each time a user edits a Concordance record, and are discussed earlier in this chapter.

  The behavior of the field varies according to the data type. If set to TEXT, the metadata for the most recent edit is stored, overwriting any previous data populating the field. If set to PARAGRAPH, metadata about each edit is stored as a separate line item in the field.

- *Creation date:* Creation date fields store the date when a record is created (or imported) into the database, and are discussed earlier in this chapter.

Authority Lists

An authority list is a way for you to restrict the types of data that can be entered into a field by requiring a user to select from a list of values. Like validation, authority lists are applied to specific fields, which you choose from the Data Entry Attributes dialog. Fields that should be restricted to a set number of values are ideal candidates to be driven from authority lists. Relying on the authority list, rather than requiring a user to type individual entries into each field, speeds data entry and reduces data entry errors.

Each authority list is stored as a separate file in the same network location as other Concordance files, and each list has an .LST extension. You set some attributes of an authority list, as they apply to a specific field, from the Data Entry Attributes dialog (from the Edit ➤ Validation menu). However, you must create the list first from a different tool. To create an authority list, use the Tools ➤ List file management menu. This opens the List File Management dialog, which allows you to create and modify several types of lists, among them authority lists (see Figure 5-11).

Note An *authority list* is a specific example of a more general Concordance object, a *list*. Other examples of lists include Concordance's stop word and synonym lists. You can modify these lists, as well, from the List File Management dialog.

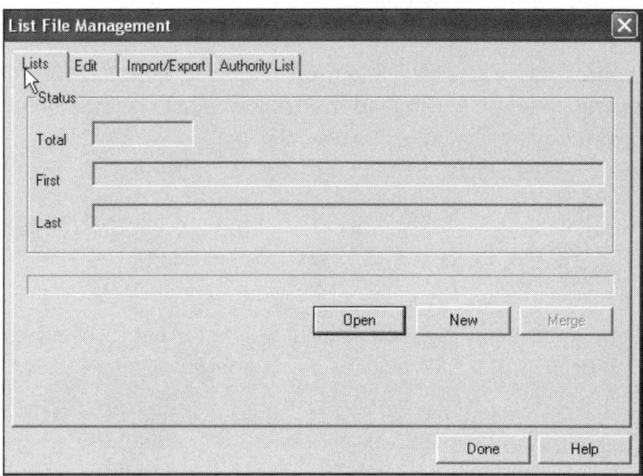

Figure 5-11. *Before you can set attributes for an authority list, you must create it from the List File Management dialog, accessible from the Tools ➤ List file management menu.*

The default tab, Lists, allows you to *Open* an existing list, create a *New* one, or to *Merge* two existing lists. Clicking the New button begins the process of creating a new list. You're presented with the option of allowing duplicates in the list file, to which you should click No, as repetitive entries in an authority list are unwanted. Next, you're given the option of creating a list that's case sensitive—this affects how the list is displayed. (Recall that searches in Concordance aren't case sensitive.)

You must now name the authority list. The Save As dialog defaults to the same network path where the current database files are stored.

Once you've named and saved the authority list, you're returned to the List File Management dialog. On creation, the authority list is empty, so the Total field displays 0, and the First and Last fields are blank.

You can add, delete, and edit entries in an authority list from the Edit tab of the List File Management dialog (see Figure 5-12).

Existing entries in the authority list are displayed in a list box on the left-hand side of the screen. The Key and "Data value" text fields refer to each entry. The Key value is the textual value that's displayed to the user when he or she brings up the list from a field that has been linked to the list, and can be no more than 1,000 characters in length. The "Data value" text field refers to a numerical value that can be assigned to each entry, and is not a requirement for entries in an authority list.

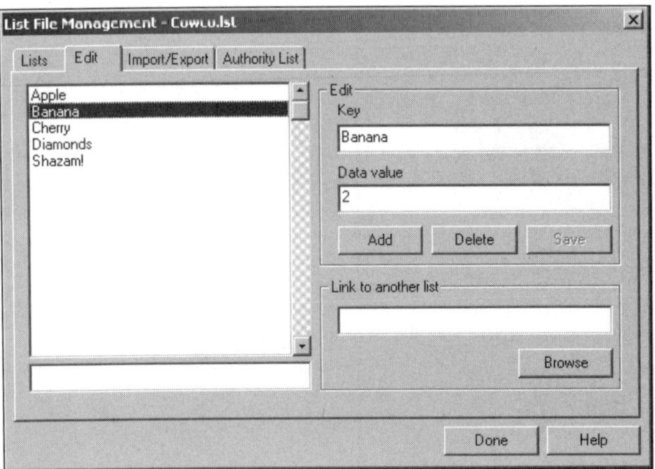

Figure 5-12. *The Edit tab of the List File Management dialog allows you to edit the individual entries of an authority list.*

To add a new line item to an authority list, type the text of the item in the Key text field, then click the Add button. Selecting a line item from the list box that displays existing entries in the authority field populates the Key and "Data value" fields with data associated with the line item. You may edit the entries (you should click the Save button after each edit) or delete the entry using the Delete key.

The text field labeled "Link to another list" allows you to link a specific value from the current list to another list. This is useful for data that follows a hierarchical chain, such as "state–county–country." The user selects a specific value from the primary list, which in turn opens another list that's dependent on the original value, and so on, until the last dependency is selected.

Import/Export Tab

Manually keying in each entry in an authority list can be time consuming. This is particularly true of common lists that may be shared among various databases (such as a list of states). For this reason, the List File Management dialog offers you a tool to import lists quickly, or to export an existing list for use in another database (see Figure 5-13).

You can prepare lists outside of Concordance in a text editor, and—if the lists have been structured properly—import them into Concordance via this tool. The proper format for a list prepared in a text editor is for each (key) value to be on a separate line. If the list contains both key values (the text of the item) and data values (a numerical identifier), the key value and data value must appear on the same line, in that order, separated by a delimiter that you can select from the Import/Export tab. An example of an appropriately formatted authority list follows:

```
APPLE,0
BANANA,0
GRAPE,0
ORANGE,0
WATERMELON,0
```

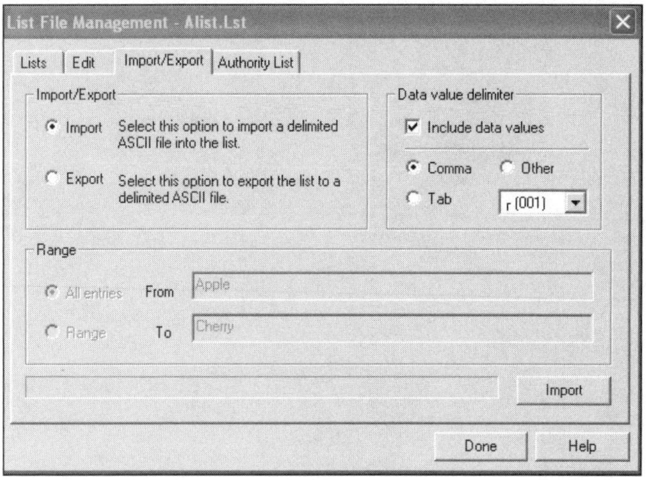

List File Management - Alist.Lst

Lists | Edit | Import/Export | Authority List

Import/Export

Import   Select this option to import a delimited ASCII file into the list.

Export   Select this option to export the list to a delimited ASCII file.

Data value delimiter

☑ Include data values

Comma   Other

Tab   r (001)

Range

All entries   From   Apple

Range   To   Cherry

Import

Done   Help

Figure 5-13. *The Import/Export tab of the List File Management dialog*

Note You can't edit .LST files created by Concordance in a text editor. To edit an .LST file, you should export the file to an external text file first, edit it accordingly, then import it via the Import/Export tab of the List File Management dialog.

The Range section of the Import/Export tab applies to exporting authority lists, and you can use it to narrow a list to a specific range. You must manually key in the From and To values, so you must take some care to avoid misspellings.

Authority List Tab

Using the methods outlined in the preceding section, you can create an authority list either by simply typing the individual entries, or importing an external and properly formatted ASCII text file. However, there might be times when you wish to create an authority list from values that are already stored in the database, perhaps in a ZIPCODE field. You can accomplish this from the Authority List tab (see Figure 5-14).

You can select a specific field in the database from the Field list box. Once you select the field, the value that's stored in that field for the first record in the current, underlying query is displayed. You can use the record selectors to move through records in the current, underlying query (see Figure 5-15).

Once you've populated an authority list from the Authority List tab, you can modify it from the Edit tab. You might find that, once the authority list is populated, it must be exported and manipulated in an external text file for values to be validated or deduplicated.

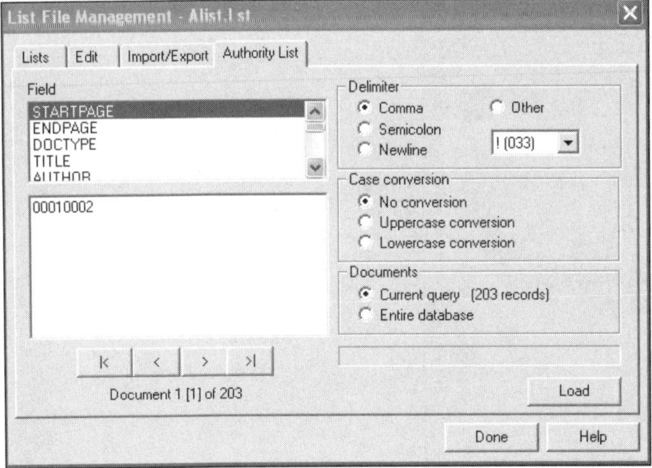

Figure 5-14. *You use the Authority List tab for creating authority lists from existing values in a Concordance database.*

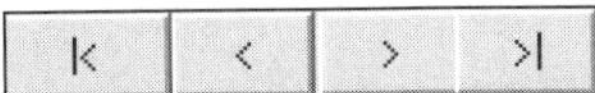

Figure 5-15. *Record selector buttons. The button on the left skips back to the first record in the underlying query. The button on the right skips forward to the last record in the underlying query. The middle buttons allow you to move forward and backward one record at a time.*

■**Note** The Authority List tab is simply a way to populate an authority list that has already been created using the Lists tab.

Assigning an Authority List to a Specific Field

Although you use the List Management tool to create and modify an authority list, you assign authority lists to specific fields from the Data Entry Attributes tool (see Figure 5-16), accessible from the Edit ➤ Validation menu.

To assign an authority list to a specific field, you must highlight the desired field from the list of fields by left-clicking it. Clicking the File button opens a dialog box that allows you to select a specific authority list (see Figure 5-17).

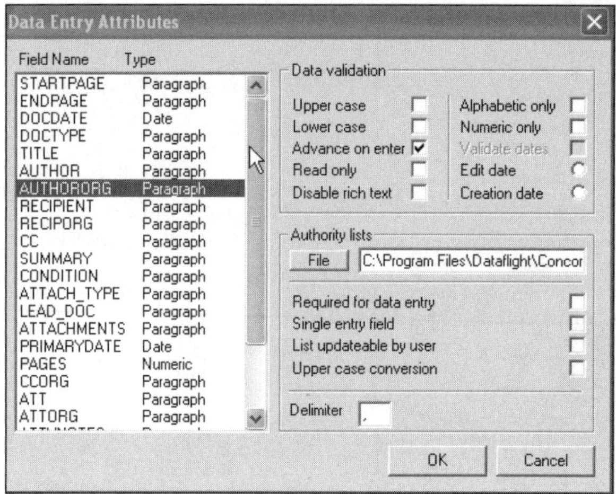

Figure 5-16. *The Data Entry Attributes tool. Note the "Authority lists" section.*

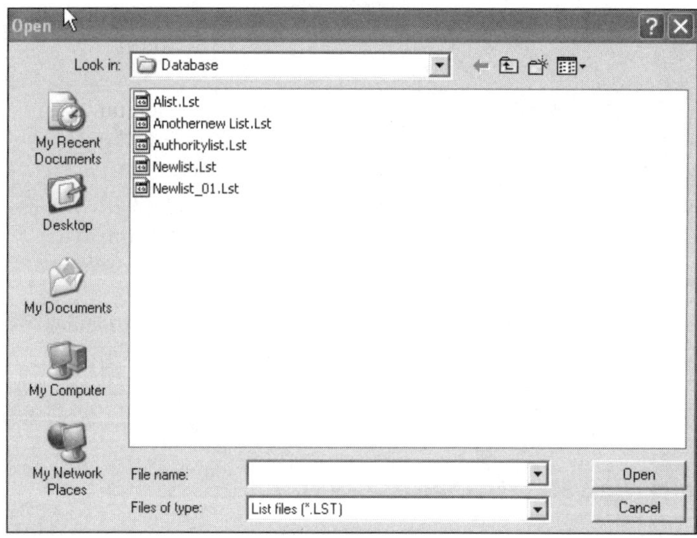

Figure 5-17. *Selecting a specific authority list to be assigned to a field. You trigger this Open dialog box by clicking the File button on the Data Entry Attributes dialog.*

Once you've assigned an authority list, you have the option of specifying attributes that control the behavior of the list as users enter data:

- *Required for data entry*: This option *requires* the user to select a value from the list before he or she can proceed. If the option is left unchecked, the user can leave the contents of the field empty.

- *Single entry field:* Fields may contain more than one entry from a list. If this option is left unchecked, separate entries are delimited by the Delimiter value, which can be modified from the text field with that label. If the option is checked, only one value from the list may be stored in the field.

- *List updateable by user:* Users can be allowed to add or remove entries from an authority list. If this option is checked, then the user has the option of manually entering a value that doesn't already appear in the list, and appending the value to the authority list with an Add button. Conversely, the user may also remove items by means of a Delete button.

- *Upper case conversion:* When clicked, this option forces all data to be converted to upper case before it's saved to the field.

Summary

Maintaining a Concordance database starts with proper planning, through consultation with both the staff who will use the database, and any outside vendors that are called on to preprocess data. To that end, it's useful to create a spec sheet for dissemination to both staff and vendors, so that deliverables conform to a specific and agreed-upon standard.

Once you've created a database and initially defined fields, you must set a series of field-level attributes that will both maintain the integrity of data in a database, and facilitate data entry for users. Some of these attributes are accessible from the Modify dialog, and some are accessible from the Data Entry Attributes dialog.

Once you've created and defined a database, the next logical step is to load it with data. The next chapter will illustrate data management procedures that apply to importing and exporting data to and from Concordance.

Importing and Exporting Data

Data management lies at the heart of Concordance administrative responsibilities. Technicians and administrators can be responsible for overseeing disparate collections of data, perhaps gathered from different sources and in different formats, and ensuring that data is properly imported. Conversely, personnel might be called upon to export data, either during routine administration, or for transmission to outside sources.

You'll find that Concordance's facilities to manage data are intuitive. You initiate all import and export tools from the Documents menu. Procedures are facilitated through the use of helpful interactive dialogs, many of which are bound together in wizards that will guide you through a procedure.

Importing into Concordance

You initiate all import routines from the Documents ➤ Import menu. This menu has five different options, each corresponding to a different import format.

Note that when Concordance imports records, no error log is created. This means that you must use some care to ensure that source data is compatible with the destination database prior to importing. Furthermore, there's no method in Concordance to undo an import or an update to a batch of records. For this reason, you should make a full backup of the Concordance database before performing data loading procedures. To back up a Concordance database, you can export the entire database to a new database, identical in structure to the source. (These methods are described in the section "Exporting As a Concordance Database.") Another way to back up a Concordance database is to make a copy of all files that define it. Restoring a database backed up in this manner means you'll replace database files with previous copies. Although a single folder can contain files supporting multiple databases, many administrators find it helpful to create dedicated folders for each database. In such an architecture, you don't have to pick and choose among a series of files to copy—just those that define the database that is to be copied.

Importing Other Concordance Databases

Other Concordance databases can be imported into a currently active database. For this to work efficiently, the source database should be similar in structure to the destination database, in that field names should match and data types should be compatible. If the source database structure deviates from the structure of the destination database, you should open the source database and use the Modify dialog from the File ➤ Modify menu to change field names and data types so that they match the destination. If field names in a source database don't match the destination, Concordance won't report any errors to the user; the fields and their data are simply ignored.

Data can either be appended as new records, or records already in the importing database can be updated, if both source and destination share one or more linking fields.

Appending Records

The Documents ➤ Import ➤ Concordance database menu activates an Import/Update Wizard that guides you through the import process.

When importing from a source database, there's no method to restrict the number of records. All records will import. In addition to fielded data, other information associated with database records is imported as well, such as document-level tags, issues, notes, and attachments.

The first screen of the wizard, Database, prompts you to locate the source database. You can use the Browse button displayed in Figure 6-1 to navigate to a network location or CD/DVD drive containing the source database.

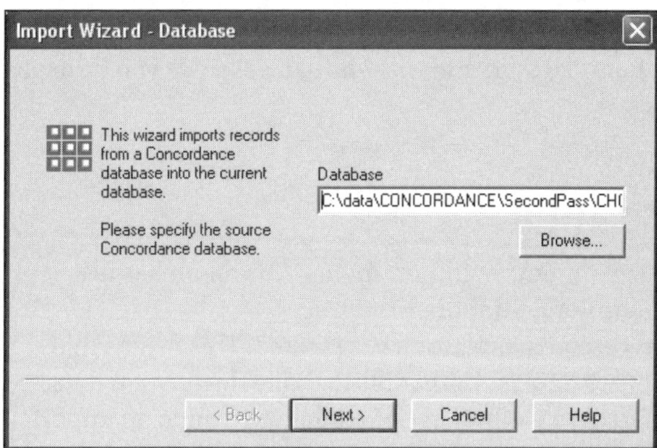

Figure 6-1. *The initial dialog of the Import Wizard used to import data from an external Concordance database. You use the Browse button to navigate to the folder where the external database's files have been saved.*

The next screen of the wizard, Fields, scans the source database, reads field names in that database, and displays them in a list box (see Figure 6-2). You can select one or more of these fields for the import. The list box supports multiple selections. Only highlighted fields will be part of the import. Fields in the destination database that have no corresponding source field will contain no data when the new database record is created.

The next screen of the wizard, Append/Replace, gives you the option to "Append all records" or "Replace matching records and append new records." It's assumed here that you wish to add records, so you should select the "Append all records" radio button (see Figure 6-3). Updating records is described in the following section, "Updating Records."

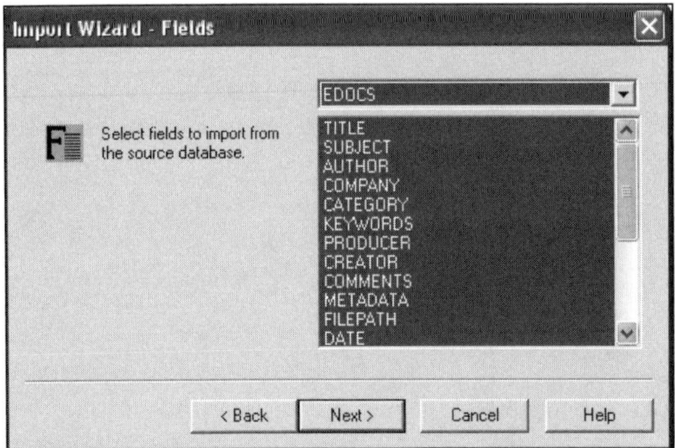

Figure 6-2. *You use this dialog to select fields that will be imported from the external database.*

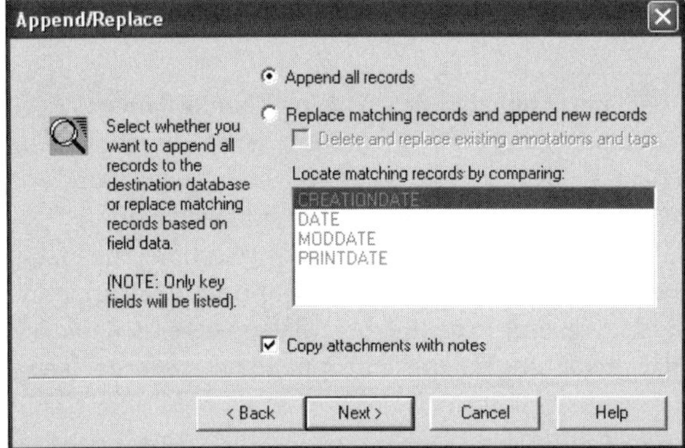

Figure 6-3. *You can use the Import Wizard either to add new data to a database, or to use data from an external Concordance database to update data. To add new records, you should select the "Append all records" option.*

The last screen of the wizard, Import, displays the file paths of the source and destination database. A status bar displays the progress as records are imported. You trigger the import by clicking the Import button. The Back button allows you to return to previous screens if any of the earlier input should be updated. You use the Cancel button to abort the procedure (see Figure 6-4).

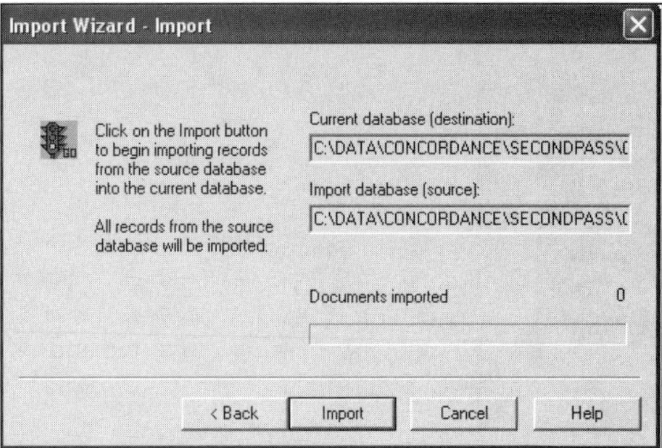

Figure 6-4. *The last screen of the wizard. Source and destination database paths are displayed, as well as a progress bar to give feedback to the user regarding how many records will be imported.*

Updating Records

Updating records is a method used to modify data that already exists in a Concordance database. This method only works if the source database and the destination database have one or more linking fields that have matching data.

You can also trigger updating from the Documents ➤ Import ➤ Concordance database menu, which activates the Import/Update Wizard described in the preceding section. The first two screens of this dialog, Database and Fields, are the same as those that appear when appending new records. You select the option to update records from the third dialog, Append/Replace, by selecting the radio button labeled "Replace matching records and append new records" (see Figure 6-5).

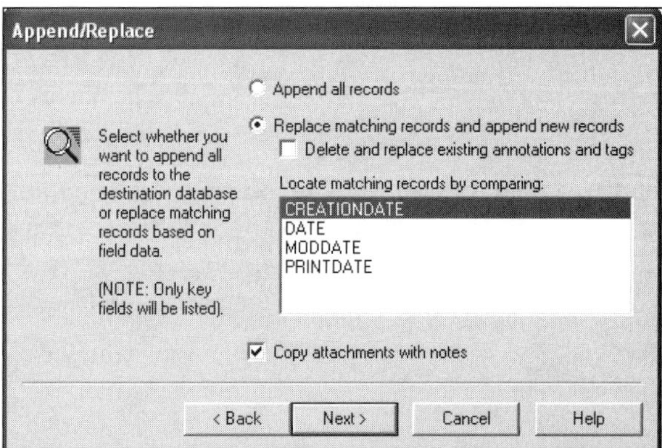

Figure 6-5. *You initiate using an external database to update fields by selecting the "Replace matching records and append new records" option. Note that the fields listed below this option are key fields in the external database. If those fields have a matching field in the destination database, a link is made and a record updated. If no link is made, the record from the external database is appended to the destination database.*

Fields listed in the list box labeled "Locate matching records by comparing:" are *key* fields in the source database. Recall that a field can be designated as a key field from the Modify dialog, activated from the File ➤ Modify menu. Highlighting a field informs Concordance that the field is to be used as a link. This list box supports multiple selections, so you can use several fields to match records. If the linking field has a PARAGRAPH data type, the linking criteria consists of the first 60 characters of the field. For other data types, the entire contents are used.

Selecting the radio button labeled "Replace matching records and append new records" instructs Concordance that the import should act to update records. It also enables the check box labeled "Delete and replace existing annotations and tags." When this option is checked, any document level *tags* and *annotations* associated with database records are deleted and replaced with those from the source database. I describe tags and annotations in more detail in Chapter 8, but to summarize: tags are information that exists outside the fields that define database records, and are assigned to sets of records to group them for quick reference. Annotations are subjective comments added by a review team to sections of text from within Concordance's Browse view.

The check box "Copy attachments with notes" is selected by default. I describe attachments in more detail in Chapter 8, but here's a summary: attachments are external files that are associated with annotated sections of text. They're actual files that can be launched from Concordance's Browse view in the native application that created them.

When the update is triggered from the final dialog of the wizard, Import, the import process updates data in fields that were selected from the Fields dialog, only if matching criteria in linked fields selected from the Append/Replace dialog are found. Unmatched records are added to the database as new records.

The Import dialog displays the file paths of the source and destination database. A status bar displays the progress as records are updated. You trigger the update by clicking the Import button.

Delimited Text

You can import ASCII delimited-text files into Concordance from the Documents ➤ Import ➤ Delimited text menu. Although delimited files often have a .TXT file extension, they might also have .DAT, .ASC, or .CSV extensions instead. As long as a delimited file is ASCII and has been structured properly, the actual file extension isn't important.

You can use delimited files either to import new records into a database, or to update existing records. When updating records, no linking criteria is used to match records from the source and destination, as with updating records from another Concordance database. When you use a delimited file to update records, data from the file is written into the Concordance database, line by line, and in the order in which data appears in both source and destination. Thus the first delimited row of data modifies the first displayed row in Concordance, the second row of delimited data modifies the second row displayed in Concordance, and so on. For this procedure to work, database records in Concordance should be sorted so that their order exactly matches the order of records in the delimited file. Updates applied in this way are often referred to as *overlaying data*.

You trigger interactive dialogs that facilitate importing delimited files from the Documents ➤ Import ➤ Delimited text menu. You have the choice of using an import wizard that will guide you through the import process, or of using an Import dialog or Overlay dialog (depending on the desired procedure). The Import and Overlay dialogs perform the same function as the Import/Update Wizard from a single screen, and are intended for more experienced users.

Appending Records

Appending records adds new records to a database. You can either use the Import/Update Wizard, described in the next section, or use the Import dialog described in the subsequent section.

Appending with the Import/Update Wizard

The first dialog of the Import/Update Wizard prompts you to choose if records are to be loaded, or if the import will be an overlay. To append new records to the database, select the radio button labeled Load (see Figure 6-6).

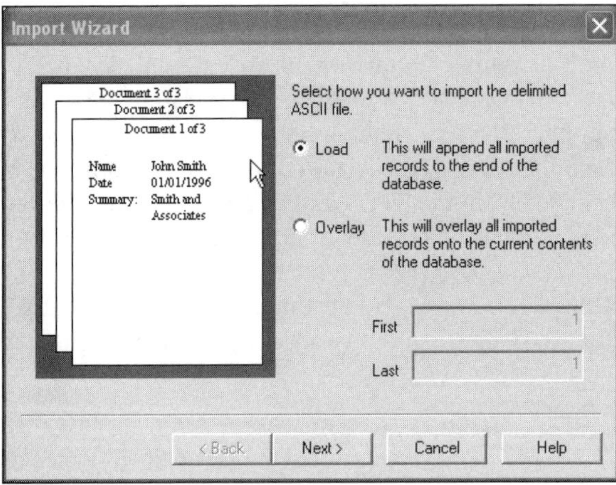

Figure 6-6. *The decision to import or update data is made from the first dialog of the Import/ Update Wizard.*

The next dialog of the wizard, Format, prompts you to choose delimiters, text qualifiers, and new line characters that are used in the source file. You can select one of the file structures from the Format drop-down box. The options are as follows:

- *Concordance default:* The developers of the Concordance software have chosen a set of characters that are highly unlikely to coincide with data contained in fields in a delimited file. The character with ASCII code 020 is used as a comma, the character with ASCII code 254 is used as a text qualifier, and the character with ASCII code 174 denotes a new line (see Figure 6-7). Many Concordance administrators and third-party vendors use these characters by default, unless otherwise instructed.

```
þSymbolþ¶þDateþ¶þOpenþ¶þHighþ¶þLowþ¶þCloseþ¶þVolumeþ
þAþ¶þ03 Mar 2004þ¶þ34.23þ¶þ34.28þ¶þ33.75þ¶þ33.97þ¶þ1823800þ
þAAþ¶þ03 Mar 2004þ¶þ37.35þ¶þ37.61þ¶þ36.83þ¶þ37.02þ¶þ4863500þ
þAAAþ¶þ03 Mar 2004þ¶þ60.53þ¶þ61.2þ¶þ60.53þ¶þ61.09þ¶þ4400þ
þAAIþ¶þ03 Mar 2004þ¶þ12.61þ¶þ12.63þ¶þ12.4þ¶þ12.5þ¶þ771300þ
þAAPþ¶þ03 Mar 2004þ¶þ39.2þ¶þ39.73þ¶þ39.04þ¶þ39.59þ¶þ973200þ
þAARþ¶þ03 Mar 2004þ¶þ21.55þ¶þ22þ¶þ21.55þ¶þ21.84þ¶þ17900þ
þABBþ¶þ03 Mar 2004þ¶þ6.22þ¶þ6.25þ¶þ6.15þ¶þ6.23þ¶þ180200þ
þABCþ¶þ03 Mar 2004þ¶þ58.15þ¶þ59.09þ¶þ58.11þ¶þ59.01þ¶þ509500þ
```

Figure 6-7. *An example of a delimited file that uses default Concordance delimiters*

- *Comma delimited (CSV)*: Comma-delimited files that use a comma as a delimiter, double quotes as text qualifiers, and a new line character with the ASCII code 013 are sometimes referred to as *CSV files*, for *comma-separated values* (see Figure 6-8). Note that although CSV files use perhaps the most commonly accepted delimiters—qualifiers and new line characters—these symbols might be poor choices when transferring files that contain the full text extracted from documents. The reason for this is that the symbols used to structure the data files, the comma and double quote, might be used *in* the data itself. If these characters are also used to denote the beginning and ending of fields, processing software will interpret a comma used in a sentence in full text as meaning that the current field terminates, and it will move on to the next field. Data will be malformed in Concordance as a result. Because of this possibility, many Concordance administrators minimize their use of this type of delimited file.

```
"Symbol","Date","Open","High","Low","Close","Volume"
"A","03 Mar 2004","34.23","34.28","33.75","33.97","1823800"
"AA","03 Mar 2004","37.35","37.61","36.83","37.02","4863500"
"AAA","03 Mar 2004","60.53","61.2","60.53","61.09","4400"
"AAI","03 Mar 2004","12.61","12.63","12.4","12.5","771300"
"AAP","03 Mar 2004","39.2","39.73","39.04","39.59","973200"
"AAR","03 Mar 2004","21.55","22","21.55","21.84","17900"
"ABB","03 Mar 2004","6.22","6.25","6.15","6.23","180200"
"ABC","03 Mar 2004","58.15","59.09","58.11","59.01","509500"
```

Figure 6-8. *An example of a comma-delimited file*

- *Tab delimited*: A tab-delimited file uses the tab character as a delimiter, a double quote as a text qualifier, and a new line character with ASCII code 013 to denote the end of a row of data (see Figure 6-9).

```
"Symbol"   "Date"   "Open"   "High"   "Low" "Close" "Volume"
"A" "03 Mar 2004" "34.23" "34.28" "33.75" "33.97" "1823800"
"AA"   "03 Mar 2004" "37.35" "37.61" "36.83" "37.02" "4863500"
"AAA"  "03 Mar 2004" "60.53" "61.2"  "60.53" "61.09" "4400"
"AAI"  "03 Mar 2004" "12.61" "12.63" "12.4"  "12.5"   "771300"
"AAP"  "03 Mar 2004" "39.2"   "39.73" "39.04" "39.59" "973200"
"AAR"  "03 Mar 2004" "21.55" "22"   "21.55" "21.84" "17900"
"ABB"  "03 Mar 2004" "6.22"   "6.25"   "6.15"   "6.23"   "180200"
"ABC"  "03 Mar 2004" "58.15" "59.09" "58.11" "59.01" "509500"
```

Figure 6-9. *An example of a tab-delimited file*

- *Custom*: The delimiters, text qualifiers, or new line characters used in a file might not be any of the choices offered in the previous discussion. If so, you can select the Custom option from the drop-down box, then select the appropriate characters from the Comma, Quote, and Newline drop-down boxes (see Figure 6-10). Each character is displayed (if it can be rendered) with its associated ASCII code.

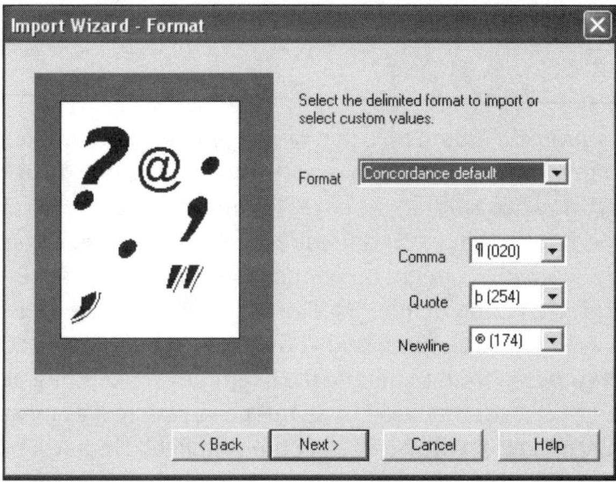

Figure 6-10. *You choose the delimiters that are used in the import file from this wizard.*

The next dialog, "Date format," prompts you to select the date format used by *all* dates in the delimited file (see Figure 6-11). All dates throughout a file, even if they are in separate columns of data, *must* be formatted in exactly the same way. If date formats are mixed, date values will appear malformed in Concordance.

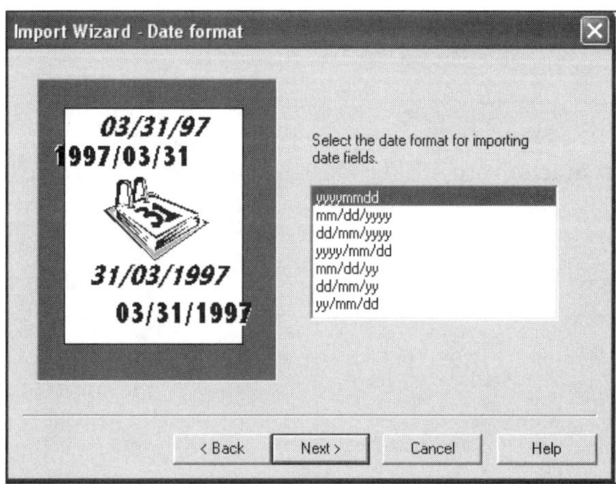

Figure 6-11. *All dates in a delimited load file must be formatted consistently. You choose the format from this dialog of the wizard.*

The next dialog, Fields, is displayed in Figure 6-12. It displays all fields in the Concordance database in a list box labeled Available Fields. You can select fields from the Available Fields list box and move them to the Selected Fields list box. Only fields that are displayed in the Selected Fields list box will be populated with data during the import. You can modify the order of fields in Selected Fields with the Up and Down buttons. The order of fields from top to bottom in this list box should match the order of fields from left to right in the delimited file.

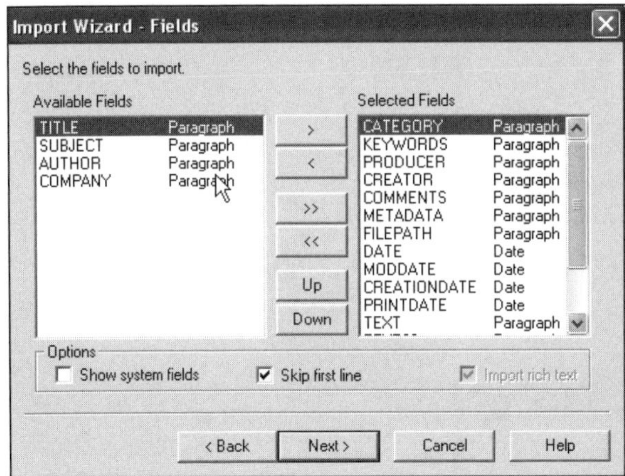

Figure 6-12. *From this dialog, you select fields in the database that will be affected by the load. Only those fields in the Selected Fields list box will have data written to them. Fields that are left in the Available Fields list box will contain no data in the new records.*

The Options area of this screen prompts you with the following choices:

- *Show system fields*: If the database contains any system fields, which are hidden by default, you can display them in the Available Fields list box by selecting this option.

- *Skip first line*: Delimited files can (and should) contain field names in the first line of the file. Vendors should be encouraged to include this line of data in files they deliver, because field names allow you to confirm the intended field for each column of data. However, you probably won't wish to import this line of data into your database. Selecting this option causes the program to skip the first line of the file.

- *Import rich text*: Any rich text formatting in the source file will be removed.

You use the next dialog, Open, to locate the load file on your computer or on a network (see Figure 6-13).

The last dialog of the Import/Overlay Wizard, Finish, displays the location of the source file, and includes a list box that displays the progress of the import (see Figure 6-14). This list box is labeled "Data overflow." This term refers to the wrong type of data being imported into a field. For example, text characters, such as letters of the alphabet, cannot be imported into a field with a NUMERIC data type. If Concordance encounters such errors, it will display the results in this list box.

Figure 6-13. *From the Open dialog of the wizard, you can use the Browse button to select the delimited file that will be loaded.*

Figure 6-14. *The last dialog of the wizard displays the path of the import file, and feedback to the user as data is processed. You click the Finish button to trigger the import.*

Appending with the Import Delimited Text Dialog

The Import Delimited Text dialog summarizes all the options displayed in the several dialogs of the Import/Overlay Wizard in a single screen (see Figure 6-15).

The "Available fields" and "Selected fields" list boxes perform the same function as in the Fields dialog of the Import Wizard. All fields in the database are displayed in the "Available fields" list box, and can be moved to the "Selected fields" list box. Only those fields in the "Selected fields" list box will be imported. You can change the order of the fields in the "Selected fields" list box by moving fields back and forth from the "Available fields" list box in the correct order. You can move fields either by double-clicking them, or by using the Select All, Select, Remove, and Remove All buttons as needed.

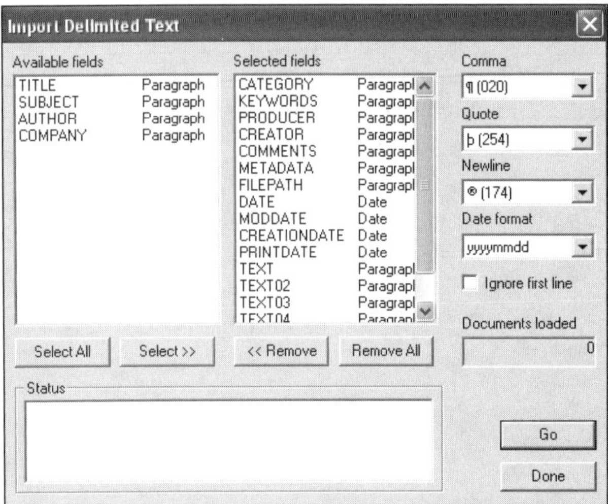

Figure 6-15. *The Import Delimited Text dialog contains all the options available from the various dialogs that define the Import/Update Wizard in a single screen.*

You select the appropriate delimiters, text qualifiers, and new line characters using the drop-down boxes labeled Comma, Quote, and Newline respectively. You select the date format from the "Date format" drop-down box. As with the corresponding check box in the Import Wizard, the "Ignore first line" check box causes the program to skip the first line of the delimited file. The "Documents loaded" and the Status fields provide feedback to the administrator during the load.

The Go button performs the same function as the Browse button in the Open dialog of the Import Wizard. Once the import has been completed, you close the Import dialog by clicking the Done button.

Overlaying Records

Overlaying records is a way to update data in a Concordance database from a delimited file. As noted earlier in this chapter, no linking criteria is used to match records from the source file to database records in Concordance. Instead, rows of data are updated in the order in which they appear, both in the delimited file and in the database. For this procedure to work, you must know what sort-order criteria was used to sort records in the delimited file, and you must apply that same sort-order criteria to records in the database. If you don't do this, the overlay will update data in the wrong order, and data in Concordance will be lost. Because there's no way to roll back a data load and restore the database to an earlier state, you're advised to make a full backup of the database prior to performing the procedure.

Overlaying with the Overlay Wizard

The first dialog of the Import/Overlay Wizard gives you the option either to import or overlay data. The first screen of this dialog is displayed in Figure 6-16. To overlay data, select the Overlay radio button. Clicking this radio button opens the First and Last text fields. The numbers in these text fields are, by default, the first and last record, referenced by ordinal position, which are accessible to Concordance from the last active search. Changing these values gives you the ability to update a subset of records. Changing the value in the First text field from 1 to 5, and changing the Last text field value to 15, means that only the fifth through fifteenth records in the database will be updated from the delimited file. If there are any records in the delimited file past the ten required to update the fifth through fifteenth database records, they're ignored.

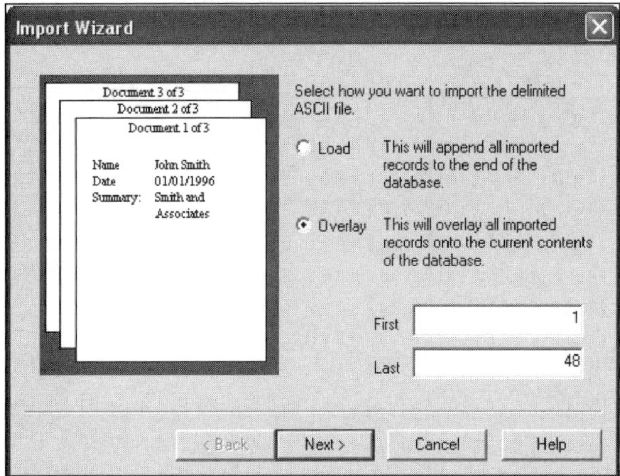

Figure 6-16. *You select the option to overlay records from this dialog. You can use the First and Last fields to specify the range of records to be updated.*

The next dialog of the wizard, Format, performs the same function as the Format dialog used when importing data, described in the section "Appending with the Import/Update Wizard." You can select the appropriate delimiter, text qualifier, and new line characters used in the file.

You use the next dialog, "Date format," to select the date format used in the delimited file. As with files used for loading data, date formats in the delimited file used for updating records must be consistent.

The next dialog is Fields. An "Available fields" list box displays accessible database fields, while a "Selected fields" list box displays only those fields that have been selected for modification. All options from this dialog are identical in purpose to those described for the corresponding dialog in the preceding section about importing.

You use the next dialog, Open, to browse your workstation or a network drive to select the delimited file. Its purpose and layout are identical to that described in the section about importing.

The last dialog, Finish, displays the file path of the delimited source file, feedback recording the number of documents processed, and any data overflows that result. Its purpose and layout is identical to that described in the section about importing.

Overlaying with the Overlay Database Dialog

The Overlay Database dialog summarizes, in one screen, all the options displayed in the series of dialogs presented by the Import/Overlay Wizard (see Figure 6-17).

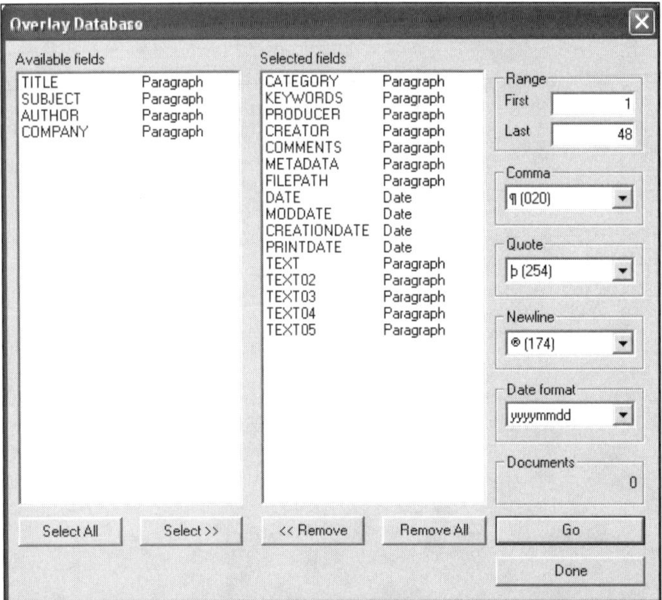

Figure 6-17. *The Overlay Database dialog contains all the options available from the various dialogs that define the Import/Overlay Wizard, though in a single screen.*

You use the Range group of text fields, First and Last, to narrow the range of records to be affected. The numbers in these fields correspond to the ordinal position of the first and last record that will be updated.

The "Available fields" and "Selected fields" list boxes perform the same function described in previous sections. All fields in the database are displayed in the "Available fields" list box, and can be moved to the "Selected fields" list box. Only those fields in the "Selected fields" list box are updated through the overlay. You can change the order of the fields in the "Selected fields" list box by moving fields back and forth from the "Available fields" list box in the correct order. As with the Import dialog, you can move fields either by double-clicking them, or by using the Select All, Select, Remove, and Remove All buttons as needed.

You select the appropriate delimiters, text qualifiers, and new line characters using the drop-down boxes labeled Comma, Quote, and Newline, respectively. You select the date format from the "Date format" drop-down box.

The Go button performs the same function as the Browse button in the Open dialog of the Import Wizard. Once the import has been completed, clicking the Done button closes the Overlay Database dialog.

E-Documents

E-documents refer to native files. Concordance can import a variety of electronic files directly. Many types of files are supported (Adobe Acrobat PDF files, most word processing documents, spreadsheets, and ASCII text files), though to import files created from Microsoft Office, the loading workstation must have the appropriate native applications installed.

The procedure imports both the text embedded in the files, and associated metadata fields, such as AUTHOR, CREATION DATE, and MODIFICATION DATE. You can create a database to store the documents from an empty database shell and add fields manually, though a Concordance template is uniquely defined for this purpose. You can access the E-Documents template database from the E-Docs tab of the "Create database from template" dialog that opens from the File ➤ New menu.

Note that, in the E-Docs template, a series of paragraph fields exists to store full-text data associated with native files: TEXT, TEXT02, TEXT03, TEXT04, and TEXT05. For most purposes, the first field, TEXT, is sufficient. In the unlikely event that full text from a document exceeds the character limit allowed by the PARAGRAPH data type—12 million characters—the excess is loaded into the next full-text field, TEXT02. If the limit of that field is exceeded, the excess is loaded into TEXT03, and so on.

You can open an E-Documents Import Wizard to guide you through the import process, from the Documents ➤ Import ➤ E-Documents menu. The first dialog of this wizard allows you to import files by type, or to import specific files from selected directories (see Figure 6-18).

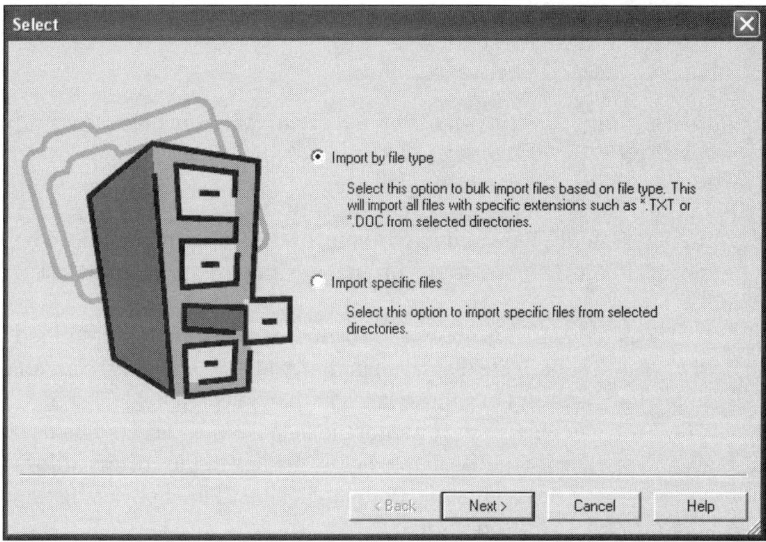

Figure 6-18. *You use this dialog of the E-Documents Import Wizard to inform Concordance if a series of files should be imported by their file type ("Import by file type"), or if you'll choose specific files ("Import specific files").*

Import Specific Files

When you select the "Import specific files" radio button from the first dialog of the wizard and click the Next button, the File dialog is opened. This feature allows you to select specific files to be imported.

This dialog has three sections (see Figure 6-19). The left-hand pane displays all drives accessible from the administrator's workstation. The nodes in the tree represent each drive. Clicking the + symbol in a node expands the drive and displays folders in it. You can expand the tree and drill down into subfolders.

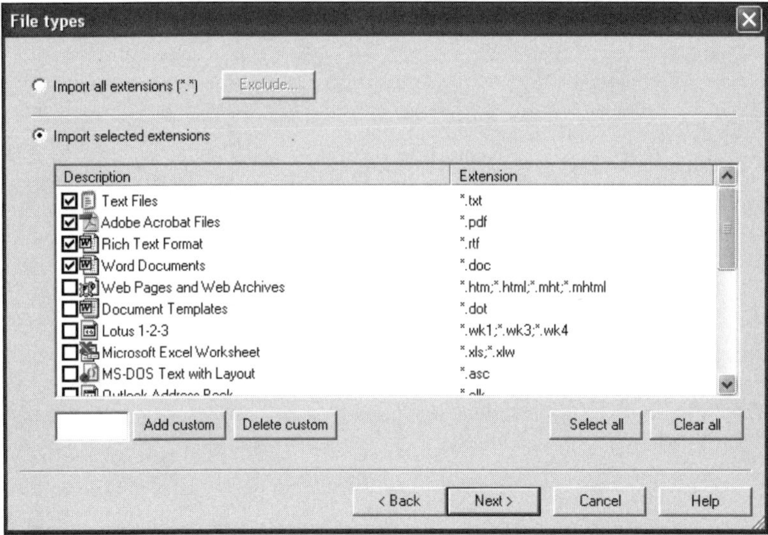

Figure 6-19. *You can choose specific files from this dialog. Entries in the right-hand pane correspond to the files contained in the selected folder in the left-hand pane. Files listed in the bottom pane will be imported.*

When you select a drive or folder in the left pane, all files in the drive or folder are displayed in the right pane. Clicking a file in the right pane and clicking the Add button lists the file path and file name in the bottom pane. Files listed in the bottom pane will be imported. To remove an item from the bottom pane, you highlight the item by clicking it, and then click the Remove button.

Import by File Type

When you select the "Import by file type" radio button from the first dialog of the wizard, and click the Next button, the "File types" dialog is opened (see Figure 6-20).

You may elect to import all extensions by default, or to import selected extensions only.

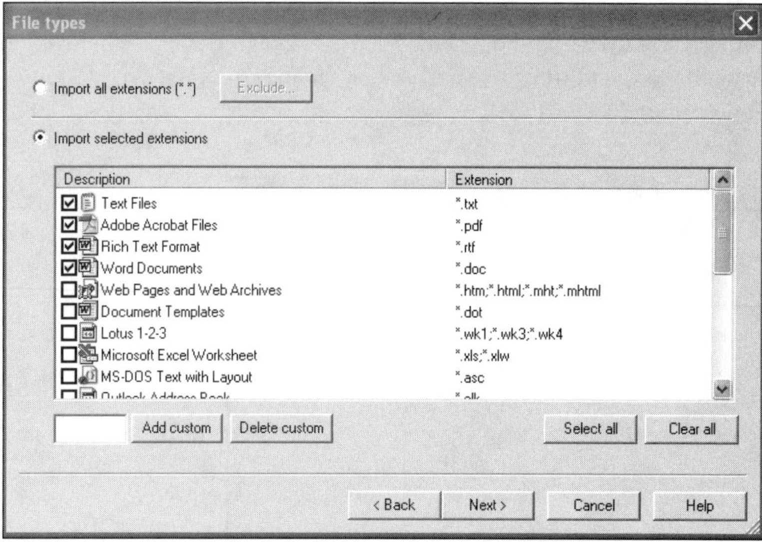

Figure 6-20. *A list of file types that Concordance can import*

Import All Extensions

Selecting the "Import all extensions" radio button causes Concordance to import every native file that it can process. Recall that some file types, such as compressed archives, must have files extracted from them first for them to be useful. Nevertheless, Concordance can process such a file by creating a record for it, if directed to.

You can explicitly define certain file extensions to be skipped, so that Concordance will ignore them, by clicking the Exclude button. This opens the "Exclude extensions" dialog (see Figure 6-21).

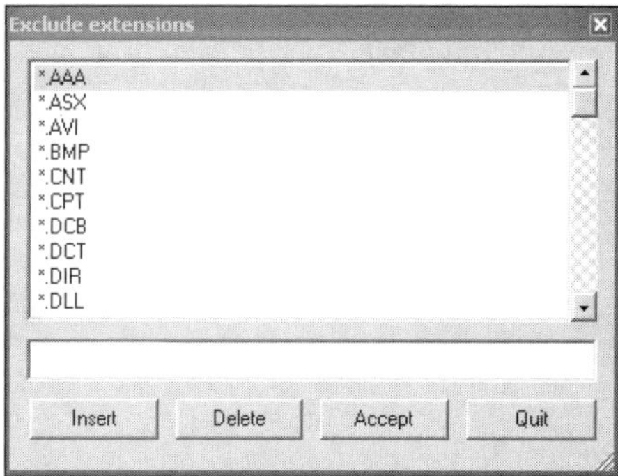

Figure 6-21. *A list of file extensions that Concordance ignores. You can modify this list using the Insert and Delete buttons.*

The list is preloaded with a series of file types that Concordance won't process. If you know of other file extensions that should be skipped that aren't already on the list, you can enter them in the open text field at the bottom of the dialog. Note that Concordance recognizes the * wildcard character, which is a placeholder for any file name. Thus, if all files with the extension AAA should be skipped, you should enter ***.AAA** in the text field. Clicking the Insert button adds the file extension to the exclusion list. You can remove any file extensions already in the list that shouldn't be skipped by highlighting the extension, and then clicking the Delete button. Deleting a file extension from the list forces Concordance to import a record associated with the file, even if the file doesn't contain searchable text. This method is useful if you want to record the existence of files, as associated metadata accompanying the files will be captured. Figure 6-22 shows the result of attempting to import a .TIF file—an image graphic that contains no searchable text.

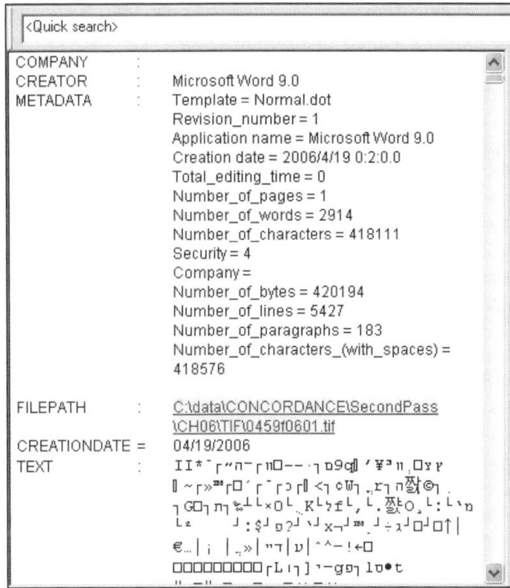

Figure 6-22. *An example of the "full text" that's extracted from an electronic file that has no actual searchable text. In this example, a .TIF image was imported. The binary format of the file is translated into indecipherable characters in Concordance.*

When you're satisfied with your selections, clicking the Accept button saves the updated list and closes the dialog. The Quit button closes the dialog without saving updates.

Import Selected Extensions

The other option available from the "File types" dialog gives you the ability to select file extensions from a list. Items that have a check mark will be imported. You can add additional file types from the text field in the lower left-hand corner of the dialog, and by clicking the

"Add custom" button. Custom items added in this way can be removed from the list by highlighting them and clicking the "Delete custom" button. Note that sometimes several file extensions are associated with the same type of file. The extensions *.HTM, *.HTML, *.MHT, and *.MHTML, for example, are all associated with a Web browser. You can add a series of custom file types in the same way by separating each extension with a semicolon. To add the file extensions *.AAA and *.BBB together, you enter ***.AAA;*.BBB** into the text field.

The "Select all" button automatically selects all extensions. The "Clear all" button clears all extensions.

The next dialog of the wizard, Folders, directs you to select one or more folders from which files should be imported. Folders can be on your own workstation, or a mapped network drive. A user selects a folder, then clicks the Add button to place a reference to the folder in the Directory list box. Multiple folders can be selected. The Remove button removes a highlighted entry from the Directory list box. Clicking the "Import files from subdirectories" check box forces Concordance to load files from all subfolders that exist under the selected folders. You can also manually key the path to a folder in the open text field under the list box on the left.

The next dialog, Fields, displays the metadata fields Concordance will import, and allows you to specify the database fields to which this metadata should be loaded. If you've created the destination database from the E-Docs template, metadata fields will already exist, and these selections are already selected by default. If you've added fields to the database, or you otherwise wish to modify these default mappings, you can select a field name from the desired drop-down box (see Figure 6-23).

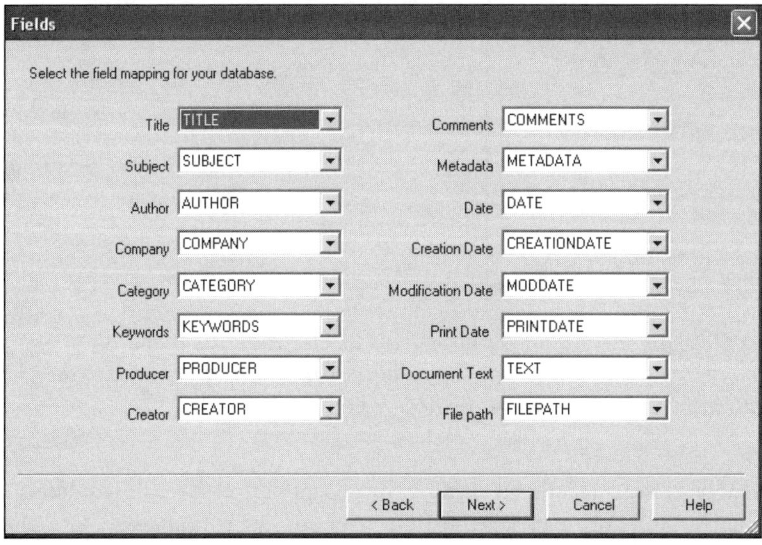

Figure 6-23. *The E-Documents database template contains field names that are associated with common metadata fields associated with most electronic file types. This dialog allows mappings from data associated with files to field names in a Concordance database.*

The next dialog of the wizard, Options, allows you to modify how Concordance will behave during the load (see Figure 6-24).

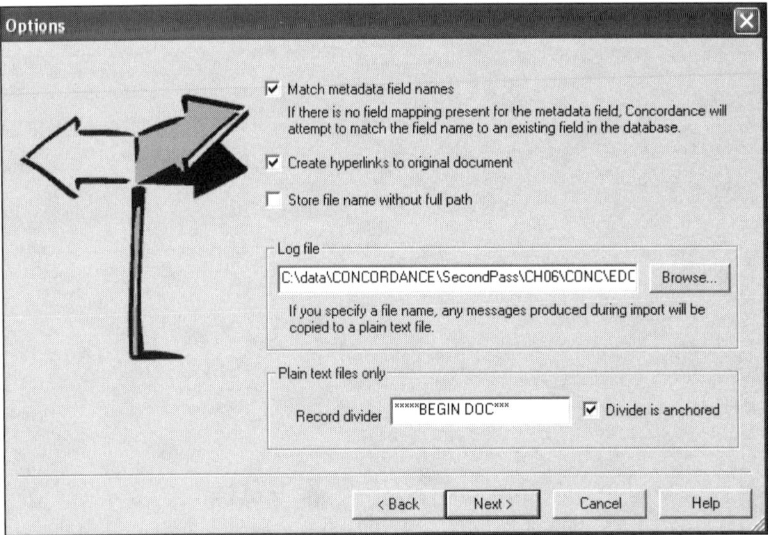

Figure 6-24. *You can set additional options from the Options dialog of the wizard.*

- *Match metadata field names*: In addition to the standard metadata values associated with native files, the users who create those files have the ability to create their own custom metadata fields. This option instructs Concordance to attempt to map any user-defined metadata fields associated with native files to the corresponding database fields.

- *Create hyperlinks to original document*: One of the fields created in the E-Docs template is FILEPATH. When Concordance loads a file, it stores the file path associated with the file in this field. If this option is checked, when a user clicks the value contained in the field in Concordance's Browse view, the file will be launched in its native application, if the application is installed on the user's computer (see Figure 6-25).

- *Store file name without full path*: If this option is selected, only the file name will be stored in the FILEPATH field, not the full file path plus the file name. This option doesn't override the preceding option, "Create hyperlinks to original document."

- *Log file*: Entering a file name in this text field causes Concordance to create a log of messages that are generated during loading. The file that Concordance creates is a clear text, ASCII file that can be opened in a text editor. The log is useful for reviewing the import process, and identifying any files that failed to import. You can use the Browse button to specify a location where the file will be created.

- *Plain text files only*: This feature is used when a file has a repeating series of characters that denote a page break. Rather than importing the entire file as a single record, Concordance creates a new database record every time it encounters the designated characters. You can enter any series of characters in the text field. This feature only works with plain text files.

```
METADATA        :      Title = Document Imaging Databases, an Overview
                       Author = None
                       Template = ApressStyles_020805.dot
                       Last_author = None
                       Revision_number = 7
                       Application name = Microsoft Word 9.0
                       Creation date = 2005/3/10 20:10:0.0
                       Last save time = 2005/3/13 19:12:0.0
                       Total_editing_time = 291
                       Number_of_pages = 1
                       Number_of_words = 4810
                       Number_of_characters = 24773
                       Security = 4
                       Company =
                       Number_of_bytes = 70656
                       Number_of_lines = 400
                       Number_of_paragraphs = 80
                       Number_of_characters_(with_spaces) = 29531

FILEPATH        :      C:\data\CONCORDANCE\FirstPass\CH01\CH01_031305.doc
MODDATE         =      03/13/2005
CREATIONDATE =         03/10/2005
```

Figure 6-25. *The FILEPATH field contains the full file path and file name of the native file to which the database record corresponds. If a user clicks this path, the file will launch in its native application, if that application has been installed on the user's workstation.*

You use the "Divider is anchored" option when the document divider characters are flush left in the document. If the divider isn't flush left, you shouldn't check this option.

The next dialog of the wizard is the last. Clicking the Import button activates the import process. The status of the load is reported to the user from the Status and Message list boxes (see Figure 6-26).

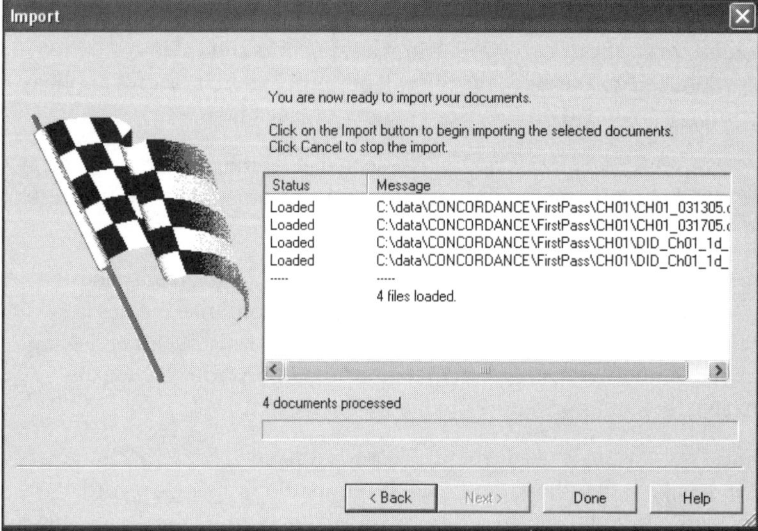

Figure 6-26. *The last dialog of the wizard reports the progress of the import as documents are processed.*

Transcripts

The Transcripts option is enabled if the active Concordance database is a Transcript database; otherwise, it's disabled. Concordance has a predefined Transcript database model that's accessible from the Legal tab of the "Create database from template" dialog.

Supported transcript formats include LiveNote's .PTF and .PCF formats. LiveNote is a popular software program that allows court reporters and those taking depositions to create real-time electronic transcripts. ASCII text files that are appropriately formatted can be imported as well.

For this feature to work, it's assumed that the transcripts to be imported are structured properly. Individual lines should be numbered and double spaced. Although there's some variation, each line usually contains no more than 60 characters, and each page usually contains no more than 25 lines. Before importing a transcript, it's helpful for you to be informed of the file's basic structure.

Choosing the Documents ➤ Import ➤ Transcripts menu prompts you to locate the folder or subdirectory that contains the transcript(s) to be imported. You can double-click a transcript name, or highlight it and click the Open button to activate the "Load transcripts" dialog. If two or more transcripts from the same folder are to be loaded, you can select them by holding down the Ctrl key on the keyboard, and left-clicking each transcript (see Figure 6-27).

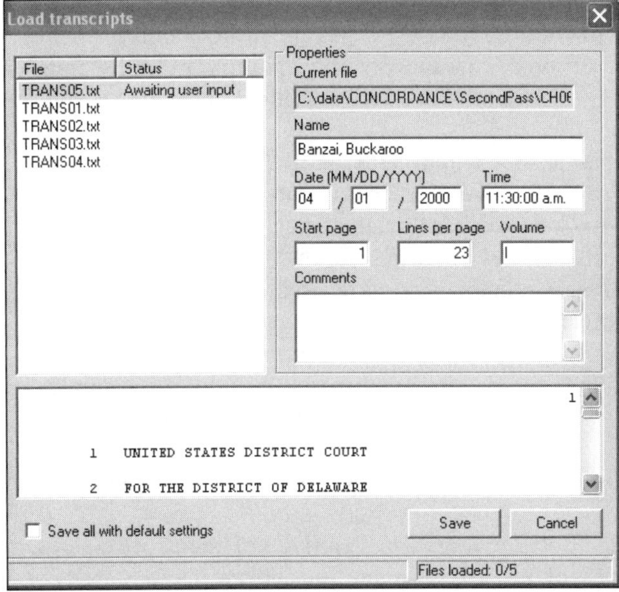

Figure 6-27. *The "Load transcripts" dialog. Each transcript listed on the left has data that appears in the Properties group of fields. You must verify that data has been correctly extracted for each transcript by clicking the Save button.*

The "Load transcripts" dialog displays all selected transcripts in a list box in the left pane. The right pane, labeled Properties, contains fields of data that Concordance will extract from a highlighted transcript. If the transcript is structured properly, this data will be correct. If not, you can scroll through the body of the transcript using the preview pane at the bottom of the dialog to locate appropriate values, and then enter corrections. If several transcripts are to be imported, you should highlight each transcript by clicking it, and verify or update the data in the Properties pane accordingly. You should click the Save button for each transcript. A progress bar at the bottom of the dialog advances as each transcript is selected, verified, and its data saved. Saving data for the last transcript in the list causes all transcripts to be loaded. The label on the Save button changes to Load. Clicking the Load button reopens the initial Open dialog so that additional transcripts, perhaps in other folders, can be loaded.

E-Mail

Concordance can import e-mail messages and other electronic objects from Microsoft's Messaging System, the Microsoft Outlook e-mail client, and Microsoft Exchange Server. When importing from one of these applications, Microsoft Outlook must be installed on the loading system.

As with e-documents, Concordance has a dedicated database template that can be used to store e-mail messages. You can access it from the E-Docs tab of the "Create database from template" dialog, from the File ➤ New menu. This template has a series of predefined fields that map to the metadata fields associated with e-mail messages. You can modify, delete, or add to these fields as needs evolve.

A common use of this feature is to import e-mail messages and attachments from the Microsoft Outlook e-mail client. For this procedure to work, the loading workstation must have Outlook installed, and the e-mail client must have access to the e-mail database file that contains the desired messages.

Microsoft Outlook can either be associated with a central e-mail server (such as Exchange), or be used as a standalone client. When Outlook operates as a standalone client, it stores messages in a .PST file. All e-mail messages, associated attachments, and other items such as Calendar, Journal entries, Contacts, and Tasks are wrapped in this single file. Concordance imports the full text and other metadata fields associated with e-mail messages, and it can extract attachments to a directory that you specify. Extracted attachment files can be associated with each e-mail record in the database, so that a user can click a link in Concordance's Browse view and launch the attachment in its native application, if that application is installed on the user's workstation. Other items stored in the .PST file, such as Journal entries and Contacts, can be imported, though e-mail messages don't share many of the metadata fields associated with these objects. As a result, the records may not contain all the data associated with these objects.

Concordance has an "Import e-mail" wizard that displays a series of interactive dialogs and that guides you through the process of importing e-mails. You activate it from the Documents ➤ Import ➤ E-mail menu.

The first dialog of this wizard displays the contents of the .PST file associated with the Outlook client in a tree view. Clicking one of the items in the tree causes Concordance to import items in that object. You may highlight only one object per import. Note that each node in the tree view might have subfolders. To ensure that all entries from every subfolder are imported, you should check the "Import subdirectories" check box. To import all entries in every object in the tree, you can click the top-level object (Personal Folders in Figure 6-28), and then check the "Import subdirectories" check box.

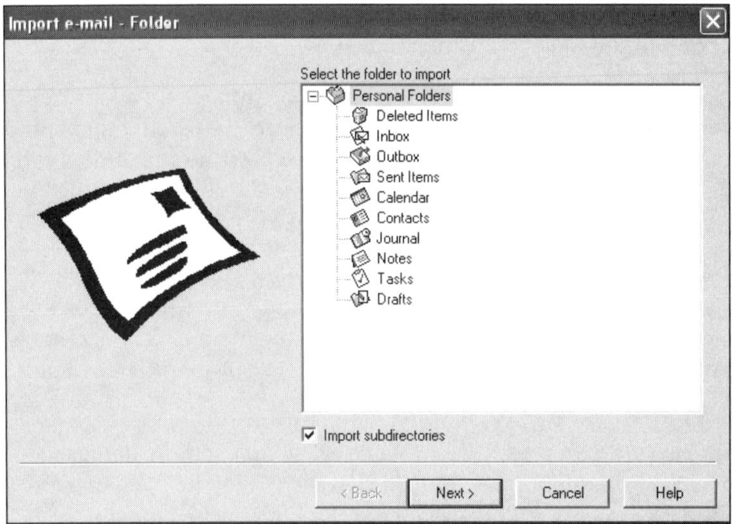

Figure 6-28. *The first dialog of the "Import e-mail" wizard. In this instance, the administrator's workstation has Microsoft Outlook installed, and has access to e-mail messages that should be imported.*

The next dialog in the wizard, Attachments, contains options that relate to e-mail message attachments (see Figure 6-29).

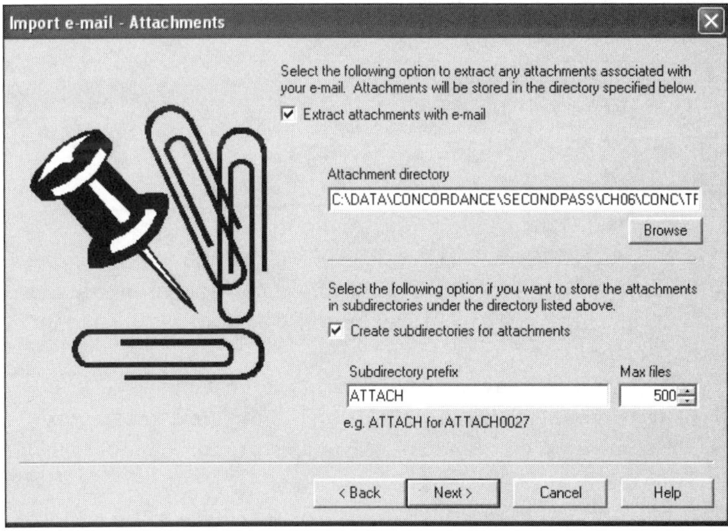

Figure 6-29. *Options from the Attachments dialog control how attachments should be handled that are associated with imported e-mail messages.*

- *Extract attachments with e-mail*: This check box enables attachment handling. When it's unchecked, other options on this screen are disabled.

- *Attachment directory*: You can use the Browse button to navigate through drives and folders to which the loading workstation is connected. You must select the parent directory in which the attachments will be stored. Note that Concordance will create attachment subfolders if you also check the "Create subdirectories for attachments" check box. If this check box isn't checked, attachments will be extracted to the parent directory only.

- *Subdirectory prefix*: The default value is ATTACH. This corresponds to the subfolder names that Concordance will create while extracting attachments, if the "Create subdirectories for attachments" check box is checked. Concordance extracts the number of attachments contained in the "Max files" field to the first subfolder (ATTACH0000), then creates a new subfolder (ATTACH0001) and continues extracting.

Note that when attachments are extracted, Concordance will assign new file names to the files. It does this to prevent the possibility that attachments with the same file name are extracted to the same folder. The names that Concordance assigns to attached files are an alphanumeric set of characters that uniquely identify the attachment across all subfolders created during the import (see Figure 6-30).

Name ▲	S...	Type	Date Modified
00000000960C0EA122102441BF64A35CD7E5F67824002000.#1.icons.gif	9 KB	GIF Image	4/16/2006 7:05 PM
00000000960C0EA122102441BF64A35CD7E5F67824002000.#2.yellowbg.doc	2 KB	Microsoft Word Document	4/16/2006 7:05 PM
00000000960C0EA122102441BF64A35CD7E5F67824002000.#3.olicon.xls	2 KB	Microsoft Excel Worksheet	4/16/2006 7:05 PM
00000000960C0EA122102441BF64A35CD7E5F67824002000.#4.ie.doc	2 KB	Microsoft Word Document	4/16/2006 7:05 PM
00000000960C0EA122102441BF64A35CD7E5F67824002000.#5.office.pdf	2 KB	Adobe Acrobat 7.0 Document	4/16/2006 7:05 PM
00000000960C0EA122102441BF64A35CD7E5F67824002000.#6.exchange.html	5 KB	HTML Document	4/16/2006 7:05 PM
00000000960C0EA122102441BF64A35CD7E5F67824002000.#7.netmeeting.gif	2 KB	GIF Image	4/16/2006 7:05 PM
00000000960C0EA122102441BF64A35CD7E5F67824002000.#8.wmt.gif	1 KB	GIF Image	4/16/2006 7:05 PM

Figure 6-30. *When files are extracted during importation of e-mail messages, Concordance assigns them new names to ensure against naming collisions.*

The next dialog of the wizard, "Date range," allows you to import all e-mails or to specify a date range (see Figure 6-31). To import all e-mails, regardless of date, you should select the "Import all e-mails" radio button. To import e-mails that fall within a date range, you should select the "Import e-mails from a specific date range" radio button. Clicking the "Begin date" or the "End date" fields opens a Calendar tool.

The next dialog of the wizard, Fields, displays a matrix of fields in the database that you can use to map to metadata fields in e-mail messages. If the E-mail Template database has been used, these mappings will be preset. If another database model is used, you must select mappings accordingly (see Figure 6-32).

The check box labeled "Do not allow duplicate e-mails" informs Concordance how it should handle e-mail messages that appear to be duplicative. If it's not checked, all e-mails will be imported. If it is checked, Concordance will compare the value in the MESSAGEID field of an e-mail message with those values contained in other e-mail messages that have already been imported. If it finds a match, only one instance of the e-mail message will be retained. The MESSAGEID value is a metadata field associated with most e-mail messages, and is used as a unique identifier.

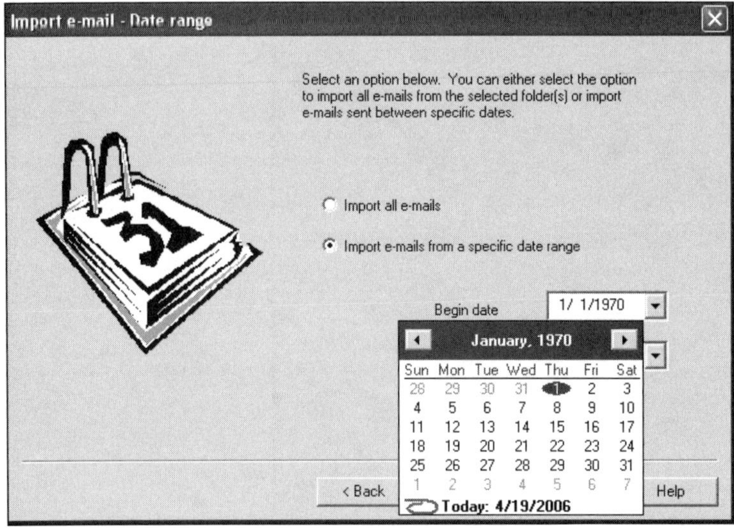

Figure 6-31. *All e-mail messages can be imported, or only messages that fall within a date range.*

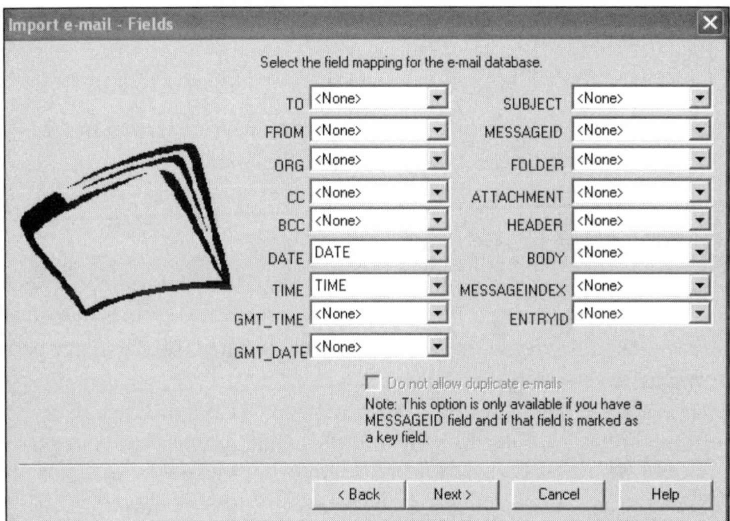

Figure 6-32. *Metadata mappings from data associated with files to field names in a Concordance database*

The last dialog of the wizard, Finish, displays a status report when you trigger the import by clicking the Import button (see Figure 6-33).

■**Note** When importing Microsoft Excel workbooks, each worksheet in the workbook is imported as a separate database record.

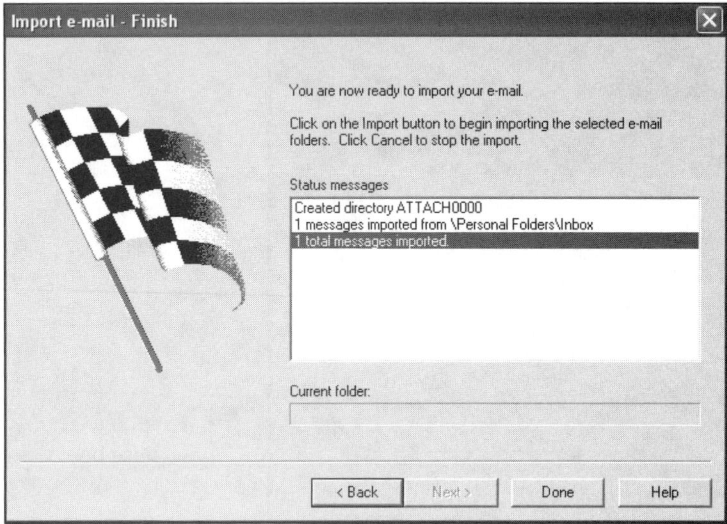

Figure 6-33. *The last dialog of the wizard reports the progress of the import as documents are processed.*

Exporting from Concordance

You initiate all export routines from the Documents ➤ Export menu. This menu item has four different options, each corresponding to a different export format.

Exporting As a Concordance Database

You can export data from Concordance to another preexisting Concordance database, or the export can create a new database entirely. If a new database is created, its structure is based on the exporting database. If exported to a preexisting database, records can either be appended or updated, if the database structures are compatible.

You access the Export Wizard from the Documents ➤ Export ➤ As a Concordance database menu. The dialogs in this wizard are similar to corresponding dialogs used in the Import/Update Wizard for Concordance data, described earlier in this chapter. However, one significant difference is the first dialog of the wizard: Database. When exporting data from Concordance to Concordance, you can use the Browse button to select the destination database. However, if the export is being performed to create a new database, you can either type the full file path and database name in the Database text field, or use the Browse button to navigate to the desired folder, enter the name of the new database in the File Name text field of the "Select database to merge" dialog, and then click the Open button. Either way, if the database name doesn't correspond to a preexisting database, a new one will be created, with field names and data types that match those of the exporting database. The final step of the export prompts you to confirm that the new database should be created in this way (see Figure 6-34).

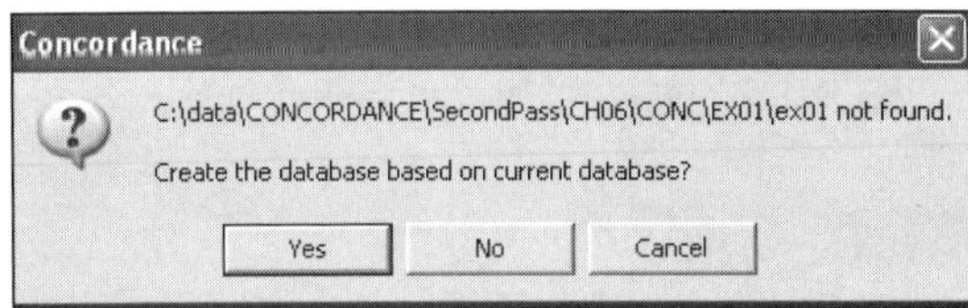

Figure 6-34. *If you've entered a destination database name that doesn't already exist, Concordance will interpret the export to mean that a new database should be created and populated with data, and that the new database's structure should be based on that of the exporting database.*

There's no way to restrict the range of records exported from the Export Wizard itself. However, Concordance only exports records accessible from the last active search. If a subset of the entire database should be exported, you must execute queries to the database before performing the export.

When an export is used to update an external database, any records that aren't matched via the linking fields are appended to the destination database as new records. When data is appended to an external database, either from the "Append all records" or the "Replace matching records and append new records" options from the Append/Replace dialog of the Export wizard, records are exported in the order in which they appear in the source Concordance database. If you wish the records to appear in a different order in the destination database, you should sort records in the source database before performing the export.

Exporting to a Delimited Text File

As with importing delimited text, you can either use an Export Wizard that guides you through the export, or an Export dialog box that summarizes the various screens of the wizard in a single screen (see Figure 6-35).

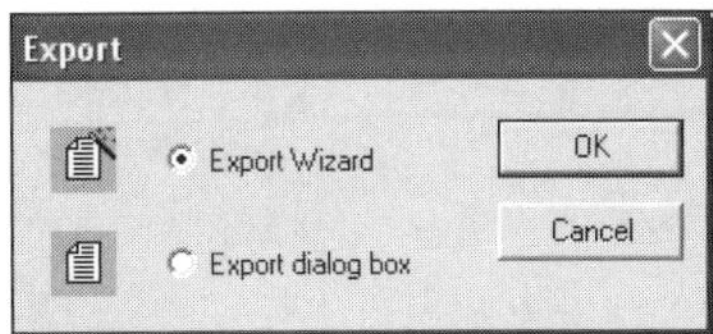

Figure 6-35. *When exporting to a delimited text file, you have the option to use a wizard or a dialog.*

Export Wizard

The dialogs in the Export Wizard are similar in layout and use as the dialogs used in the corresponding delimited-data Import Wizard.

The first dialog of the Export Wizard prompts you to specify a range of documents (see Figure 6-36). The First and Last text fields correspond to the ordinal positions of database records that can be accessed from the last active query in Concordance. If the last active query represents all records in the database, these values will correspond to every record.

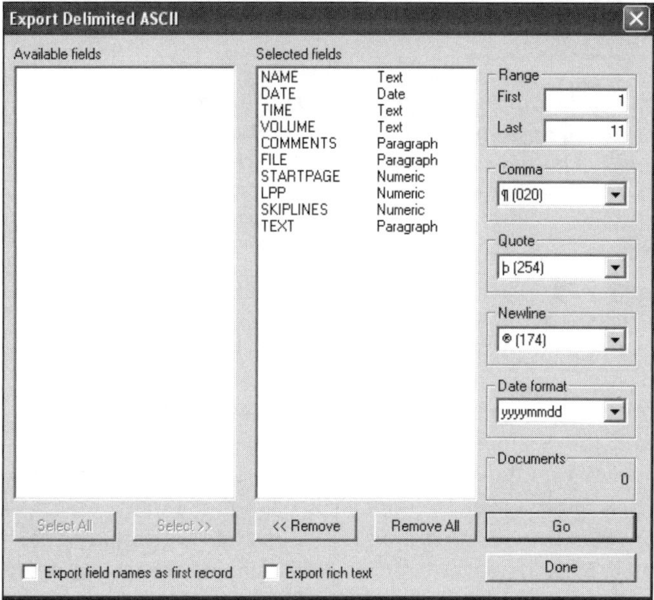

Figure 6-36. *You use the Export dialog when exporting data from Concordance to an external delimited file.*

The next two dialogs, Format and Date Format, are exactly like their counterparts in the delimited Import Wizard. However, note that the formatting choice made from the Date Format dialog controls the export format of every selected date field, regardless of how fields are formatted to appear to end users from the Modify dialog used to set field names, formats, and data types.

The next dialog in the Export Wizard, Fields, is similar to the Fields dialog of the Import Wizard (see Figure 6-37), with the following distinctions:

- The "Skip first line" option in the Import Wizard appears as "Export field names" in the Export Wizard. In the Export Wizard, this option is used to write the names of fields as the first line of the delimited file.

- The "Import rich text" option in the Import Wizard appears as "Export rich text" in the Export Wizard.

Figure 6-37. *Options in the Fields dialog of the Export Wizard that differ from corresponding options in the Import Wizard*

Export Dialog

The Export dialog box's layout is almost identical to that of the Update dialog described earlier in this chapter, with two distinctions that are displayed in Figure 6-38.

- *Export field names as first record*: This option writes the names of fields as the first line of the exported delimited file.

- *Export rich text*: Rich text formatting will be exported if this option is selected. In general, when transferring data between programs by using delimited text, you shouldn't check this option unless the software that will use the data is programmed to understand rich text formatting instructions.

Figure 6-38. *Options in the Fields area of the Export dialog that differ from corresponding options in the Import dialog*

Database Transcripts

When transcripts are exported from the Documents ➤ Export ➤ Database transcripts menu, they're saved in LiveNote's Portable Case Format (.PCF). This method of exporting transcripts is used when you know that data is to be shared with that program.

The Export Transcripts dialog has options to export just the currently displayed transcript, or to export a range (see Figure 6-39).

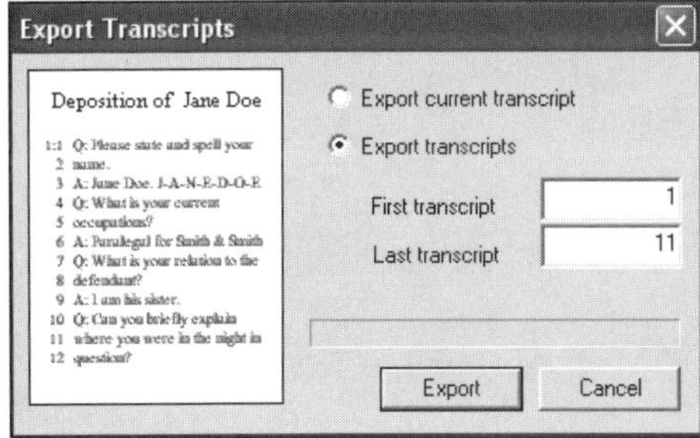

Figure 6-39. *The Export Transcripts dialog. You can export the currently active transcript, or select a range.*

The "First transcript" and "Last transcript" fields correspond to the ordinal positions of transcript records accessible to Concordance via the last active search. When several transcripts are exported, they're saved in a single .PCF file. All annotations are exported into the file, including hyperlinks. However, the files that hyperlinks reference aren't exported to the .PCF file and must be copied separately as individual files.

Clicking the Export button opens a "Save as" dialog, which allows you to select the location where the transcripts should be saved.

Database Structure

You can do a few things with the empty shell of an existing database, including field names, attributes, and data types. You can export it to serve as a new database, it can be an administrator-defined database template, or it can be used for reference purposes. When the new database structure is created, document-level tags aren't exported unless they're *persistent*, a method of making tags a permanent fixture to a database. Also, user account information in Concordance's security model doesn't carry over to the empty shell.

Summary

This chapter has dealt with the methods used to import and export data to and from a Concordance database.

You can import data into Concordance from a variety of sources. You can use Concordance databases and delimited files either to append new records to a database or to update existing records. Other compatible data formats include e-documents (native electronic files), e-mail messages from Microsoft e-mail and messaging products, and appropriately structured electronic-transcript files.

Records can be exported to a new Concordance database, or can be used to update records in an existing Concordance database. You can also export data as delimited text files. If the source database has been created from a Transcripts database template, you have the additional option of exporting transcript records in LiveNote's proprietary .PCF format. (LiveNote is a popular software product used to manage electronic transcripts.) You can export a database's actual structure as well—either as a new, blank database, or as a database template that can be recycled for later use.

Previous chapters have summarized how a Concordance database is designed, created, deployed, and secured. At this point, you should be able to create a fully functional database and prime it with data. The next chapter details how a Concordance database is actually used.

CHAPTER 7

Administrative Functions

Concordance databases are rarely static. You can reasonably expect to receive new sets of data; data is often corrected and requires updating; document records are occasionally deleted; users are regularly editing and annotating records; the number and roles of users change—these and other requirements mean you'll be faced with a series of daily or weekly tasks that are necessary to keep Concordance running efficiently.

Indexing Databases

When dealing with full text, data must be indexed before it can be searched. *Indexing* refers to a process in which Concordance scans appropriate fields and identifies textual units; that is, *words*. When a search is applied to a Concordance database, the search is made of the database's index, not the actual underlying record data itself. This method is what causes Concordance to search data so quickly: the index is a simplified roadmap of where data is stored. The existence and position of a word is stored in the index, which contains a pointer to the record or records that match the search criteria.

The concept is familiar to anyone who has searched for information in a book that contains an index. If you were to search for a given topic by starting at the beginning of the book and reading through to the end, finding the actual topic could take some time. If you refer instead to an index in the back of the book, you can find the topic listed with a corresponding page, and locate the appropriate subject matter quickly. This is similar to how Concordance locates words according to a user's search criteria.

Concordance identifies textual units in the following way: strings of alphanumeric characters that are separated by white space or common punctuation marks are considered to be words. Numbers, single letters, indefinite and definite articles, and prepositions are ignored. Consider the following quote:

Lady in thy orizons, be all my sinnes remembred.

It contains seven words that Concordance regards as meaningful: Lady, in, thy, orizons, all, sinnes, remembred.

The words "be" and "my" are ignored because they're so common in the English lexicon; a search that included them would likely produce many false positives. The words would be a valid hit from a technical perspective, but not useful to the user. For a list of all words that are ignored, you can access and modify the Stopword list from the File ➤ Dictionaries ➤ Stopword list menu.

Punctuation can be important in terms of how Concordance recognizes textual units. Concordance recognizes the characters in Table 7-1, by default, as common punctuation.

Table 7-1. *Characters That Concordance Uses As Punctuation*

Character	Description
-:	Hyphen
/:	Forward slash
.:	Period
,:	Comma
;:	Semicolon
':	Single quote apostrophe

You can modify this list from the File ➤ Modify menu (see Figure 7-1). You might wish to exclude the hyphen character to retain searches of hyphenated last names, such as Mary Scott-Smith. By default, Concordance treats this name as three words: Mary, Scott, and Smith. If the hyphen is removed from the punctuation list, Concordance will treat the name as two words, Mary and Scott-Smith.

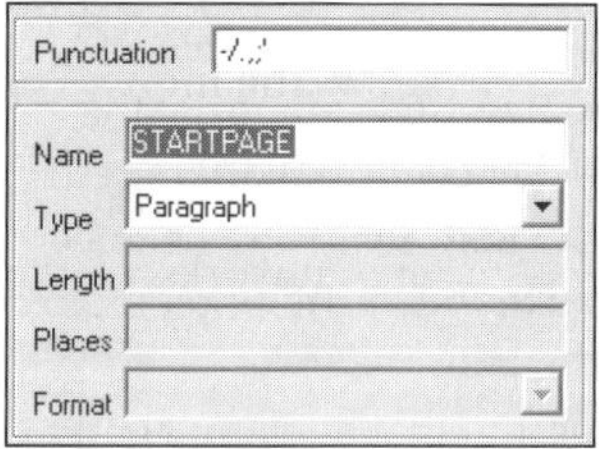

Figure 7-1. *You set punctuation that's used during indexing to identify textual units from the File ➤ Modify menu.*

■**Note** Modifying the punctuation list requires a full reindex of a database for changes to take effect, and for searches to return accurate results.

Dictionary and Inverted Text Files

Concordance uses two files to facilitate searches, the *dictionary* and *inverted text* files. Both files have the same name of the database being indexed, but have file extensions .DCT and .IVT, respectively.

The dictionary file is a list of every textual unit identified by the index process. Each unique word is stored in the dictionary file only once. In this way, Concordance will build a full vocabulary of every word used in the database, akin to a dictionary.

The inverted text file contains information that identifies the location of each occurrence of a word as it appears in document records that define a Concordance database. This means that a word listed in the dictionary file will have one or more entries in the inverted text file, depending on how many times that word appears through any record in the entire database.

Working in conjunction, these two files identify the following:

- That a word exists in the database

- Where that word appears in the document records

Indexing vs. Reindexing

To index a database means to rebuild the dictionary and inverted text files completely. To *reindex* a database means to update them. Indexing is always necessary when data is first loaded into an empty database. Reindexing is necessary when indexed fielded data is edited, when data has been deleted, or when more data has been added to a database. Note, too, that actions you take to modify the contents of a database, such as altering a database's synonym or Stop-word lists, mandates a reindex before these changes are incorporated into searches.

You're provided with a visual cue from the File ➤ Reindex menu by means of a small check mark that appears next to the word "Reindex." If the check mark is there, the database must be reindexed.

Optimizing Indexing

Indexing and reindexing are resource-intensive procedures. Because of the way that Concordance is configured, you should be aware that the machine that performs the index is the client workstation that calls the procedure, not the server on which database files are stored. (This statement assumes a client/server network installation.) This means that the performance of an index is commensurate with the speed of the calling client workstation's hardware, and how much Random Access Memory (RAM) the client workstation has allocated for indexing—a setting made from within Concordance itself.

You can configure a workstation's RAM from the Tools ➤ Preferences menu. This opens a multi-tabbed Preferences dialog. The tab labeled Indexing contains options that you can use to optimize the procedure (see Figure 7-2).

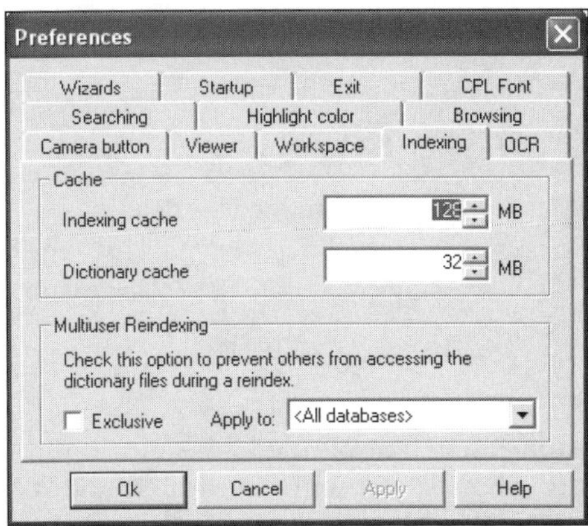

Figure 7-2. *The Indexing tab of the Preferences dialog*

- *Indexing cache*: The value in this field corresponds to the amount of RAM, in mega-bytes, devoted to indexing by the client workstation. RAM is used for this purpose only while the index procedure is running. When an index has completed, RAM is returned to the workstation and will be used by other programs. In general, the higher this value, the less time it will take an index to complete. However, the value shouldn't equal the total amount of available RAM in the workstation, as the machine's operating system itself requires RAM. How much RAM a workstation's operating system needs varies by operating system. Microsoft recommends that Windows XP be allocated at least 128MB of RAM for it to function properly. This means that if a workstation running Windows XP has 512MB of RAM installed, 128MB should be reserved for XP, leaving 384MB to be divided between the Indexing and Dictionary caches.

- *Dictionary cache*: Unlike RAM used during indexing, Concordance uses RAM allocated for the Dictionary cache continuously, to store data pertaining to various list files, security files, database key files, and—when invoked—by indexing procedures. This RAM isn't released back to the operating system while Concordance is active. Dataflight recommends a setting of 4MB for the Dictionary cache. In the preceding example, where 384MB was calculated to be the amount of RAM that could be split between the Indexing and Dictionary caches, 380MB can be allocated for indexing.

- *Multiuser Reindexing*: Users can continue using a Concordance database while it's reindexing, though this will cause the reindexing itself to proceed more slowly. The effect is small, but if the speed of a reindex is at a premium, you can override this default setting using the Exclusive check box. A database in exclusive mode locks the dictionary file, preventing users from accessing it so that searches cannot be initiated. You can apply the setting to the current database or to all databases using the "Apply to" drop-down box.

Scheduling Indexing Tasks During Times of Nonusage

No damage will be done to a database if an index is triggered during normal work hours when users are actively querying and using Concordance. Administrators and users should be aware, though, that until an index is complete, searches aren't accurate. It's only when the indexing is completely finished that searches can be fully trusted. To this end, you might find that it's best to perform this administrative task at a time when users don't need a database.

Packing Databases and Dictionary Files

Packing is a Concordance-specific term that refers to removing records marked for deletion (when packing the database itself) or updating a database's dictionary files (when packing the dictionary) so that they operate more efficiently. Both are accessible from the File ➤ Pack menu.

Packing a Database

When a Concordance database is packed, those records that have been marked for deletion are removed from the underlying data files, in effect removing document records from the database. Deleting records from a Concordance database is a two-step process: records are marked for deletion first, then—at a later time—the database is packed. Records aren't completely removed from a Concordance database until the pack has been completed. This separation of steps means that the administrator (or another user with appropriate rights) can audit and verify the records marked for deletion before they're actually removed.

Deleting records is a terminal process, and should be invoked with care. Because document records can contain subjective metadata (document-level tags and annotations), removing a record can also remove the intellectual effort of a user. The deletion cannot be undone.

You can mark records for deletion from the Edit ➤ Delete and Undelete menu. This opens the Delete/Undelete Records dialog (see Figure 7-3). This tool grants the user the ability either to mark records for deletion, or to reset documents that had been previously set for deletion, so that they won't be removed.

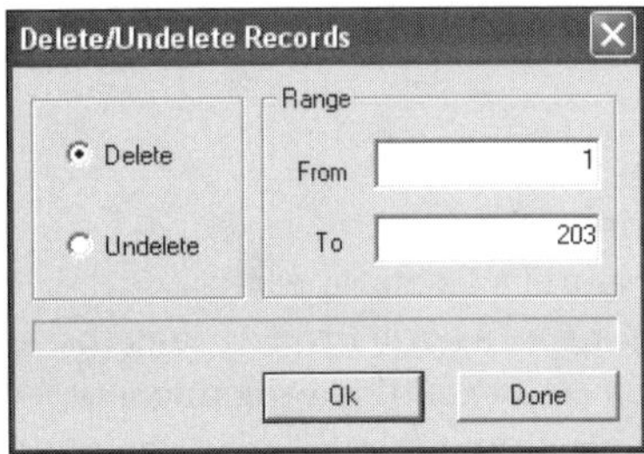

Figure 7-3. *Selecting records for deletion or undeletion*

A user must enter a document range. The document range refers to the ordinal position of the records that are displayed with the last active query issued to the database. If no query has been issued to the database so that all records are visible, the From and To values correspond to the first and last records in the entire database. If the last active query refers to some subset of records in the database, the First and Last values correspond to the first and last records in that query.

If, out of all records in a given database, you wish to mark the third record for deletion, you must set the From and To fields to be the same value: 3.

When a record is marked for deletion, the record will display the letters DEL in the lower right-hand border of the Concordance window. To display only those records that have been marked for deletion, you can click the tagging icon located at the top of the Concordance screen. This opens the Tag/Issue Management dialog (Figure 7-4). Clicking the "Deleted records" button invokes a search of all records in the database that have been marked for deletion, and is the active query when the tool is closed.

You should create a complete backup of the database before records are deleted. This is an additional layer of insurance if records are determined to have been erroneously removed. Because deletions cannot be undone, if it's determined that some or all of the records must be restored, you must either reactivate the backup as the primary database, or move deleted records from the backed-up version of the database to the primary version.

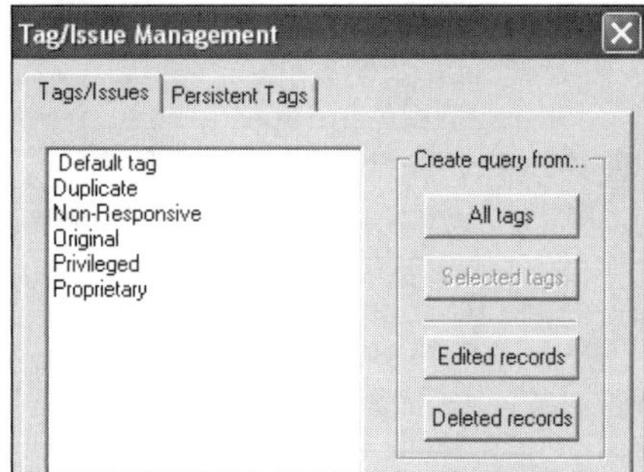

Figure 7-4. *You can use the "Deleted records" button to query for just those records that have been marked for deletion.*

Packing the Dictionary Files

Choosing File ➤ Pack ➤ Database causes the dictionary and inverted text files, essential for speedy search and retrieval, to be compacted. During the life cycle of a database, as it's indexed and reindexed, these files can contain entries that are scattered across a hard drive. Packing these files causes entries to be physically ordered on a drive so that successive entries are contiguous. This reduces the amount of time that the drive head must span the drive to retrieve data. In other words, the hardware itself is able to find data more quickly.

Zapping a Database

Zapping a database means erasing all records. It's the equivalent of marking all records for deletion, and then packing both the database itself and its dictionary file. You trigger zapping from the File ➤ Zap menu. You're prompted to confirm the operation. Zapping a database cannot be undone. When the zap is complete, the database is an empty shell, leaving only field names and data types. Note that any settings applied to Concordance's security model aren't affected.

If no security is applied to a database, the menu item is accessible to all users. Given the potential for catastrophe, users should be blocked from accessing this menu item. You can restrict menu access using the Concordance security model, described later in this chapter in the section "Menu Access."

Before zapping a database, it's best to make a complete backup of all database files.

Deduplicating Records

When a single document is represented by two or more distinct rows in a Concordance database, duplication occurs. Although this concept might seem obvious, you must use some care when identifying duplicates. Because a Concordance record is represented by a series of fields, the question must be asked: what combination of fields that contain equivalent data causes two or more records to be regarded as duplicates? The answer can vary depending on how document records are interpreted.

Selecting Duplication Criteria

We might regard records that contain exactly the same full text to be duplicates. This might
be true in terms of our intuition, but what if the SOURCE field of two documents that have the
same full text are different, where the SOURCE refers to the individual from whom documents
were collected? If it's important to users to know who had the same document in their posses-
sion at the time of document collection, records with the same full text, but with different
SOURCE values, are not duplicates. The test of duplication depends on the values in both fields.

Another method to identify duplicates might be to locate those records that have the
same data across *all* fields in a database. At first glance, this appears to be an absolute method
of identifying duplicates, but what if the database contains an accession field, so that each
document record has a unique, numerical identifier? If the test for duplication involves the
comparison of every field in the database, no records will be identified as duplicates because
the autonumber field will have a unique value in each field.

Because of varying interpretations of what criteria should be used to identify duplicates, you
should refer the question to end users, so that those who are intimately familiar with the matter
represented by the Concordance database can define how duplicates should be identified.

Concordance provides a tool to mark records as *original* or *duplicate* (or other values you
specify). You can open it from the Tools ➤ Check for duplicates menu. The Duplicate Detection
dialog lists all fields in a database (with data type), so that you may select one or more to be used
in the duplicate checking process (see Figure 7-5). Once you highlight the desired fields, the Ok
button triggers the procedure. A running total of the number of duplicates identified is displayed
under the Duplicate Count label.

Note When fields that have a PARAGRAPH data type are selected as part of the criteria, only the first
60 characters of those fields are used during the comparison. This means you cannot, in fact, analyze the
entire contents of a database record that contains PARAGRAPH fields to determine duplication.

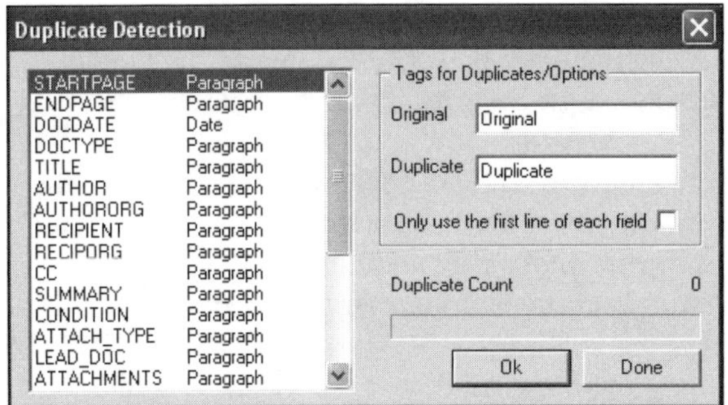

Figure 7-5. *Selecting records to be identified as duplicates*

Original vs. Duplicate Tags

When document records are identified as duplicates, they're given document-level tags that, by default, are labeled original or duplicate. The assignment of these tags is arbitrary, in that the first record used as the record to be compared to is given the original tag, and other records that appear later in the database and that fit the duplicate criteria are given the duplicate tag. You can change the names of these tags from the Duplicate Detection tool, and you should, in fact, change these values for subsequent checks for duplicates, as the labels are reused. For example, if two unrelated checks for duplicates are run against the database, and if the labels of the original and duplicate tags aren't changed, both batches will share these tags, making it difficult to group duplicates together according to criteria.

Security

By default, a new Concordance database doesn't have any security applied. If a database contains data that isn't of a sensitive nature, it might not be necessary to enable security at all. However, in many applications it's necessary to restrict the information that users can view, and more importantly, to prevent unauthorized users from accessing data. However, until you explicitly enable security in a Concordance database, any user that has access to the program and possesses the appropriate network permissions can open a Concordance database and view Concordance.

When enabled, Concordance adds a layer of security over regular network permissions and enforces that security from within Concordance itself. This means that users who have full network rights to read, write, execute, and delete files in the Concordance directory can still do so, but when they open a Concordance database that's secure, they're restricted by Concordance itself from modifying or viewing data from within the program. For example, while users in Concordance might be prevented from deleting an entire database from the File ➤ Zap menu, they can still delete all Concordance files from the database's directory if their network permissions allow them to do so. A thorough treatment of security in Concordance involves both Concordance's own security model and users' network permissions as well.

Concordance's security model is applied to each database instance. To administer security for a specific database, you must open that database first. There's no external tool for administering security, nor is there a method to apply security across several sessions of multiple databases.

Security in Concordance affects a user's ability to read (and search) data from specific fields, or to access menu items. Restrictions are placed on fields within records, not on the records themselves. If a database contains records that a user shouldn't view, you must remove those records from the database entirely or prevent the user from accessing the database.

When security is applied in Concordance, passwords and other security settings are stored in the database's .SEC file. If a database is named DOCREVIEW.DCB, its security file will be named DOCREVIEW.SEC. This file won't exist until security has been enabled. Once security is activated, deleting this file will lock all users out of the database, thereby rendering it unusable.

Managing Security

You manage security from the File ➤ Administration ➤ Security menu, which opens the Security dialog. Because security isn't applied by default on a new Concordance database, any user will be able to access this tool. A login screen is displayed with the user name OWNER. The password is initially blank (see Figure 7-6).

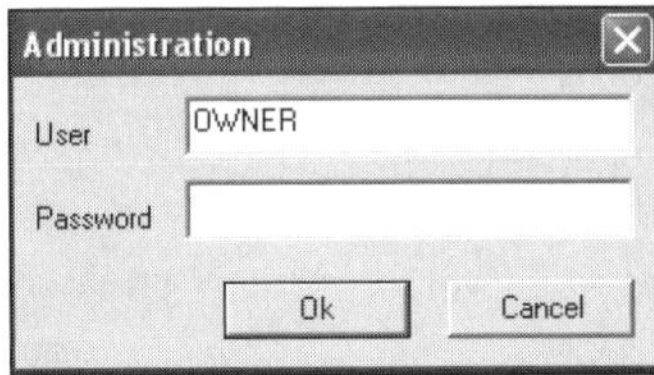

Figure 7-6. *When "Login required" is enabled from the Modify dialog, this login screen will pop up after a user has activated Concordance, but before the program opens.*

When the Security dialog is opened for the first time, there will be two preexisting accounts: *default* and *owner* (see Figure 7-7). Owner is an actual account that should be reserved for the administrator. Default is an account that's used when an individual provides Concordance with a login name that isn't recognized by the database. Removing this account effectively locks out all unauthorized users.

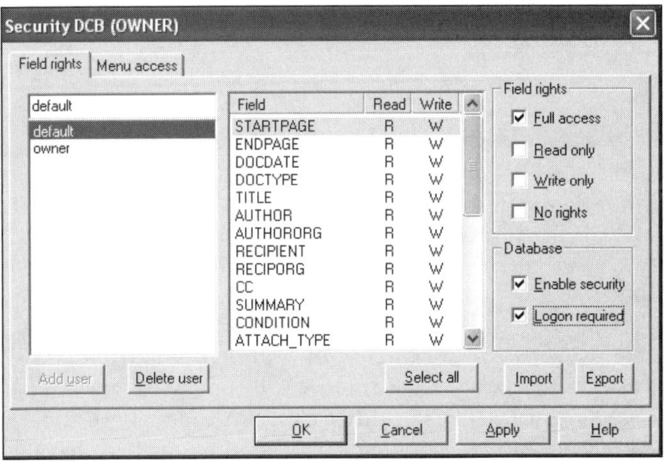

Figure 7-7. *The Security dialog, accessible from the File ➤ Administration ➤ Security menu item*

■ Note Although the default and owner accounts are preset by Concordance, they aren't activated until you check the "Login required" check box.

Managing Users and Field-Level Permissions

You can use two settings, individually or in combination, to secure a database. They are to "Enable security" or to require a login ("Login required"). When "Enable security" is selected, field-level permissions are enforced. When "Login required" is selected, users are required to submit a valid login and password before a database will open. The most secure method combines these features: security is enabled and a login is required. If the default account has been deleted, this will grant access only to those users with user names that you've added, and will prevent those users from viewing or writing to fields for which they have no permission.

Note If both "Login required" and "Enable security" are checked, but no field-level permissions have been set, users will be unable to view any fields in the database.

Managing Users

You add or delete users from the "Field rights" tab of the Security tool (see Figure 7-8). To add a user, click into the text field that appears on the left-hand side of the tab just under the label "Field rights," add the desired user name, and then click the "Add user" button. The user's name is added to the list box. To delete a user, select the name from the list, and then click the "Delete user" button.

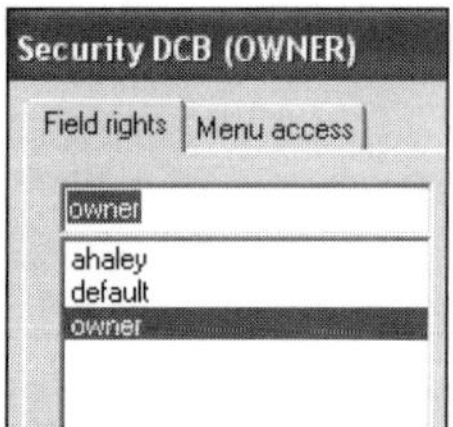

Figure 7-8. *User names that have been added to the database*

When "Login required" isn't checked, Concordance will capture the user's network login name, if there is one. If "Enable security" is checked, Concordance will attempt to match the user's network name with the list of names saved in Concordance's security model. If Concordance finds a match, the user will proceed with the field- and menu-level settings that have been stored in Concordance under his or her name. If Concordance doesn't find a match, it will grant the user permissions defined by the default user. If there's no default user account name, the user cannot use the database.

When an account is initially created, its corresponding password is blank. There's no menu item or button to change or set a password; this feature is built into the login screen if the user enters his or her password in a specific way.

To change an existing password, at the login prompt the user should enter his or her old password, a forward slash (/), and the new password, in this form:

```
oldpassword/newpassword
```

This indicates to Concordance that the user wishes to change his or her password. Concordance responds with a new login/password screen with the title Confirm New User/Password. The user should type the new password, and then click the Ok button. The new password is now set.

To set a password for the first time, the process is slightly different. When an administrator creates an account, that account's password is initially blank. The first time the user attempts to log in to the Concordance database, he or she should enter the desired password and then click the Ok button. A confirmation login screen appears that prompts the user to type the desired password again. Clicking the Ok button sets the password and opens the database. In future sessions, the user is required to use this same password. If the user wishes to change the password, the preceding method is used, with the following form:

```
oldpassword/newpassword
```

Setting Field-Level Permissions

Field-level permissions are applied uniquely to each user. This means that, each time you create a new user account, if "Enable security" is checked, you must take the time to determine how the user can interact with every field in the database. You must apply this same care when modifying the structure of a database. After creating a new field, you should immediately set permissions for that field, for all users. You must reset existing field-level permissions for a field that's renamed via the File ➤ Modify menu, for each user. Because of the additional overhead involved in modifying the structure of a database for which the security model is mature, you'll want to approach structural changes to a database methodically.

To set permissions for a field, click the desired field, highlighting it, and then select one of the four options—Full access, Read only, Write only, and No rights—described in the following sections. Pressing the Ctrl key on the keyboard allows for multiple selections. The interface also provides a Select All button to highlight all fields.

Four security settings are available for each field. These settings are exclusive, despite the check boxes that appear next to the respective labels (check boxes usually indicate multiple selections are possible). For example, a field cannot be both "Read only" and have "No rights."

Full Access

The user can both read and write to the field. Note that field-level permissions affect administrative functions as well. For example, a user granted the ability to index the contents of a field can't do so successfully unless he or she is granted full access to the field.

A byproduct of the fact that changing the name of a field resets its permissions means that, when the field has been renamed, even the owner account loses full access to it. Changing the name of a field prevents you from modifying a database unless you use the Security tool to grant your account full access to the renamed field.

Read Only

The user is able to search and view data in the field, but not modify it in any way. Even administrative functions such as loading data are affected, so that when a user attempts to load data into a Concordance database, those fields for which he or she has read-only access won't appear in the list of fields available in the database.

The effect of setting a field to read only for an individual user is similar to the effect of setting the field to read only for all users from the Data Entry Attributes dialog, accessible from the Edit ➤ Validation menu: the field is locked, though visible, when a record is opened for editing. However, setting a field to read only from the Data Entry Attributes dialog supersedes individual field rights. A field set to read only from the Data Entry Attributes dialog remains locked to a user even if he or she has full rights to the field from the Security tool.

Note Whether a user can load data to a field is determined by the field-level permissions set using the Security dialog, not from the Data Entry Attributes dialog.

Write Only

The field is hidden to the user from the Concordance graphical user interface, though the user can interact with the field via administrative functions such as loading or overlaying data. Otherwise, the field isn't available for searching, viewing, or editing.

This setting also prevents a user from modifying a database.

No Rights

The user may not search, edit, or view the field.

Menu Access

You can apply security to menu items in the same way that it's applied to fields, enabling items for some users and disabling them for others. This is particularly important, given that some of the items accessible from Concordance's menus can permanently alter data. To safeguard a database, you should take the time not only to control which fields a user can view, but also which menu items a user can access.

Modifying menu-level access can be accomplished from the "Menu access" tab of the Security tool (see Figure 7-9). Here, all menu items are displayed in an expandable tree. You can navigate through this tree to select the lowest-level menu item, then activate or deactivate it per user as needed. Each node on the tree has a check box. When a check box for a particular node in the tree appears with a gray color, this indicates that the node contains sub elements—other menu items—and that some of them have been disabled.

You should be careful when modifying menu access, as you can render the database unusable. For example, if you remove access to the File menu, you'll lose the ability to modify the database or administer security. As a result, you should ensure that your account has access to *every* menu item.

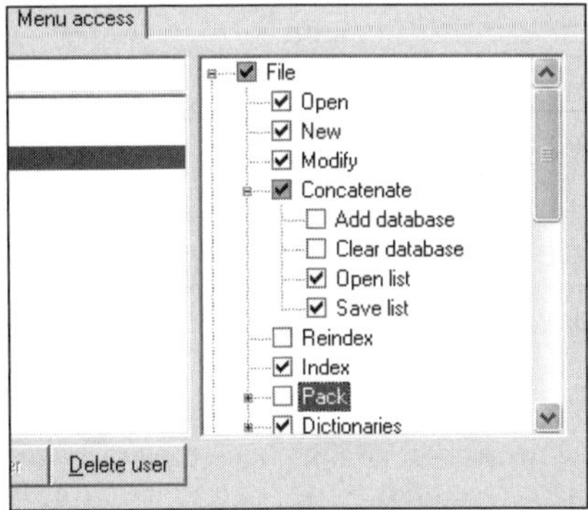

Figure 7-9. *Menu-level access, from the Security tool. Note that items that have a check mark but that also have a gray color indicate that they have child menu items that have been disabled.*

For regular users who should have no access to the administrative features contained in Concordance, you should hide the following menu items:

- *File menu:* New, Modify, Concatenate, Reindex, Index, Pack, Dictionaries, Status, Administration, Zap, Begin Program, Edit Program

- *Edit menu:* Validation

- *Documents menu:* Import, Export, Replication

- *Tool menu:* Convert to V8, List file management, Preferences

However, Concordance offers a series of presets that will aid you in assigning menu item privileges to users according to the role they assume when using the database. Table 7-2 summarizes each role.

Table 7-2. *Preset Roles Provided by the Concordance Security Model*

Role	Disabled Menu Items	Purpose
Supervisor	None	The Supervisor role is one of a super user. The Concordance supervisor is an administrator with complete access to all menu items, and therefore, all administrative tools in the database.
Administrator	*File:* Administration (and all submenus), Added menu items	The Concordance administrator has access to most administrative functions in the database, but cannot set security or modify menu items. This role is appropriate for one who oversees the daily function of a Concordance database.

Continued

Table 7-2. *Continued*

Role	Disabled Menu Items	Purpose
Editor	*File*: New; Modify; Reindex; Index; Pack; Administration (and all submenus); Zap; Begin Program, Edit Program *Edit*: Validation, Delete and undelete *Documents*: Replication (Enable replication, Create a replica, Purge events) *Tools*: Check for duplicates, List file management	This is the most common role for users who both read and write to document records. All menu items relating to administration are disabled, while all menu items relating to the editing of individual document records are enabled.
Researcher	*File*: New; Modify; Reindex; Index; Pack; Administration (and all submenus); Zap; Begin Program, Edit Program *Edit*: Append, Edit, Validation, Global edit, Delete and undelete, Find, Find again, Replace, Send to *Documents*: Import (Delimited text, E-documents, Overlay); Export (Structure) *Tools*: Toolbar (Edit toolbar), Check for duplicates, List file management, Preferences	Users who are researchers have the ability to search and view data. They cannot edit document records, and they have no access to Concordance's administrative features.
No access	*File*: New; Modify; Concatenate (and all submenus); Reindex; Index; Pack (and all submenus); Dictionaries (Database dictionary, Stopword list); Administration (and all submenus); Zap; Page Setup; Print Preview; Print; Begin Program, Edit Program *Edit*: Append, Edit, Validation, Global edit, Delete and undelete, Undo; Cut; Copy; Paste; Find, Find again, Replace *Search*: All submenus disabled *Documents*: Import (Delimited text, E-documents, Overlay); Export (To a delimited text file, Structure); Print documents *Reports*: Report writer *Replication*: All submenus disabled *Tools*: Bell; Empties; Split screen; Toolbar (Main, Browser toolbar, Edit toolbar, Report toolbar, Review toolbar, Table toolbar), Check for duplicates, List file management, Preferences	This role is appropriate for the *default*, or unknown, user. When a user attempts to open a Concordance database where security is enabled, if Concordance doesn't recognize the user's login, it will grant the user default access. The "No access" role allows the user to open other databases, or close Concordance.

Carrying Security Between Databases

When records from a secure database are exported to another Concordance database, the source database's security model doesn't export with the document records. This means that an administrator could export data from a database for which security has been carefully prepared to an unsecured database, thus circumventing Concordance's security model. You should use care when transferring data between databases to ensure that security isn't breached.

Security settings are portable, though, using the Security tool. The Export button allows you to save user names, field-level permissions, and menu item permissions to an external, comma-delimited file. This file can then be imported into other databases using the Import button. For a company or firm with a large user base, keeping a basic template of user permissions can save you a great deal of time.

Adding Custom Menu Items

The File ➤ Administration ➤ Added Menu Items menu opens the Added Menu Items dialog displayed in Figure 7-10. You can use this tool to create new menu items, set their placement on the menu bar, and configure them to trigger customized actions, such as to open another database, to print a report, or to activate a program written in the Concordance Programming Language (CPL). CPL programs are described in greater detail in the section "The Concordance Programming Language," later in this chapter. Top and second-tier–level menu items can be added. Menu items can be configured to appear only in the currently active database, or in all databases, and menu items can be configured only to appear to certain users.

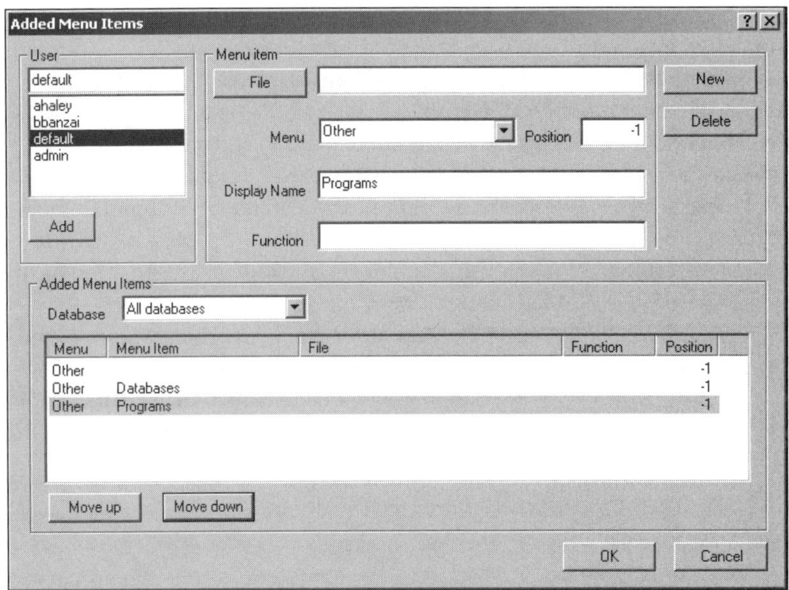

Figure 7-10. *The Added Menu Items dialog*

You must define the database in which the menu item will appear. You determine database scope by the Databases drop-down box under the Added Menu Items label in the middle of the dialog. If the menu item should appear in all databases, you should select the "All databases" option.

You must also select the users to whom the menu item will appear by clicking and highlighting user names in the User list box. Note that the contents of this list box aren't prepopulated with entries from a database's security settings. You must add users by entering their login names in the empty text field under the User label, and by clicking the Add button. You should use some care when entering login names, as they should match the users' actual names as defined by the Concordance security model (if it is used) or as defined by a network security model. (Recall that if security in a Concordance database is enabled, but a login isn't required, Concordance will capture a user's network login and use that value when determining how security should be applied for the user.)

Note that any menu item associated with a default user will be accessible to all users. To use this feature, you must create the default user with the methods described in the previous paragraph.

You must define access for custom menu items for each user from the Added Menu Items dialog. The other method of configuring menu-level security, from the "Menu access" tab of the Security dialog (accessed from the File ➤ Administration ➤ Security menu) applies only to Concordance's default menu items.

To add a top-level menu item, select the database scope and the user to whom the menu will be visible. Enter the menu name in the Menu drop-down box. If the menu item is to appear at the end of the menu bar, the Position of the menu item should be -1. Otherwise, the number in this field corresponds to the vertical position of the menu item on the menu bar. For example, if the File menu is the first top-level menu item, and your custom menu item is to appear next to it, the value in the Position field should be 2. The Display Name field is left blank. If the top-level menu is to trigger an action, you can associate a file with the item by clicking the File button and selecting a program to run. If the top-level menu item is to take no action and will contain other menu items, this field should be left empty.

To add a submenu item under a parent, select the database scope and the user to whom the menu will be visible. You select the parent menu name from the Menu drop-down box. The value in the Position field is irrelevant. The name of the submenu item is entered in the Display Name field. If the submenu item is to trigger an action, you can associate a file with the item using the method described in the previous paragraph. You can set the position of submenu items using the Move Up and Move Down buttons.

You can enter the path and name of a valid CPL program in the File text field. You use the Function text field when CPL programs are invoked by menu items. Some CPL programs contain *functions* (a section of programming code). If the name of a function in the CPL program referenced in the File text field appears in the Function text field, it's activated by the menu item.

Concatenation

Concordance features a way to conjoin up to 128 databases so that they appear to the user as a single, virtual database. One database is designated as primary (Concordance refers to it as the *main* database); when a user opens it, he or she sees all records in that database, plus all records in other databases that appear in the primary database's *concatenation* file. The concatenation file is an ASCII text file that contains file paths to the .DCB files of other Concordance databases. It has the same name as the .DCB file for the main database. For example, if the main database file is DOCREVIEW.DCB, the concatenation list, if there is one, will be named DOCREVIEW.CAT.

Both indexing and searching are applied on all records in all databases that have been concatenated if those actions are triggered from the main database. The concatenated databases themselves aren't altered in any way, and can be opened and used individually.

When Is It Necessary to Concatenate a Database?

There are times when it may be useful for you to create several databases to represent a single matter. The reasons for this might be for performance or purely administrative.

The theoretical limit of a single Concordance database is 32 million document records, although you'll find that, in practice, users will experience database performance issues before a database becomes that large. For example, if the database contains several PARAGRAPH fields, indexing will take longer. When index time becomes prohibitive, regardless of the number of records in the database, you should consider splitting the database into parts. You can index each database individually, perhaps at separate workstations, and the procedure will complete more quickly. Though searching across a series of concatenated databases can take a little longer, the concatenation itself will otherwise be invisible to the user.

There might also be times when security that is to be applied to a series of related databases isn't uniform: fields for some records should be restricted, while others may not be. Here, you may segregate groups of records that share security characteristics into different databases, apply security to each one individually, and then concatenate them into a single, virtual database. The scope of security is specific to each database, so that the security model applied to the primary database doesn't supersede that of secondary, concatenated databases.

Another reason to concatenate databases is one of simple management: it might be easier for you to create separate databases that are related to the same matter, but that represent slightly different material per database, or that come from a variety of sources. You can color code records in each database so that users may see, at a glance, which records come from which database, and therefore, from which source.

Note To change the color of records in a Concordance database, use the Font button F*f* from Browse or Table view.

How Concatenation Works

Concatenation works like this: one database is designated as the main database. If other databases have been concatenated, they'll appear in a database concatenation file—a file that has the same name as the primary database, and that has a .CAT extension. Note that there are no restrictions as to where the individual databases are stored across a network. As long as users have the appropriate permissions to read and write to files in all folders referenced in the concatenation file, the virtual database will behave normally. However, concatenated databases spread over a Wide Area Network (WAN) might experience latency issues, and perform more slowly than a series of concatenated databases that reside on the same network server.

Note For each user, you should consider placing each database in its own dedicated folder.

Databases with different structures can be concatenated. Users can use Concordance's table layout from the primary database to alter the appearance and order of fields of all concatenated databases (see Figure 7-11).

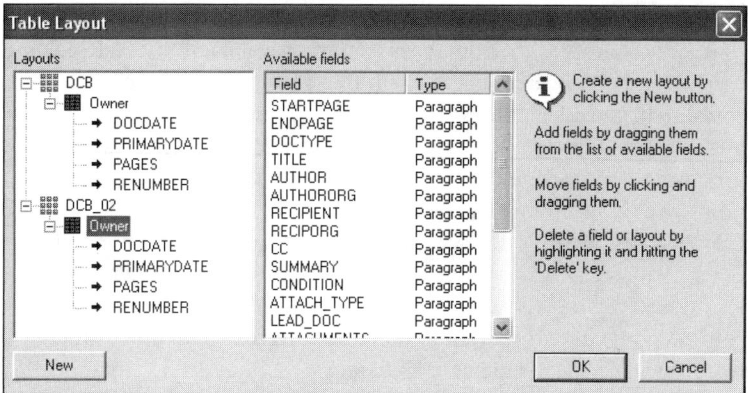

Figure 7-11. *When databases are concatenated, the user can alter the fields that appear in the Table view of Concordance, for each database. In this configuration, the fields displayed for both the DCB.dcb and the DCB_02.dcb databases are the same, though this isn't a requirement. The user could elect to see fields in a different order when records appear from different databases.*

Unless the structure of all databases is exactly the same, it's recommended that you perform data maintenance on each database individually. For example, say the main database contains ten fields while a secondary, concatenated database contains only five. Exporting data from the main database will export *all* records from both databases, though data from the second database won't line up properly with the first. Despite this caveat, indexing from the primary database will trigger across all secondary databases, regardless of each database's structure.

To group databases together, you should open the designated primary database first. Until a concatenation list for a database is created, there is no .CAT file, so when you create a Concordance database for the first time, you won't see it. Only after the list has been created and saved will Concordance create the appropriate file. Once it has been created, you'll find that the .CAT file is an ASCII text file that can be edited from any text editor. However, all modifications to the .CAT file can be accomplished from the Concordance interface.

The following options are available from the File ➤ Concatenate menu, or from the Join button ⬚ that appears at the top of the Concordance screen:

- *Add Database.* This option opens the Concatenated Databases tool (see Figure 7-12). The Concatenated Databases tool lists the main database and all secondary databases that will open with the main database. You may use this tool to both add and delete entries from the .CAT file.

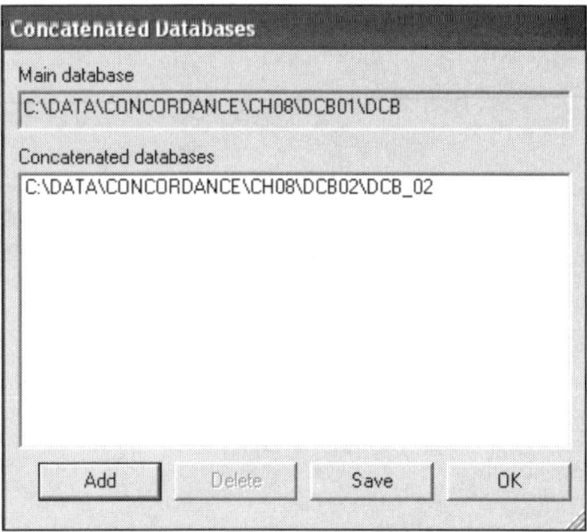

Figure 7-12. *Deleting and adding databases to the main database's concatenation file*

- *Clear Database*: Selecting this option doesn't delete a .CAT file. Rather, it closes all concatenated databases except for the main database. It's a quick way to search just the main database.

- *Open List*: This allows the user to select any concatenation file, which then opens all databases in that list. Any database currently open and active is first closed.

- *Save List*: A concatenation file is created and all currently opened databases are added to it.

The Concordance Programming Language

The Concordance Programming Language (CPL) was created specifically for the purpose of augmenting Concordance's native functionality. CPL programs can perform useful procedures not otherwise available from the tools that can be opened and invoked from within Concordance, or you can use the CPL programs to automate existing Concordance procedures.

During installation, Concordance creates several CPL programs, and places them in a folder named CPL off the main installation directory. These programs have been written and tested by the manufacturer, and can be quite useful to an administrator. Other CPLs are available for download from the CPL Library section on Dataflight's Web site at `http://www.dataflight.com/cpl.library.html`. Programs in the library are grouped according to their use: Administration, Import/Export, Printing, and so on (see Figure 7-13).

Programs written in CPL can have a .CPL extension, and are ASCII text. They can be opened by a text editor, or opened by Concordance from the File ➤ Edit Program menu. When you use this menu item to open a CPL program, you're prompted for the program's location. When you select it, Concordance opens the program in its own simple text editor (see Figure 7-14).

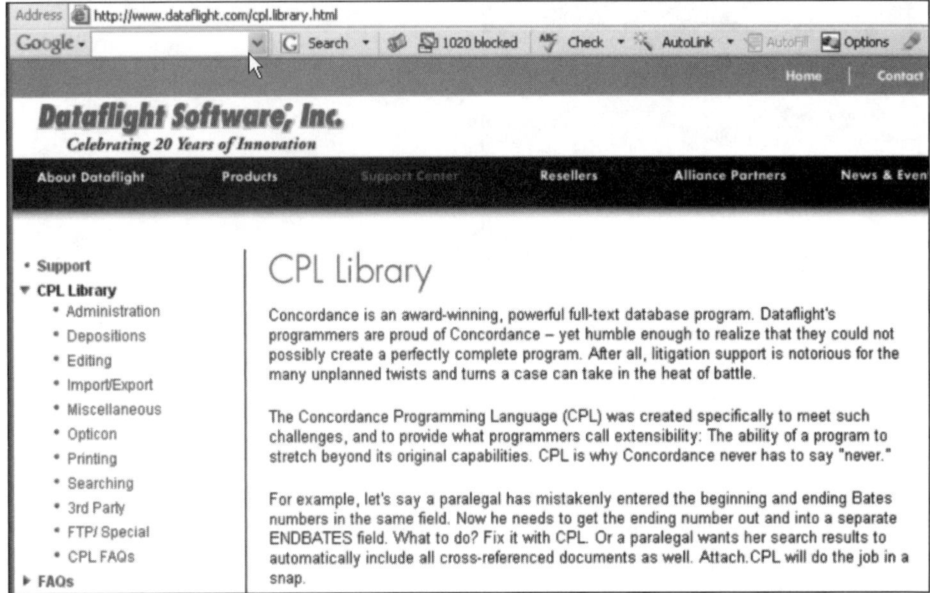

Figure 7-13. *The CPL section of the Dataflight Web site*

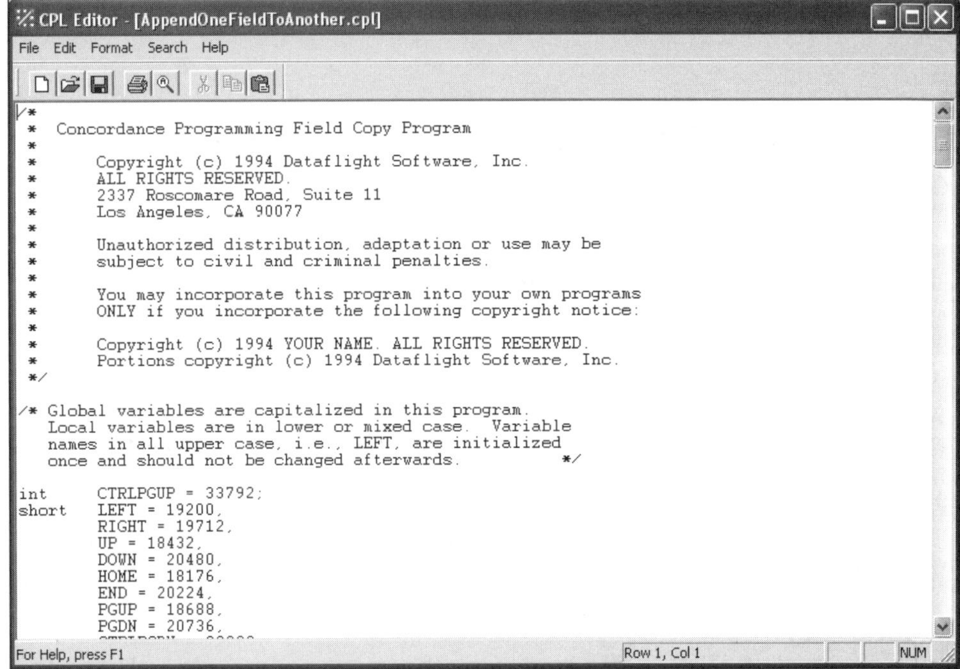

Figure 7-14. *A CPL program opened from the File ➤ Edit Program menu*

CPL programs can also have a .CPT extension. .CPT program files are created the first time Concordance successfully runs a program with a .CPL extension. A .CPT program file is a compiled equivalent to a .CPL file, and runs more efficiently because it has been converted to machine code. Note that if a .CPL file contains a programming error so that it cannot run to completion, Concordance will be unable to compile the file into a .CPT equivalent.

CPL programs can perform a variety of useful procedures. A sampling of CPL programs available at Dataflight's CPL Library include the following:

- *Indxpack.cpl*: Indexes and then packs a database.

- *Userid.cpl*: Displays a user's network login.

- *Send-to-Excel.cpl*: Sends data from the last active query to an Excel file.

- *Calender.cpl*: Displays a calendar. Can be used to augment other CPL programs.

The Structure of a CPL Program

A complete discussion of CPL structure exceeds the scope of this book, as it's a full-fledged programming language. However, you should know that CPL programs are divided into functions, where a *function* is a series of programming lines. Functions can perform many tasks, such as executing other functions, performing calculations, activating features otherwise accessible from Concordance's menu items, modifying data in a database, or providing a user with feedback. Sometimes all these actions are executed from within a single function. Programmers define one function within a CPL program to be the *main* or *entry* function. Such a function is the first set of code to be run in a program, and it often does most of the work, calling other functions in the program to perform related tasks.

Recall in the section "Adding Custom Menu Items" that the Added Menu Items dialog has a File text field that you can use to link a CPL program to a menu item. You can use the Function text field in this dialog to call a function from within the CPL program file referenced in the File text field. The function that's called doesn't have to be a CPL's entry function; it may be a function that tests some condition that must be met before the CPL is run.

Executing a CPL Program

You run CPL programs from the File ➤ Begin Program menu. You're prompted to locate the CPL from an Open dialog. When you select and open a .CPL or a .CPT file, the program begins execution. Many CPLs will first prompt you for input parameters needed for the program to run. This is best illustrated using the example in the following section.

Readocr.cpl

Readocr.cpl is created in the CPL folder during the initial installation of Concordance. The purpose of this program is to load full text data into a field that has the PARAGRAPH data type. The program is appropriate when OCR has been extracted for each document record and saved in separate text files, one file per database record. This method of transmitting data is often used when full text extracted from records is potentially voluminous. A delimited load file that contains both fielded and OCR data can be quite large, and difficult to open and examine using a text editor. A vendor might instead provide a single delimited file that contains fielded data (BEGDOCNO, ENDDOCNO, CUSTODIAN, DOCDATE, and so on), and provide OCR data as separate text files. (Other methods exist of transmitting data—a vendor might provide a Concordance database instead of a delimited text file and also provide OCR in separate text files, with the understanding that you can use these files to reload OCR at some later date if necessary.)

For this program to work, the individual text files must have file names that match some field in the delimited file (assuming that is the structure of the load file). A candidate for this information is the beginning document control number. For example, if the first record in a load file has a BEGDOCNO that is PX000001, its OCR data will be stored in a text file named PX000001.txt. Another requirement is that all OCR text files be in the same folder. No sub-foldering is allowed.

Running the Program

This example uses the COWCO.DCB database that's created during Concordance's initial installation. The beginning document control number in this database is called STARTPAGE. Several text files have been created and stored in a folder named TEXT_TO_LOAD under the Database folder, itself under the Concordance root (see Figure 7-15). These text files have been created specifically for this example, and aren't part of the Concordance installation. The first five records of the COWCO.DCB database have STARTPAGE values of 00010002, 00010003, 00010004, 00010007, and 00010008. The TEXT_TO_LOAD folder contains five text files: 00010002.txt, 00010003.txt, 00010004.txt, 00010007.txt, and 0010008.txt. Note the relationship between file names and STARTPAGE values, a prerequisite for this program to successfully load OCR data. Note also that the last file in the sequence, 0010008.txt, doesn't match the STARTPAGE value 00010008. This error has been introduced on purpose so that the OCR for this record won't load successfully—a failure that's recorded by the CPL in a log file and described later in this section.

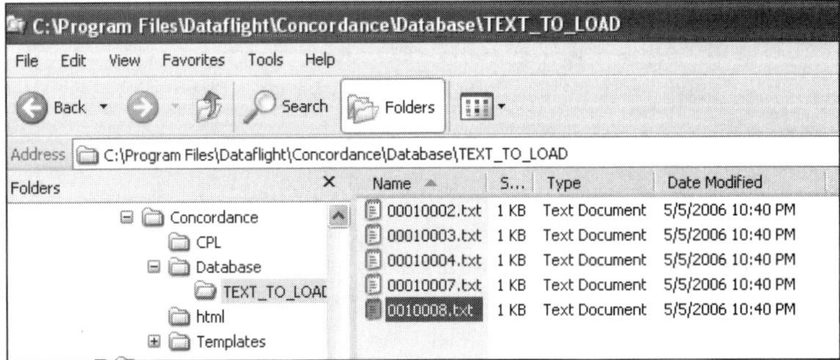

Figure 7-15. *Text files created for this example. Each file name matches a value in the STARTPAGE field of a record in the database, with the exception of 0010008.txt, an error that has been purposely introduced.*

The first step is to select the File ➤ Begin Program menu item. This opens an Open dialog that prompts you to select the CPL to be run (see Figure 7-16).

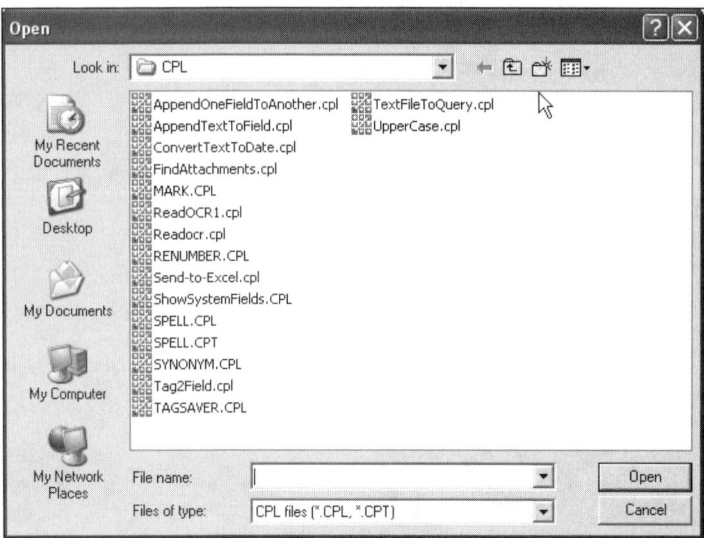

Figure 7-16. *The Open dialog triggered from the File ➤ Begin Program menu. The dialog defaults to the CPL folder under the Concordance folder created during installation.*

Selecting the Readocr.cpl program and clicking the Open button starts the program. Alternatively, you can double-click the program file. The program begins by displaying a message box that describes its purpose (see Figure 7-17).

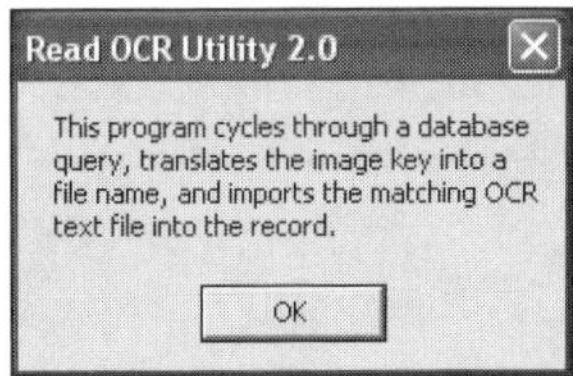

Figure 7-17. *An initial message box created by the Readocr.cpl program describes its purpose.*

When this particular CPL is activated, it provides an interface that prompts you for information needed for the program to run successfully. This interface is created by the CPL itself and is integrated with Concordance; it isn't part of the Concordance software itself (see Figure 7-18).

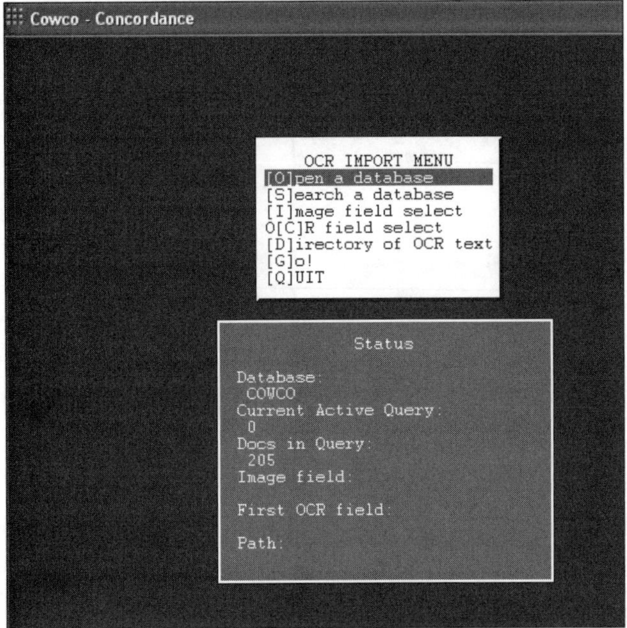

Figure 7-18. *The Readocr.cpl interface. Letters between square brackets are keyboard hotkeys.*

The interface has seven options. The label of each option has a letter between square brackets. This indicates that you can either click the option to activate it, or press the appropriate letter on the computer keyboard.

- *[O]pen a database*: Selecting this option activates an Open dialog. You can select a different Concordance database than the one that's active. If no database is selected, the program assumes the currently active database will be used for the loading procedure. The selected database name is displayed in a status window (see Figure 7-19).

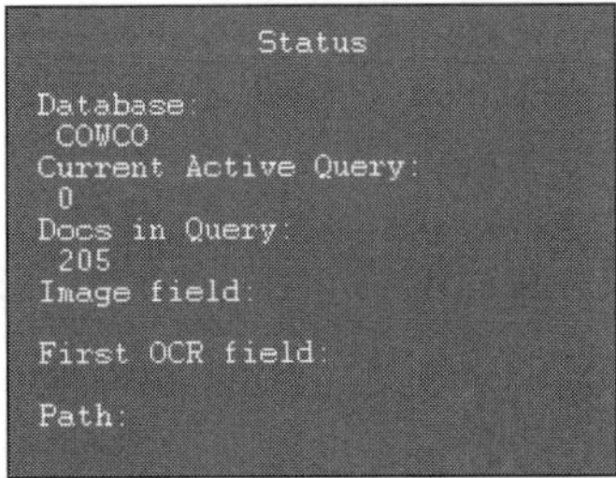

Figure 7-19. *The CPL status window. Note the Database entry—in this example, it's the COWCO.DCB database.*

- *[S]earch a database*: Selecting this option opens a search tool that you can use to select records that will be affected by the loading procedure (see Figure 7-20). When the search is completed, clicking the Done button closes the tool and returns focus to the CPL interface. If you have already queried the database to select appropriate records to be loaded, no search is required. The status window displays the numerical alias of the last active query and the number of records in that query.

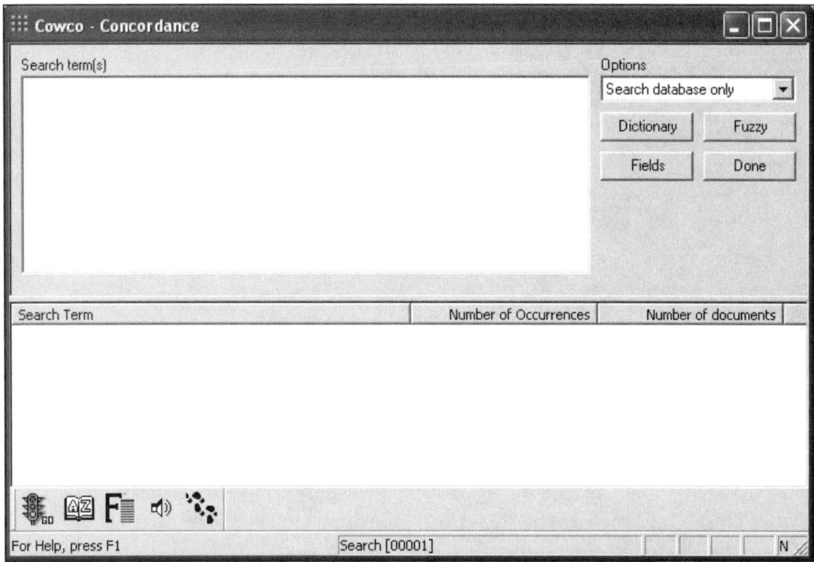

Figure 7-20. *The search tool opened by the "[S]earch a database" option*

- *[I]mage field select*: Selecting this option presents all fields in the database in a list (and each field's data type). You can click the field, or use the up and down arrows on the keyboard to scroll through the list until the desired field is displayed. To select a specific field, click the field name, or scroll to it and press the Enter key. For example, a database may have a field named STARTPAGE that contains the beginning document control number for document records—values that should match OCR text file names. This information is also displayed in the status window.

- *O[C]R field select*: Selecting this option presents all fields in the database in a list (and each field's data type). You select the field to which OCR should be loaded by clicking on the required field or by using the up and down arrows on the keyboard to highlight it.

- *[D]irectory of OCR text*: Selecting this option opens an Open dialog. You should use this tool to navigate to the folder that contains OCR text files. Recall that all files must be in a single folder. Once the appropriate folder is displayed, you must select one of the text files—by double-clicking it or by highlighting it and clicking the Open button—to set the file path. All text files will be loaded, but at least one text file must be selected in this way for the CPL to understand the file path containing OCR text files.

As with the preceding options, your selection is displayed in a status window (see Figure 7-21).

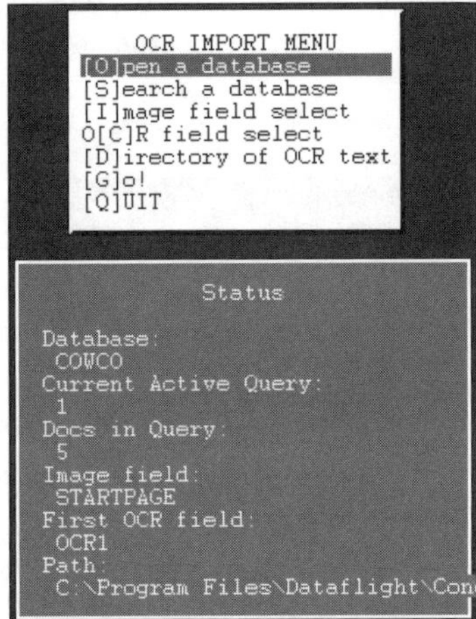

Figure 7-21. *The status window displays the file path selected using the "[D]irectory of OCR text" option.*

- *[G]o!*: Selecting this option prompts you to select a file path for a log file. The log file augments feedback provided by the status window, and is a separate ASCII text file that creates one row per processed file, regardless of success. You can use the log file to locate any OCR text files that failed to load during the procedure. You enter the name of the log file (of your choosing) and then click the Open button. This triggers the actual load.

When the load procedure is activated, the CPL takes over and processes each database record and each associated OCR text file. The CPL displays a running tally of the number of database records processed. As the CPL attempts to load each database record, the results of the procedure are recorded in the log file. If the CPL encounters a value in the field selected from the option "[I]mage field select" that doesn't have a corresponding text file of the same name, an error message is created as a separate row in the log file. The log file created by this particular load is displayed in Figure 7-22; recall that the file 0010008.txt was purposely misnamed to generate an error message.

```
log.txt

Loaded C:\Program Files\Dataflight\Concordance\Database\TEXT_TO_LOAD\00010002.TXT successfully.
Loaded C:\Program Files\Dataflight\Concordance\Database\TEXT_TO_LOAD\00010003.TXT successfully.
Loaded C:\Program Files\Dataflight\Concordance\Database\TEXT_TO_LOAD\00010004.TXT successfully.
Loaded C:\Program Files\Dataflight\Concordance\Database\TEXT_TO_LOAD\00010007.TXT successfully.
Could not open 00010008.rtf as .txt or .rtf
```

Figure 7-22. *The log file created by the Readocr.cpl in this example. The last line of this log file records the fact that the program was unable to locate a file matching the STARTPAGE value 00010008.txt.*

- *[Q]UIT*: Selecting this option closes the CPL and returns focus back to the Active Workspace screen in Concordance.

Interacting With Other CPL Programs

The interface created by Readocr.cpl is unique to that program. Other CPL programs that perform different procedures will prompt you for different information and will use different interfaces. You might wish to create a sample database, and activate various CPLs, to test how they work and to examine their results. As with any procedure that involves bulk processing and modification of data, you're strongly advised to make a complete backup of a database before a CPL is invoked.

Summary

Because Concordance databases usually involve a dynamic set of underlying data and a dynamic set of users, you'll find that you must interact with databases on a frequent basis to keep them operating at peak efficiency. In this chapter, some basic administrative functions were described: indexing and packing databases, deduplicating records, applying security and concatenating databases, creating custom menu items, and running CPL programs. Although the descriptions in this chapter will give you some insight as to how a Concordance database should be administered, there's no better way to learn than by doing. I recommend that you create test databases and practice the various administrative techniques described in this chapter.

At this point, you should have a good grasp of how databases are created, designed, and deployed. Chapters thus far haven't delved too deeply into how you and end users actually *use* a database, though. The next chapter addresses just that. Among other things, it covers how to view, sort, and edit records, and how to group them using document-level tags. The chapter also introduces the important concept of document *annotations*—subjective comments created by end users to qualify the data presented to them by Concordance.

CHAPTER 8

Using a Concordance Database

This chapter will cover the basic usage of a Concordance database, such as opening a database, viewing and navigating through records using Concordance's Browse and Table views, editing data, using document-level tags, and adding annotations (you'll learn about advanced searching in Chapter 9). Both you, as an administrator, and end users will find these functions useful. The purpose of this chapter is to give you a detailed understanding of how to use a Concordance database to view and manipulate document records.

Opening a Database

A single Concordance database is defined by a series of files that work in conjunction. These files are stored in the same directory in which the database was created (see Figure 8-1). The names of these files are similar, and depend on the name of the database when it was created. For example, a database named DocReview consists of several files, each named DocReview. However, the file types and file extensions will be different. The DocReview database might consist of a dozen separate files, such as DocReview.dcb (a file that contains the structure of the database), DocReview.tex (a file that contains text data stored in fields), DocReview.sec (security settings, if security has been enabled), and so on.

Name	Size	Type
Docreview-Notes.Dcb	12 KB	Concordance Database
DOCREVIEW-NOTES.INI	1 KB	Configuration Settings
Docreview-Notes.Key	4 KB	Registration Entries
Docreview-Notes.Ndx	1 KB	NDX File
Docreview-Notes.Tag	4 KB	TAG File
Docreview-Notes.Tex	1 KB	TEX File
Docreview-Notes.Trk	4 KB	TRK File
DOCREVIEW.DCB	12 KB	Concordance Database
Docreview.Ini	2 KB	Configuration Settings
Docreview.Key	88 KB	Registration Entries
Docreview.Ndx	27 KB	NDX File
Docreview.Tag	4 KB	TAG File
Docreview.Tex	754 KB	TEX File
Docreview.Trk	4 KB	TRK File

Figure 8-1. *A single Concordance database is defined by a series of separate files, similarly named. Each file has a separate purpose, defined by the file's extension.*

Of these files, it is the data control block (.DCB) ▦ that Concordance uses to open a database. You and end users should ignore all other files, opening only the database's .DCB file. However, note that the folder that contains the database's files might contain two or three additional files with a .DCB extension. Only one of them is used to activate the database. The database uses the other .DCB files as system files. These files are named in a similar manner to the main .DCB file, with the suffixes -notes and -redlines embedded in their names. You should ignore them. For example, for the DocReview database, DocReview.dcb uses the files DocReview-notes.dcb and DocReview-redlines.dcb in its normal operation. -notes.dcb and -redlines.dcb are valid Concordance data control bocks, but you never interact with them directly.

■**Note** -notes.dcb contains the text of annotations added to document records from Concordance's Browse view. -redlines.dcb contains metadata about image annotations added to document images via Opticon. Concordance creates a -notes.dcb file when a database is created. However, -redlines.dcb isn't created until an annotation on an image is made via Opticon.

To open a Concordance database, select the File ➤ Open menu or click the Open button located on the button bar at the top of the Concordance screen.

This opens an Open Database dialog (see Figure 8-2). You can navigate through your computer or through a network to locate the appropriate .DCB file. To open a Concordance database, either highlight the file name (by left-clicking on it once) and then click the OK button, or double-click the file name.

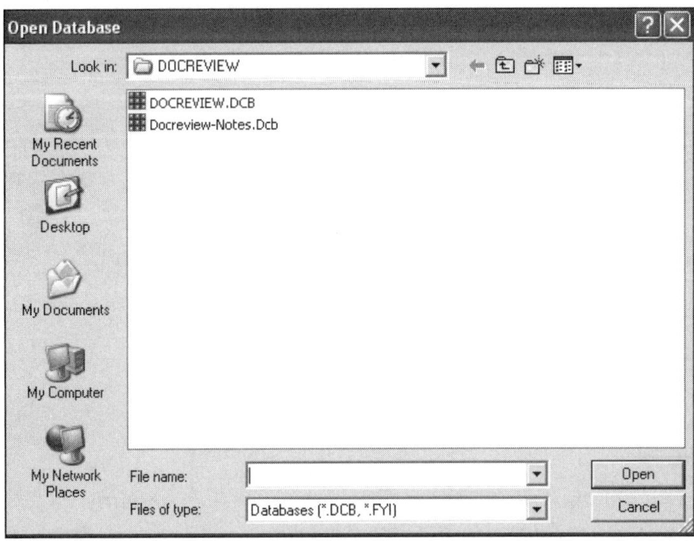

Figure 8-2. *The Open Database dialog. To open the DocReview database, you should select the file DOCREVIEW.DCB.*

If the option "Logon required" is enabled (from the Security tool), you're prompted to provide a valid login and password. If you have no login, you're logged in as the `default` user, if that account exists; otherwise, the database won't open.

■Note If "Logon required" isn't enabled for a particular database, anyone can open it. Concordance captures your network login name, and uses that to compare against the list of names in the Security tool for field-level and menu item permissions.

If the database is the main database of a series of concatenated databases, it—and all secondary databases—will open. The main and secondary databases behave as a single, extended database. Searches span all records from all databases.

Concordance remembers recently opened databases, and displays them in the default Active Workspace view (see Figure 8-3). You can click the name of a database and it opens.

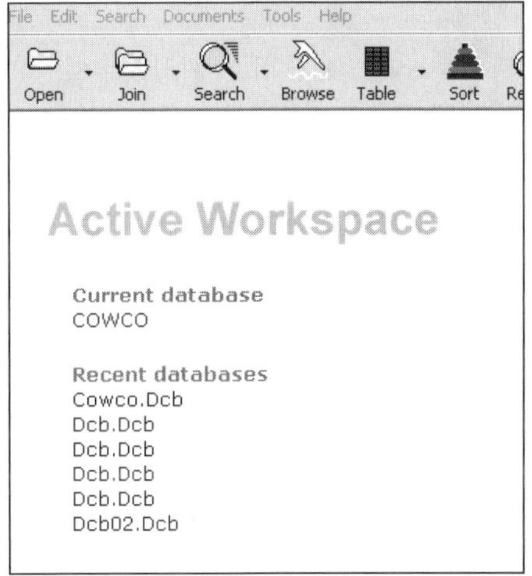

Figure 8-3. *The default Active Workspace view*

You can configure the "Recent databases" history from the Preferences tool, opened from the Tools ➤ Preferences menu. You can use the tab labeled Startup, displayed in Figure 8-4, to set the number of links that appear on the Active Workspace. The default setting is 6. You can also use this tool to control the default view that's displayed when a database is first opened: Browse, Table, or None. The following sections describe Browse and Table views. Selecting the None option causes the Active Workspace to be the default view when a database is opened.

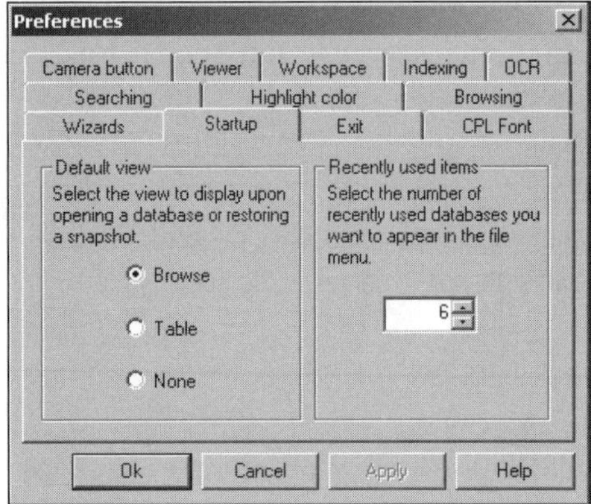

Figure 8-4. *Concordance's Preferences dialog. The Startup tab controls the program's behavior when it's first opened.*

Browse View

Concordance's Browse view displays the contents of a single record (see Figure 8-5). Field names are listed on the left-hand side of Browse view, with field values next to them. The Browse button that appears at the top of the Concordance window activates or deactivates Browse view.

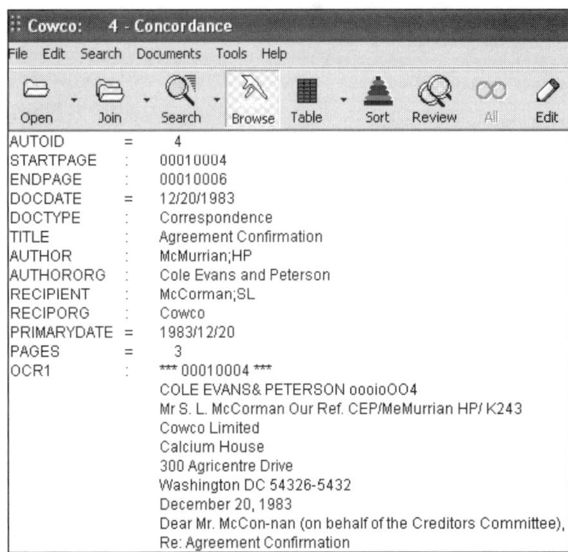

Figure 8-5. *Concordance's Browse view, which displays the contents of a single record*

You can navigate sequentially through records, forwards and backwards, using advance and retreat buttons located at the bottom of the Browse view window (see Figure 8-6).

Figure 8-6. *Navigation buttons, displayed at the bottom of the Concordance screen*

- *First* ◄ : Retreat to the first record of the underlying query. Also, Ctrl+Home from the keyboard.

- *Previous* ◄ : Retreat to the previous record. Also, Ctrl+Page Up from the keyboard.

- *Next* ► : Advance to the next record. Also, Ctrl+Page Down from the keyboard.

- *Last* ►| : Advance to the last record of the underlying query. Also, Ctrl+End from the keyboard.

■**Note** These navigation buttons are only visible when Browse view is enabled, either by itself, or in combination with Concordance's Table or Edit views.

Note the use of the phrase *underlying query.* With an open Concordance database, there's always a currently active underlying query that is some subset of all records in the database. When a database is first opened and no search has been applied, the default query displays all records. As searches are applied, results are returned that represent some subset of all records, even if a search yields no records (the subset is zero) or all records (the subset represents every record in the database). When navigating through records in Concordance's Browse view, the last record is from the most recently applied query. This record might or might not be the last record of the entire database. It's important to remember the context of your navigation, if a search criteria has been applied to the database or not. A visual cue will aid you. The current record (actively displayed in Browse view), the absolute position of the record in the database (relative to all records), and the number of records that result from the most recently applied query are displayed in the lower right-hand corner of the Concordance screen (see Figure 8-7).

```
Document 1 [1] of 205
```

Figure 8-7. *Record counts, displaying the total number of records in the database and the current record position*

For example, if a database has 100 records, if no search has been applied, if the currently active record is the first record in the entire database, and if no sort has been applied, the numbers will look like the following:

```
Document 1 [1] of 100
```

The first number represents the currently active record, the second number in square brackets represents the position of the currently active record displayed in Browse view relative to all other records in the database, and the third number represents the total number of records that result from the last active query.

If a search yields 50 records and you navigate to the second record in that set, the numbers will change. If that second record is the 25th record in the entire database, Concordance will display the following:

```
Document 2 [25] of 50
```

Reading from the left, the number 2 means that the second record of the last active query is displayed in Browse view. The number in the square brackets, 25, represents the position of the current record relative to the entire database. The value 50 represents the total number of records returned from the last active query.

The relative, absolute, and total number of records represented by the currently viewed record are also displayed for Concordance's Table view, as well. This view is described in the later section, "Table View."

■**Note** If the database has an accession number field, the number in the square brackets will represent the numerical value stored in the accession field, not the absolute position of the record.

At any time, you can review your search history from the Search ➤ Review menu, by clicking the Review button, or by pressing the F3 key. This opens the Search Review view. Each successive search is displayed, and is represented by a numbered alias. The currently active search is highlighted (see Figure 8-8). The search history is for the current session only, and disappears when an end user closes and reopens Concordance.

Search Number	Number of Hits	Number of Docs	Search Term(s)
00000	205	205	<Entire Database>
00001	2	2	smith
00002	19	19	DOCTYPE = MEMORANDUM
00003	21	20	1 or 2

Figure 8-8. *The current search history. Each search is given a numeric alias, which can be used as a shortcut to reference the search.*

Note that, within a given set of records, you can skip around if you know the relative position of a record in the current query. For example, you might wish to jump from the first record directly to the tenth record in the query. While in Browse view, pressing the G (for Go) key or clicking the Go To button opens the Go To dialog. You can enter a number that represents the position of a desired record, and then click the OK button. That record is made current and active.

Next and Previous Hit Buttons

Another method for navigating through records after a search has been applied is to use the Next Hit and Previous Hit buttons. Assuming that a search produces results (the result is not zero records), the keywords found in indexed fields are highlighted red, as a visual cue to aid you in locating positive results (see Figure 8-9). Because PARAGRAPH fields might contain so much text that you must scroll vertically through the results, positive hits might not be immediately displayed. Clicking the Next Hit button shifts the focus to the next highlighted search term, effectively scrolling through a document record for a user. Focus will shift to the next document record if there are no highlighted terms in the current document. Similarly, the Previous Hit button shifts the focus to the previous highlighted search term.

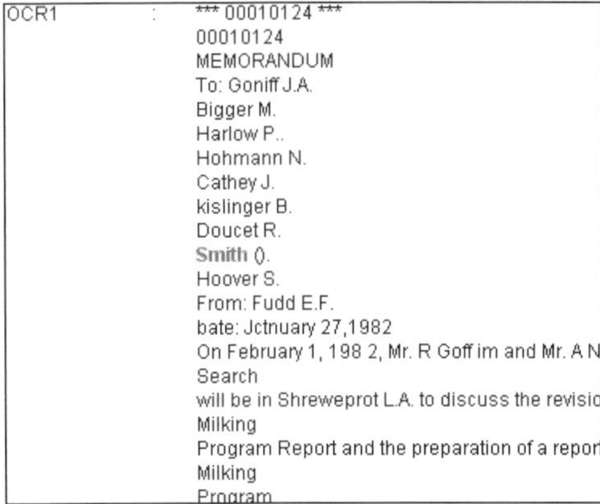

Figure 8-9. *The name Smith is highlighted as a hit from a search.*

You can change the highlight color to suit your preference, using the Preferences dialog, opened from the Tools ➤ Preferences menu (see Figure 8-10).

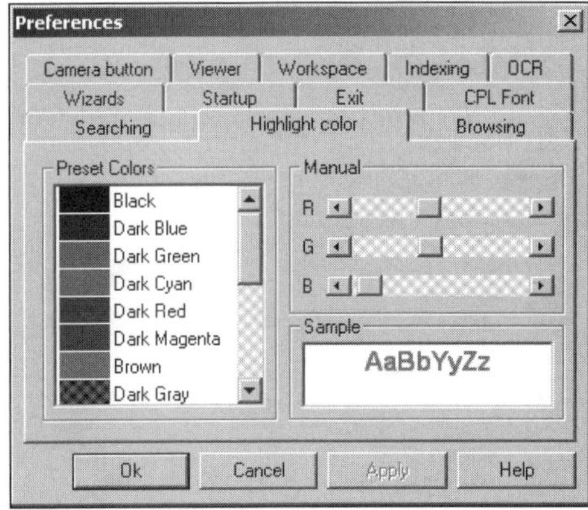

Figure 8-10. *You can use the Preferences dialog to set the highlight color of hits displayed in Browse view.*

Empties

Browse view either displays every field, regardless of whether or not a field contains data, or it displays only those fields that contain data, in effect suppressing blank (empty) fields. You can toggle the setting from the Tools ➤ Empties menu.

Determining Field Types from Browse View

For the purposes of searching, there are two types of fields in Concordance: *indexed* fields and *fixed width* fields. Indexed fields are fields that have a PARAGRAPH data type, or that have their index attribute set to True from the File ➤ Modify menu. Indexed fields are scanned during indexing or reindexing, and their contents are stored in the database's dictionary and inverted text files.

Nonindexed fields—fields with a TEXT, NUMBER, or DATE data type—aren't scanned during indexing or reindexing. To search these fields from the <Quick Search> bar, you must use relational operators, such as equals, greater than, and so on.

Chapter 9 describes search techniques in detail. As an example, for a database containing two fields, FULLTEXT and LASTNAME, the following search only produces records where the LASTNAME field is identically equal to the value SMITH:

```
LASTNAME eq SMITH
```

The following search produces records where the field FULLTEXT contains the value SMITH anywhere in the field:

```
SMITH
```

Records that result from searches depend on the data type of the fields defined for the structure of the database. Concordance's Browse view offers a visual cue to you as to how each field is data typed (see Figure 8-11). Field names next to a colon (:) are indexed. Field names next to an equals sign (=) are fixed width fields.

```
STARTPAGE    :    00010124
ENDPAGE      :    00010124
DOCDATE      =    01/27/1982
DOCTYPE      :    Memorandum
TITLE        :    Untitled
AUTHOR       :    Fudd;EF
RECIPIENT    :    Goniff;JA, Bigger;M, Harlow;R, Hohmann;N, Cathey;J, Rislinger;B,
                  Doucet;R, Smith;D, Hoover;S
PRIMARYDATE  =    1982/01/27
PAGES        =    1
```

Figure 8-11. *From Concordance's Browse view, you can determine if a field is indexed or not. The field STARTPAGE is indexed, as denoted by the colon (:). The field DOCDATE isn't indexed, as denoted by the equals sign.*

Table View

Concordance offers an alternative to Browse view that allows you to view several rows of data simultaneously. You can toggle Table view in three ways: by using the Table button located on the button bar at the top of Concordance's screen, by selecting the

Search ➤ Table ➤ Table view menu, or by pressing the F5 key. Field names appear above each column, and each row represents a document record (see Figure 8-12).

STARTPAGE	ENDPA...	DOCDATE	DOCTYPE	TITLE
00010158	00010158	12/15/1983	Correspondence	V BAP, et al, vs Cowco 81-2 Milking Progr
00010159	00010160	10/11/1983	Correspondence	Adohr Farmout Agreement
00010161	00010161	05/31/1983	Table	MMC Records on Cowco D19830531
00010162	00010186	11/23/1983	Report	Cowco, Report of Agreed Upon Procedur
00010187	00010188	07/13/1983	Memorandum	Reserve and Economic Analysis, Tuscalo
00010189	00010189	10/31/1983	Memorandum	Out of Cycle Examination of Cowco 81-02
00010190	00010190	05/12/1983	Correspondence	Cowco
00010191	00010192	05/02/1983	Correspondence	Cowco
00010193	00010193	05/23/1983	Correspondence	Farmout Agreement, Cowco and Adohr U

Figure 8-12. *Concordance's Table view, which displays multiple records*

You can scroll through several screens of records by using the vertical scroll bar that appears to the right of the Table view. For large databases, scrolling can cause performance issues and screen flicker if all fields have been selected for viewing in the Table view. If this happens, you can elect to remove PARAGRAPH fields. These fields contain a great deal of data, and Concordance might struggle to display them quickly, as scrolling causes your screen to repaint. The later section, "Table Layout," describes this method of altering the layout of fields.

You can also skip to records directly using the Go To button or by pressing the G key. This is the same feature available from Concordance's Browse view.

Sorting

Column names allow you to sort records quickly by the contents of a field. When a database is first opened, no sort order is applied. Records appear in the order in which they were loaded. Sorting toggles between ascending and descending, so that clicking a column name once sorts records in an ascending manner based on only the contents of the column that was clicked. Clicking that same column name again sorts records in a descending manner. Clicking it a third time re-sorts records in an ascending manner once again.

■**Note** For PARAGRAPH fields, only the first 60 characters in the field are used for the sort.

Concordance gives you a visual cue to indicate how records are sorted, by means of a small up/down arrow embedded in the column name. When a database is opened such that no sort order is applied, the arrow doesn't appear in any column name.

Clicking a column name sorts only on the contents of that column. To create a composite sort of two or more columns, you can click the Sort button located on the button bar at the top of Concordance's screen. This opens the Database Sort tool. Available fields appear in a list on the left. You can add fields by highlighting them, then clicking the Ascending or Descending buttons. Sort order may be mixed so that, in the composite sort, the first field sorts ascending and a second field sorts descending. To remove a field, highlight the desired field and click the Remove button.

Once you've selected the desired fields and their respective sort orders, clicking the Sort button sorts records (see Figure 8-13). A progress bar appears at the bottom of the Sort tool to indicate the status of an ongoing sort.

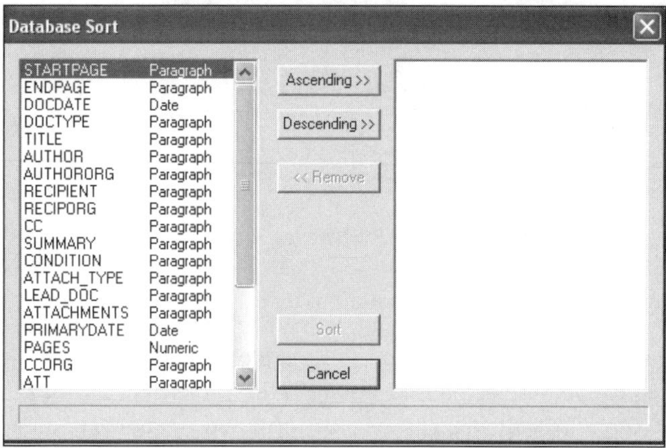

Figure 8-13. *Concordance's Sort tool. Fields on the left can be added to the sort list box on the right, and sorted in ascending or descending order.*

Table Layout

Each user can set the number of fields that are visible in Table view and the order in which they appear. Furthermore, Concordance can store the details of several layouts (in a file with a .LAYOUT extension), so that a user may select a view of fields that most efficiently displays only those fields that are useful at a given time.

To modify the order and appearance of fields in Table view, right-click anywhere in the Table view, then select the Table Layout option. This opens the Table Layout tool, which displays a list of the currently saved views and a list of all fields in the database (see Figure 8-14). Highlighting the name of a layout and clicking the OK button returns you to Table view, with the highlighted layout ordering and hiding fields as defined in the layout.

If a database has been concatenated with other databases, each database will appear as a different node in the view (see Figure 8-15). Clicking a database name expands a node so that layouts available to you will appear. When working with concatenated databases, it's recommended that the layout of each database display the same number of fields, in the same order. Although this isn't a requirement, mixing field positions can confuse users as they cross from one database to another as they scroll through records.

Each layout has a unique name, defined by a user. Clicking the name of a layout expands the tree further, so that the fields that can be viewed from the layout are visible. Users can modify the order in which the fields appear by clicking and dragging a field up or down the list. To remove a field from a layout, users can highlight it, then press the Delete key, or click and drag the field off the list entirely. Removing a field in the Table Layout tool doesn't delete the field from the database. Rather, it causes the field to be hidden in Table view. To add a field to the list, users can drag and drop from the list of remaining field names on the right to the desired position in the layout on the left.

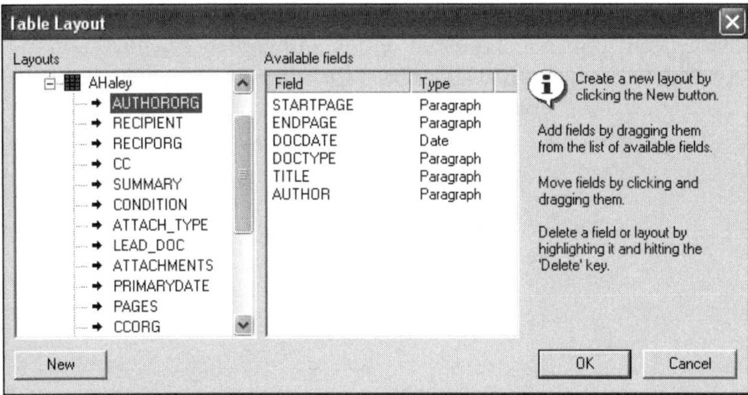

Figure 8-14. *Specifying a table layout. The fields displayed on the left appear in Concordance's Table view. The fields in the "Available fields" list box are not displayed.*

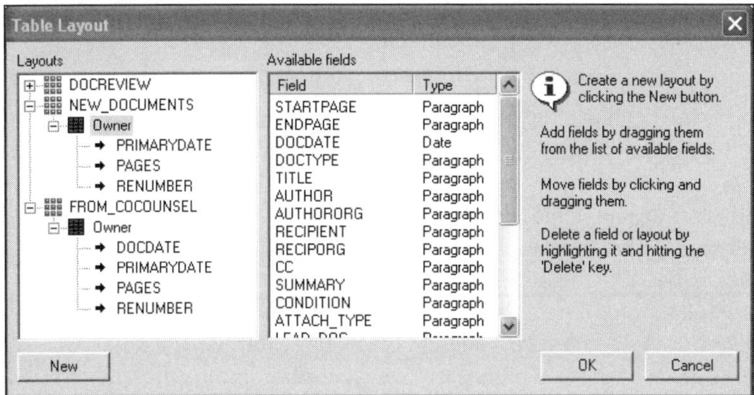

Figure 8-15. *Table layouts for concatenated databases*

To add a new layout with its own collection of fields, users highlight a database name, right-click, and then select the New Layout option.

If no layout has been created for a database, the Table view displays all fields by default, in the order in which the fields were created. When one or more layouts have been created, users may select among them by right-clicking anywhere in the Table view, and by selecting the name of the layout they wish to view.

Tallying Fields

Table view offers the ability to select a field, and then count the number of unique instances of values in that field across all records in the currently active query. For example, in a database that has a field LASTNAME, you might wish to know how many SMITHS, how many JONES, and how many other names appear in the field, as well as the count of each name. This process is known as *tallying*.

To accomplish this, you click into a record visible in Table view, hover your mouse over the contents of the field to be tallied, and then select the Tally option. Concordance begins counting the contents of the field. A tally window opens just above the Table view where ongoing results of the tally are displayed (see Figure 8-16). A progress bar appears at the bottom of the screen to give you a status of the tally as it progresses.

Item	Count
0000/00/00	39
1980/01/27	3
1980/09/09	3
1980/10/24	3
1980/12/15	3
1980/12/17	3
1981/02/00	3
1981/02/28	3
1981/03/06	9
1981/03/11	3

Tallied 126 items   Print   Reset   Close

Figure 8-16. *The Tally screen. The field that was tallied has a DATE data type. The Item column represents unique values stored in the field. The Count column represents the number of times the value appears in the database. The value 1980/01/27 appears in three records.*

∞ **All** A tally applies only to the results of the currently active query. If you wish to tally the entire database, you should click the Infinity button located on the button bar at the top of Concordance.

Tallying counts unique values in a field. In most fields, this is a straightforward calculation: the tally counts each value. By default, Concordance treats values separated by a comma as multiple values. When a field contains multiple values, the tally counts each value in the field. This means that for a field that contains two distinct values, separated by a delimiter, the tally will count the contents of the field twice. For example, if a database contains a field named LASTNAME, and if one of the database records contains the value SMITH, JOHN, Concordance will count SMITH and JOHN separately. For another record in which the field contains the value SMITH, JOHN, BROWN, JOHN, the tally will count four separate values.

To minimize confusion, you might wish to change the default delimiter for a field. You can accomplish this from the Data Entry Attributes tool, opened from the Edit ➤ Validation menu. You can set different delimiters for different fields. To set a delimiter, click the desired field, then update the value in the Delimiter field (see Figure 8-17).

■**Note** Tallying a database can be resource intensive, as the counting occurs on the client workstation.

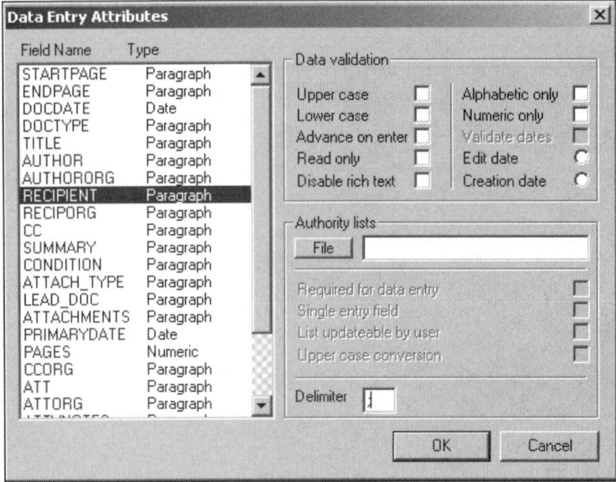

Figure 8-17. *You can set the delimiter for a field from the Data Entry Attributes tool. In this example, the delimiter for the field has been changed to a semicolon.*

Split Screen

An effective way to view records in a Concordance database is to use the Browse and Table views concurrently. Concordance allows you to activate both views by clicking both Browse and Table buttons. In this way, you can see several records laid out horizontally in Table view, and the contents of one of those records—the highlighted one—in Browse view. When configured in this way, Concordance is said to use a *split screen*. You can toggle this option from the Tools ➤ Split screen menu. When this menu item has a check mark, Concordance can operate in a split screen mode. If the menu item isn't selected, the option is turned off, so that clicking the Browse button when Table view is active closes the Table view, and Concordance's Browse view opens exclusively.

Clicking the Browse and Table buttons opens and closes the views, respectively. When neither view is selected, Concordance displays the Active Workspace. By toggling the Browse and Table buttons, you can place Browse view on the left and Table view on the right, or vice-versa (see Figure 8-18).

A.	DO...	PR...	P	R
58	01/27/1982	1982/01/27	1	0123
188	02/26/1982	1982/02/26	23	0021
01/27	1982/01/27		1	0123
02/26	1982/02/26		23	0021
01/27	1982/01/27		1	0123
02/26	1982/02/26		23	0021

```
AUTOID        =   58
STARTPAGE     :   00010124
ENDPAGE       :   00010124
DOCDATE       =   01/27/1982
DOCTYPE       :   Memorandum
TITLE         :   Untitled
AUTHOR        :   Fudd;EF
RECIPIENT     :   Goniff;JA, Bigger;M, Harlow;R, Hohmann;N, Cathey;J, Rislinger;B, Doucet;R, Smith;D, Hoover;S
PRIMARYDATE   =   1982/01/27
PAGES         =   1
```

Figure 8-18. *In this split screen view, Table view is on the left; Browse view is on the right.*

Editing Data

Assuming he or she has the appropriate permissions, a user has the ability to add records or modify data in existing records by editing fields. Clicking the Edit button or selecting the Edit ➤ Edit menu opens Edit view, in which all fields for which the user has viewing rights (regardless of the current table layout) for the current record are displayed and will be populated with field values (see Figure 8-19). To add a record, end users can select the Edit ➤ Append menu. This opens Edit view, with empty fields. Fields for which users have read-only permissions have a gray background, and are locked for editing. Users can modify open fields, with a white background.

AUTOID	58
STARTPAGE	00010124
ENDPAGE	00010124
DOCDATE	01/27/1982
DOCTYPE	Memorandum
TITLE	Untitled
AUTHOR	Fudd;EF
AUTHORORG	
RECIPIENT	Goniff;JA, Bigger;M, Harlow;R, Hohmann;N, Cathey;J, Rislinger;B, Doucet;R, Smith;D, Hoover;S

Figure 8-19. *Concordance's Edit view. Fields with a gray background cannot be edited. Fields with a white background are open for editing.*

Edits are automatically saved to Concordance in response to a user navigating to another record, closing the database, or activating another Concordance tool, such as Form Search. There's no Save button, per se, as it isn't needed.

When Edit view is activated, a series of buttons is made visible on the bottom of the Concordance screen. Record navigation buttons, as described in the "Browse View" section earlier in this chapter, allow you to advance or retreat through records. The Go To button is available as well. Other buttons useful during Edit view are the following:

- *Ditto* ❚❚ : Allows you to create a new record in Concordance, duplicating values from fields that you select. Clicking this button opens the Duplicate tool—a dialog that displays all fields in the database—and offers other options (see Figure 8-20). To select fields to be duplicated, click the field name, highlighting it. To select two or more fields, press the Ctrl key, and then click field names while the Ctrl key is depressed.

  When you select the "Append new" radio button, a new record is created, with field values duplicated from the values of the record that was active when the Duplicate tool was opened. If you select the "Copy previous" radio button, values will be copied from the previous record. If you select the "Copy from another" radio button, you must specify the numerical position of an existing record that will provide data for the new record.

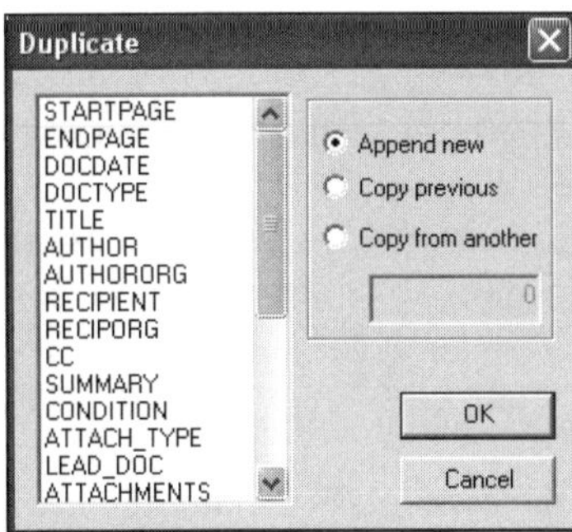

Figure 8-20. *Concordance's Duplicate tool. You can copy the contents of a record into a new record.*

- *Delete/Undelete* 🖹 : Allows you to mark a record for deletion. When a record is marked for deletion, the code DEL appears in the lower right-hand corner of the Concordance screen. If a record has already been marked for deletion, clicking this button will remove the mark, so that the record will no longer be deleted.

  Records aren't removed until you *Pack* a database, from the File ➤ Pack ➤ Database menu.

- *Undo* 🗑 : Clicking this button activates the Edit Options tool, which allows you to reset edits in a record (see Figure 8-21).

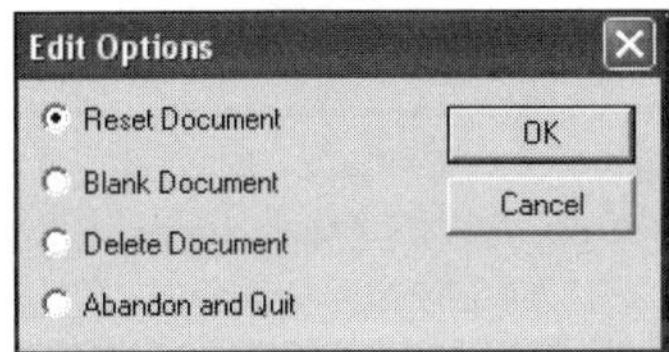

Figure 8-21. *Undo options available from clicking the Undo button*

The choices available in the Edit Options tool are as follows:

- *Reset Document*: All edits to the record are removed, and the field values are reset to their original values.

- *Blank Document*: Nulls out all data in all fields in the record. Accession fields aren't affected.

- *Delete/Undelete Document*: Marks the record for deletion or undeletion, depending on the record's active state.

- *Abandon and Quit*: Resets all fields to their original values, closes both the Reset Document tool and Edit view, and returns you to the Active Workspace view.

After a record has been edited, changes aren't available to searches until the database is reindexed, if those edits occur to a PARAGRAPH or indexed field. Edits made to fixed fields—that is, fields that have a data type of TEXT, NUMBER, or DATE, and that aren't indexed—are available for searches as soon as Concordance saves the edit.

Because of a user's ability to modify data, some fields in a Concordance database should *always* be read only. For example, a user should never have the ability to modify the contents of an accession field. Other fields you should consider as read only for all users include beginning and ending document ID fields, creation date fields, edit date fields, and full text fields that represent the contents of a document.

There might be times when you wish to edit the contents of a field in so many records that editing each one individually becomes a hardship. Concordance offers a global edit feature that grants you the ability to overwrite or otherwise modify the contents of one or more fields in batches of records. You can activate the Global Replace tool using the Global button or the Edit ➤ Global edit menu (see Figure 8-22).

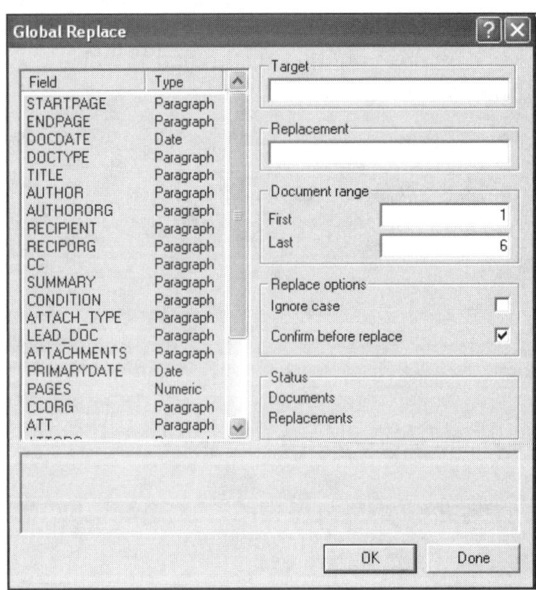

Figure 8-22. *Global Replace tool. You can modify the contents of one or more fields over a set of records by highlighting field names in the list box.*

Available fields are listed in a list box on the left-hand side of the tool. You may select one or more fields; to select multiple fields, you should press the Ctrl key, and keep it depressed as you select field names.

The Target field represents the text that is to be replaced. In the fields that are to be updated, note that only the text that appears in this field is modified. Thus, if you enter the letter S here and no replacement value is provided in the Replacement field, the value Smith will be updated to mith.

■**Note** There's no method in Concordance to blank out the contents of a field using the Global Replace tool.

The "Document range" fields give you the ability to update some subset of records from the currently active underlying query. When the tool is opened, the First value is always 1, representing the first record in the query. The value in the Last field depends on the active query—if the last search yielded 50 records out of a database that contains 10,000 records, the value in this field will be 50. To reduce the possibility of error, you should query the database to display only those records that you wish to edit.

The "Ignore case" check box, unchecked by default, causes Concordance to pay attention to case when replacing data.

The "Confirm before replace" check box, checked by default, prompts you to confirm each update before the update is made, for each record. If you wish to update a large number of records, this option should be unchecked.

Replacements are written when you click the OK button. As Concordance finds fields that contain the Target value, a count is updated onscreen in the Status area (see Figure 8-23). The total number of document records scanned is displayed next to the Documents label, while the Replacements label shows a count for only those document records that contain data that matches the Target.

Figure 8-23. *The Status section of the Global Replace tool gives you visual feedback about how many records are being scanned, and how many replacements are made.*

Clicking the Done button closes the Global Replace tool and returns you to the Active Workspace.

Tagging Records

Tags are document-level markers. Tags are useful in that you can use them to group a set of documents that have no common feature, and that cannot be found using a series of logical searches. Even if you can find a set of records using a series of searches, you might find the use of tags to isolate records preferable to conducting a search, because querying tags takes place much faster than completing a full text or relational search of fields. Tag data exists outside the data stored in document record fields, and is stored in a file with a .TAG extension. Compared to a search that must scan through every record and perform field-by-field comparisons of large sets of data, a search of tags refers to the .TAG file alone, which compared to Concordance's ancillary search files, is small. Also, unlike edits made to indexed fields, adding, deleting, or modifying tags doesn't require a database to be reindexed.

You may create as many tags as you wish, which grants you the ability to group disparate sets of documents according to different criteria. Tags are available to all users, so that an administrator—who might be more adept at constructing Concordance searches than users—can group records together according to complex search criteria, and then tag the results for other users to use.

You can combine tags with full text and relational searches so that you may begin with a known grouping of documents (those that are tagged), and narrow down to subgroups of the tagged documents according to a fielded search. Combining searches in this way takes advantage of the speed of selecting tagged documents, and the flexibility of searching according to criteria contained in specific fields.

Viewing Tags

You can view document-level tags in Concordance by clicking the Tag button located on the button bar at the bottom of the Concordance screen (see Figure 8-24). An area of the Concordance screen opens, displaying document-level tags; each tag has a label (the name of the tag) and is represented by an open check box. When a tag is enabled for a document, the check box contains a small, red check mark. The check box toggles, so that clicking it causes the check mark to disappear, thus untagging the document.

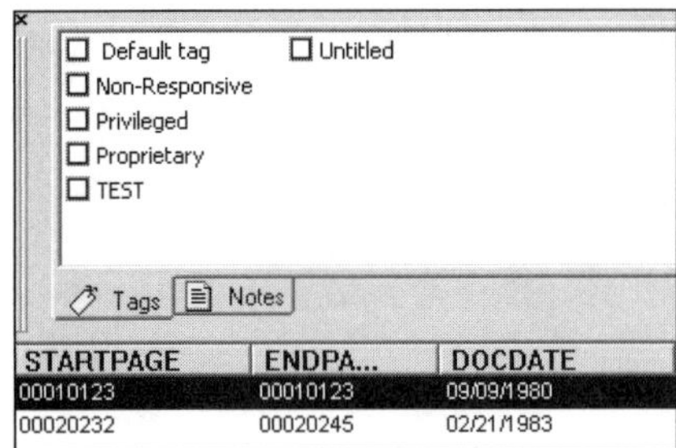

Figure 8-24. *Tags/Issues screen. Document-level tags are created and applied from this window.*

By default, Concordance creates a persistent tag with the label "Default tag," so even if no user has created a tag in a new Concordance database, the Default tag will exist. (See the following section for a discussion of persistence.) This tag may be used for miscellaneous purposes, or in an ad hoc way, to group and ungroup documents quickly during your session.

Types of Document-Level Tags

Tags are either *persistent* or *non-persistent*. A persistent tag exists in the database and is available even if no document uses that tag. Non-persistent tags only exist in the database as long as at least one document has the tag. If you remove a non-persistent tag from all records in a database, then close and reopen the tag screen, the tag will disappear. You set persistence from the Tag/Issue Management dialog described in the following section. When a tag is persistent, a reference to it is stored in the database's .INI file, in ASCII text, so that you can edit that file with a text editor to copy and paste persistent tags quickly from one database to another.

Note You should use care when editing a database's .INI file. Before making an edit to the file, you should make a full copy of the file, then verify that the database operates properly with the edited .INI file before releasing the database to users. Users should never be allowed to edit this file.

Managing Tags

  You can create tags, set them to persistent or non-persistent, and query them from the Tag/Issue Management dialog, which can be opened by clicking the Tagging button located in the button bar at the top of the Concordance screen. Note the difference between the Tagging button at the top of the Concordance screen and the Tag button at the bottom of the Concordance screen. The Tagging button opens the Tag/Issue Management dialog, which allows for advanced management of tags. The Tag button displays tags in a section embedded in the Concordance screen itself.

The Tag/Issue Management dialog (see Figure 8-25) grants you more advanced features than the Tag window embedded in the Concordance screen. However, the Tag window is always open (assuming you've enabled it by clicking the Tag button) and affords an overview of how the current document is tagged at a glance.

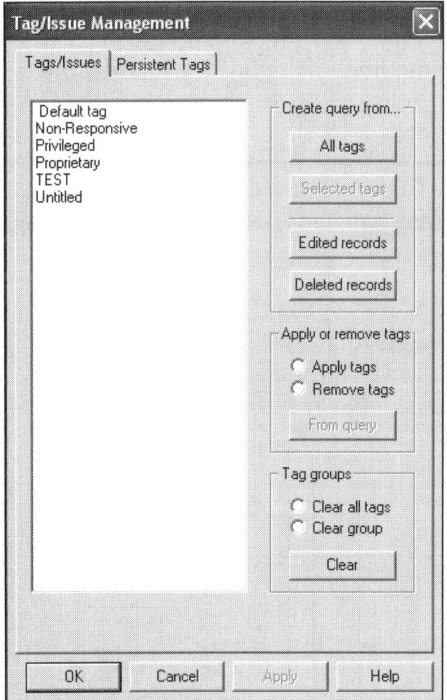

Figure 8-25. *The Tag/Issue Management dialog has two tabs. You can use the Tags/Issues tab to locate records with selected tags. You can use the Persistent Tags tab to enable a tag's persistence.*

Creating New Tags

There are two ways to create a new tag: from the Tag window (see Figure 8-24) embedded in the Concordance screen or from the Tag/Issue Management dialog.

To create tags from the Tag window, right-click anywhere in the white area between tags, select the "New tag" option, then enter the name of the tag. Tags created in this way are non-persistent. When a new tag is created, it's automatically applied to the currently active document. You should take care when creating tags on a random document; that document will contain the tag. To minimize errors, you should navigate to a record that should receive the tag, and then create it.

To create a tag using the Tag/Issue Management dialog, open the tool, click the Persistent Tags tab, and then click the New button. You may also right-click in the list box containing field names, and then select the "New tag" option. Note that a new tag created in this way is automatically set to persistent, as indicated by the red check mark in the check box adjacent to the new tag name. Note that, if you create a tag in this way, remove the tag's persistence, and then close the Tag/Issue Management dialog, the tag won't be saved. You must apply non-persistent tags to at least one document record to exist in a database.

Applying Tags

You can apply tags from both the Tags/Issues screen and the Tag/Issue Management dialog.

- *From the Tag window:* To apply a tag to a single document, navigate to the desired document, open the Tag window, and click the tag so that a red check mark appears in the check box adjacent to the tag label. An alternate method is to right-click in the white area between tags and select the Tag Document option.

  To tag several documents at once, you can right-click in the white area between tags, and then select the Tag Every Document option. This tags every document in the currently active query. (In a like manner, you can untag batches of documents by selecting the Untag Every Document option.)

- *From the Tag/Issue Management dialog:* The Tags/Issues tab has an area labeled "Apply or remove tags." You should select one or more tags from the tag list (this list allows for multi-selection by means of the Ctrl key), then select "Apply tags" or "Remove tags" accordingly. Clicking the "To query" button either applies or removes tags to all records in the currently active underlying query.

Deleting Tags

You can remove tags from either the Tag window (if they're non-persistent) or the Tag/Issue Management dialog (for both types of document-level tags).

- *From the Tag window:* If a tag is not persistent, you can right-click over a tag, then select the Untag Every Document option. Although the tag will still appear in the Tag window for the remainder of your session, it will disappear when the database is reopened. Users who open Concordance won't see the tag. Recall that tags removed in this way affect the last active underlying query. To ensure a tag is removed from every record in the database, you should ensure that the last active query corresponds to all records.

- *From the Tag/Issue Management dialog:* From the Tags/Issues tab, you can use the section of the tool labeled "Clear all tags" to remove one, several, or all tags from the database. Selecting one or more tags from the list, selecting the "Clear group" radio button, then clicking the Clear button removes the selected tags from the database. The "Clear group" radio button removes every tag from the database when the Clear button is clicked.

Querying from Tags

You can query tags from either the Tag window or the Tag/Issue Management dialog. When one or more tags are queried in this way, all document records that have the tags selected are grouped together, and those records are visible in Concordance as the currently active underlying query. Concordance adds an item to its search history to represent the search. As with full text or fielded searches, the tag query is given a numerical value that can be used as an alias and combined with other searches in Concordance's search history.

Note that in both of the following methods, when you query for two or more tags, the resulting documents must have *any one* of the tags selected. The search is, in effect, an *or* search, so that documents will look like the following:

```
tag1 or tag2 or ... or tagn
```

To locate documents that have all tags selected, you must conduct a search of each tag separately, and then refer to each search's query number alias in the <Quick Search> search field as follows:

```
1 and 2 and 3 ... and n
```

- *From the Tag window:* You can multiselect one or more tags from the Tag window using the Ctrl key. Once the desired tags have been highlighted, you can right-click, and then select the "Create query from tag(s)" option. Records are displayed that have the tag, or that have all the highlighted tags if multiple tags have been selected.

- *From the Tag/Issue Management dialog:* From the Tags/Issues tab, you can select one or more tags (using Ctrl to multiselect), then click the "Selected tags" button. The "All tags" button queries documents on the basis of all tags that appear in the tag list box.

Combining Tagged Searches with Full Text and Fielded Searches

You can combine results from a tagged search with full text or fielded searches by means of the numerical alias Concordance gives to each search. You can view these aliases from Concordance's Review screen. To combine searches in this way, you should conduct the tagged searches separately from the full text and fielded searches. You should then click the Review button so that you can determine what numbers have been assigned to each tagged search. Using these numerical aliases, you can enter search terms in the <Quick Search> search field and use relational operators to join or exclude records.

For example, say that search alias 00001 represents a tagged search for all documents that have been tagged as Nonresponsive, and that the database contains a field named LASTNAME that's a nonindexed TEXT field. The following search locates those records with the tag Nonresponsive that contain the value SMITH:

```
1 AND LASTNAME = SMITH
```

When searching for terms that appear in full text fields, no relational operator is needed in the search for the term itself. If the database contains a PARAGRAPH field DOCTEXT, the following search locates those records with the tag Nonresponsive in which the name SMITH appears anywhere in the DOCTEXT field:

```
1 AND SMITH
```

Annotations in Browse View

Annotations are sections of text in Browse view that contain additional information provided by a user. Users can use annotations to highlight a section of text in Browse view, and then add subjective comments, perhaps about the relevance of a block of text. Annotations are either free-form comments (known as a *Note*) or a tag. These tags are the same document-level tags described in the preceding section. However, the scope of how a tag is used in this way is different: it applies only to the section of text that has been highlighted for the annotation. Tags used in this more narrowly defined way are known as *Issues*.

In addition to comments and Issue tags, annotations grant you the ability to attach an external file or URL to the note. In this way, files and programs outside Concordance, such as an Adobe PDF document or a Microsoft Excel workbook, can be linked to the annotation if the file is relevant to the block of text that has been highlighted. Each note can have only one attachment, and the attachment can be launched as an external process or by an image viewer.

Adding and Deleting an Annotation

To add an annotation, you must have Browse view active. Highlight a block of text, then right-click and select the option "New note." The Notes tool opens (see Figure 8-26).

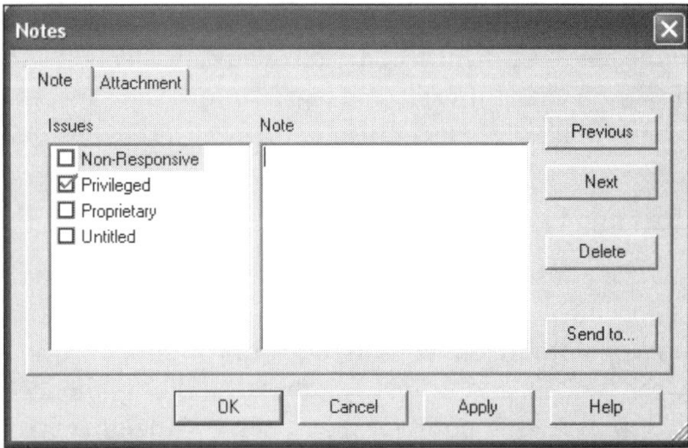

Figure 8-26. *In the Notes tool, the Issue-level tags that appear on the left of the tool also appear in the Tag window. Issues and Tags differ only in scope in how they're applied: Issues to sections of text, Tags to entire document records.*

The Notes tool has two tabs: Note and Attachment. In the Note tab, there are two panes, Issues and Note. Issues are tags that have been created using the methods described in the previous section. In addition, you can add tags from this tool by right-clicking in the white area between tags, selecting the "New issue" option, and then naming the tag accordingly. Tags added from this tool become available as document-level tags as well, and can be viewed from the Tags pane of the Tags/Issues screen. You can click one or more Issue-level tags to apply them to the highlighted text.

The Note area of the Note tab is a text field in which you can enter comments. This is free-form text, and is stored in a database's -notes.dcb file. As a result, the text in notes is indexed, added to Concordance's dictionary files, and can be searched. Data in the -notes.dcb file is indexed automatically when an administrator indexes or reindexes data from the main database. There's no reason you should open the -notes.dcb file, as this data is accessible from the main database .DCB file.

Note You can search for full text in the database's fields, in annotation notes, or both using the following options: Concordance's Search tool, accessible from the Search ➤ Search menu; the Search button ; or by pressing the F2 key. The default is "Search database only."

Once you enter Issue tags or comments, you can click the Apply button to save the annotation. The highlighted text now has a yellow background and is underlined, indicating that an annotation is attached to it. When you hover your mouse pointer over the highlighted block of text, the first line of the Note assigned to the annotation is displayed.

After you've created an annotation, you can double-click the highlighted text to open the Notes tool.

To delete an annotation, you can open the Notes tool for a given annotation, and then click the Delete button.

Navigating Through Multiple Annotations

The Notes tool gives you the ability to scroll through annotations within a document (see Figure 8-27). The Previous and Next buttons cause the Notes tool's focus to shift to the previous or next annotation within the document, respectively. The annotation that's active in the Notes tool is highlighted in Browse view in the background.

Another way to see all annotations in a document at a glance uses the Tags/Notes screen, toggled by means of the Tag button at the bottom of Concordance. The Notes pane in this screen displays the text of the note, one of the Issue tags assigned to the annotation, and the path to any attachment that has been added to the annotation (see Figure 8-28). Column headers sort in the same way column headers in Concordance's Table view sort: clicking once sorts the annotations by the field in an ascending order. Clicking again sorts in a descending manner.

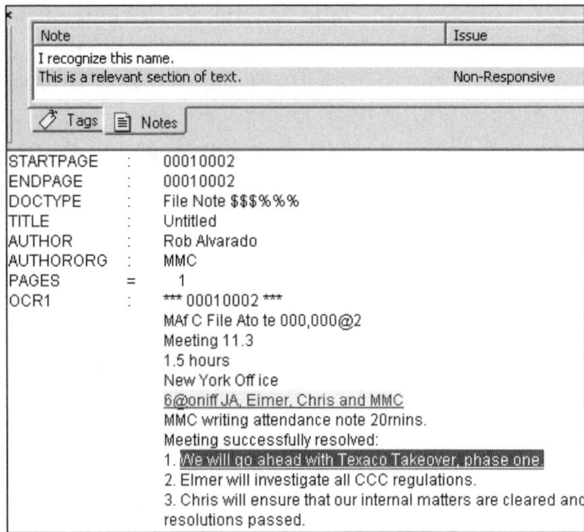

Figure 8-27. *The annotation attached to the text "We will go ahead with Texaco Takeover, phase one" is highlighted blue because a user has selected that note in the Notes pane of the Tags/Notes screen.*

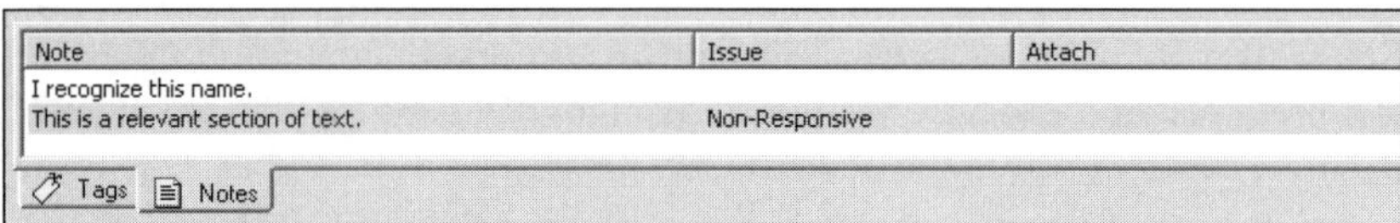

Figure 8-28. *The Notes pane of the Tags/Notes screen*

Attachments

An external file can be associated with an annotation from the Attachment tab of the Notes tool (see Figure 8-29). An annotation can have only one attachment. The attachment can be an actual file located on a user's PC, it can be on a network, or it can be the URL to a web page. Depending on how an attachment is applied, it can be launched as an external process separate from Concordance (that is, the file launches in its own, native application), the file can be opened by the viewer that's registered in Concordance from the Tools ➤ Preferences menu, or the actual file path of the file is copied to your clipboard. This last option allows you to paste the path into a different application.

The "Attachment type" options available from the drop-down box control how the attachment is handled when you double-click the annotation text from Browse view, if the "Open attachment when note is clicked" check box is checked. Note that, when this option is checked, the normal behavior of double-clicking the annotation from Browse view is overridden, so that the attachment is launched instead of the Notes tool. To edit an annotation that has an attachment, you can right-click over the annotation and select the "Edit note" option.

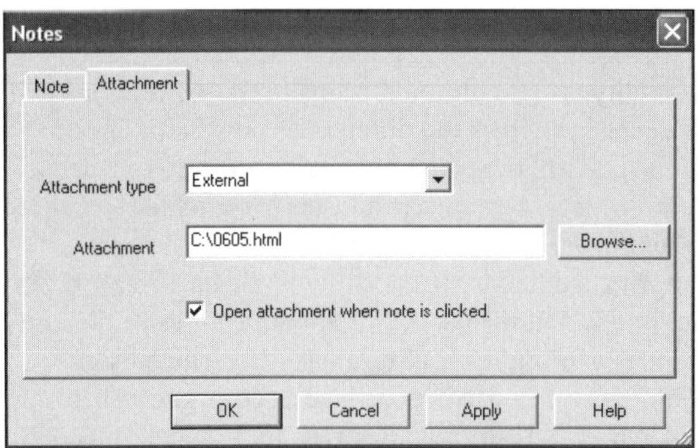

Figure 8-29. *On the Attachment tab, the "Attachment type" drop-down box controls how Concordance responds when the attachment path is clicked in Browse view, if the "Open attachment when note is clicked" check box is enabled.*

The following options are available from the "Attachment type" drop-down box:

- *<none>*: No attachment has been selected. The Attachment text field is locked.

- *External*: The attachment is launched as a separate process.

- *Viewer*: The attachment is opened from the registered viewer.

- *Clipboard*: The file path of the attachment is copied into your clipboard.

If a file has been associated with an annotation but "Open attachment when note is clicked" isn't checked, you can still launch the attachment by right-clicking over the annotation from Browse view, and selecting the "Run attachment" option. The preceding options define how the file is handled.

When any option is selected other than <none>, the Attachment field unlocks, and you can click the Browse button to navigate through a network and locate the file you wish to attach.

Note Although it's possible for a user to select an attachment stored on his or her hard drive, other users won't be able to launch and view the attachment unless the file is also stored on their computer and in the same location on their hard drive. In practice, attachments should be stored on a shared network location accessible to appropriate users.

The option "Save attachment as," accessible from Browse view when right-clicking over an annotation, allows you to save a copy of the attached file to some other location, perhaps onto your hard drive, or to separate media for offline review.

Summary

This chapter has covered the basic functionality of Concordance. Many of these functions will be readily apparent to users as soon as they see it, such as the differences between Concordance's Table view and Browse view. Other aspects of the program aren't so obvious, such as combining result sets from searching document-level tags with result sets from fielded searches.

Although you can configure security features to prevent users from deleting records, modifying sensitive fields, or otherwise altering a database irrevocably, some basic features in Concordance must be enabled at all times and can, if misused, corrupt data; for example, the Global Replace tool. It's best that users "learn by doing" only after they've been given some exposure to the software by means of a training regimen. Never, ever grant users access to a database if they've never used Concordance. Even a 15-minute tutorial can alleviate the need for tedious and costly administrative repairs down the line.

However, "learning by doing" is often the most effective way of learning how a program works. To that end, after users have been given an overview of how Concordance works, you might wish to grant users access to a sample or test database, for them to practice.

An important part of Concordance usage is locating database records. Concordance has a powerful search engine, a variety of methods to retrieve records, and an advanced search syntax. Although this chapter has touched on a few methods to locate records, the next chapter explores search methods in detail.

■ ■ ■

Searching

Storing and viewing data is fundamental to data management. However, data is of no use if it cannot be queried appropriately. In the context of managing large sets of data, intelligent searching and grouping of database records is the primary purpose for using a full-text information retrieval system such as Concordance. In a likely scenario, a research team might face the challenge of sifting through a million documents to evaluate only those pages that make reference to a relevant topic in certain contexts and within various time frames. In the past, this kind of discovery was either resource consuming or impossible. However, with a properly designed Concordance database and with an adequately trained staff, this kind of discovery can be accomplished quickly and efficiently.

Things to Know About Searching

Understanding the scope of a search is essential for proper management of large sets of data. Concordance maintains both objective data (file metadata, text contained in documents) and subjective data (annotations). Searches can span both. Users may initially search objective data, and then add their own subjective comments. Later in a project's life cycle, users may search objective data *and* subjective data to retrieve only those documents that are of interest.

Understanding the way that Concordance stores data is as important as understanding the scope of a search. Techniques vary according to the type of data being searched. Using the right search syntax on the wrong type of data can cause a search to return unintended results.

Subjective vs. Objective Data

Data that has been gleaned from documents, whether from an OCR process or by document coding, is often referred to as *objective data*. For example, an electronic file's creation date isn't usually subject to interpretation. Data added to documents during discovery, such as tags or annotations, can be referred to as *subjective data*. You might tag a document as "Hot document—must review," which reflects your subjective opinion. Subjective data gives documents meaning within the context of a project's scope.

Functionally, Concordance supports two types of subjective data: document-level tagging and phrase-level annotation (see Figure 9-1). You can tag an entire document as "Interesting," and in that document, annotate a specific phrase as "Requires further research."

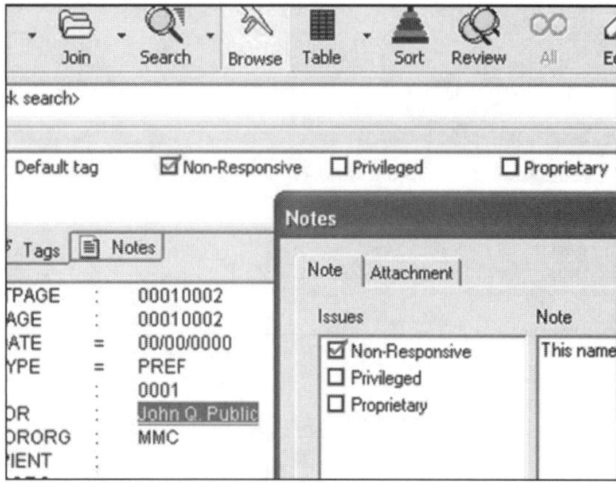

Figure 9-1. *Document-level and issue-level tagging: the document record has been tagged as Non-Responsive, while the name "John Q. Public" has been tagged as Non-Responsive as well. This is an example of subjective data.*

Searches in a Concordance database may be on objective data, on subjective data, or on a combination of both types of data. In this way, a user can select only those documents in which certain phrases appear in the full text and for which other users have added specific comments.

Indexed vs. Nonindexed Data

As noted in previous chapters, when a Concordance database is indexed or reindexed, Concordance creates a dictionary file of every word used in every PARAGRAPH, TEXT, NUMERIC, or DATE field with the index attribute set to True. Figure 9-2 displays the Modify dialog, where field-level attributes such as the Indexed property are configured for fields.

You search PARAGRAPH fields using a syntactical structure that's different from the syntactical structure used to search nonindexed TEXT, NUMERIC, and DATE fields. You can combine these syntactical structures. Searches on PARAGRAPH fields are often referred to as "free text searching," while searches on nonindexed fields are often referred to as "relational searching." Table 9-1 displays a list of each type of data field in a Concordance database, with the appropriate syntactical method for searching.

Table 9-1. *A Summary of Field Types and Acceptable Search Syntax*

Field	Type of Syntax
Paragraph fields (indexed by default)	Free text syntax to locate words or phrases within the field Relational search syntax to perform comparisons (first 60 words only)
Date, text, and number fields that are indexed	Free text syntax to locate words or phrases within the field Relational search syntax to perform comparisons
Date, text, and number fields that aren't indexed	Relational search syntax

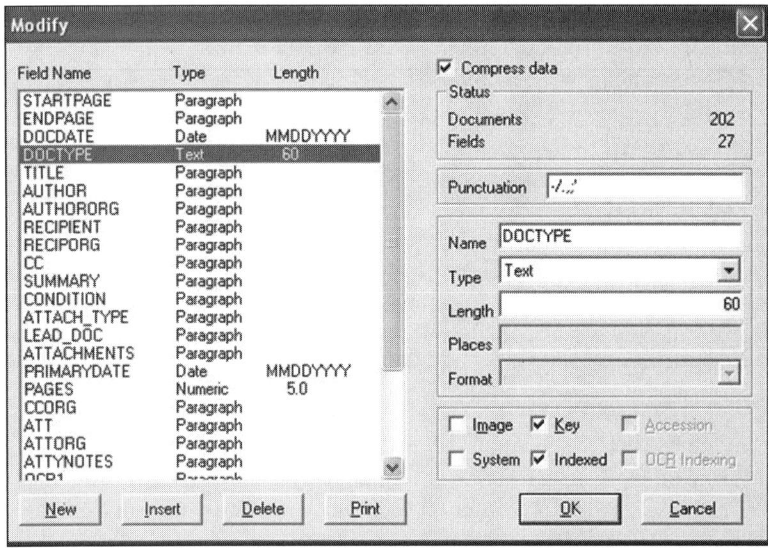

Figure 9-2. *Field-level attributes, set from the File ➤ Modify menu. Field names and data types are usually defined at the time of database design, before any data is loaded. Note that the DOCTYPE field is a fixed text field, set to 60 characters, and it's indexed so that words in the DOCTYPE field are added to Concordance's dictionary file.*

The rest of this chapter will discuss search techniques, how search syntax is constructed, and how searches may be combined, reviewed, and saved.

Referencing and Saving Searches

When a search has completed, Concordance saves it as a query, and it's given an alias in the form of a five-digit number. Before any search has been invoked, 00000 refers to all records in the Concordance database. 00000 is a permanent reference in all Concordance databases; even if a search history is cleared (Search ➤ Clear menu), 00000 remains. Successive searches are numbered sequentially from 00000 as 00001, 00002, . . ., n, where n refers to the last search invoked. Figure 9-3 shows a Search History window, which is activated by clicking the Review button on Concordance's top button bar.

Search Number	Number of Hits	Number of Docs	Search Term(s)
00000	202	202	<Entire Database>
00001	69	69	DOCTYPE = CORRESPONDENCE
00002	1	1	AUTHOR = "JOHN Q. PUBLIC"

Figure 9-3. *Search results viewed in the Review screen. Each line represents a different search. Note that query 00000 represents all records in the database. You open the Search History screen by choosing the Search ➤ Review menu, by pressing the F3 key, or by clicking the Review button.*

The numerical alias allows you to track a search history, and to refer to previous searches by number, minimizing the potential for typographical errors when reentering query logic. The following search logic filters query 00002 for records in which the AUTHOR field contains the value "JOHN Q. PUBLIC":

```
2 AND AUTHOR = "JOHN Q. PUBLIC"
```

Note that if the last half of the search were passed to the database search engine alone, it would be applied to all records in the database:

```
AUTHOR = "JOHN Q. PUBLIC"
```

It could be written as follows:

```
0 AND AUTHOR = "JOHN Q. PUBLIC"
```

Query 00000 is a permanent artifact of a Concordance database. It's the active query displayed when a database is first opened, unless a startup routine has been defined that overrides this behavior. All searches can be said to involve query 00000, even if it isn't written out explicitly. Take the following search:

```
2 AND AUTHOR = "JOHN Q. PUBLIC"
```

It could be written as follows:

```
0 AND 2 AND AUTHOR = "JOHN Q. PUBLIC"
```

You should understand that each search is applied to all database records, and that combining searches is the key to narrowing results.

You can save dynamic searches as *query files* (from the Search ➤ Keep menu), which will refresh each time data is loaded or deleted. You can also save dynamic searches as *snapshots* (from the Search ➤ Snapshot ➤ Save Snapshot menu), which are static results, regardless of how data has been modified since the snapshot was initially created. The section later in this chapter "Saving Searches as Snapshots and Queries" describes these techniques in more detail.

The Importance of Training: Computers vs. Humans

Effective searching of a Concordance database involves both technical and human factors. A badly designed database or a badly trained user can obscure otherwise intuitive search results. A Concordance administrator who spends a great deal of time deploying properly designed databases might find that his or her efforts are frustrated by an impatient user base, unwilling to learn the techniques for sophisticated searching. Conversely, a willing user base might be disappointed by search results if the Concordance administrator doesn't actively seek to design Concordance databases in as efficient a manner as possible.

Both users and administrators require a rudimentary understanding of the ways in which Concordance stores data. An important reason is that PARAGRAPH fields are searched differently from fields with other data types. Another reason is that you can use Synonym and Stopword lists to broaden useful searches by matching similar words, and to restrict useless searches by ignoring words that have no value during review. An example of a synonym may be the matching of the word automobile when the word car is used in a search. An effective list of stop words would exclude pronouns, prepositions, and definite and indefinite articles.

Training Concordance: The Computer Factor

Concordance supports lists of synonyms and lists of stop words that you can use to increase the accuracy of search results. You can modify these lists using the File ➤ Dictionaries menu. *Synonyms* refer to a series of words that Concordance can be trained to recognize as equivalent, while *stop words* refer to those words that should be ignored. Concordance will build a default Stopword list, but the Synonym list for a new database will be empty. For maximum effectiveness, the Concordance administrator may build or fine-tune both lists.

Synonym Lists

By default, the Synonym list in a new Concordance database is empty. There's no way to build a de facto thesaurus that will intelligently consider possible synonyms within multiple contexts. A project involving the fashion industry might equate the word `model` with the words `male` or `female`. A project involving a technical issue might equate the word `model` with the phrase `mathematical treatment`. Other potential synonyms might not be so obvious. Consider the phrase "Four-score and seven years ago." Should documents containing this phrase be included in search results, if instead of `four-score`, you search for 55? As the Concordance administrator, you must coordinate with review team members to build a list of meaningful synonyms within the lexicon of a project.

In addition to the contextual meanings of words, the Synonym list also provides you with the means to broaden searches with words that are considered to be equivalent (see Figure 9-4). For example, a principal in a matter might have the legal name `John Q. Public` but be referenced in document records as `JQP`. When you want to find all memos that reference `John Q. Public`, you should include records that contain the value `JQP` in the query output. Again, the Concordance administrator must liaise with the review team on a project to identify words that should be treated as equivalent.

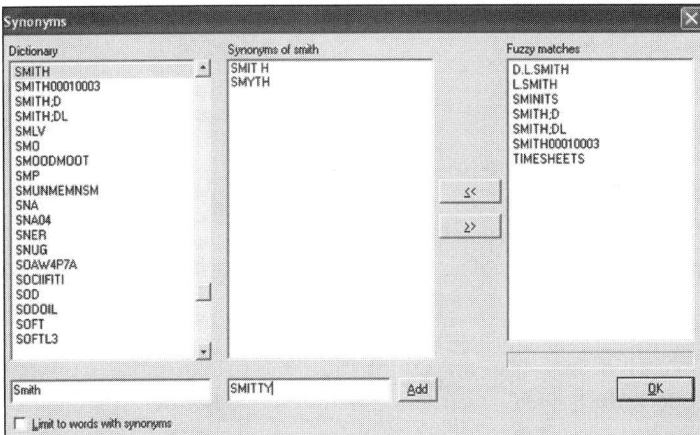

Figure 9-4. *The Synonym list tool. Concordance scans words in the dictionary file and suggests potential matches in the "Fuzzy matches" list on the right. The middle list, "Synonyms of smith," displays words that the user has added as synonyms. Any search for the word SMITH returns hits for SMIT H and SMYTH.*

■**Note** A database's Synonym list is an effective way to ensure that searches for important keywords capture not only the instances of the keywords, but also any common misspellings. For example, because the U and I keys on a standard computer keyboard are adjacent, the word "big" is often misspelled as "bug" (and vice versa).

Stop Words

By default, the Stopword list in a new Concordance database isn't empty. The software manufacturer has identified a series of words that are so common that they're of no use in the intent of a search. Examples of stop words that Concordance includes by default in a new database are the words and, for, and the. If you want to search for the value Four-score and seven years ago, Concordance will ignore the word and, and will only provide matches for records that contain the words four-score, seven, ago, and years.

Concordance prevents stop words from being included in a search by preventing those words from being written to the dictionary file. It's the dictionary file that's searched when you query indexed or PARAGRAPH fields. This means that the larger the Stopword list, the smaller the dictionary file, and the faster searches will execute. You must use some caution—a Stopword list that's too restrictive will skew search results. For most purposes, the default list Concordance provides is sufficient. Figure 9-5 displays the Stopwords dialog, opened from the File ➤ Dictionaries ➤ Stopword list menu.

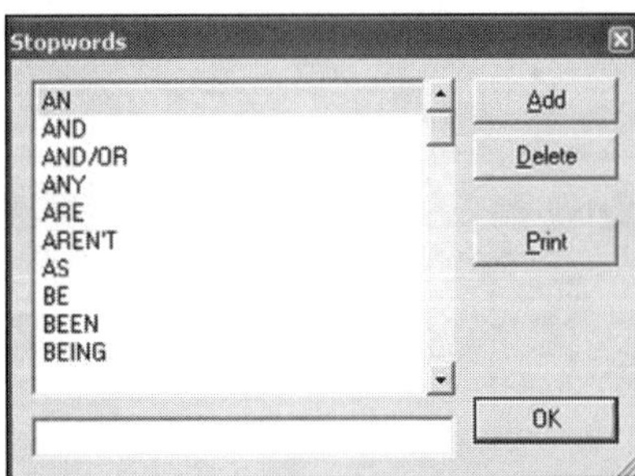

Figure 9-5. *You can modify, add, or delete words using the Stopword list tool.*

Training Users: The Human Factor

Querying a Concordance database is a conversation: you ask the database a question, and it provides an answer. With a properly designed Concordance database that has been loaded with a clean set of data, it's never true that "the database gave the wrong answer," a statement often heard from frustrated users. Concordance's search engine will always answer exactly the question that it's asked, even if that question—the search syntax provided by the user—doesn't convey the user's intentions. No software program can intuitively guess what a user wants; it can only work with the search syntax provided.

For this reason, it's important that users know how to construct questions that convey to the database what they intend. Sometimes this isn't intuitive. Training of users should be fundamental to the administration of Concordance databases. Unfortunately, when a set of data has been freshly delivered and a review team is eager to begin its review, training is often overlooked.

The Importance of Accurate Data—Garbage In, Garbage Out

In the previous discussion, it was assumed that a database has been loaded with a clean set of data. If it's never true that "the database gave the wrong answer," it's always true that "a question presented to a database will receive an answer only as accurate as the data itself." Ensuring that underlying data is accurate is fundamental to the usefulness of a Concordance database.

For the Concordance database administrator, policing huge sets of imported data can be a challenge. That oversight begins before documents are sent to a vendor for scanning and coding. For example, how are documents physically grouped—in folders, boxes, or both? Should the database contain a field that records these divisions? If the records originated as e-mail, should they be deduplicated? A member of the review team intimately familiar with the details of a matter should be consulted before boxes or electronic media are sent to a vendor.

When data does arrive, another layer of quality assurance is required. Has the vendor supplied data precisely in the format stipulated by the administrator? As the administrator, you might wish to build a quality control workflow in which you review data before it's released to end users. Most problems can be prevented before a database is deployed by means of vigilant quality assurance.

Viewing Search Results

Concordance provides several visual tools and onscreen controls to assist you with managing search results. Besides highlighting hits, Concordance also maintains a search history (see Figure 9-6). Given that the desired result might require several intermediate queries, Concordance also manages and indexes queries to allow you to refer back to, and build upon, previous searches easily.

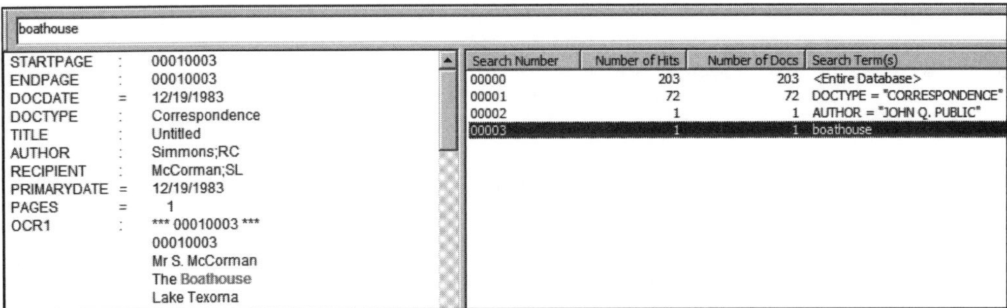

Figure 9-6. *The highlighted word Boathouse is a hit from search 00003 for that word. You open the Search History screen by using the Search ▸ Review menu, by pressing the F3 key, or by clicking the Review button.*

Subsets vs. All Records

Even when all records are being displayed, Concordance considers a valid query to be one that returns all rows. Concordance names this query 00000, which you can use in your searches to refer to the entire database. When opening a Concordance database, 00000 is the default query.

After 00000, successive searches are named 00001, 00002, and so on. Unless you combine queries, each new search is based on 00000. This can be confusing to some users; it means that if you open a database, then search the field DATECREATE for a date range, the rows that are returned are a subset of 00000:

```
PRIMARYDATE >= "1/1/1980" AND PRIMARYDATE <= "1/1/1985"
```

This subset is named 00001. If you then proceed to search the RECIPIENT field for any entries that contain Goniff;JA, the records that are returned are a filtered subset of 00000, not 00001:

```
RECIPIENT = "Goniff;JA"
```

This filtered subset is named 00002. If you had wanted to query only those records contained in 00001, the following search accomplishes this:

```
1 AND RECIPIENT = "Goniff;JA"
```

Figure 9-7 shows this search, with the results displayed in Concordance's Table view.

DOCTYPE	RECIPIENT		Search Number	Number of Hits	Number of Docs	Search Term(s)
Correspondence	Goniff;JA		00000	203	203	<Entire Database>
Correspondence	Goniff;JA		00001	192	192	PRIMARYDATE >= "1/1/1980" AND PRIMARYDATE <= "1/1/1985"
Memorandum	Goniff;JA		00002	41	41	RECIPIENT = "GONIFF;JA"
Correspondence	Goniff;JA		00003	41	41	1 AND RECIPIENT = "GONIFF;JA"
Correspondence	Goniff;JA					
Correspondence	Goniff;JA					
Correspondence	Goniff;JA					
Correspondence	Goniff;JA					

The query box above the table reads: `1 AND RECIPIENT = "GONIFF;JA"`

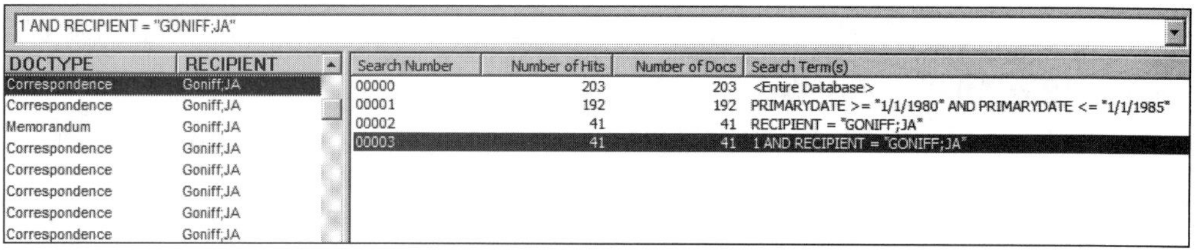

Figure 9-7. *Combining a named query with other search logic. Note that the left-hand pane is Concordance's Table view, while the right-hand pane is Concordance's Review screen.*

You can combine query aliases:

```
(1 OR 2) AND DOCTYPE = "MEMO"
```

The preceding query groups all records contained in 00001 and 000002, and of those records, only returns those documents that have a DOCTYPE value of MEMO.

Referencing a query by its number causes a query to execute more quickly than if you use the full search syntax. Take the following query:

```
(1 OR 2) AND DOCTYPE = "MEMO"
```

It's faster than explicitly writing out the entire logic for 00001, 00002, and DOCTYPE = "MEMO".

Concordance maintains a complete history of searches in a session, until you specify that it should clear the history and return to 00000. You accomplish this from the Search ➤ Clear menu. When referring to a previous query in a search phrase, the resulting query is given its own alias. Consider a database that displays 00000: all records. You enter the following search, which retrieves 54 records:

```
TITLE = "Untitled"
```

The last query alias is now 00001. Next, you perform the following search (CO means "contains," and is described later in this chapter):

```
AUTHOR CO "ROB"
```

This search retrieves one record. Next, you perform the following search:

```
1 AND PAGES = 1
```

Concordance interprets this as: *Take the results of query 00001, and of those records, find those where the PAGES field is equal to a value of 1*. The results of this search are given the alias 00003. The alias 00002 (AUTHOR CO "ROB") hasn't been overwritten.

At any point in the search history, you can enter the following:

```
0
```

The database interprets this as: *Return to all records in the database*.

To search specifically for a number, instead of referencing a query index, you should contain the number in double quotes, as follows:

```
PAGES = "1"
```

Note You can change the double-quote character used to delimit search phrases to another character from the Searching tab of the Preferences dialog, opened from the Tools ➤ Preferences menu.

Understanding Highlighting

Depending on the type of search, actual *hits* are highlighted in Browse view to indicate to you where in the document the search word or phrase appears (see Figure 9-8). By default, the highlight color is red. You can change this color via the Tools ➤ Preferences menu, on the Highlight Color tab in the Preferences dialog.

Because Concordance unitizes on the document level (that is, one record in Concordance represents several pages of a bound document), it's possible for a search word or phrase to appear in several places within the same document record. Instances of the search word or phrase are highlighted throughout the document. For documents that contain hundreds of pages (bound in one Concordance record), navigating between hits can become a chore; hence the Next Hit and Previous Hit buttons.

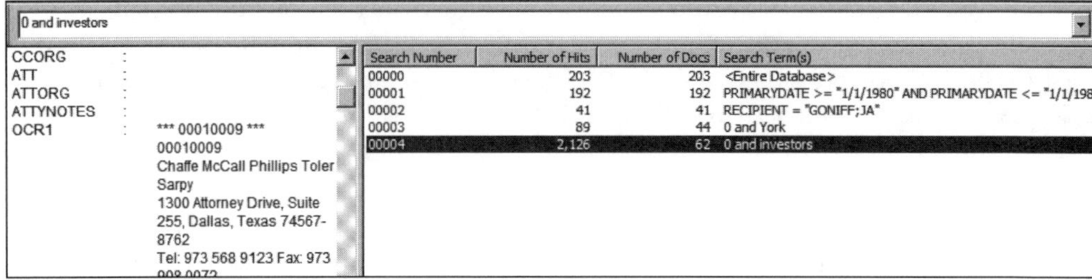

Figure 9-8. *Search 00004 for the word "investors" results in 2,126 hits scattered throughout 62 documents (right-hand pane). For the document displayed in Browse view in the left-hand pane and for the page displayed, there are several hits.*

You should be aware that words and phrases are highlighted in fields that have a PARA-GRAPH data type, or in fields that have been indexed. Words and phrases aren't highlighted in fields that haven't been indexed. Furthermore, for those fixed fields that have been indexed, highlights will only appear if the search syntax doesn't use relational operators (used for comparisons). All words in all PARAGRAPH fields are added to the dictionary file by default, but only those words in fixed fields with the index attribute set to True are added. For example, say you want to find all documents that have a modified date that's earlier than 1/1/2002. The modified date field is named MDATE, and has a data type of DATE. It hasn't been indexed. The search syntax is as follows:

```
MDATE <= "1/1/2002"
```

The hits in the MDATE field in the resulting records aren't highlighted.

If the index property of the MDATE field is set to True, and then the database is reindexed (so that the dictionary file is updated), all dates in the MDATE field are added to the dictionary file. When you enter the following search, the contents of the MDATE field in Browse view will be highlighted:

```
"1/1/2002"
```

■**Note** It's also true that more records might result from this search because the field name hasn't been specified. Searches without a specific field name perform a search of every PARAGRAPH field and every field that has been indexed. If the string `"1/1/2002"` appears in a DOCTEXT field in a record, this record will be included in the output—and the hit in that record will be highlighted.

Hits aren't highlighted in searches that use relational operators, and that are performed on fixed fields that are indexed. Relational searches don't refer to the dictionary file (even if a field has been indexed), and instead compare the values contained in fields. If the MDATE field has been indexed, the following search will return records, but the date "1/1/2002" won't be highlighted:

```
MDATE <= "1/1/2002"
```

Form Search (Query by Example)

Although freehand searches entered into Concordance's <Quick Search> search field offer the most flexible way of searching records, Concordance provides a graphical user interface to assist users: the Query by Example search builder (see Figure 9-9). This interface lists all fields in the database in drop-down boxes, applicable operators (also in drop-down boxes), and empty fields for words or phrases you supply. It also provides a quick way to examine the actual words that are contained in the dictionary file, by means of a Dictionary button. You can use this list to select search words by double-clicking them.

Novice users might prefer this interface, given the ease of selecting fields and operators. It's also a useful training tool, as searches built in this way will be translated into the appropriate search syntax, and displayed each time a search is executed. You can even type searches directly into this field, to fine-tune the syntax suggested by Concordance in response to the values you select from drop-down boxes.

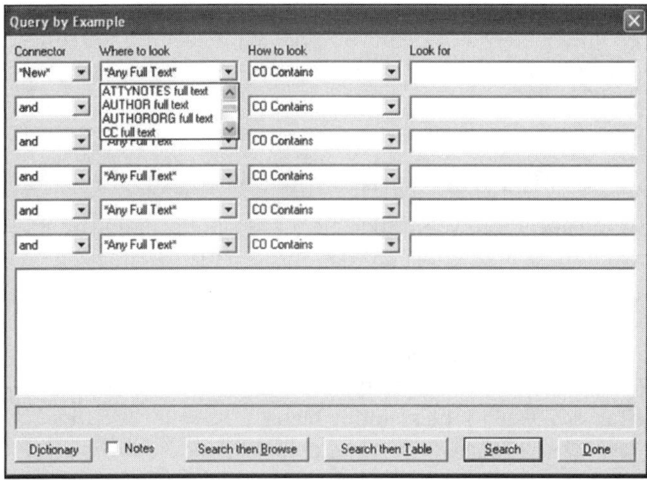

Figure 9-9. *Query by Example, activated from the Search menu, Form search submenu item*

Building Searches with Connectors

The Connector drop-down box allows you to build more complex searches by combining or excluding fields. The following search operators are available: AND, OR, NOT, ADJ, ADJ5, ADJ25, NEAR, NEAR5, NEAR25, SAME, NOTSAME, and XOR. The section "Relational Searches" discusses these search operators in greater detail.

Specifying Fields

Every field in the database is listed in the "Where to look" drop-down box. Field names are displayed in all caps. The field's data type is displayed as well. In addition to all field names, the option *Any Full text* searches any paragraph field and any other field that has been indexed.

The available options in the "How to look" drop-down box change depending on what's selected in the "Where to look" drop-down box. If *Any Full text* is selected, only the CO operator is listed. If a specific field is selected, the following operators are available: CO, EQ, GE, GT, LE, LT, NC, NE, OL, and WL. The section "Operators" discusses these relational operators in greater detail.

Entering Search Values

Each row of fields in the Query by Example dialog provides you with a blank text field to enter search words and phrases. You must take some care when searching for entire phrases. Concordance interprets the phrase NEW YORK as NEW ADJO YORK, which returns hits for all instances of NEW YORK where the two terms are directly adjacent. (The default operator Concordance uses is ADJO, described later in this chapter in the section "Proximity Operators.") If you wanted all hits where either the word NEW or the word YORK appeared, even if the words aren't adjacent, you'd have to provide the text NEW in the first search row, select the OR connector, then enter YORK in the second row. A document that contained the word NEW would be part of the result set, even if the word YORK wasn't in the document.

If you wanted all documents where the words NEW and YORK appear (that is, both words must appear in the document), even if they aren't adjacent, you'd have to select the AND connector. A document that contained the word NEW but not the word YORK would be excluded from the result set.

Search Then Browse vs. Search Then Table

Clicking the Search button executes the query, but keeps the Query by Example dialog open. The number of records that result from the search is displayed in the lower left-hand corner of the Concordance window when Browse, Table, or Edit views are active. Clicking the "Search then Browse" button executes the search, closes the Query by Example dialog, and then opens the Browse view to the records that resulted from the search.

In the same way, clicking the "Search then Table" button closes the Query by Example dialog and then opens Concordance's Table view with the resulting records. The view is either Browse or Table (see Figure 9-10), regardless of the way you had defined Concordance's layout prior to opening the Query by Example dialog. That's because opening the dialog forces Concordance to return to the Active Workspace view. This behavior of the software forces you to click the Browse or Table button to view the results of your search. However, if the search results in no records, the Query by Example dialog will remain open, even though "Search then Browse" or "Search then Table" was clicked.

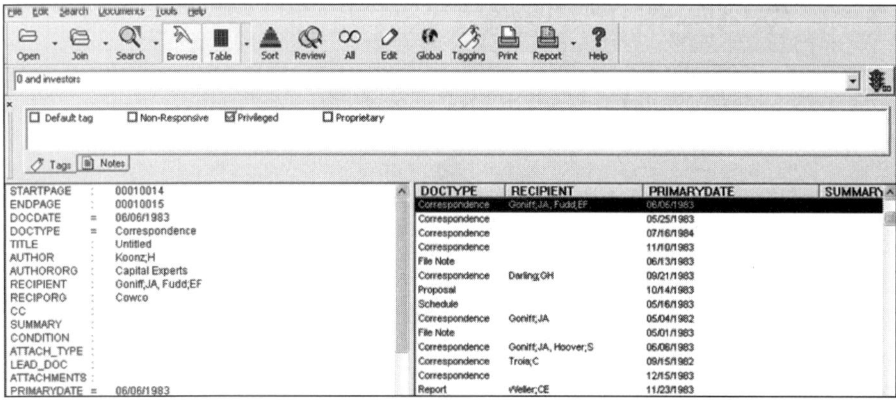

Figure 9-10. *Browse view (left) and Table view (right) in split screen mode. You may go from the Query by Example dialog directly to either Browse view or Table view by clicking the appropriate button.*

Search Syntax Window

The search syntax window is a large field located beneath the query builder rows (see Figure 9-11). It shows you how Concordance interprets the search you specify with the query builder fields. It also allows you to bypass the query builder fields and enter search text directly. Functionally, this means that you can return to all records from the Query by Example dialog by clearing out all search text from the query builder fields, entering **0** in the search syntax window, and clicking the Search button. However, the query builder fields take precedence: if you've entered **0** in the search syntax window and have entered text in a "Look for" field, the text in the search syntax window will be ignored.

Figure 9-11. *From the Query by Example dialog, the user has entered 0 in the search syntax window to return to all records.*

Searching Subjective Data

Subjective data is information provided by the review team to describe document records or document text in Concordance database records. You can attach descriptions to sections of text in a document page (notes), tag entire documents to create families of records, or apply tags to sections of text (issues). The Concordance search engine can search subjective data. In this way, one member of a research team can locate just those documents that have been declared "Of interest" by other members of the team.

Tags

A tag is a reusable descriptor that can be applied to a document. Tags are created by users, and can be applied to documents in combinations.

You manage tags with the Tag/Issue Management dialog (see Figure 9-12), which you can open by clicking the Tagging button. A list of all tags that are available in the database is displayed. You can select several tags simultaneously (by pressing the Ctrl key while clicking tag names), and then create a query to retrieve records that share the tags. Queries created from the Tag/Issue Management dialog are given aliases, like those described in earlier sections of this chapter. This means you can use the Tag/Issue Management dialog to build a query that locates documents with selected tags, and then reference that query's alias in combination with keyword searches.

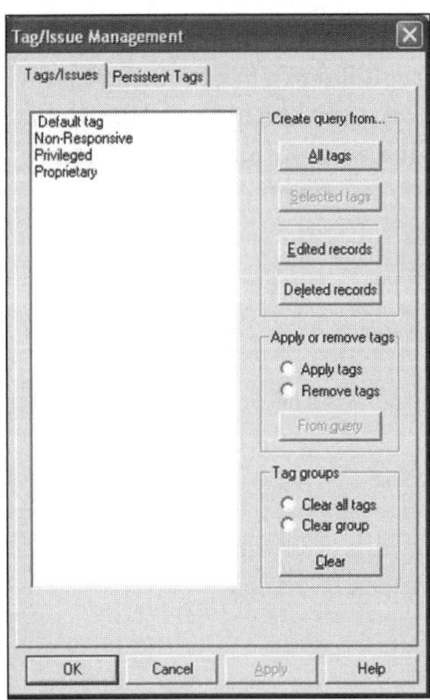

Figure 9-12. *You can use the Tag/Issue Management dialog to query tags in a database.*

Queries applied from the Tag/Issue Management dialog are always applied to query 00000: all records. However, each new query is given a new alias. This affects how you can narrow sets of records based purely on tag management. It isn't immediately obvious from the Tag/Issue Management dialog how to query records that contain the following:

```
tagA AND tagB AND tagC AND ... AND tagN
```

When you create a query by selecting two or more tags, the resulting search logic uses the operator OR. Records in the resulting query contain any database record marked with any one of the tags that have been selected.

To find the intersection between two or more tags, you must query each tag separately. Because each query is given an alias, you can return to Concordance's Table or Browse view, and combine the queries that were created to narrow records using the <Quick Search> search field. For example, if you want to find only those documents that have been tagged as "Confidential" and that have been tagged as "Redacted," you should query each tag separately using the Tag/Issue Management dialog. Then you should click the Review button to determine what aliases the queries have been given. If the aliases are 1 and 2 respectively, the following search syntax will locate just those records that have both tags:

```
1 AND 2
```

Issues

Issues are tags, and are applied to sections of text rather than to entire documents. The available family of issues is the same as the available family of tags. You apply issues by highlighting a section of text in Browse view, right-clicking, and selecting the New Note popup menu item. You can use an available list of tags to select one or more tags to apply to the highlighted text.

Because issues are tags, they're searched using the same method described in the preceding section. There's no way to discriminate between text-level issues and document-level tags when using the Tag/Issue Management dialog to query records.

Notes

Notes are user-defined descriptions that are attached to sections of highlighted text. You apply notes by highlighting a section of text in Browse view, right-clicking, and selecting the New Note popup menu item (see Figure 9-13).

You can search notes exclusively, or in conjunction with other database fields, by using the Search window that you open by clicking the Search button (see Figure 9-14). The following options are available from the Options drop-down box: "Search database and notes," "Search database only," and "Search notes only."

Notes aren't available to the search engine until a database administrator indexes or re-indexes a database. For this reason, you'll want to coordinate with a research team to reindex the database at strategic times to ensure that searches are accurate and up to date.

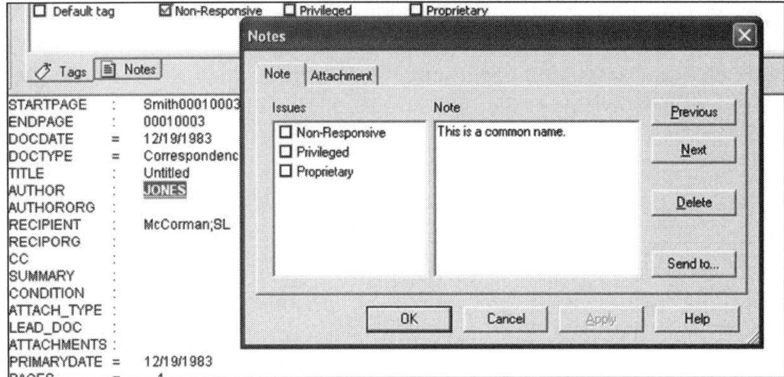

Figure 9-13. *The author JONES has been given the note "This is a common name."*

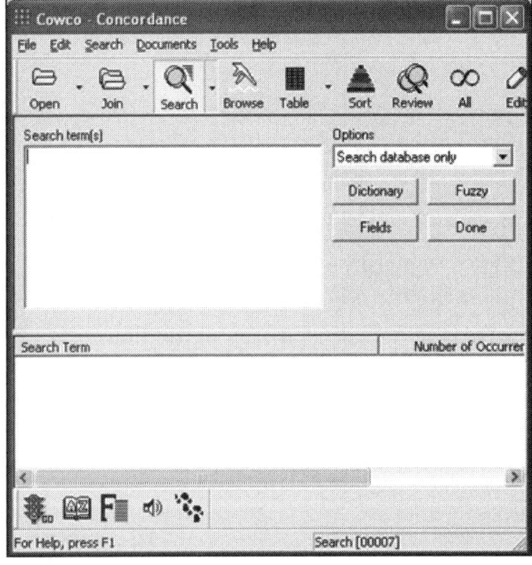

Figure 9-14. *You open the Search window by clicking the Search button. No search terms have been entered yet. Note the Options drop-down box. "Search database only" is selected.*

Using the Search Window

The Search window, opened by clicking the Search button, is another way to search database records (see Figure 9-15). It allows you to enter search terms; to view result statistics; and to gain quick access to field names, Concordance's dictionary file, and Concordance's Fuzzy feature (a way to locate similar words).

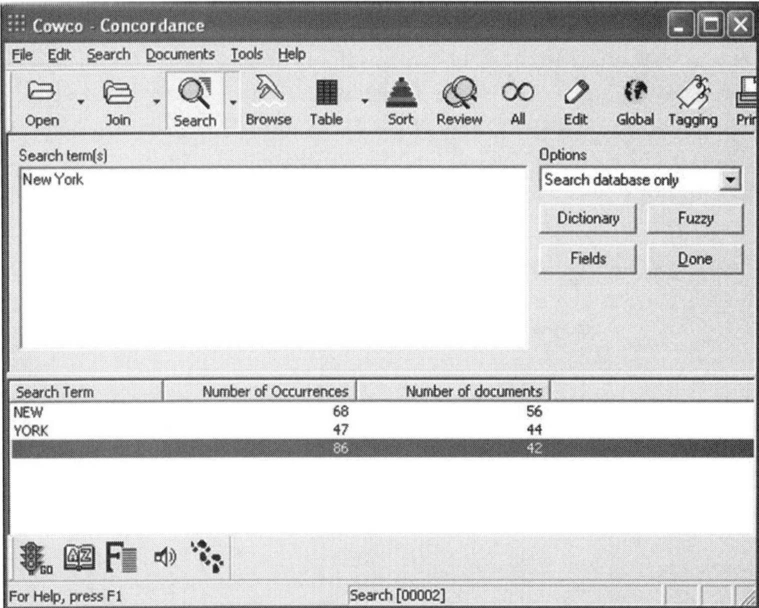

Figure 9-15. *The user has entered New York as a search phrase in the Search window. The number of hits (occurrences) and number of documents containing those hits for each word of the search phrase is displayed.*

Purpose of the Search Window

Although you can enter search queries into the <Quick Search> field displayed by default when a Concordance database is opened, Concordance provides a Search window that adds additional search features. You can open this window by clicking the Search button, by selecting the Search ➤ Search menu item, or by pressing the F2 function key.

The Search window allows you to specify if the entire database should be searched, if just notes should be searched, or both. Other features include displaying a field list, displaying the contents of the dictionary file, and defining fuzzy searches.

The Search window displays a history of searches, with search terms that have been used, the number of occurrences of the search terms, and the number of documents across which those search terms appear. You shouldn't confuse this summary with the query history that Concordance retains with each new search.

Scope of Searches

Recall that notes created by users and associated with sections of text in Browse view are stored in a separate Concordance database that shares the primary database's name, with a -notes.dcb suffix. You can search this data from the Search window by selecting "Search notes only" from the Options drop-down box. You may instead choose to search just the database itself by selecting the "Search database only" option, the default setting. You can search both the database and associated notes using the "Search database and notes" option.

Entering Searches

You enter search syntax in the "Search Term(s)" field. Note that, in contrast to the Query by Example dialog, the Search window doesn't guide you in constructing a valid search syntax.

As each search is executed, a search history is shown at the bottom of the screen. Search terms, number of hits (occurrences), and number of documents are displayed on separate lines, where each line corresponds to a separate search (see Figure 9-16).

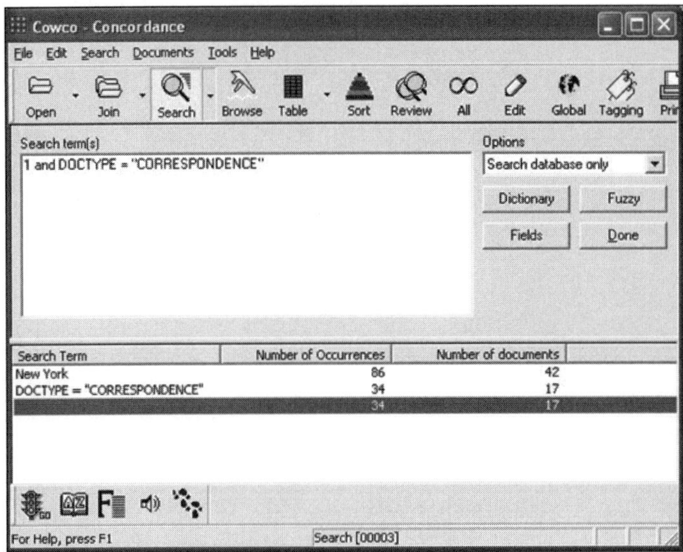

Figure 9-16. *In the Search window, the user has built on the previous query by referencing its query number, 1.*

Tracking Searches

For each search, results are tallied at the bottom of the screen, as in Figure 9-17. The hits for each search term are displayed on each line, and a combined total of all hits across all documents is displayed in the last line. The number of hits on the combined-total line depends on the search logic used. Say you enter the following:

```
NEW YORK
```

If NEW appears in 55 documents and YORK appears in 44 documents, the grand total on the last line will display the number of documents in which both NEW and YORK appear. This number may be less than the numbers corresponding to the individual search terms.

Say you enter the following:

```
NEW NOT YORK
```

The first two result lines for NEW and YORK will display the same number of hits (55 and 44 respectively, in this example). The grand total line will display the number of documents in which the word NEW appears, but in which the word YORK doesn't appear.

The combined-total line isn't a simple addition of all hits, but the true number of hits according to the logic of the search.

Search Term	Number of Occurrences	Number of documents
New York	86	42
DOCTYPE = "CORRESPONDENCE"	34	17
	34	17

Figure 9-17. *Viewing the search results history from the Search window*

Accessing the Dictionary File

The Dictionary button opens the Dictionary dialog (see Figure 9-18). This dialog gives you direct access to a database's dictionary file, and you can use it to minimize typing errors: you can add a term to the Search Term(s) field in the underlying Search window by highlighting it and clicking the Accept button. Double-clicking a term produces the same effect.

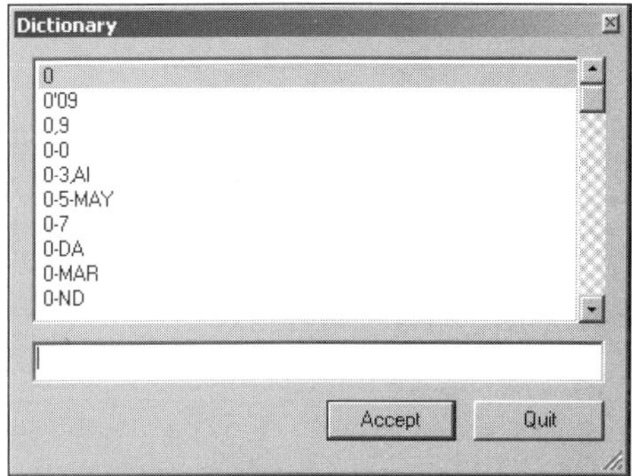

Figure 9-18. *The Dictionary dialog is a direct interface to a database's dictionary file. You can add, edit, or delete terms.*

Accessing Field Names

Clicking the Fields button opens a Fields dialog (see Figure 9-19). Every field in the database is displayed in a list box, with each field's data type. Highlighting a field name and clicking the OK button adds the field's name to the Search Term(s) field in the underlying Search window. Double-clicking a field name produces the same effect.

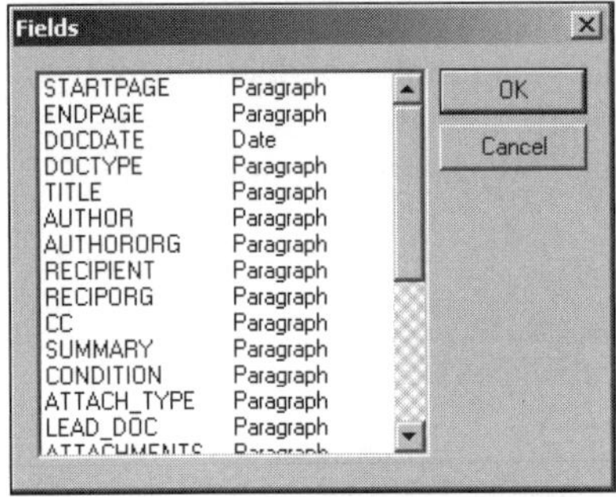

Figure 9-19. *The Fields dialog displays every field in a database. Double-clicking a field inserts the field name in the "Search term(s)" text area in the Search window.*

Fuzzy Searches

Concordance maintains a list of words that are similar to words contained in the dictionary file. This list is unique to each database, and is created each time a database is indexed or reindexed. It's accessible from the Search window by clicking the Fuzzy button (see Figure 9-20). You can highlight a specific search term—for example, the word york—and see Concordance's suggestions for similar words. In one instance of a database, the list might display fork, morkm, pork, and work. In another instance of a database, the list might be different.

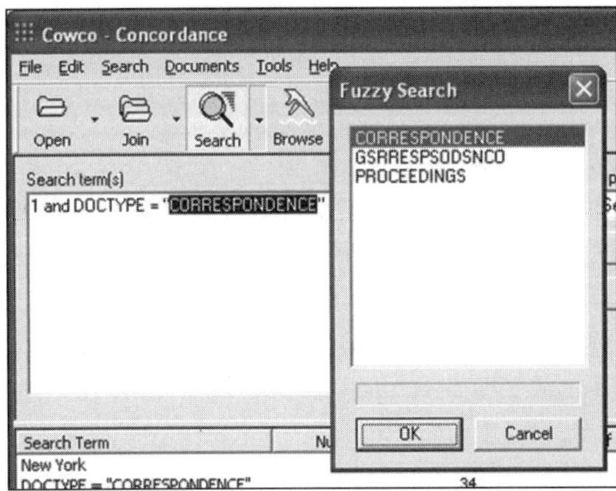

Figure 9-20. *Variations of the word CORRESPONDENCE identified by Concordance's Fuzzy Search feature*

Fuzzy searches are particularly useful given misspellings, typographical errors, and OCR scanning errors. Because of errors in data that are native to the data itself, it might be desirable to broaden searches to include these other words. For example, because the "U" key on most standard computer keyboards is directly adjacent to the "I" key, you might broaden searches for the word "big" to include the word "bug."

Using the <Quick Search> Field

Locating all documents is as easy in Concordance as typing a word or phrase in the <Quick Search> field and pressing the Enter key (see Figure 9-21). For many teams, research starts with retrieving documents that contain words or phrases. When you wish to locate documents that exclude words or phrases, or documents in which some words appear within a defined proximity of other words, searches can become quite sophisticated.

Note Keyword and comparison searches are not case sensitive.

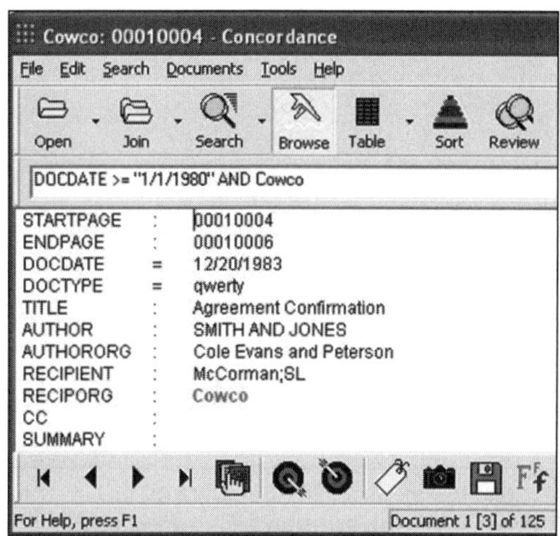

Figure 9-21. *An example of search logic entered directly into the <Quick Search> text field. Note the highlighted hit in the document itself.*

Overview of the <Quick Search> Field

During indexing, Concordance identifies individual words by means of leading and trailing white space: if a string of characters is preceded by a space and is followed by a space, Concordance recognizes the characters between the spaces as a complete word. When words are separated by punctuation, Concordance follows the same logic. For example, a string of characters preceded and followed by a comma becomes a word. When a string of characters is preceded by a space and is followed by punctuation, the characters are treated as a word.

Note that Concordance treats the hyphen (-) as punctuation by default. This can cause problems with hyphenated names. If a hyphen is to be treated as punctuation, Concordance will identify "Mary Todd-Lincoln" as three words: "Mary," "Todd," and "Lincoln." What if a discovery team must locate documents that contain the continuous string of characters "Todd-Lincoln"? You can construct searches to do just that, if it's assumed that "Todd" and "Lincoln" are two words. Further, you can set up a Synonym list to address this. However, it might be easier for you—the database administrator—to tell Concordance explicitly not to use a hyphen as common punctuation. You can accomplish this from the File ➤ Modify menu.

Full text searches use a database's dictionary file. To search for terms that appear in the dictionary file, you simply enter the word or phrase in the <Quick Search> field and press the Enter key. You must search fields that haven't been indexed using a specific syntax described in the following section. Concordance provides visual cues of the data type of a field. In Browse view, field names that are followed by a colon (:) are paragraph fields. Field names that are followed by an equals sign (=) aren't paragraph fields; they might or might not be searched by entering a word or phrase in the <Quick Search> field with no qualifier. There's no visual cue to indicate that a field has a NUMERIC, DATE, or TEXT data type and that it has been indexed. As the Concordance administrator, you must coordinate with a research team so that the team understands the basic structure of the database it's using.

Basic Syntax

To locate all documents in which the word NEW occurs, use the following syntax:

NEW

Without specifying a field name, Concordance assumes the desired search is of PARAGRAPH fields and other fields that have been indexed. To locate all documents in which the phrase NEW YORK appears, use the following syntax:

NEW YORK

This example is a simplification of the following more formal search statement:

NEW ADJO YORK

ADJO is an example of the *proximity operator, adjacent.* (ADJO is the default operator assumed when no explicit operator is given. You can change it to another operator via the Tools ➤ Preferences menu, or from the Searching tab.) Operators serve to apply logic between individual search words or phrases. In general, the proper syntax of a search query of indexed fields is as follows:

WORD OPERATOR WORD OPERATOR WORD ...

For example, to locate all documents in which the word NEW appears but the word YORK doesn't appear, the syntax is as follows:

NEW NOT YORK

Concordance recognizes the operator NOT as a reserved word, and uses its meaning to exclude search words, instead of interpreting it as another search term. To search for a word that's reserved by Concordance for other uses, you should enclose the word(s) in double quotes. Hence, the following search phrase locates all documents that actually contain the word NOT:

"NOT"

You can nest words, phrases, and operators to facilitate more powerful searches. You separate groups of words and phrases by means of parentheses. Hence, the following search locates documents that contain either the word OLD or the word NEW directly adjacent to the word YORK; that is, documents that contain either OLD YORK or NEW YORK:

```
(OLD OR NEW) YORK
```


Formally, you could write the preceding search as follows:

```
(OLD OR NEW) ADJO YORK
```

You could also write it as follows:

```
(OLD YORK) OR (NEW YORK)
```

Or you could write it as follows:

```
(OLD ADJO YORK) OR (NEW ADJO YORK)
```

This last example—(OLD ADJO YORK) OR (NEW ADJO YORK) —is the most explicit form of this search, and is the easiest for you to interpret.

Subnesting search words and phrases and operators is allowed. Hence, the following search locates documents that contain either OLD YORK, NEW YORK, OLD MEXICO, or NEW MEXICO:

```
((OLD ADJO YORK) OR (NEW ADJO YORK)) OR ((OLD ADJO MEXICO) OR (NEW ADJO MEXICO))
```

Relational Searches

Concordance's ability to assign data types to fields in a database allows you to retrieve records by comparing data in fields with fixed values. You can combine relational searches with other searches to locate documents that contain keywords and that have data that fits user-defined criteria.

Overview of Relational Searches

Data in Concordance databases is divided into separate fields. These fields are given specific data types that describe the data in those fields. A CDATE field might describe the creation date of a document, and be given a DATE data type. Describing the type of data that's contained in a field enables Concordance to perform comparisons more easily. You might want to locate records where CDATE contains date values that are at least 1/1/2003 but no later than 1/15/2003, and every record that contains CDATE values between those boundaries.

These types of searches are fundamentally different from searches that locate documents on the existence of keywords. Keyword searches rely on Concordance's dictionary file to locate hits. No sort of comparison is required. Whereas keyword searches require a full index to be completed on the database being searched, relational searches of fields that have data types DATE, NUMBER, or TEXT (up to 60 characters, nonparagraph) don't require a full index.

Scanning documents and converting the contents of those documents into digital characters is an automatic process. Scanning equipment is unable to make any sort of intelligent decision about what kind of document is being scanned, when the document was created, or who the author of the document might have been. These data elements require the evaluation of each document, and the direct intervention of a human who creates values or codes to represent properties of the documents. For this reason, fielded data in Concordance is often referred to as *coded data*. Searching coded data involves the use of comparison operators such as less than, greater than, contains, and outside limits. The section "Relational Operators" describes all the applicable operators.

Basic Syntax

Relational searches target specific fields in Concordance for evaluation (comparison) to specific values or ranges. The structure of a relational search can be summarized as follows:

```
FIELDNAME OPERATOR value
```

For example, to locate all documents with a CDATE (created date) of 1/1/2003, use the following syntax:

```
CDATE = "1/1/2003"
```

CDATE is the field name, = is the operator, and 1/1/2003 is the value.

When searching for key phrases in fields that have a TEXT data type, you must take some care with search phrases that contain white space, such as NEW YORK. You should enclose search phrases in double quotes. Write the search for documents that contain NEW YORK in a CITY field as follows:

```
CITY = "NEW YORK"
```

Without the opening and closing double quotes, Concordance interprets white space as the default operator—ADJO in most Concordance installations. Take the following search:

```
CITY = NEW YORK
```

Concordance would interpret it as follows:

```
CITY = NEW ADJO YORK
```

You can use double quotes when comparing DATE fields and NUMERIC fields, so that the following is a valid syntax:

```
CDATE = "1/1/2003"
```

The following is also a valid syntax:

```
TOTALPAGES = "32"
```

Searches can combine fields, so that groups of records where different fields adhere to various criteria are returned. For example, in a database that contains a CDATE field and an AUTHOR field, you could use the following search syntax to locate all documents created on 1/1/2003 that have the name JOHN Q. PUBLIC as an author:

```
CDATE = "1/1/2003" AND AUTHOR = "JOHN Q. PUBLIC"
```

To locate any document created on 1/1/2003 or that has been authored by JOHN Q. PUBLIC regardless of the creation date, the following search is valid:

```
CDATE = "1/1/2003" OR AUTHOR = "JOHN Q. PUBLIC"
```

You can reference the same field name more than once in a search. For example, to locate documents that have been created on 1/1/2003 and on any successive date that's no later than 1/1/2004, the syntax is as follows:

```
CDATE >= "1/1/2003" AND CDATE <="1/1/2004"
```

To search for multiple values in a single field, you can separate values by use of a comma. The following search locates records where the TOTALPAGES field contains the values 1, 10, or 100:

```
TOTALPAGES = 1, 10, 100
```

Notice that the OR operator is equivalent, so that the preceding search could be written like this:

```
TOTALPAGES = 1 OR TOTALPAGES = 10 OR TOTALPAGES = 100
```

The ability to retrieve multiple values, where each value is separated by a comma, allows for the construction of searches that are more concise, easier to read, and less prone to typographical errors.

The use of parentheses aids creation of complex statements involving different fields and ranges within those fields. Use the following syntax to locate records that have been created on 1/1/2003 and on any successive date that's no later than 1/1/2004, and that have been authored by JOHN Q. PUBLIC:

```
(CDATE >= "1/1/2003" AND CDATE <="1/1/2004") AND AUTHOR = "JOHN Q. PUBLIC"
```

Wildcards

Sometimes the exact contents of a field might not be known. For example, in a database that contains an AUTHOR field, and in which it's known that there are variations of the name JOHN Q. PUBLIC contained in this field, it's possible to use *wildcards* to look for patterns. This is sometimes known as *masking*. Two wildcard characters are installed by default in a new installation of Concordance: the question mark (?), which stands for a single character, and the asterisk (*), which stands for a series of characters.

> **Note** You can change the wildcard character (*) from the Searching tab of the Preferences dialog, opened from the Tools ➤ Preferences menu.

To locate documents in a database that contains the field CITY and in which the values STAMFORD and STANFORD are desired, the syntax is as follows:

```
CITY = STA?FORD
```

The use of the ? wildcard is most useful when searching for dates. For example, the following search locates any document with a CDATE in the year 2004:

```
CDATE = ??/??/2004
```

To locate records in which the CITY field contains the stem STA with any permutation of characters following (Stamford, Stanford, Standard, Station, and so on), the following syntax is correct:

```
CITY = STA*
```

You can combine wildcards, so that the following search locates values including JEFF, JAFF, JEFFREY, and JAFFREY:

```
AUTHOR = J?FF*
```

You must treat double quotes, used to group search phrases, with care when using wildcards. Consider a field CITY with the literal value NEW YORK*. Here, there's an asterisk in the field itself. The following search won't return this record:

```
CITY = "NEW YORK"
```

The following search locates the record on the basis of the exact match NEW YORK*:

```
CITY = "NEW YORK*"
```

> **Note** The * is an actual character in the field.

The following search locates the record, because the search phrase NEW YORK is masked with the *:

```
CITY = "NEW YORK"*
```

You can use wildcards with keyword searches as well.

Operators

Operators are reserved words and symbols that Concordance uses to expand the facility of searches. With operators, you can apply basic AND/OR/NOT logic, specify ranges, or search for words within a proximity of other words. Operators fall into four basic classes: Boolean, context, proximity, and relational.

An operator requires both a scope (that is, a field name) and a range (that is, a value). An operator without a scope or a range is meaningless. Hence, the following search causes Concordance to display an error message:

```
AND 22
```

The following search doesn't generate an error message, but it isn't a useful search:

```
>= 22
```

Concordance interprets this as *any indexed field greater than or equal to the number 22.*

Boolean Operators

The term *Boolean* honors the contributions of George Boole, a mathematician who lived in the 19th century. Concordance recognizes the Boolean operators AND, OR, NOT, and XOR, described in the following sections.

The AND Operator

The AND operator combines the statement on the left of the operator with the statement on the right of the operator, resulting in only those records in which both statements are true. The following syntax locates only those records in which the CDATE field contains the value 1/1/2003, and in which the AUTHOR field contains the phrase JOHN Q. PUBLIC:

```
CDATE = "1/1/2003" AND AUTHOR = "JOHN Q. PUBLIC"
```

Documents in which either side of the operator fails—that is, CDATE isn't equal to 1/1/2003 or AUTHOR contains something other than JOHN Q. PUBLIC—aren't returned.

The OR Operator

The OR operator considers the statement on the left of the operator and the statement on the right of the operator, resulting in those records in which either statement is true:

```
CDATE = "1/1/2003" OR AUTHOR = "JOHN Q. PUBLIC"
```

This locates those records in which the CDATE field contains the value 1/1/2003, or in which the AUTHOR field contains the phrase JOHN Q. PUBLIC. Documents in which either side of the operator succeeds—that is, CDATE is equal to 1/1/2003, or AUTHOR contains JOHN Q. PUBLIC—are returned.

The NOT Operator

The NOT operator considers the statement on the left of the operator and excludes the statement on the right of the operator, resulting in those records in which the left-hand statement is true and the right-hand statement is false:

```
CDATE = "1/1/2003" NOT AUTHOR = "JOHN Q. PUBLIC"
```

This locates those records in which the CDATE field contains the value 1/1/2003 and in which the AUTHOR field doesn't contain the phrase JOHN Q. PUBLIC. Documents with a CDATE equal to 1/1/2003, and for which the AUTHOR field doesn't contain JOHN Q. PUBLIC, are returned.

The XOR Operator

XOR is shorthand for the phrase "exclusive or," and can be thought of as an extension of the OR operator. You use it to locate records that contain either the left-hand or the right-hand statement, but that don't contain both the left-hand and right-hand statements. In short, *either A or B but not both A and B*:

```
CDATE = "1/1/2003" XOR AUTHOR = "JOHN Q. PUBLIC"
```

This locates all records in which the CDATE field contains 1/12003, or where the AUTHOR field contains JOHN Q. PUBLIC, but it won't return those records in which both CDATE = "1/1/2003" and AUTHOR = "JOHN Q. PUBLIC" appear in the same record.

For an example that uses indexed paragraph and text fields, take the following search:

```
APPLES XOR ORANGES
```

It locates records that contain APPLES or ORANGES in the dictionary file, but not those records that contain both APPLES and ORANGES.

Context Operators

You use context operators to locate documents that contain some combination or exclusion of keywords. There are four context operators: SAME, NOTSAME, the single period (.), and the double period (..).

Limiters

The term *limiter* is used when discussing context operators, and refers to a method to specify a specific field. The symbol for a limiter is a period (.). You can use the limiter to tell the database to include a field, or to exclude a field. When specifying that a field should be included in a search, the field name must begin with and end with a period.

.AUTHOR. indicates to Concordance that the AUTHOR field should be searched. Conversely, there might be times when you want to search all fields except for a specific field. To accomplish this exclusion, you should precede the field with two periods, and follow it with one period.

..AUTHOR. means to search every indexed field, but don't include the AUTHOR field as part of the search. The double period used in this way is referred to as a *not limit* operator. This means that searches that can be written as FIELDNAME = VALUE can also be written as follows:

```
VALUE.FIELDNAME.
```

For example, take the following search:

```
CDATE = 1/1/2003
```

It's equivalent to this search:

```
1/1/2003.CDATE.
```

Or this one:

```
("1/1/2003").CDATE.
```

The following search locates instances of the word SMITH in all indexed fields, but ignores any record with the exact value SMITH in the AUTHOR field:

```
SMITH..AUTHOR.
```

This type of search is useful when, for example, a researcher wishes to find any document that refers to SMITH, but that isn't authored by the individual SMITH.

The SAME Operator

Syntactically, the SAME operator supports the use of search limiters. The proper usage of the SAME operator takes the following form:

```
(Term1 SAME Term2).FIELDNAME
```

Used in this way, the SAME operator locates records where both search terms appear in the same field as specified by FIELDNAME.

If no search limiter is used, and a fieldname isn't referenced, you can use the SAME operator in the following way:

```
Term1 SAME Term2
```

Used in this way, the SAME operator locates all documents in which both Term1 and Term2 appear in any field, as long as that field is indexed.

The NOTSAME Operator

Syntactically, the NOTSAME operator supports the use of search limiters. The proper usage of the NOTSAME operator takes the following form:

```
(Term1 NOTSAME Term2).FIELDNAME
```

Used in this way, the NOTSAME operator locates those records in which either Term1 or Term2 appear in FIELDNAME, but not both, and where the search term that doesn't appear in FIELDNAME also appears in another field. For example, if a database has fields AUTHOR and FULLTEXT where both fields are indexed, the following search won't match records that contain both SMITH and JONES in the field name AUTHOR:

```
(SMITH NOTSAME JONES).AUTHOR.
```

Hence, a document with the value THIS IS AUTHORED BY BOTH SMITH AND JONES in the AUTHOR field is ignored. Documents with either SMITH or JONES in the AUTHOR field are candidates for the result set, but they're only matched depending on which of the two terms are contained in the AUTHOR field. A document in which the name SMITH appears in the AUTHOR field and the name JONES appears in the FULLTEXT field will be matched. A document in which the name JONES appears in the AUTHOR field and the name SMITH appears in the FULLTEXT field will also be matched.

It's possible to create this same behavior but with more explicit (to the user) operators. Take the following logic:

```
((AUTHOR CO SMITH AND AUTHOR NC JONES) AND JONES) OR
((AUTHOR CO JONES AND AUTHOR NC SMITH) AND SMITH)
```

It's equivalent to the following, which is more compact:

```
(SMITH NOTSAME JONES).AUTHOR.
```

Furthermore, because the latter notation references the operator NOTSAME only once, Concordance is spared the work of translating each AND, OR, CO, and NC operator in the former expression. The more compact notation returns results more quickly.

Used without search limiters, the NOTSAME operator locates records where one term appears in any indexed field and the other term appears in any other indexed field. The following search ignores records in which both words, SMITH and JONES, appear in the same field. It includes records in which SMITH appears in a field, and JONES appears in another field:

```
SMITH NOTSAME JONES
```

Proximity Operators

Proximity operators allow a researcher to locate documents where words appear within ranges of each other, where *range* refers to the number of terms between the search words. There are two proximity operators—ADJ*n* and NEAR*n*—and although their use is similar, the results of searches that use them can be quite different. The similarity between the two operators is that both search for the proximity of words; the difference between the two operators is that NEAR matches any order of words—*A to B* or *B to A*—while ADJ matches a specific order of words— only *A to B.*

ADJ and NEAR take a number between 0 and 99 to define how many words are allowed between the search terms. When 0 is used, this indicates that the words should be directly next to each other. If no number is used with a proximity operator, or if a number is used that is greater than 99—for example NEW ADJ YORK or NEW ADJ150 YORK—Concordance uses 0 as the range argument.

You use proximity operators to locate search term proximity where the search terms appear in the same field. ADJ and NEAR have no meaning across separate fields.

The ADJn Operator

ADJ*n* only matches documents in which the second search term appears within the range specified by *n* of the first search term, and in that order. This means that for documents that contain the phrase I live in New York City. in a LOCATION field, the following search logic locates those documents:

```
NEW ADJ1 CITY
```

However, the following search logic won't locate the documents:

```
CITY ADJ1 NEW
```

The NEARn Operator

NEAR*n* locates search terms within the specified range, regardless of the order of the search terms. The following search logic locates documents where NEW YORK and YORK NEW are matched:

```
NEW NEAR YORK
```

Recall that when no range is specified, the NEAR operator assumes a range of 0—no intervening words. You can write NEW NEAR YORK as NEW NEAR0 YORK.

Relational Operators

Ten relational operators in Concordance allow for evaluating and comparing fielded data. Most of these relational operators have both a symbolic representation (for example, < for "less than") and a two-letter abbreviation that's exactly equivalent to the symbolic representation (for example, LT for "less than). Take the following search:

```
CDATE < "1/1/2003"
```

It's the same as this one:

```
CDATE LT "1/1/2003"
```

To search for the two-character abbreviation as a search term; for example, documents that contain the actual characters LT, use double quotes to enclose the search term. For example, the following syntax forces Concordance to use LT as a search term, not as the operator "less than":

```
TITLE CO "LT"
```

Table 9-2 lists the relational operators and their abbreviations.

Table 9-2. *Relational Search Operators, Symbols, and Abbreviations*

Symbol	Abbreviation	Description	Applicable Data Type
<	LT	Less than	Date, numeric
<=	LE	Less than or equal	Date, numeric
=	EQ	Equal	Date, numeric, text
>	GT	Greater than	Date, numeric
>=	GE	Greater than or equal	Date, numeric
<>	NE	Not equal	Date, numeric, text
&	CO	Contains	Text
!	NC	Doesn't contain	Text
(no symbol)	WL	Within limits	Date, numeric
(no symbol)	OL	Outside limits	Date, numeric

Although many of these operators are self explanatory, some require clarification.

- CO: The "contains" operator locates records that contain a search term. The following search locates documents in which the word SMITH appears anywhere in the DOCTEXT1 field:

```
DOCTEXT1 CO SMITH
```

- NC: The "not contains" operator locates records that don't contain a search term. The following search locates documents in which the word SMITH doesn't appear anywhere in the DOCTEXT1 field:

```
DOCTEXT1 NC SMITH
```

- WL: The "within limits" operator examines values in a field that appear within a specified range. It's particularly useful when locating documents that originated within a date range. The following search locates documents in which the MDATE field has a date that's between 1/1/1980 and 1/1/2004:

```
MDATE WL 1/1/1980, 1/1/2004
```

- OL: The "outside limits" operator examines values in a field that appear outside a specified range. The following search locates documents in which the MDATE field has a date that's earlier than 1/1/1980 and later than 1/1/2004:

```
MDATE OL 1/1/1980, 1/1/2004
```

Combining Keyword Searches with Relational Operators

A complete Concordance database contains fields that have been indexed, and fields with DATE, NUMERIC, or TEXT data types. Thus far, the discussion has treated the methods to search indexed fields separately from the methods used to search nonindexed fields. Documents can be searched effectively through a combination of these search techniques. Consider the example in which a researcher wishes to find any e-mail in which the company name ACME is referenced in the body of an e-mail, where the recipient is JOHN Q. PUBLIC, and the date the e-mail was sent was between 1/1/2003 and 1/1/2004. The first part of this search—to locate documents in which the name ACME appears—involves a keyword search of indexed fields. The second and third parts of this search—where the recipient is JOHN Q. PUBLIC and the date the e-mail was sent was between 1/1/2003 and 1/1/2004—are fixed field or relational queries. Although it's possible to build each search separately and refer to them by their query number, it's also possible to combine the entire search into a single search phrase:

```
ACME AND ("JOHN Q. PUBLIC").RECIPIENT. AND
(SENTDATE >=1/1/2003 AND SENTDATE <=1/1/2004)
```

Note You use search limiters to specify the field RECIPIENT, and you use parentheses to group the SENTDATE comparisons.

Concordance doesn't recognize the word ACME as a reserved word, and it isn't attached to a specific search field. Because of this, Concordance interprets the word as a search term, and assumes you want to search all indexed fields for that term. In this way, by combining search terms and phrases with additional search logic that does specify fields and comparison values, you can combine indexed searches with fixed field searches.

Combining Keyword and Relational Searches with Subjective Data

You can tag records at a document level (tags) or a phrase level (issues). Additionally, you can highlight and annotate sections of text (notes). You can search both subjective and objective data separately, and you can combine those searches using Concordance's numbered query history. In this way, you can locate records that have been tagged "For review," and within that specific set of documents, search for records that contain desired words or phrases.

Although you can combine searches of subjective and objective data, the mechanisms to complete the searches are different. There's no search syntax to search tags and issues directly from the <Quick Search> text field. Grouping records with tags requires you to click the Tagging button, select the desired tags, and then click the "Create query from" Selected Tags button. Records with the desired tags are given a query number, and this set of records is displayed in Table or Browse view. Indexed or relational searches performed from that point on are of the entire database (query 00000), unless you specify the named query that has resulted from the tagged search.

For example, say you open a database so that query 00000, all records, is the only query in the query history displayed by clicking the Review button. You first want to locate all documents that have been tagged "For review." To narrow down to these records, you click the Tagging button, select the "For review" tag, and then click the "Create query from" Selected Tags button. In this hypothetical example, ten records result, and this result set is given the alias query 00001.

You review the output in Concordance's Table view. Then you might decide that of the ten records that are tagged "For review," only those records with a DOCTYPE = MEMO are of interest. If you enter the following search, the entire database will be searched, not the ten records in query 00001:

```
("MEMO").DOCTYPE.
```

This isn't what you wanted. To locate the intersection of the ten records tagged "For review" and records with a DOCTYPE = "MEMO", you must combine query 00001 with the following relational search logic:

```
1 AND ("MEMO").DOCTYPE.
```

Combining search results from annotations with tagged searches involves a similar process. Here, you want to search annotations first. To accomplish this, you must click the Search button to open a more advanced Search window. You can select an option to "Search notes only." The set of records that results from a search of annotations is given a query number. To search tags, you must click the Tagging button. Any search using the Tag/Issue Management dialog is also given a query number. Finally, to locate the intersection of these two searches—one of annotations and one of tags—you must enter the query numbers in the <Quick Search> text field. If the annotations search was given a query number 1 and the tag search was given a query number 2, the following search is the intersection of the two queries:

```
1 AND 2
```

The challenge for a novice user is to know which search mechanism applies to which set of data. Table 9-3 summarizes the various methods.

Table 9-3. *Summary of Search Methods: Objective vs. Subjective Data*

Type of Search	Options
Searching subjective data	For tags and issues, click the Tagging button to open the Tag/Issue Management dialog. For annotations, click the Search button and select "Search notes only."
Searching objective data	Enter search logic directly into the <Quick Search> text field. Click the Search button, select "Search database only." Select the Search menu item, then the Form search submenu item (or click F4).

Viewing Search Results

There are two methods in Concordance to view document records: Table view and Browse view. Table view, activated by clicking the Table button, displays each document in a single row and in a tabular format. Browse view, activated by clicking the Browse button, displays a single document. You can view the two modes singly or in a split screen format. (see Figure 9-22). To view these two modes side by side or one on top of the other, you must specify to Concordance that you desire a split screen, by selecting the Tools ➤ Split screen menu. When the split screen option is activated, you may click the Browse and Table buttons to lay the two views side by side. When split screen isn't activated, clicking either button fills the screen with the particular view corresponding to the button that was clicked.

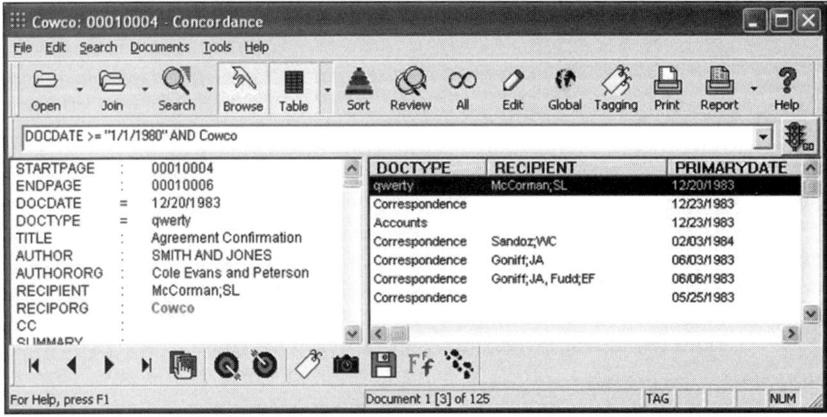

Figure 9-22. *Browse view (left) and Table view (right) in split screen mode*

Saving Searches As Snapshots and Queries

There are two methods in Concordance to save the results of searches between sessions: queries and snapshots. Both a query and a snapshot save data about a search in a separate file so that you can retrieve them for later use. Queries save search logic, while snapshots save information about your search session at the time the snapshot was saved.

Snapshots

A snapshot stores information about how you've elected to search, sort, and view records at a given instant in time. If there's any search history in effect prior to the restoration of a snapshot, it's destroyed and replaced with the search history stored in the snapshot itself. Any sort order applied to records when the snapshot was saved is also restored.

Snapshots are useful when you want to save a search history and settings between Concordance sessions. Because the snapshot saves information *about* a Concordance session, you can know that, when a snapshot is restored, you're viewing the same search history, with the same sort order as when you left off from a previous session. The snapshot even saves information about which record was active when the snapshot was saved. In this way, you can create a search profile, and return to that profile each time you use a particular Concordance database. This saves you from having to reconstruct the parameters about a previous search session, even if a significant amount of time has elapsed since your last use of a specific Concordance database.

You can make this effect transparent by means of the Auto restore feature, activated by means of the Search ➤ Snapshot ➤ Auto restore menu. Auto restore automatically saves a snapshot of your Concordance session when the program is closed, and automatically applies the snapshot each time the Concordance database is opened. Any snapshot file is available for use with the Auto restore feature—when the Auto restore is first activated, you'll be prompted to select a snapshot file for use with Auto restore. You can later change this snapshot file by deactivating, then reactivating the Auto restore feature.

Information about Auto restore is saved for each computer user. This means that multiple users of the same workstation can designate their own Auto restore snapshot file, provided that the workstation has been set up with multiple user login accounts.

Given that users can update and delete records, and given that a Concordance administrator may modify Concordance data, end users should be aware that when a snapshot is restored, the number of records that qualify in each entry in the search history at the time the snapshot was last saved might *not* still be accurate. This behavior applies to every query in the snapshot except for query 00000—all records. For every other query in the search history, rows that have been deleted between the time that a snapshot was last saved and when it has been reinvoked appear as blank lines in Concordance's table view. Furthermore, when data has been edited between a user's Concordance sessions, words that had previously been highlighted as hits might no longer exist.

This might or might not be a useful tool: although it does allow you to track which records have been deleted or edited since your last session, it's also impossible to refresh the queries in the search history to exclude mismatches. For that reason, you might find that the most useful application of a snapshot is either to save an exact image of your search session if your work is interrupted, or to use the snapshot to preserve sort order alone in conjunction with the Auto restore feature.

Saving a Snapshot

You can save a snapshot file by means of the Search ➤ Snapshot ➤ Save snapshot menu. You're prompted to save the snapshot in a specific location from a Windows "Save snapshot" dialog box. The default location for saving a snapshot is in the same directory as the database itself.

Depending on the number of snapshot files created by the administrator and the database users, as the Concordance administrator, you might find it useful to create a separate subfolder specifically to store snapshot files. Snapshot files are saved with an .SNP extension. Unlike an external query file (described below), you can't open the snapshot file in a text editor.

Restoring a Snapshot

One way to restore a snapshot is by means of the Auto restore feature. This forces a specific snapshot to restore when you open a Concordance database, and forces the snapshot to save when you close the database.

You can restore snapshots during a Concordance session by means of the Search ➤ Snapshot ➤ Restore snapshot menu. You're presented with an Open dialog box.

Because snapshots are specific to a Concordance database, the first action that takes place when a snapshot is restored is that the currently open database is closed. Next, all queries and sort orders in the snapshot are applied to the database or databases (if databases are concatenated) referenced in the snapshot. Finally, the focus shifts to the set of hits (highlighted text) that were active when the snapshot itself was last saved. Given that underlying data in the database might have been modified or deleted, the hit list and the search results summarized in the Review screen might no longer be accurate.

Queries

The term *query* is often used to refer to a specific instance of a search. In a broader sense, a *query* can also refer to an external file that saves the search logic of an entire search history. These files are given a .QRY extension, and are saved and executed from within Concordance by means of the Search ➤ Execute submenu items.

Unlike a snapshot, a query references the data that's in a database at the time that the query is executed, not when the query is saved. If a query had resulted in no records when it was saved, and then that query is executed a week later—after data has been modified or added to the Concordance database—the number of matches might be different. In this way, you can use a query to determine how data in a database has changed.

As described in the earlier section, "Snapshots," when a snapshot is opened, any current search history is destroyed and replaced by the search history saved in the snapshot. However, when a query is opened, the behavior is different: any current search history isn't destroyed, and the search logic contained in the external query file is appended to the current search history and numbered accordingly. Thus, if the current search history displays queries 00000, 00001, and 00002, and a query with two entries is opened, those entries are assigned numbers 00003 and 00004.

The format of an external query file is highly structured, and may be modified in a text editor. The format is as follows, where search logic refers to an actual search phrase that must be syntactically correct:

```
SEARCH: search logic
SEARCH: search logic
SEARCH: search logic
...
SEARCH: search logic
```

Each `search logic` entry can be no longer than 200 characters in length. Concordance ignores any line in the external query file that doesn't begin with exactly the characters `SEARCH:`, and may use them as comment lines.

From the user's perspective, external queries can reference complex chains of previous search logic. Because the search phrases are saved in the file, you're not required to retype long or tedious strings of search logic. If certain aspects of research are similar across databases, and those databases are structured appropriately, external queries can provide a starting point in a trail of discovery. You can also use queries to check for "hot documents" that match a string of search logic as data in Concordance is modified or added. There's no way to cause a query to auto-load in the same way that snapshots can be automatically loaded by means of the Auto restore feature.

Saving Queries

You can save queries to an external file by means of the Search ➤ Keep menu. This opens a Keep Queries dialog box, where you can name and save the query accordingly. Queries are stored by default in the same folder in which the primary database files are stored.

Executing Queries

You open (execute) queries from the Search ➤ Execute menu. Concordance responds with a Keep Queries dialog box that allows you to navigate to the appropriate folder that contains the desired query.

Summary

Concordance offers several methods to search both objective and subjective data. Each search is saved in a history and is given a numerical alias, starting with query 00000 (all records). Using query aliases to refer to previous searches means that separate queries can be combined. Reviewers can select records based on keywords and comparisons, and then join those results against records that have subjective annotations.

Using the Query by Example dialog, you can select field names from a list, specify comparison criteria, and enter search terms or values. This is an excellent tool for new users. The Search window allows you to select the scope of a search (database, notes, or both) and enter search syntax directly. The <Quick Search> search field also allows you to enter search syntax directly. Unlike the previous two methods, the <Quick Search> field is embedded in the main Concordance screen itself when Browse view or Table view are active, and you can view retrieved records immediately.

Concordance searches use a specific syntax and make use of a range of operators. You can use relational operators such as less than (`LT`) and greater than (`GT`) to test data against specific values. You can use Boolean operators such as `AND`, `NOT`, and `OR` to include or exclude documents by comparing them against conditions. You use the proximity operators `ADJ` and `NEAR` to locate words within a specified distance from each other. The context operators `SAME` and `NOTSAME` and search limiters locate documents that include or exclude combinations of keywords.

To search document-level tags, you can either use the Tag/Issue Management dialog, or use the "Create Query from tags(s)" right-click option from the tagging screen.

You can save one or more searches and run them against a database in later sessions. You use a *query file* to retain the logic of one or more searches. The query file can produce varying results if underlying data evolves. You use a *snapshot* to retain the results of one or more searches; it's a static picture of a database.

Although users might be content to review records onscreen, Concordance provides several methods to create printed output. The next chapter explores these facilities.

CHAPTER 10

Printing

This chapter shows you how to print document records from the Concordance interface, not through Opticon. Opticon allows administrators and report designers to print a digital image of a document; the Concordance interface prints document records more or less as they appear in Concordance's Browse view. Concordance can print reports of document records and of associated annotations, or it can print a special kind of report that groups like values from multivalued fields together ("exploded sort" reports).

Depending on the software that's installed on a user's computer, the report can either be directed to a standard printer, or be output as an electronic file. Some manufacturers, such as Adobe, offer additional support that creates a printer driver that, although selectable as a printer, redirects output to a digital file.

There are three ways to print reports from Concordance:

- You can print the current document from Concordance. You can use the File ➤ Print menu, press the Ctrl+P key combination, or right-click in Browse view and select the Print Record option from the shortcut menu. This is a quick way to print just the current record displayed in Concordance's Browse view.

- You can print sets of records by clicking the Print button located on the button bar at the top of the Concordance screen. This allows more flexibility than the preceding method, as you can select specific fields (or sections of fields) for the report.

- You can create formal reports by clicking the Report button located on the button bar at the top of the Concordance screen, or by selecting the Documents ➤ Report menu. This requires some design time to select and place fields, and to structure the overall appearance of reports. However, this is the most precise and powerful way to create a formally structured report. To aid you in designing reports, Concordance features helpful *wizards*, a series of interactive dialogs, which guide you through the process of building a report.

Printing the Current Document

Printing the current document is the easiest and quickest way to print a document record. Printing in this way affects only the currently displayed document record. Printing the current document from Concordance by using the File ➤ Print menu, by pressing the Ctrl+P key combination, or by right-clicking in Browse view and selecting Print Record opens the printer dialog associated with your default printer (see Figure 10-1). Note that the precise type of dialog might vary according to the printer selected. Options available usually refer to the number of copies to print and the number of pages within the current document to print (range). Additional options are usually accessible from the Properties button located next to the selected printer combo box.

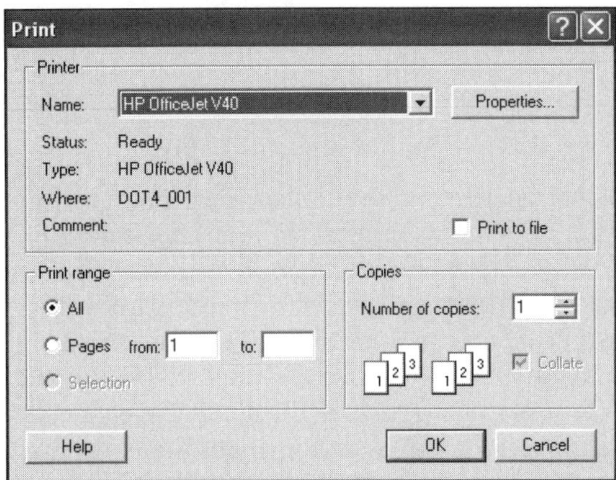

Figure 10-1. *An example of a printer dialog. This particular dialog is specific to the printer attached to a user's computer. In this example, the dialog pertains to an HP OfficeJet V40 printer.*

You can use the File ➤ Print Preview menu item to open a new window that displays a representation of what the printed document will look like (Figure 10-2). It's usually a good idea to open the Print Preview screen first, to get a feel for how the document record will appear. Buttons on this screen allow you to send the result to a printer (Print), advance or retreat among pages (Next Page, Prev Page), split the view so that two pages are displayed for each preview screen (Two Page), zoom in or zoom out (Zoom In, Zoom Out), and close the window (Close).

You can find additional options by selecting File ➤ Page Setup (see Figure 10-3). The Page Setup dialog allows you to select the size of paper that will be used, the source of the paper feed (such as multitray printers), the orientation of the page (Portrait vs. Landscape), and the Left, Right, Top, and Bottom margins. You can also switch printers using the Printer button.

Note that annotations embedded in a document appear highlighted in a printed output, just as they do in Concordance's Browse view. Terms that are highlighted in Browse view as a result of a search are underlined in the printed output. However, search terms that are part of an annotation won't be underlined, as they're part of the highlighted annotation.

Printing in this way synchronizes with the Empties option (select Tools ➤ Empties). Recall that, when the Empties item has a check mark next to it from the Tools menu, all fields will be displayed in Browse view, even those that have no data. Toggling Empties by selecting it from the menu again suppresses empty fields, and only displays those fields that contain actual data.

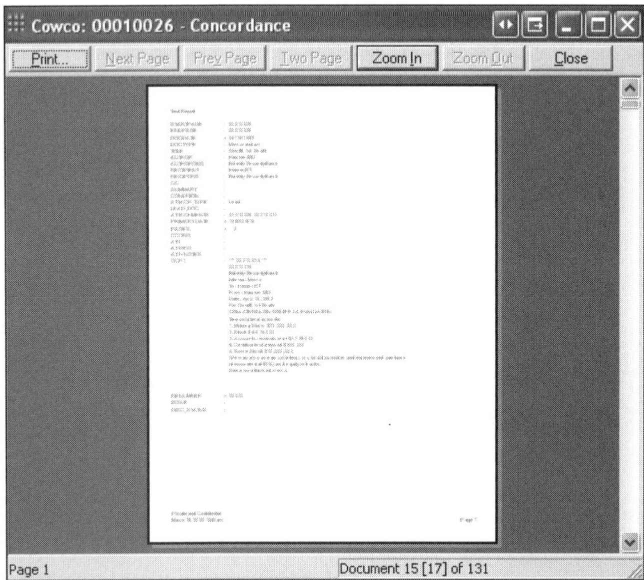

Figure 10-2. *In this example of print preview, the One Page option is selected, so that only one page appears on each screen.*

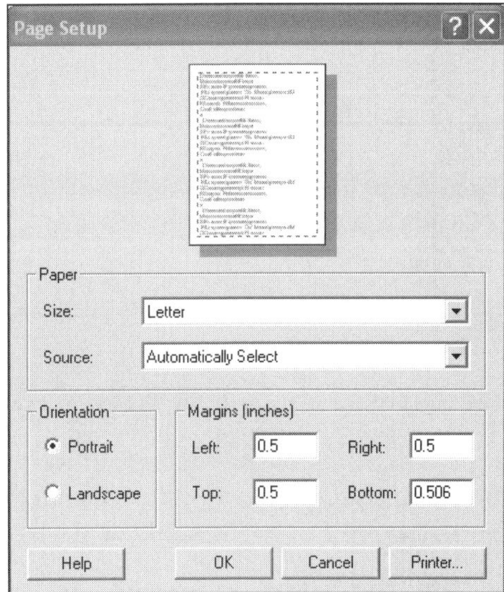

Figure 10-3. *Options in the Page Setup dialog pertain to the type of paper that will be used, page orientation, and margins.*

Printing Sets of Records

You can print sets of records by clicking the Print button located on the button bar at the top of the Concordance screen. This opens the "Print documents" dialog, which has several tabs that display various options for formatting the output. This method differs from printing a single document in that you can select batches of documents to print, which fields to print, and how the output will be displayed.

The "Print documents" dialog has the tabs Fields, KWIC, Formatting, and Print, described in the following sections.

Fields Tab

You use the Fields tab to select which fields to display in the output (see Figure 10-4). All available fields are displayed in a list box on the left of the screen. You can use buttons to move fields back and forth from "Available fields" to "Selected fields." You can use the "Select all" and "Remove all" buttons as a quick way to include or remove all fields. Another way to move fields is to highlight them, then double-click them in either list. Double-clicking a field in the "Available fields" list box moves that field to the "Selected fields" list box.

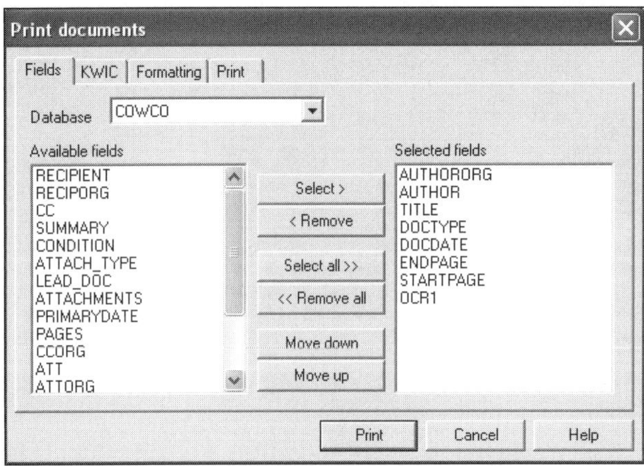

Figure 10-4. *The Fields tab of the Print documents dialog*

You can set the order of the fields here, as well. "Move up" and "Move down" buttons alter the order of the fields, and this order is reflected in the output report. Moving a field up the list causes the field to appear to the left of a printed page.

The printed report synchronizes with the Empties option from the Tools ➤ Empties menu, so that fields with no values can be suppressed.

KWIC Tab

KWIC means *keywords in context.* It's a way to make otherwise lengthy reports more manageable and concise by displaying just those sections of indexed fields that contain selected keywords. The selected keywords are the highlighted sections in Concordance's Browse view that have resulted from the previous search (see Figure 10-5).

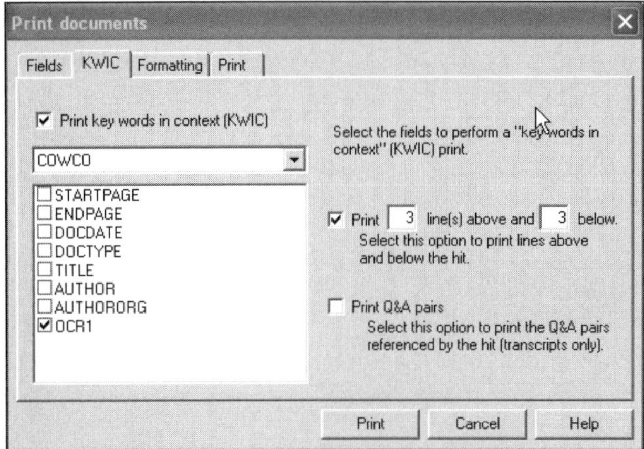

Figure 10-5. *The KWIC tab of the Print documents dialog*

The "Print key words in context (KWIC)" check box enables the feature. When this check box isn't selected, all the other KWIC options are disabled.

Fields that appear in the list box under the Databases combo box refer to those fields that you've selected for the output to the report from the Fields tab. Clicking a field's check box enables the KWIC feature for that field. Fields with no check mark will have their entire contents printed, if they have data.

Additional options allow you not only to see the line that contains the keywords, but also to print *n* number of lines before and after the line that contains the keywords. This means that the report will output a section of text in and around the keywords, enabling someone who views the report to understand the context of the paragraph that contains the hit (hence the *context* part of KWIC).

"Print Q&A pairs" refers to transcripts and depositions, where questions and answers are denoted by "Q" and "A." Selecting this option alone displays the entire text of a Q/A couple, but selecting this option and selecting the number of lines to be displayed before and after a hit limits the output to just the number of lines you specify. When used in this way, Q/A pairs can be displayed, with a set number of lines of text around them, to convey to a reader the context in which the keywords were used in the transcript or deposition.

Formatting Tab

The Formatting tab allows you to select more advanced options for how a report will be displayed (see Figure 10-6).

The Header and Footer fields accept text that will display at the top and bottom of each page. Document records that span several pages will have the header and footer on every page. Headers and footers are left justified.

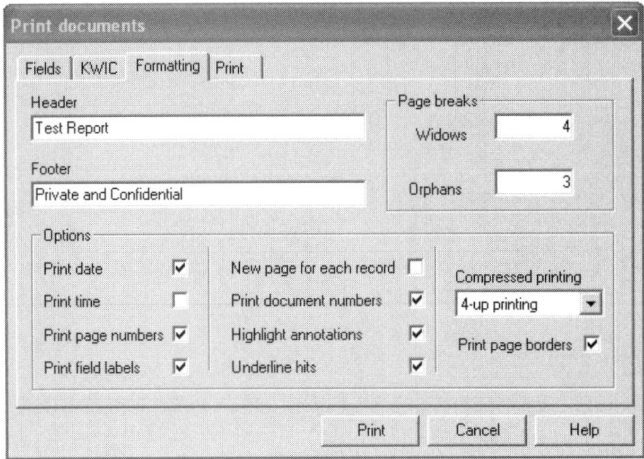

Figure 10-6. *The Formatting tab of the Print documents dialog*

The Options area of this tab controls other formatting features:

- *Print date and Print time*: Prints the current date or time, as defined by the user's PC clock.

- *Print page numbers*: The current page number appears at the bottom right of the page.

- *Print field labels*: The name of a field appears in the report. If unchecked, only values will appear.

- *New page for each record*: Determines if the end of a document record forces a new page break. If this option is unchecked, new data for the next document record will appear just after the last record. If checked, the end of a document record will force a page break.

- *Print document numbers*: Displays the document number of the document itself on each page, as it appears in the last active query in Concordance. For example, every page of the 12th document of a 50-record result set will display "Document 12 of 50."

- *Highlight annotations*: Forces any annotations highlighted in Browse view to be highlighted in the report as well.

- *Underline hits*: Causes the keywords that are highlighted in Browse view and that result from the last active search to be underlined in the report. This option only affects indexed fields; that is, fields that have a PARAGRAPH data type (which are indexed by default), or that have one of the other available data types (DATE/TEXT/NUMERIC) and are indexed.

- *Compressed printing*: Gives the user the ability to force document records with multiple pages to print on a single sheet of paper. This is often referred to as *n-up* printing. For example, selecting 4-up printing causes the first four pages of a document record to appear on the first page of the report (see Figure 10-7). This is often useful when printing large sets of data, such as transcripts or depositions.

- *Print page borders*: If checked, will draw a thin border around each page in the output.

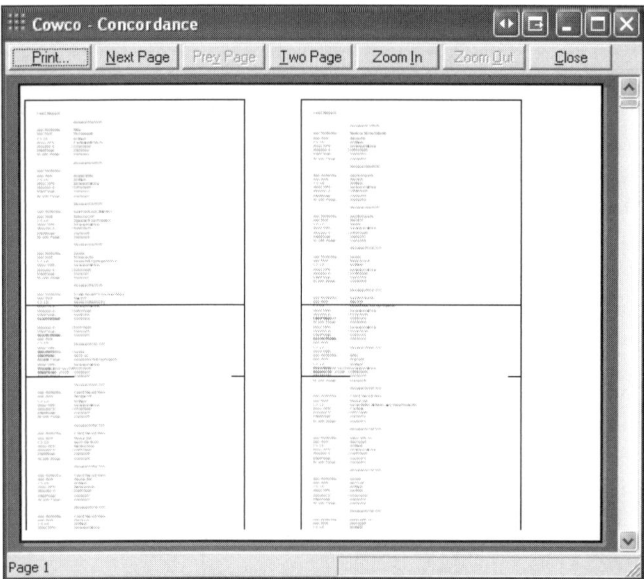

Figure 10-7. *An example of n-up printing, with n=4. Four pages of the report are compressed so that they appear on a single page of the report.*

The "Page breaks" text fields accept the number of lines for Widows and Orphans. These terms refer to lines that appear before and after a page break when a document record spans more than one page. *Widows* are the number of lines left at the bottom of a page when Concordance ends one record, and begins printing the next. *Orphans* refer to the number of lines at the top of the next page.

These options are relevant if the "New page for each record" option is not checked. When this option is not checked, new document records will be added to an existing page in the report, at the end of the last document record; more than one document record can appear on a single page. When this option is checked, the end of a document record forces a new page break; no one page will contain more than one document record.

If the "New page for each record" option is not checked, then the possibility exists that when a document record reaches its last few lines near a page break, a handful of lines will spill over to a new page. When this happens, the main body of the document record that appears on the previous page is the Widow, and the few lines that appear on the new page are the Orphans.

This might seem like a trivial formatting concern, but it can affect how a report appears to an end user. If only a single line at the end of a document record appears on a new page, the report isn't visually continuous.

These "Page breaks" options that pertain to Widows and Orphans give the report designer the ability to control how many lines are allowed for a new document record at the end of a page, and to control how many lines of text are allowed to spill over into a new page from the previous page.

The number in the Widows text field controls how much of a new document record is allowed to appear at the bottom of a page. For example, if the number entered here is 5, and available space at the end of the page where the record will start only allows for three lines to appear, the entire record is forced down to a new page.

The number in the Orphans field "borrows" lines from a previous page until the specified number of lines appears at the top of the next page. For example, if a document record spans into a second page so that only a single line appears on the new page, the number in the Orphans field will force the report to move lines from the previous page to the new page until the numbers match. Note that this borrowing of lines might cause the number of lines on the previous page to fall under the threshold set by the Windows text field. When this happens, the entire document record is moved to a new page.

Print Tab

The Print tab allows you to make final formatting changes, and to save current print settings as a profile that can be retrieved later (see Figure 10-8).

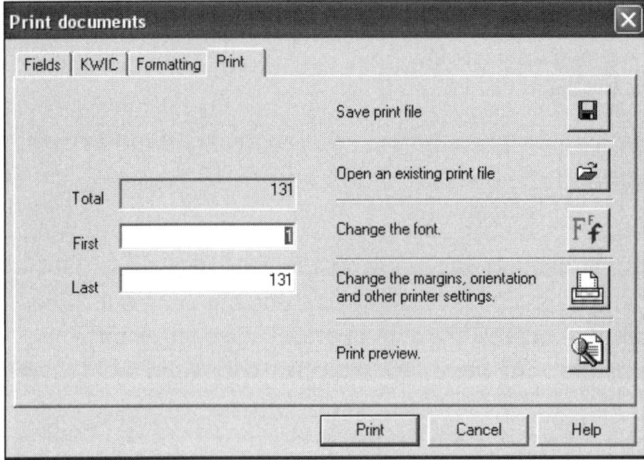

Figure 10-8. *The Print tab of the "Print documents" dialog*

- *Total, First, and Last text fields:* The Total text field displays the number of document records that are accessible to the report. Note that the number that appears here depends on the number of document records available to Concordance from the last active search. However, you can narrow the number of records that are output by entering values in the First and Last text fields.

- *Save print file* ▣ : Saves the current formatting selections you made to a file that can be later recalled by clicking the "Open an existing print file" ☞ button. This can save time when printing the same types of reports between Concordance sessions. The formatting profile is saved as a file with an .FMT extension. It's stored in a raw text format, and can be opened and modified using a text editor.

- *Change the font* F𝐟 : Selects the font to be used in the report. However, this selection is subordinate to any font modifications made to Concordance directly via Browse view.

- *Change the margins, orientation and other printer settings* : Opens a printer dialog and allows you to modify the orientation of the page and to set page margins. Note that the actual window that appears is dependent on the selected printer.

- *Print preview* : Allows the user to see an onscreen representation of the report before sending it to a printer.

Creating Formal Reports

You can generate two types of structured formal reports from Concordance. You can access these reports by clicking the Report button or from the Documents ➤ Reports menu. When using the button, clicking the small tick mark adjacent to this button displays the options Report Writer and Annotation Report.

The Report Writer option allows you to create a report to display fielded data from the Concordance database. You can use the Annotation Report option to create reports to display Concordance's various annotations: issues, attachments, notes, and Quick marks.

When creating a report, you'll select fields that will be displayed, set print margins, enter headers and footers, and choose other formatting options. You can save these selections as external metafiles that can be reused and rerun in later sessions. Annotation report profiles are saved as .ARF files; Report Writer profiles are saved as .ARP files.

Report Writer

Selecting the Report Writer option opens a Report Writer dialog (see Figure 10-9), which displays three options: Report Writer Wizard (to guide you through creating a report), Report Writer (to create a report directly from a report design mode, bypassing the wizard), and "Open existing report" (to open a previously saved report profile).

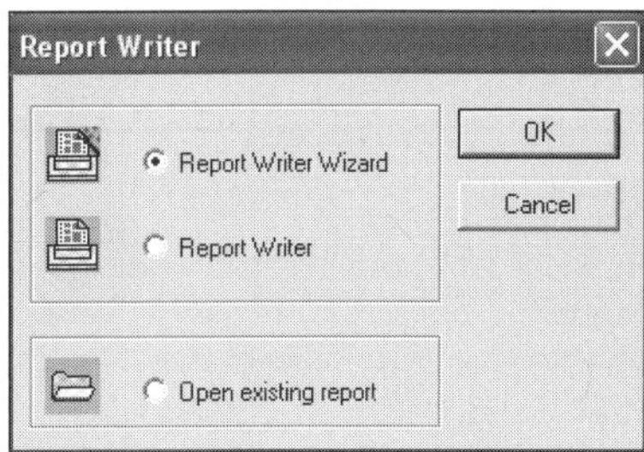

Figure 10-9. *The Report Writer dialog that first appears when you open the Report Writer*

Using the Report Writer Wizard

The Report Writer Wizard guides you through the process of creating reports by means of interactive dialogs. This is usually a good first step in creating a report: you use the wizard to create a profile of a basic report that you can modify further using Concordance's report designer environment.

The wizard has ten different interactive dialogs, described in the following sections.

Documents Dialog

The first dialog asks you which documents should feed the report (see Figure 10-10). The First and Last values displayed in this dialog depend on the result of the last active query that's displayed in Concordance. You can elect to print all documents of a database, or you can select a subset of those records. If the most active query itself represents a subset of all records in the database, you can elect to print all those results, or a subset of that subset.

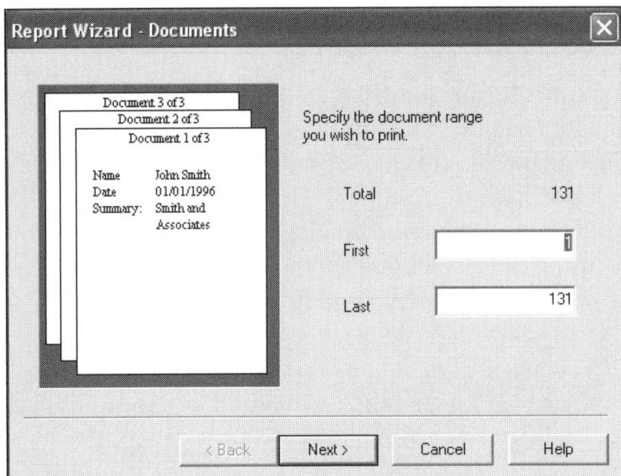

Figure 10-10. *The range of documents to be printed. The total number of records that will appear in a report is defined by the number of records that appear in the last active query in Concordance.*

Page Numbering and Dates Dialog

The next dialog controls how page numbers, date and time, and fonts should be displayed in the report (see Figure 10-11). Page numbers are printed in the lower right-hand corner of each page. Date and time values are printed in the lower left-hand corner of the report.

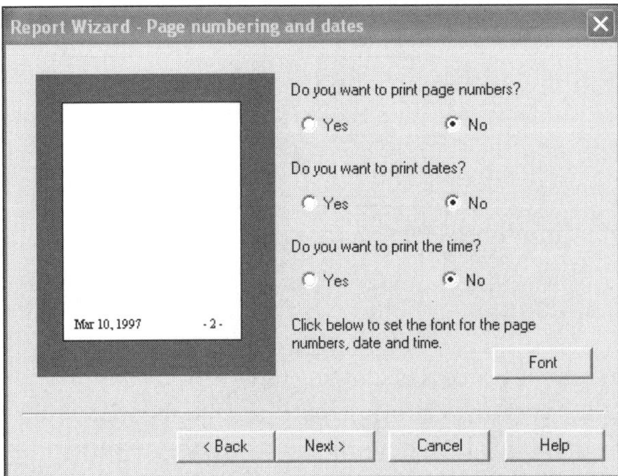

Figure 10-11. *"Page numbering and dates" dialog*

Header/Footer Dialog

The text fields in the Header/Footer dialog accept static text that appears at the top and bottom of every page in the report (see Figure 10-12).

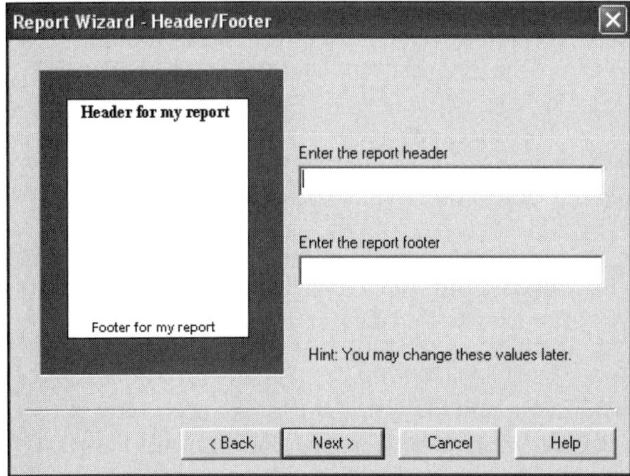

Figure 10-12. *Header/Footer dialog*

Options Dialog

The Options dialog displays a series of Yes/No formatting options that control the basic structure of the report (see Figure 10-13).

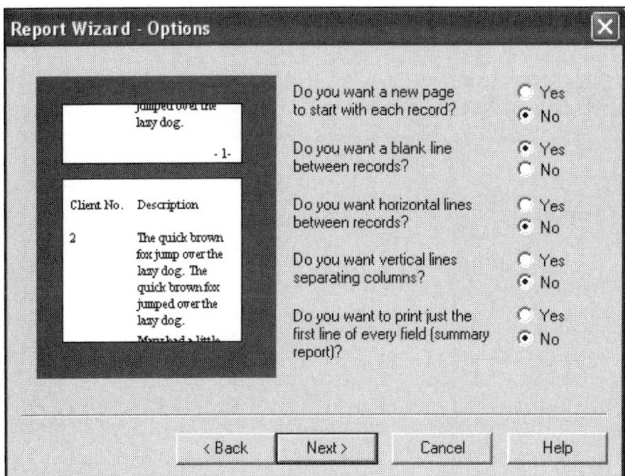

Figure 10-13. *Options dialog*

- *Do you want a new page to start with each record?* Controls how document records appear on each page. If you select this option, the start of a new document record will force a page break. Otherwise, continuous records will flow down a page, even if several records appear on a single page.

- *Do you want a blank line between records?* This option is appropriate if new document records don't force a page break: It inserts space between records to act as a visual cue so that the breaks between the end of one record and the beginning of the next record can be easily identified.

- *Do you want horizontal lines between records?* This option inserts a single horizontal rule in the blank space between records, only if blank space has been enabled by the preceding option.

- *Do you want vertical lines separating columns?* This places vertical rules between fields to act as a visual cue so that that the bounds of fielded data can be easily identified.

- *Do you want to print just the first line of every field (summary report)?* You should select this option if the report will display paragraph fields, and if the length of the report should be kept to a minimum. This affects multiselect fields as well, and suppresses entries if the delimiter in the field is a carriage return or line feed.

Margins Dialog

You set top, bottom, left, and right margins in the next dialog (see Figure 10-14). Margins are measured in inches. Keep in mind that some printers have built-in margins that are always present on a printed page, even if you've set margins to zero. The Intercolumnar (1/10th″) value controls how much space is inserted between fields in the report. This value is measured in tenths of inches. Having a small padding between fields usually makes for a report that is easier to read.

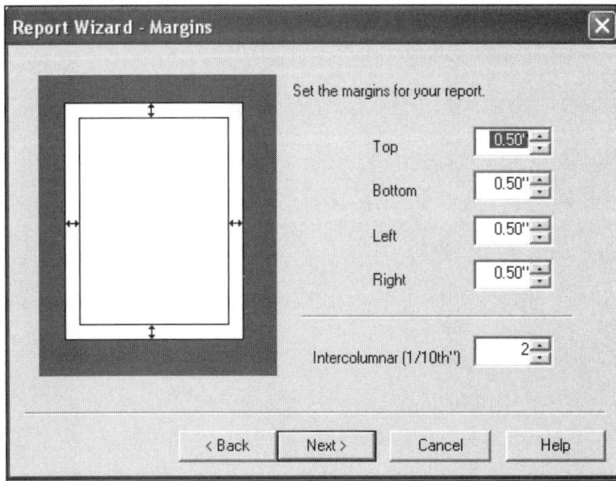

Figure 10-14. *Margins dialog*

Printer Dialog

The Printer dialog controls printer-specific options and gives you the ability to define Widow and Orphan lines. Clicking the Printer button opens a new dialog that displays options specific to the user's printer (see Figure 10-15): the size of the output page (letter, legal, and so on), the page orientation (portrait or landscape), and page margins.

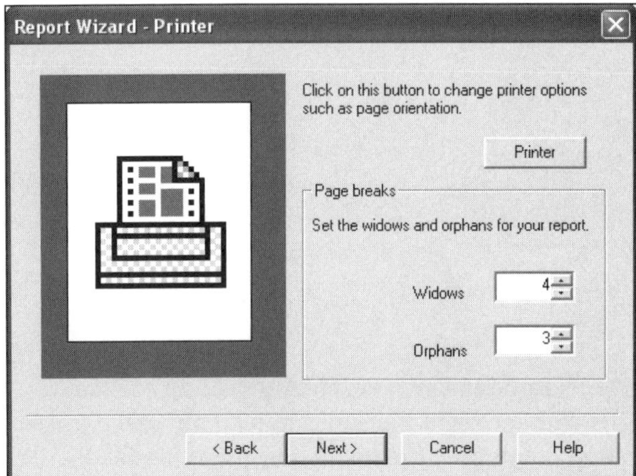

Figure 10-15. *Printer dialog*

Exploded Sort Dialog

You use an *exploded sort report* to structure and sort data from fields that contain multiple values, separated by a delimiter. As an example, for a database that contains document records that represent e-mails, the CC field might contain multiple e-mail recipients, with each name separated by a semicolon. Normally, this field—which can contain quite a bit of text—is displayed on one or more lines in the report, and is read from left to right. If a person using such a report is interested in specific recipients, it can be a challenge to locate only those records that contain a certain name. Visually, it's easier to locate any one of the values in this field if they're sorted alphabetically, and displayed vertically in the report.

You can select only one field as the field to be exploded, which you choose from the drop-down box labeled "Select the field you want to explode sort" (see Figure 10-16). You can select other fields for display in the report, but they won't be sorted in the same way as the exploded field. The field to be exploded always appears first in the row of fields across the page.

You specify the delimiter in the text field with the label "Set a delimiter to base the exploded sort." By default, this is set to a comma. Regardless of which delimiter you select, it's important that the field that drives the sort use the delimiter consistently. In other words, "dirty" data with inconsistent delimiters can throw off the sort.

An exploded sort report differs from a standard report in that a standard report groups fielded data together for each document record. The report starts with the first record of the database, with each document record then fed to the report in the order in which it appears in Concordance. If each document record fits on a single page, and if page breaks for new records are enforced, there will be one document record for each page of the report. Group boundaries are defined by document record boundaries.

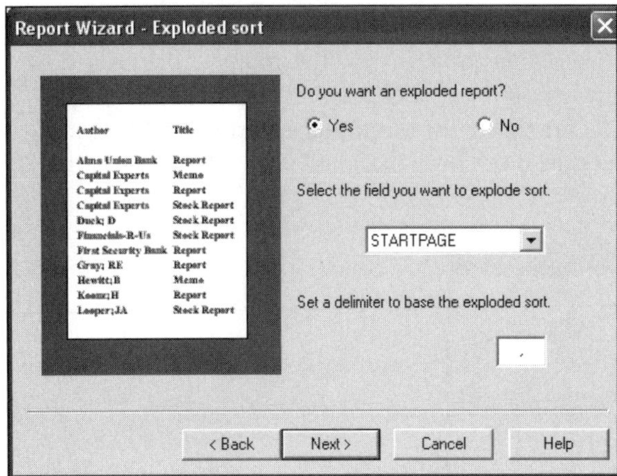

Figure 10-16. *In the "Exploded sort" dialog, one field is selected for the exploded sort.*

However, an exploded sort report groups values from the exploded field. In a CC field, if the same recipient appears in 12 records, that recipient name will appear on 12 separate lines on the report, grouped together. Group boundaries are defined by the exploded field. Figures 10-17 and 10-18 display the same data in a nonexploded sort (see Figure 10-17) vs. an exploded sort (see Figure 10-18).

Unexploded report

AUTHOR	STARTPAGE	ENDPAGE	DOCDATE	DOCTYPE	TITLE
John Q. Public	00010009	00010011	02/03/1984	Correspondence	Cowco In Bankruptcy
Koonz;H	00010014	00010015	06/06/1983	Correspondence	Untitled
Koonz;H	00010016	00010017	05/25/1983	Correspondence	Cowco
McDonald;JE	00010018	00010018	07/16/1984	Correspondence	Untitled
Koonz;H	00010019	00010020	11/10/1983	Correspondence	Cowco Cow Milking Programs
Hauser;MD	00010070	00010070	06/13/1983	File Note	Conversation Between Gary B and Hauser M
Weller;CE	00010083	00010084	09/21/1983	Correspondence	Untitled
	00010087	00010090	10/00/1983	Proposal	Terms of New Proposal

Figure 10-17. *An example of a report that doesn't use an exploded sort*

			Exploded report		
AUTHOR	STARTPAGE	ENDPAGE	DOCDATE	DOCTYPE	TITLE
	00010008	00010008	11/23/1983	Accounts	Audit of D19831121 and D19831123 Moroney J of Stockments Bank & Trust Company £000,000s
	00010023	00010024	04/00/1983	Financial Paper	Table of Data Concerning Loans to GRC and Gama Trust
	00010031	00010032	00/00/0000	Schedule	Cow Security
	00010033	00010034	00/00/0000	Schedule	Property Real
	00010036	00010064	00/00/0000	Financial Report	Untitled
	00010065	00010066	00/00/1983	Note	Goniff JA Cash Flows for 1982-83

Figure 10-18. *An example of an exploded sort report. This is the same data that is displayed in Figure 10-17.*

Fields Dialog

Use the Fields dialog to select the fields that will appear in the report by highlighting desired fields and using the Select ▸ and Remove ◂ buttons (see Figure 10-19). You can also double-click a field to move it from the left list box (fields to select from) to the right list box (fields that will appear in the report).

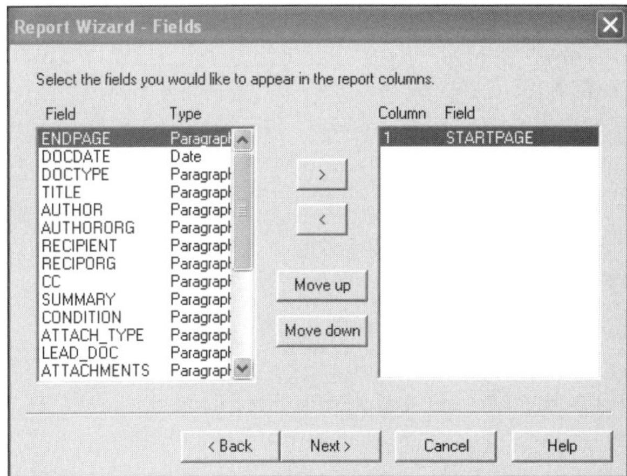

Figure 10-19. *Fields dialog*

You can modify the order in which the fields appear using the "Move up" and "Move down" buttons. Although the list of fields is stacked from top to bottom, the order they appear on the report is left to right. Moving a field higher up the list forces the field to move to the left side of the report.

If the report relies on an exploded sort, the field that has been selected for exploded sorting will always appear first (on the left side of the page in a report). No other field can occupy this position.

Field Options Dialog

The Field Options dialog controls several useful features that pertain to each selected column for the report (see Figure 10-20). You must select each field individually. This means that you can uniquely define the options for each field.

Figure 10-20. *In the Field Options dialog, you apply options to each field, individually. First, you must highlight the first option in the list box, then set the options for that field.*

The Sum section of the Field Options dialog contains the following settings:

- *Total*: Calculates a total at the end of the report for the selected column. This option is appropriate for fields that have a NUMERIC data type.

- *Subtotal*: When the value in the "Break column" selection changes, a subtotal will be calculated. A report can span several pages without calculating a subtotal if the data contained in the "Break column" is the same for many records. For this option to be used effectively, you should sort the report on the "Break column" field. Like the preceding Total option, this option applies to fields with a NUMERIC data type.

- *Width*: Controls the number of digits that are displayed in totals and subtotals.

- *Decimals*: Controls the number of digits that appear to the right of a decimal place in totals and subtotals.

- *Break column*: Defines how subtotals should be calculated, as described earlier.

- *Style*: You set the format of how a total or subtotal appears using one of the following values:

    - *<none>*: No specific formatting is applied.

    - *Comma*: Uses a comma to separate hundreds, thousands, and millions.

    - *Currency*: Formats the total or subtotal to display as a monetary value.

    - *Zero filled*: Works in conjunction with the value selected in the Width field so that leading zeroes are used to pad out a value to fit to the specified width.

Other options control the handling of data specific to a field:

- *New page on new entry*: Forces a page break when data in the field changes value. For this option to work effectively, you should sort the report by this field.

- *Suppress repetitive entries*: For fields that contain repetitive values, you can use this option to display the repeating value only once. As with the "New page on new entry" option, this feature works most effectively if you sort the report on this field.

- *Underline hits*: The report underlines search terms that result from the last active query applied to Concordance. This is analogous to highlighting hits in Browse view.

Finish Dialog

The Finish dialog is the last dialog of the wizard (see Figure 10-21). You can elect to go back to previous dialogs using the Back button. The Finish button doesn't actually run the report—it constructs it. It then shifts the view to Concordance's report designer. From the designer, you can modify the selections made by Concordance, or view the formatted output of the report by clicking the Print Preview button.

Figure 10-21. *Finish dialog*

Report Designer

The report designer is a design environment that enables you to make formatting changes to a report. You can access this design environment directly by selecting the "Report writer" option from the Report Writer dialog. The report designer is also active at the end of a Report Wizard session, once you click the Finish button and the wizard builds the report.

Before the design environment is opened, Concordance opens a Report Options dialog, intended to gather basic information about how the report should be structured (see Figure 10-22). The options accessible from this dialog are the same options presented during a Report Wizard session. Although formatting options presented by the Report Options dialog are the same as those accessible from the Report Wizard tool, the layout of the Report Options dialog is different. The wizard has separate dialogs that prompt you with questions about the report; the Report Options dialog is more compact, in that all options are accessible from one dialog that has multiple tabs. Each tab corresponds to the different dialogs in the wizard. The Report Options dialog contains the following tabs:

- *Report*: Select document range and number of columns; set blank lines and rules between records

- *Printer*: Set page margins, spacing between columns, and widow/orphan limits

- *Footer*: Select options to print page numbers and dates, and select the output font

- *Exploded sort*: Select exploded fields and set the delimiter

- *Options*: Set totals, subtotals, and repetitive entries for each column

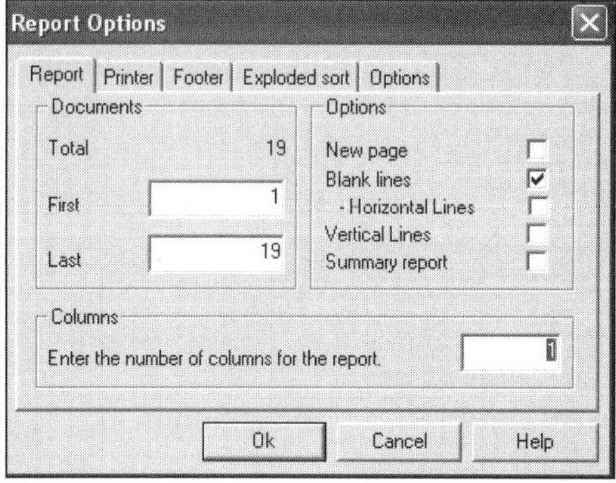

Figure 10-22. *In the Report Options dialog, the various types conform to the different screens in the Report Writer Wizard.*

Note You don't select fields that appear in the report from this tool initially. The fields are inserted into the report after this tool is closed and the report designer environment is opened. The Options tab of the Report Options dialog lists fields in a drop-down box. Until fields have been inserted into the report from the design environment, these options aren't relevant. You should use the Report Options dialog when it opens initially to define basic parameters for the report, such as the number of columns and margin settings, and then use the design environment to refine the report further.

You can reopen the Report Options dialog from the design environment by clicking the Options button located on the button bar at the top of the Concordance report designer environment (see Figure 10-23).

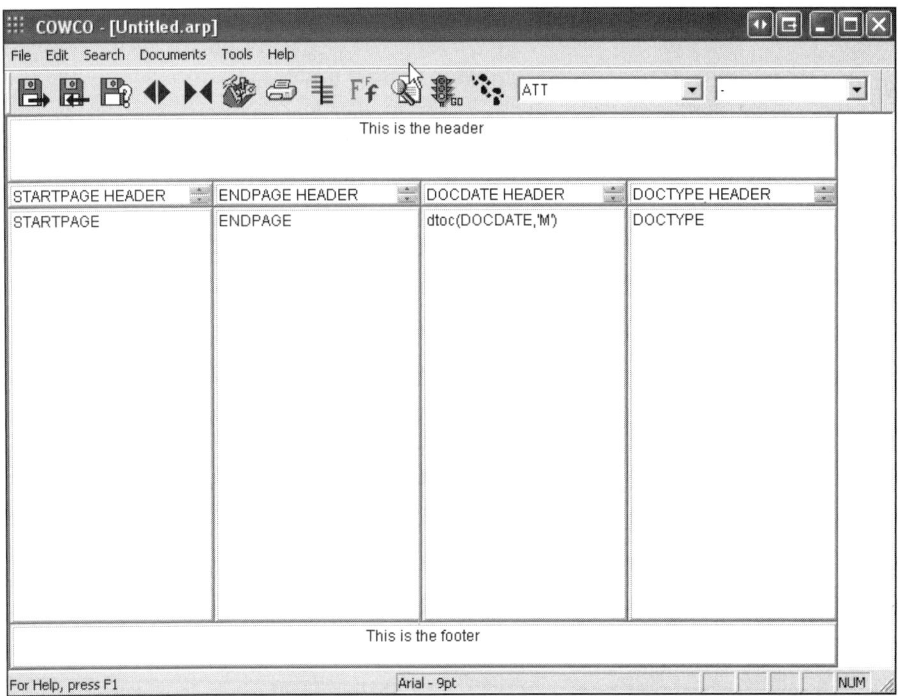

Figure 10-23. *The report designer*

The report designer environment displays the basic structure of a single page in the report. There are open areas for the header and footer, and the body of the report is divided into cells that represent the number of columns that have been selected to appear in the report. You can click into these areas and type text directly.

A new button bar appears at the top of the designer screen, replacing the button bar that's displayed in Concordance's Browse and Table views (see Figure 10-24). These new buttons are specific to the construction of reports. Included in the button bar are drop-down selections that represent the available fields in the database. Selecting a field adds it to the report. A list of additional and useful functions—commands that alter the appearance of data in a field—is also displayed (see Table 10-1).

Figure 10-24. Report designer button bar

Table 10-1. *Buttons Accessible from the Report Designer*

Name	Button	Description
Open		Opens an existing report profile. Profiles are saved as external files and are given an .ARP extension. They're convenient, in that the time spent in structuring a report isn't lost between user sessions. A user can create an annotation report, save the profile, then call it in a later session.
Save		Saves the current report settings to a report profile. If the report profile has already been saved, clicking this button updates the .ARP file to reflect report settings that have been changed. If the report is new and no report profile has been saved previously, you're prompted to give the profile a name and to specify a location where the profile should be saved.
Save as		Saves the current report settings. You're prompted to give the profile a name and to specify a location where the profile should be saved.
Insert		Inserts columns. You specify the number of columns to add. Select a column by clicking into it first. Columns that are added are inserted into this position, pushing the selected column to the right.
Delete		Deletes columns. You specify the number of columns to delete. Select a column by clicking into it first. Columns that are deleted are removed from this position, so that adjacent columns to the right of the deleted columns are pushed left.
Options		Opens the Report Options dialog. This is the same tool that opens by default when you select the Report Writer option after clicking the Report button.
Page Setup		Opens a printer dialog that allows you to set printer properties, such as the orientation of the pages of the report, and the paper source.
Justify		Justifies report cells for the report's header and footer, and cells for column labels and column data, left, right, and center. You control alignment by selecting the cell to be justified first, then clicking the Justify button. A dialog opens that asks you if you want to apply the alignment to the currently selected cell, or to other report objects. The next Text Alignment dialog is where you select left, center, or right justification.
Font		Report cells for the report's header and footer, and cells for column labels and column data, can have different fonts. You select a specific cell first, then click the Font button. As with the Justify button, a dialog opens that prompts you to confirm that the font selection will apply to the currently selected report item, or to other objects in the report. The next Font dialog displays settings such as font name and size, with additional options pertaining to italicizing, underlining, or setting font weight. You can underline or strike (strikeout) fonts as well. Font types are applied to the entire contents of a cell, but not to sections of text within a cell. This means that all text in a cell is formatted in the same way; you cannot mix font styles inside the cell.
Print Preview		Activates the report, altering the view from the design environment to a view that emulates how the actual report—with actual data—will appear when sent to a printer. Print preview allows you to scroll from page to page in a report, to survey the results. However, it's limited to the first 100 pages of the report.
Print		Prints the report.
Exit		Closes the report designer environment and returns to Concordance's Active Workspace view.

In addition to the buttons, the button bar contains two select boxes, one that displays every field in the database, and one that displays common formatting functions that you can use to modify the underlying data in a field.

To display data in a column from a specific field, you must first click into the cell corresponding to the placement of the desired column. Each column has two sections: a header, which displays static text, and a data cell, which displays data from fields (see Figure 10-25).

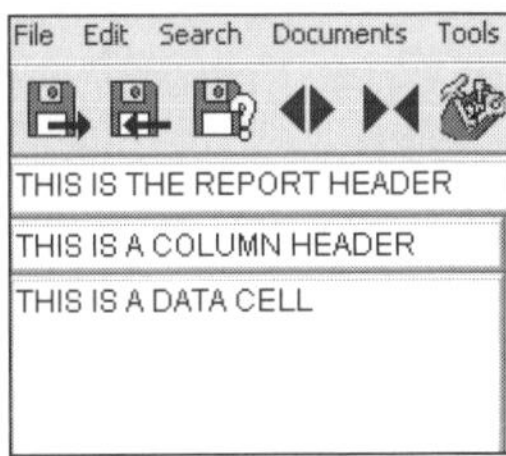

Figure 10-25. *Concordance's design mode, with report header, cell heading, and data cell labeled. Note that the text "THIS IS A DATA CELL" is meant to indicate to you what the cell is used for. If this report were run, it would generate an error. Data cells should contain the names of fields, operators, or functions.*

Often, the column header is simply the name of the field that is displayed. You can either manually key the name of the field into the column header, or click into the header cell itself, then select the column name from the select box on the button bar. However, you can enter any text in the column header, so if the name of a field doesn't intuitively describe its contents, you can enter a title that's more informative.

When the name of a field is either typed or inserted by means of the select box into the data cell of a column, this indicates to Concordance that the actual data from the field, not the label itself, should appear in the cell. The information in the data section of a cell is dynamic.

The report header and footer cells are like column header cells in that they only accept static text. Dynamic data from the database *only* appears in the data cells of a column.

If you choose to key the field name manually into the data cell of a column, you must ensure that you type the name of the field exactly as it is referenced in the database, and that you enter the name of the field using capital letters. Concordance won't match a field name entered with lower case letters with a field in the database, and an error will be generated when the report is activated.

You can modify how the dynamic data in a data cell is displayed in the report by means of additional labeling, or with Concordance functions. You can combine the dynamic data, the additional labeling, and these Concordance functions in the same cell to display complex interpretations of data.

For example, with a column labeled CC and a corresponding database field that represents the carbon copy list of an e-mail document record, you might wish for each entry to have an additional "Recipient:" label. The column header will appear as CC; the data in the field will be displayed under that column header, and the text "Recipient:" will appear to the left of each set of data (see Figure 10-26).

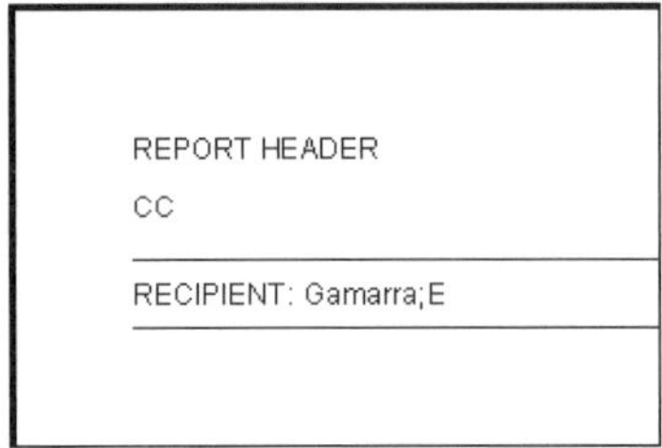

Figure 10-26. *An example of adding a label to dynamic data in a report data cell*

The syntax for displaying information in this way is as follows:

```
"Recipient: " + CC
```

This section of text represents three things: the label, Recipient, which must be bracketed by double quotes; the + symbol, which concatenates sections of text; and CC, which represents dynamic data from the CC field (see Figure 10-27).

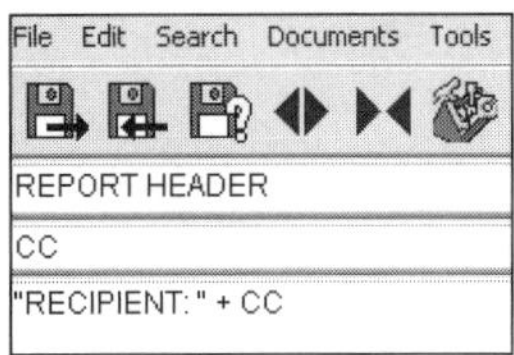

Figure 10-27. *In report designer mode, the data part of a cell can include items other than just the name of a field, such as labels, denoted by the use of double quotes.*

In addition to extra labeling in a data cell, the Concordance report designer makes available a series of useful operators and functions that you can use to modify the formatting of dynamic data in a cell. An example of an operator is the + symbol, used earlier to concatenate the values of the CC field with the label Recipient. An example of a function is capitalize(ARGUMENT), which capitalizes the first letter of the ARGUMENT placeholder. The function capitalize("robert") is displayed as Robert when a report is activated. The function capitalize(DOCTYPE) converts the first letter of every value contained in the field DOCTYPE to upper case.

Using the concatenation operator (+), values from several fields can appear in a single column in a report. Consider a database that has a CC field and a BCC (blind carbon copy) field. Both these values can appear in a single column with the title "CC and BCC," and will include descriptive labels that will appear in each line of the report, if you use the following syntax in the column's data cell:

```
"CC: " + CC + newline() + "BCC: " + BCC
```

In Concordance's report designer mode, the report looks like Figure 10-28.

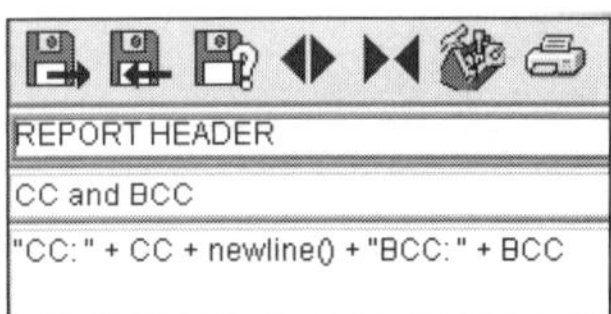

Figure 10-28. *Using labels, operators, and functions to concatenate different fields from a Concordance database into a single report cell*

The report looks like Figure 10-29 when viewed in Print Preview mode.

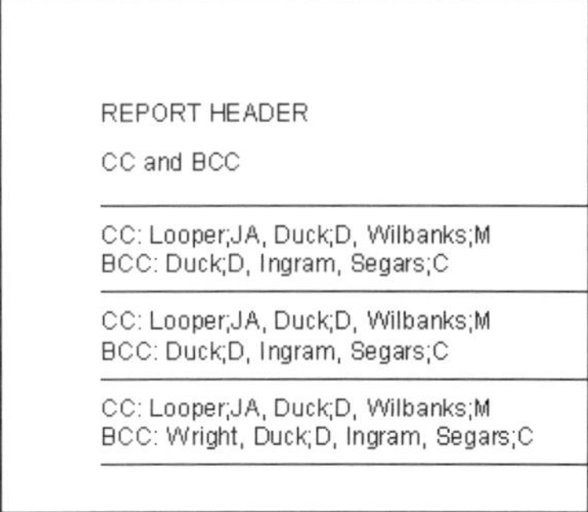

Figure 10-29. *An example of using functions to concatenate different fields in a Concordance database into a single data cell*

In the example displayed in figure 10-29, the `newline()` function is concatenated between the `CC` field and the `BCC` label. This function forces a line break between these values.

When designing a report, you should bear in mind that, when building a report, data cells aren't restricted only to the unformatted contents of a single field from the database. Consider the fields `FIRST_NAME`, `LAST_NAME`, `ADDRESS_1`, `ADDRESS_2`, `CITY`, `STATE`, and `ZIP`. You could lay out each of these fields across a report as separate fields, from left to right. This is a perfectly valid way to display this data. As the report designer, you might wish to consolidate the fields to save space, and to present names and addresses in a more familiar way by stacking the data from top to bottom in a single column. You can accomplish this with the following syntax:

```
trim(FIRST_NAME) + " " + trim(LAST_NAME) + newline() +
trim(ADDRESS_1) + newline() +
ADDRESS_2 + newline() +
trim(CITY) + ", " + trim(STATE) + " " + trim(ZIP)
```

With this data in separate columns, the report looks like Figure 10-30.

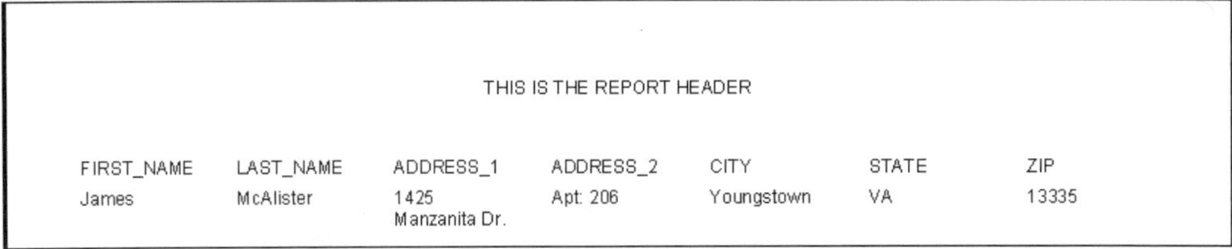

Figure 10-30. *Name and address fields laid out horizontally, as separate fields, across a report*

When field names are concatenated with functions, the report looks like Figure 10-31.

Figure 10-31. *A more concise way of presenting names and addresses*

■**Note** When concatenating text fields, you'll find that the length of the field set in the field properties from the File ➤ Modify menu causes unused white space to pad out to the full length of the field. For example, if a text field is given a length of 60, and a field only uses 10 characters of actual text, the field will appear with extra white space. The function `trim(ARGUMENT)` removes white space from the contents of a field.

You can fully exploit the power of Concordance's report designer through the use of functions and operators, and use them to create reports that are concise, logical, and visually appealing. You can find a full listing of the available functions and operators in the *Concordance Language Manual* that ships with the product, as well as in Concordance's internal help files.

Annotation Report Wizard

The "Annotation report" option, which you can choose by clicking the Report button, activates a wizard that guides you through a series of interactive dialogs that enable you to build a report that displays annotations, as displayed in Figure 10-32.

00010004

Note:
    Is this the guy we're looking for?

Mr S. L. McCorman Our Ref. CEP/MeMurrian HP/ K243

00010003

Note:
    This opening paragraph is just useless pablum. WHo writes like this?Jeeze.

It was wonderful seeing you and Rita on Sunday. You
certainly have the perfect garden for a summer drinks party.
Rita's looking stunning, she's obviously recovered from
Jeremiah's birth very quickly.

00010004

Attachment:
    C:\DATA\DOC\Active_10069207_1_Feedback Request Form for Offsite Document Review and
    Collection.DOC

Issue:
    •   HOT_DOC

Note:
    See attached

Re: Agreement Confirmation

Figure 10-32. *An example of an annotation report. Highlighted sections in the report correspond to highlighted sections of text in Concordance's Browse view.*

You can also select this option from the Documents ➤ Reports ➤ Annotation report menu. Recall that annotations are applied to sections of text in Concordance's Browse view, and are categorized in four ways:

- *Issues*: Issues are tags that are applied to sections of text. These are the same tags that are applied to a document from Concordance's Tags/Notes window. When used as an annotation, the scope of the tag applies to the highlighted text, not necessarily the entire document.

- *Attachments*: Attachments include the entire path to an external file, and the file name.

- *Notes*: Notes are free-form comments added by a user to describe sections of text.

- *Quick marks*: Quick marks are linked to a line number in a transcript.

The structure of an annotation report is straightforward: each document record is identified by a selected field in the database. Annotations are labeled and appear under this identifier. Annotation reports are continuous, in that there is no page break between records. Annotations for several document records can appear on the same page. *N-up* printing is supported, so that several screens of annotations can be forced to appear on a single page, to save paper.

Before the wizard itself is activated, and in response to you selecting the "Annotation report" option, Concordance first prompts you to start the wizard itself, or to open a previously saved annotation report profile. These profiles are saved as separate files and given an

.ARF extension. They're convenient, in that the time spent in structuring an annotation report isn't lost between user sessions. A user can create an annotation report, save the profile, then call it in a later session.

There's no corresponding report designer for annotation reports. You use the interactive dialogs in the Annotation Report Wizard to create a report, and if further modification is required, you can use an Annotation Report dialog, with tabs that correspond to the various dialogs of the wizard, to update the report's profile and regenerate the report.

The first dialog of the wizard has four options: Issue report, Attachment report, Note report, and Quick mark report (see Figure 10-33). Choose one of the annotation types to govern which records appear in the report. This means that, if the report is defined as an Attachment report, other records that have issues and notes, but that lack attachments, won't appear in the report. An Attachment report only displays annotations that have attachments; a Note report only displays records that have notes. However, that doesn't mean that multiple annotation types are exclusive. If desired, an Attachment report will display other annotations such as notes and issues, but only if a given annotation also has an attachment associated with it.

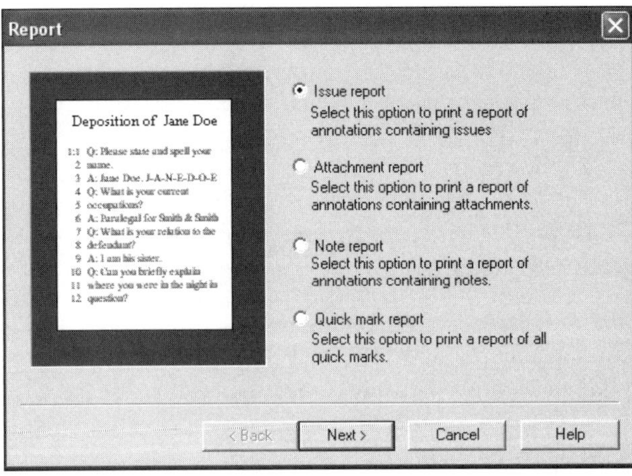

Figure 10-33. *The first dialog of the Annotation Report Wizard. Use these options to determine the primary annotation to drive the report. You add other annotation options later.*

Issues Dialog

The Issues dialog gives you the option to select all issues in the database, or only selected issues (see Figure 10-34). If you desire only some of the issues for the report, you should select the "Print selected issues" radio button, then highlight the desired issues from the list box. You can use the "Clear" and "Select all" buttons as a quick way to highlight all issues (helpful if there are numerous issues to choose from) or to remove the highlight from all issues. Although the "Select all" button is equivalent to selecting the "Print all issues" radio button, it can be useful when most, but not all, issues are to appear in the report. You can select all, then remove highlighting from the issues that aren't required for the report.

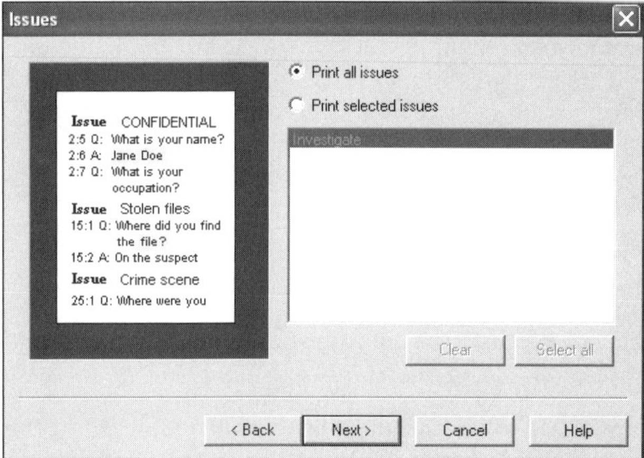

Figure 10-34. *Issues dialog*

Annotations Dialog

The next dialog in the Wizard, titled Annotations, controls what annotations appear in the report, and how they appear (see Figure 10-35).

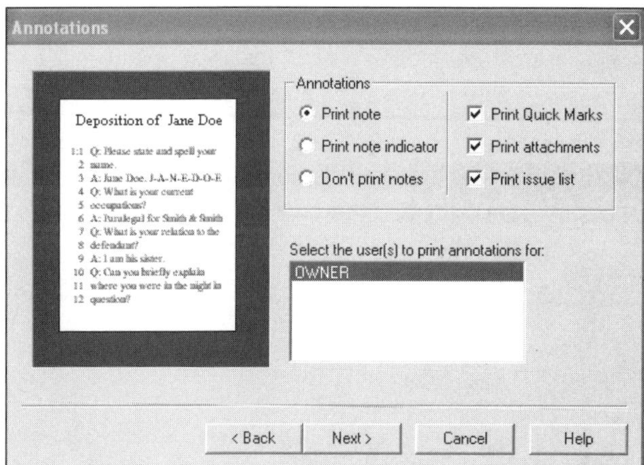

Figure 10-35. *Annotations dialog*

The first set of options, controlled by radio buttons, determines how notes are treated:

- *Print note*: Recall then when you add an annotation to a block of text in Concordance's Browse view, you can enter a comment—a note—to the annotation. If you select this radio button, the entire comment will appear in the report. This option is exclusive of the other options, "Print note indicator" and "Don't print notes," so if it's checked, these other options aren't available.

- *Print note indicator*: The snippet of text that pops up when you hover your mouse over an annotation in Browse view is known as the note indicator. It's the first 60 characters of the note. If you select this radio button, this snippet of text will appear in the report. This option is exclusive of the other options, "Print note" and "Don't print notes," so if it's checked, these other options aren't available.

- *Don't print notes*: Notes and indicators won't appear in the report.

- *Print Quick Marks*: This option applies only to transcript databases. When selected, the Quick mark associated with a line number in a transcript database will appear in the report.

- *Print attachments*: Selecting this option causes the file path and file name of the attachment associated with a note to appear in the report.

- *Print issue list*: If selected, this option will print a list of issues. Note that deselecting this option for a report that's otherwise defined as an Issue report causes issues to be suppressed in the final output.

The list box labeled "Select the user(s) to print annotations for" lists all users who have created annotations in the database. These are the same users set through Concordance's security model. By applying or removing a highlight to users listed in this list box, the person designing the report can control which notes appear in the database by the user who created them.

Context Dialog

You use the Context dialog to control how much text surrounds an annotation (see Figure 10-36). As the name implies, using these features gives an annotation some context as it appears in a document record.

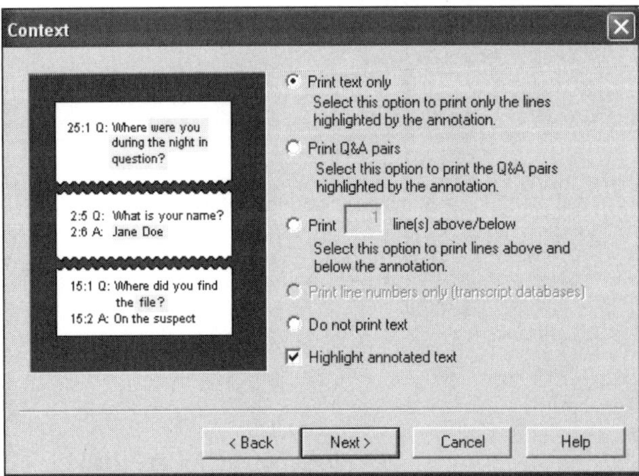

Figure 10-36. *Context dialog*

- *Print text only.* Displays only the highlighted section of text.

- *Print Q&A pairs:* Used with transcript and deposition databases, this option prints a Q/A pair.

- *Print n line(s) above/below.* Includes *n* number of lines both above and below the highlighted section of text that contains the annotation.

- *Print line numbers only.* Prints the line number of an annotation in a transcript or deposition database, but no text.

- *Do not print text.* Suppresses the section of text that's highlighted, but prints the annotations associated with the text.

- *Highlight annotated text.* Emulates the highlighting that's applied to a section of text in Concordance's Browse view when an annotation is applied.

Formatting Dialog

The Formatting dialog determines how pages in the report will appear (see Figure 10-37). Options allow the person designing the report to include page numbers and date and time values. You enable compressed printing (*n-up*) from this dialog.

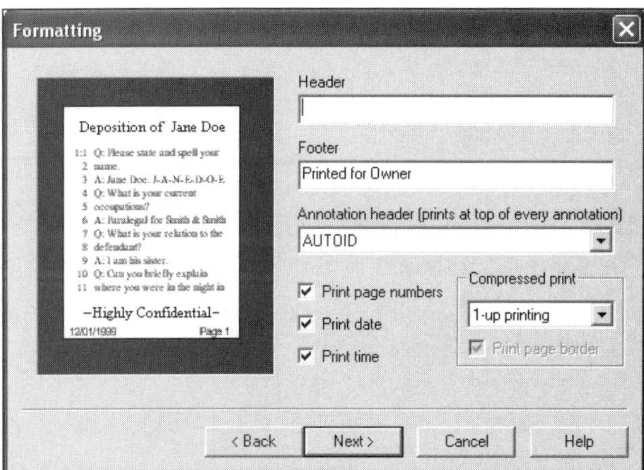

Figure 10-37. *Formatting dialog*

- *Header and Footer.* Text entered here appears in the header and footer of each page of the report.

- *Annotation header.* This field from the database appears at the head of each annotation, and identifies the document record that contained the annotation. Ideally, it's some unique identifier, such as an accession field, or a document control number. If the Concordance database that drives the report is a transcript or deposition database, this option defaults to NAME, DATE, and VOLUME fields.

- *Print page numbers*: Prints page numbers at the bottom right of each page of the report, in the format *Page n.*

- *Print date*: Prints the user's system date in the lower left corner of each page.

- *Print time*: Prints the user's system time in the lower left corner of each page.

- *Compressed print*: This is often referred to as *n-up* printing. For example, selecting 4-up printing causes the first four pages of a document record to appear on the first page of the report. This is often useful when printing large sets of data, such as transcripts or depositions. If checked, the check box "Print page border" will draw a thin border around each page in the output.

Print Dialog

The Print dialog is the final dialog of the Annotation Report Wizard (see Figure 10-38). The selections that the report designer has made up to this point can be saved from this dialog to an external file. Additional formatting options, such as the font type and margin size, are accessible here (see Table 10-2).

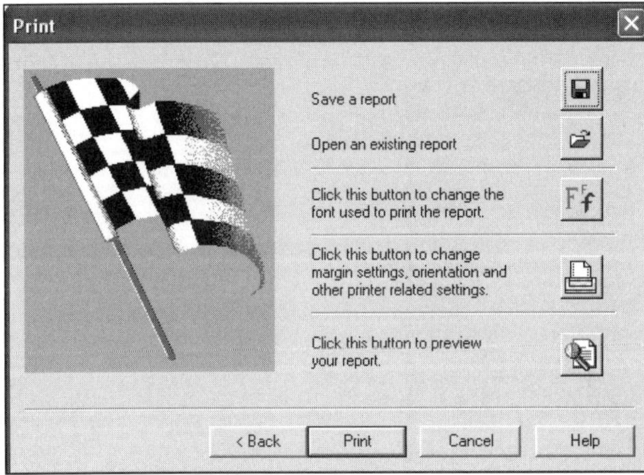

Figure 10-38. *Print dialog*

Table 10-2. *Buttons on the Print Dialog*

Name	Button	Description
Save a Report		Saves the current report settings. You're prompted to give the profile a name and to specify a location where the profile should be saved.
Open an Existing Report		Opens an existing report profile.
Font		Selects the font to be used in the report. However, this selection is subordinate to any font modifications made to Concordance directly through the Browse view.

Name	Button	Description
Margin Settings and Orientation		Opens a Page Setup dialog that allows you to set the size of the paper to be used when printing the report, the paper source, orientation (portrait or landscape), and page margins.
Preview		Opens a new window that displays a representation of what the printed document will look like.

If the person designing the report is satisfied with the report, pressing the Print button will send the report to the selected printer.

Annotation Report Dialog

The Annotation Report dialog compresses the various dialogs from the Annotation Report Wizard into a single dialog, with multiple tabs (see Figure 10-39). You can set each option that's accessible from each dialog of the wizard from the corresponding tab in the tool. This dialog is opened directly when you open an existing report profile. It also opens when you close the Print Preview screen while viewing the formatted output of an annotation report.

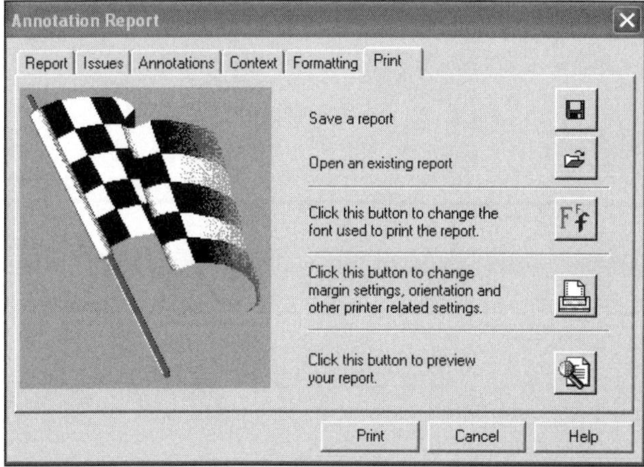

Figure 10-39. *The Annotation Report dialog offers the same features as the various dialogs that open in sequence during the Annotation Report Wizard.*

Summary

This chapter has described the various ways to present data in Concordance as printed reports. You can print just the current document, with minimal formatting specifications, or build a complex report that presents only selected fields. You can streamline otherwise unwieldy data using the formatting options available from Concordance's functions and operators, such as `capitalize(ARGUMENT)` and the concatenation operator, +. This data, easily accessible from Concordance's Browse view but otherwise difficult to present on a printed page, can also be made visually appealing.

Document annotation reports are available as well, though Concordance presets the structure of those reports: you use a wizard and a corresponding tool to select which types of annotations to present and how they should appear, but not *where* the annotations will appear in the report. There's no report designer environment for annotation reports, and Concordance functions aren't applicable. However, you'll find that the layout of these annotation reports is logical, and additional design specifications beyond those that are accessible from the Annotation Report Wizard and the Annotation Report dialog aren't needed.

Users who create and design reports will find that, although the steps required to build a basic report are simple, precise formatting concerns can take some time. Although Concordance's wizards gather required basic information about a report, and build the report itself, this is just a first step. End user specifications regarding font type, field placement, and page formatting usually require the person designing the report to refine the report several times before the end result conforms exactly to what the end user desires.

Report design is simple in practice, but potentially time consuming to make a reality. However, given that reports can narrow a forest of data to only the information that an end user finds most valuable, both users and report designers will find that the time spent designing them is time well spent.

■ ■ ■

CHAPTER 11

Opticon: Introduction, Overview, and Installation

Opticon is optional software that's manufactured by Dataflight, the same company that markets Concordance. You use it to view graphical images that represent individual pages of Concordance database records. Associating images with document records in a Concordance database isn't a requirement. However, you can augment the use and value of database applications by granting end users the ability to view exact digital representations of the documents they retrieve in Concordance. By viewing associated images, an end user might discover that a document contains valuable information not captured through an OCR process, such as handwritten marginalia.

Opticon is a full-featured program. End users can scroll through images one by one or jump to specific images. Users can increase or decrease image magnification as needed; they can also annotate images with subjective comments, known as *redlines*. Users can search, print, or export images and annotations to external data files. Chapter 12 describes these features.

Opticon is opened as an external program, outside Concordance. However, it can link to Concordance. An end user launches it by clicking a button located on the bottom edge of Concordance's Browse, Table, or Edit views. Many users find it useful to toggle between the two programs, or to place them side by side. Opticon reads *image key* data from the current database record in Concordance, and uses that information to locate corresponding images that represent the database record. The link is continuous. When a user moves to a new record in Concordance, Opticon will update and display images associated with the new record. The link is also two-way. If a document boundary is crossed in Opticon, Concordance will react by making the corresponding database record active. Linking Concordance database records to associated images through Opticon makes possible an important feature used to create and rename new sets of images that Concordance has retrieved and sorted first. Chapter 14 covers exporting—or producing—images in this way.

For Concordance and Opticon to link and synchronize, image file name and file path information must be loaded into a database's *imagebase*. An imagebase is a Concordance file used by Opticon to determine the file path and file name of an image. Chapter 13 describes administrative tasks relating to imagebases.

Working with Graphical Images

Document data loaded into a Concordance database must be converted into a series of graphical images that represent document records. Of course, if database records originated as Opticon-supported images, no actual conversion is needed. If database records represent physical documents or electronic files, a Concordance administrator might ask a vendor assigned to scan, code, and extract OCR from documents to provide corresponding images as well.

Broadly speaking, digital images can be divided into two types: *vector graphics* and *raster graphics*. These terms refer to the basic conceptual methods to create an image.

Vector Graphics

Vector graphics translate the visual detail of an object into simple geometric shapes, such as lines, points, and curves. A vector file contains data about the shapes that combine to produce a visual approximation of the source object. Opticon isn't compatible with vector files. If the source images for a Concordance database originate as vector-based files, they must be converted to raster graphics, described in the following section.

Raster Graphics

Raster graphics are digital representations in which visual details are distilled into a matrix of dots. These dots are often referred to as *pixels*, an abbreviation for the term *picture elements*. Each pixel in an image contains information that defines its appearance, such as its color. In general, a higher number of pixels in a fixed area translates into a more detailed image. A common way of referring to image quality is to use the phrase *dots per inch* (dpi). An image containing 300 dpi is more detailed than an image containing 200 dpi. Images that are more detailed contain more pixels, and therefore more data. Image detail and file size correlate: the more detailed the image, the larger the file.

Raster File Formats

The act of creating a digital image from an object is known as *scanning*. The hardware used during this procedure is known as a *scanner*. Many different types of hardware exist, from small units intended for personal use, to high volume scanners that can process many thousands of documents or files quickly. Although some photocopiers are capable of scanning a physical document and saving an image in a format that's acceptable to Opticon, many Concordance administrators who oversee a large volume of documents rely on a third-party vendor to create associated raster images corresponding to coded and OCR data intended for a Concordance database.

A scanner is commonly connected to a workstation, so that scanning personnel can review the results of a scan, and select an output *image format*. This term refers to the specific way in which image data is organized in a file. Several different types of image formats exist. You can determine a file's format from its file extension. You might be familiar with some of the more popular file formats that are used to transfer image data on the World Wide Web, such as the Graphics Interchange Format (GIF) and the Joint Photographic Experts Group format (JPEG). These two particular file formats are well suited for use on the Web, in that they produce files that are comparatively small in size as a result of data *compression*.

Compression

The term *compression* refers to a method of reducing a file's size. Several types of compression methods exist. Compression methods employ a mathematical algorithm—a series of codified steps used to determine how a file should be compressed.

If some data in a file is lost as a result of a compression method, its algorithm is said to be *lossy*. If no data in a file is lost, an algorithm is said to be *lossless*.

Lossy algorithms don't automatically imply inferior file quality. For example, a compression algorithm applied to an audio file might remove data corresponding to frequencies that lie outside the range of human hearing. The resulting file will be smaller than the original and information will have been lost, though this fact will be undetectable to the human ear.

Lossless compression algorithms also reduce file size, but the compressed file is considered to be an exact copy of the original, uncompressed image. These algorithms are often used when the resulting quality of a digital file is more important than reducing its overall size.

Supported File Types

Opticon can open a variety of digital file formats. The following sections summarize each one. File extensions corresponding to a format appear in parentheses. Note that some image file types are associated with more than one file extension.

Tagged Image File (*.TIF; *.TIFF)

The Tagged Image File Format (TIFF) uses electronic markers or "tags" in a file's header to define characteristics about an image. The TIFF format was originally designed in the 1980s to be a standard for manufacturers of scanning equipment. This format has improved over time, and is often used by full-text information retrieval systems to store image data. Unless there are extenuating circumstances, most scanning and coding vendors will provide monochrome (black and white) TIFF images. Monochrome images tend to be smaller than their full-color counterparts. When the volume of images associated with a database is high, the space saved in lieu of color images can be significant. Unless otherwise noted, explanations and examples in the remainder of this book will assume that Opticon is linked to TIFF images.

You can create TIFFs using a variety of compression algorithms. One of the most common is the Group 4 compression method, which is lossless. Although you can use Opticon to save or export TIFF images using a variety of compression methods, *Opticon will only open Group 4 compressed TIFFs.*

An important characteristic of a TIFF file is that it can be single-page or multi-page. A single-page TIFF represents a single page from a document or file. If a document has many pages, it's represented by many single-page TIFFs. Although there's some variation, the file size of a single-page TIFF can be as small as 25 kilobytes. A multi-page TIFF is a single file that represents an entire document. All pages of the document have been wrapped into the one file, and page breaks are digitally signed. Image viewers that are compatible with multi-page TIFFs recognize page breaks, and allow a user to advance or retreat, page by page, within a document. TIFFs are the only format compatible with Opticon that has this feature.

Joint Photographic Experts Group (*.JPG; *.JPEG)

The phrase *Joint Photographic Experts Group* refers to the original name of the body that developed the format. JPEGs can represent millions of colors, and are well suited to storing image data about highly detailed, photo-realistic images. The JPEG standard uses a lossy compression algorithm that takes advantage of the fact that the human eye can recognize changes in brightness more readily than changes in color. Artifacts in the original image that are unimportant to visual interpretation are discarded. Despite the loss of information, image quality is retained. Compression ratios as high as 20:1 are achievable.

Because of the relatively small size of JPEG compressed images, and because of the rich color palette and resulting image quality, JPEG images are ideal for use on the Web, where limited bandwidth might be a concern.

Graphics Interchange Format (*.GIF)

CompuServe created the GIF method of compressing images in 1987 as a way to minimize file size. The GIF format uses a lossless data compression algorithm, so there's no loss in image detail. However, the GIF format is limited to the display of 256 individual colors, whereas the JPEG format described in the preceding section supports 16 million separate hues. For this reason, GIF images are ideal for symbols, logos, and images that have a limited amount of color variation. Like JPEGs, GIF images have found widespread use on the Web.

Bitmap files (*.BMP)

Microsoft Corp. invented the Bitmap image format. It's the standard image format for Windows operating systems. Many non-Windows applications support it as well. Bitmapped images sometimes have a .DIB (device-independent bitmap) file extension.

Images stored in this format can display a wide range of colors, from simple monochrome to 16.7 million colors. Although the bitmap format does support a compression method, it is rarely used. As a result, BMP files can be quite large.

PC Paintbrush Bitmap (*.PCX)

ZSoft Corp. invented the PCX method of digitizing images. It was used by the PC Paintbrush program, a popular graphics program for early PCs.

PCX files use a compression algorithm, though it isn't efficient when used with images that have a high pixel density. As a result, PCX image files aren't preferred for creating images from photographs and other detailed graphics.

In modern computer usage, PCX files are rare. This image format has been superseded by formats that support better compression (and hence, smaller file sizes) such as JPEG and GIF, described in earlier sections.

Computer Aided Acquisition and Logistics Support Raster (*.CAL, *.MIL)

.CAL and .MIL image files represent a format defined by the Department of Defense. Raster images of this type are two color, and are used primarily in Pentagon archives. The DoD formally defines this format in two separate standards documents, *MIL-STD-1840A, Automated Interchange of Technical Information*, and *MIL-R-28002A, Requirements for Raster Graphics Representation in Binary Format*. You can obtain these documents from the CALS office of the DoD:

CALS Management Support Office (DCLSO)
Office of the Assistant Director for Telecommunications and Information Systems
Headquarters Defense Logistics Agency
Cameron Station
Alexandria, VA 22314 USA

Using a Vendor to Create Images

When a vendor is used to scan, code, and extract OCR data from document records, the vendor might be asked to provide associated graphical images as well. This is a standard practice. Vendors will deliver image data in conjunction with Concordance data, often on the same media. Image data consists of individual images and metadata (often referred to as *log files*) about image file paths. This metadata is a requirement if Opticon is used to view images. It often takes the form of ASCII comma-delimited files (Chapter 13 describes the format of these files). Log files are used to update a database's imagebase with the file paths and file names of newly delivered data, also described in Chapter 14.

Deliverables

When interacting with a vendor, you should take care to outline the format of expected deliverables:

- *The media on which images are to be delivered*: As of this writing, many vendors continue to use CDs and DVDs as the transmission media of choice. In most circumstances, you'll be required to copy image data from the delivery media to a network (see the section "Workflow"). If image data spans multiple CDs or DVDs, this can add to overall processing time, as you must copy each media separately. If you expect a particularly large set of documents to be scanned and converted to images, you might prefer a vendor to use an external hard drive as the delivery media, so that processing can be performed in single steps.

- *Image formats*: Supported formats are described earlier in this chapter in the section "Supported File Types." If the TIFF format is used, you should specify that the TIFF files should be compressed using the Group 4 method of compressing TIFF files.

- *If images should be single- or multi-page*: Only the TIFF format allows several images to be combined into a single file.

- *Image name schema*: Image names can be the same as the values contained in the associated Concordance database's image key field, or can follow an alternative naming scheme.

  Image names must be unique in each Windows directory. Two files in a single Windows directory with the same name will cause a naming collision. Images in different Windows folders can share the same name. As long as subordinate folders are different, no naming collision occurs. However, when working with or speaking of images in separate subfolders with identical names, confusion can follow. You might wish to specify that image names throughout a delivery be unique.

- *Processing Excel files*: Excel files can present challenges when converted to images. An Excel workbook can contain two or more separate worksheets. Each worksheet can contain a defined print area so that parts that lay outside the area won't appear on a page when the worksheet is printed. Each worksheet contains cells in columns and rows, and these cells might or might not contain actual data. The width and height of columns and rows can be smaller than the total amount of data contained in cells, so that some data isn't visible. Rows and columns can be resized so that their width or height is zero, an effect that serves to hide the row or column from a user.

These characteristics can affect the appearance of images created from worksheets. If a worksheet's associated image is simply identical to what an end user might see if the workbook is opened using Excel, the image might not display all data. To ensure this doesn't happen, the vendor should preprocess Excel workbooks prior to conversion so that hidden rows and columns are resized and all data in cells is visible. If the defined print area's dimensions exceed that of the standard 8.5″ × 11″, you might wish the vendor to use larger image sizes.

You might want to have a conversation with a vendor beforehand to confirm these and other preprocessing steps.

Workflow

When you're provided with media containing Concordance and image data, you can do the following:

1. Load an existing Concordance database or create a new Concordance database with Concordance load files provided on the media.

2. Index or reindex the database loaded in the preceding step.

3. Copy images and a log file from the media to a workstation or network location.

4. Open and edit the log file so that file paths are updated to the workstation or network location in step 3.

5. Load a database's imagebase from the log file using Opticon's Imagebase Management dialog.

6. Test Concordance and Opticon to ensure that database records can be searched, and that associated images are linked properly.

A log file created by a vendor might contain file paths that represent image locations on the vendor's network. Because the vendor's network architecture is probably different from your network, you can update the log file to reference new file paths. Because log files are ASCII files, you can view them in a text editor and use a global find and replace to update file paths.

A vendor might provide an Opticon log file with root file paths stripped out. File paths referenced in the log will reference subordinate folders. Again, you can open the log file in a text editor and use a global find and replace to insert root file paths that represent a valid location on your network.

When files are copied from a CD or DVD to a network location, their *read-only attribute* is set to TRUE, and they cannot be edited. Although it isn't usually necessary for you to reset the read-only attribute for images, it's necessary to reset the attribute for a log file if it will be modified prior to loading an imagebase. (The same is true for any Concordance database files provided on fixed media.) You can view and modify a file's properties by selecting the file in a file explorer window, right-clicking, then selecting the Properties option. Figure 11-1 displays the Properties dialog that opens.

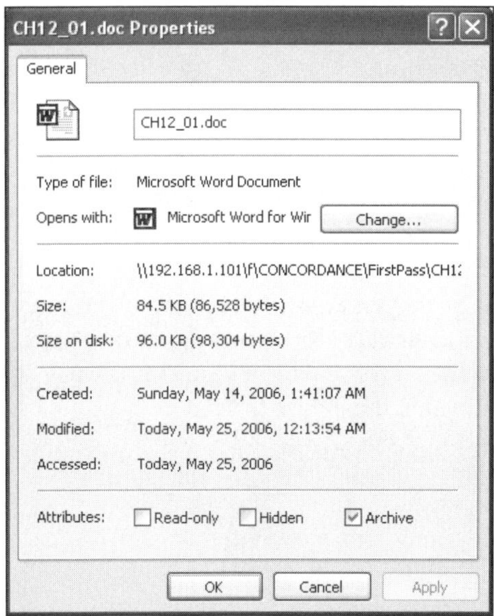

Figure 11-1. *This particular Properties dialog is from a Windows XP operating system. The Properties dialog of other versions of Windows might look slightly different.*

Another option is for you to load the log file into an imagebase, then use the Directory tab of the Imagebase Management dialog to update file paths. Chapter 13 describes this tab of the Imagebase Management dialog in detail.

Installing Opticon

When a firm or company purchases Concordance from the software manufacturer, Dataflight, a decision is made about the number of users allowed to use the software. Like the Concordance licensing model, Opticon licensing uses a per-seat model, so that a concurrent number of users are allowed to activate the program at any given time. The Opticon executable, Opticon.exe, contains licensing information embedded within its source code. The program tracks the number of users actively using the program, and denies access to additional users when the limit of allowed users is reached. This fact can affect how the program is likely to be installed.

During most installations, you must decide if the program will be installed locally on a workstation, or onto a networked server. This decision will determine where installation files and the Opticon executable are stored.

For example, if a firm has a ten-seat license, a common installation method would be to install files and the executable on a network server. In this paradigm, you won't install the program on individual workstations, but rather, on a networked server. You'll eventually run a workstation setup file, provided with Opticon's installation disks, on each client PC. This setup file informs the client of the network location of Concordance data files.

If an individual has a single license copy, he or she may install the program on a network, or on his or her own workstation. If installed on a network, this architecture is similar to that described earlier, with an end-user base of just a single user. If installed on the individual's workstation, all program files are stored on the client computer.

If, instead, your firm has purchased an Enterprise license—a scheme appropriate for large organizations—you're at liberty to install the program on as many workstations and servers as needed, and in whatever configuration desired.

You can and should consult with Dataflight regarding the optimal method of installation that ensures the maximum number of users are allowed to access databases within the appropriate licensing model.

Before Opticon can be installed, you should ensure that end users have the appropriate permissions to read and write to files stored in folders designated for Concordance databases.

You'll also want to confirm that the hardware on the server or workstation that will use Concordance conforms to minimum standards, outlined in the following section.

Hardware Requirements

Dataflight recommends the following hardware configuration on workstations that will use Opticon:

- Microsoft Windows 95/98/2000/NT/XP

- Personal computer with a Pentium 100 or higher processor

- 32MB of RAM on Windows 95/98

- 128MB of RAM on Windows 2000/NT

- 20MB of available hard disk space

- 800 × 600 display, 256 colors

- Windows-compatible mouse

- CD-ROM drive

For additional information about hardware requirements that pertain to both Concordance and Opticon, see Chapter 2.

Opticon Server Installation: Step by Step

Installation itself is easy: you insert the CD provided by the manufacturer into a computer's CD-ROM drive, and follow the onscreen prompts (detailed in Figures 11-2 through 11-8).

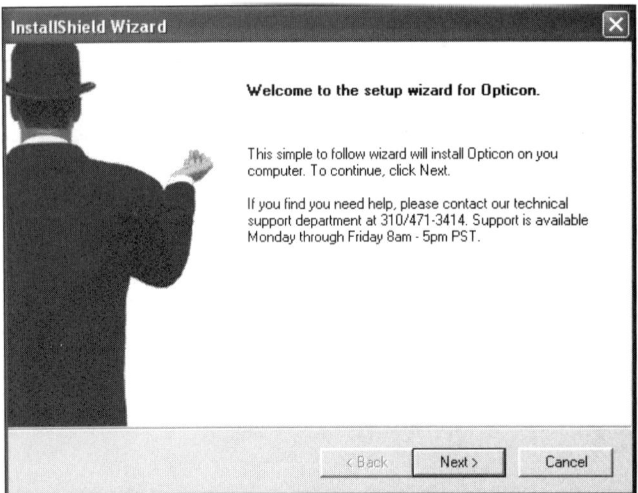

Figure 11-2. *After inserting the installation CD, you're prompted with a splash screen.*

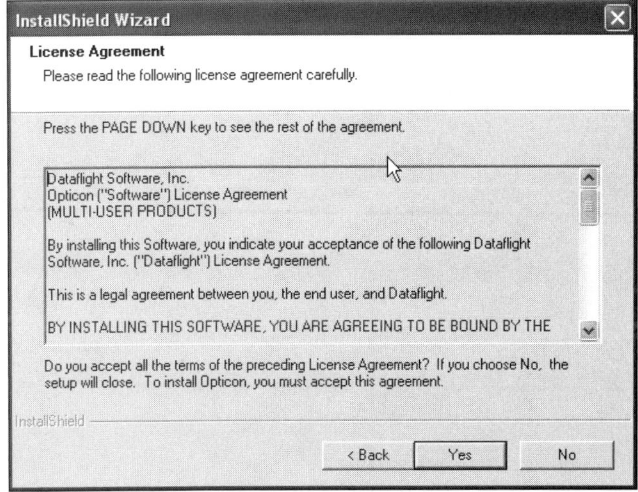

Figure 11-3. *The first dialog of the installation wizard (after the initial splash screen) displays the End User License Agreement (EULA).*

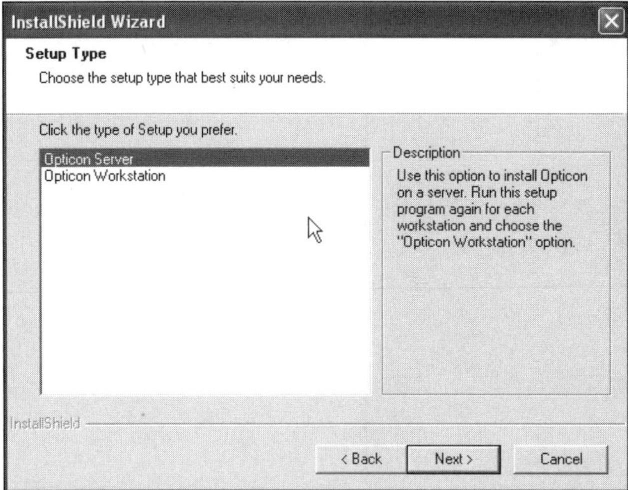

Figure 11-4. *To install Opticon on a server, you should highlight the Opticon Server option. You use the Opticon Workstation option to configure client workstations to interact with a server-side installation.*

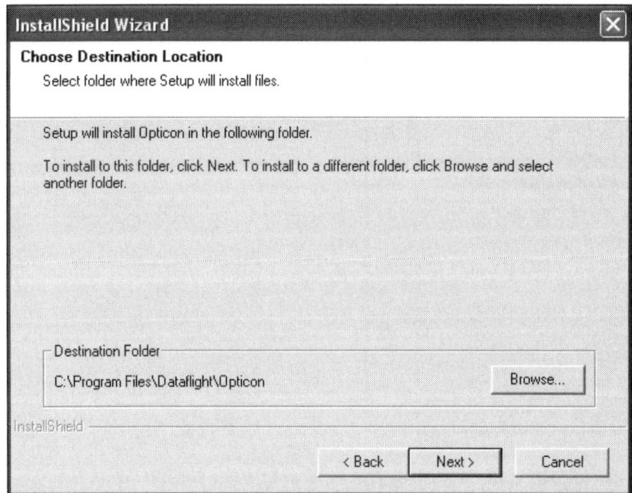

Figure 11-5. *You select the destination folder where Opticon will be installed from this dialog. The default is C:\Program Files\Dataflight\Opticon. If you desire another location, click the Browse button.*

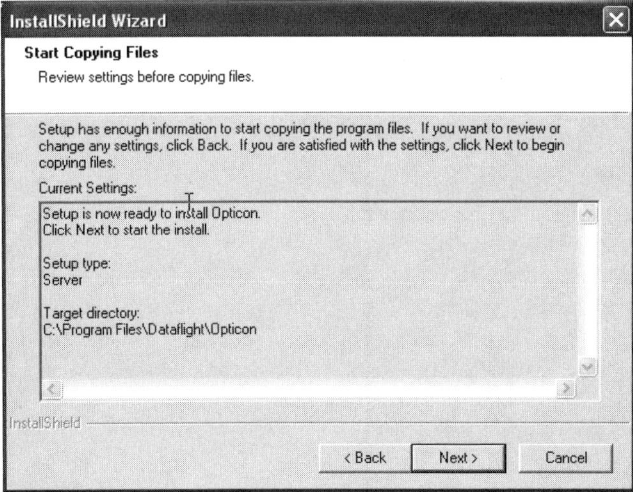

Figure 11-6. *This is a confirmation screen. If any of the parameters are incorrect, you can click the Back button and update the location of installation files, or change the type of installation (server or workstation).*

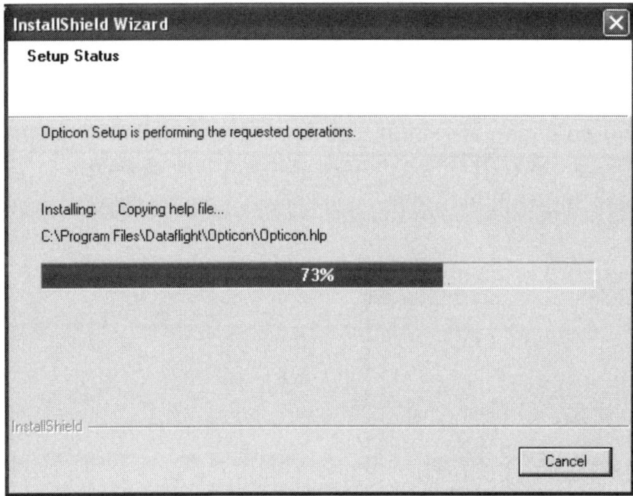

Figure 11-7. *A progress bar displays the status of the installation.*

Figure 11-8. *The final dialog of the Opticon Server Installation Wizard*

Opticon Workstation Installation: Step by Step

You run the workstation installation routine on each client workstation that will connect to a networked installation of Opticon. The workstation setup doesn't install the Opticon program on the client PC. Instead, it configures the client to connect to the server installation.

The Splash, EULA, and Setup Type dialogs that open during the Workstation Installation Wizard are the same as those detailed earlier in the section "Opticon Server Installation: Step by Step." You'll want to highlight the Opticon Workstation entry in the Setup Type dialog. Figures 11-9 through 11-13 describe the remaining dialogs.

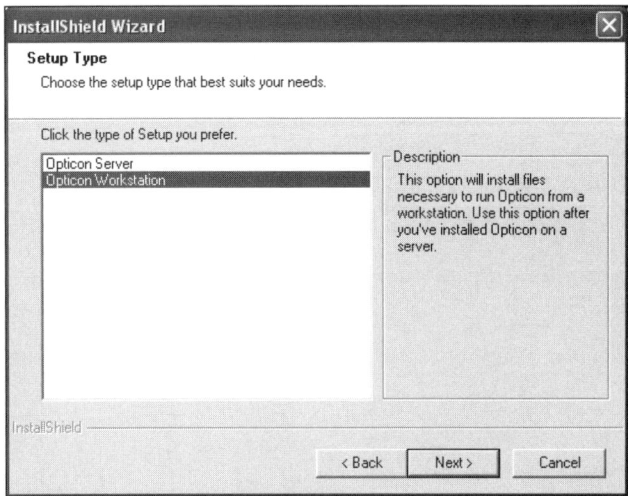

Figure 11-9. *You must highlight the Opticon Workstation option to run the Workstation install.*

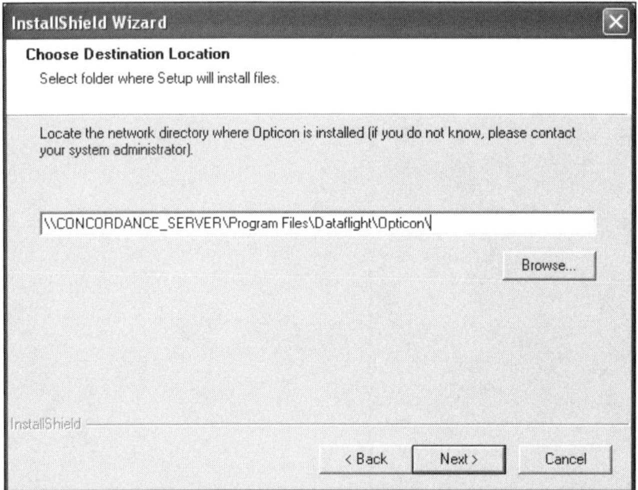

Figure 11-10. *Use the Browse button to open a Choose Folder dialog. You select the network location where Opticon is installed here.*

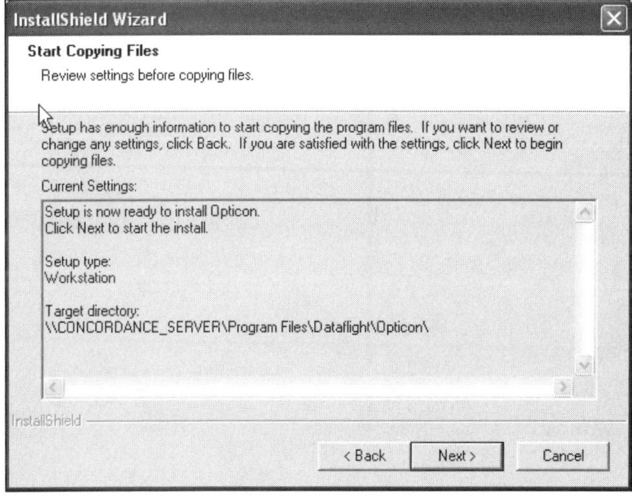

Figure 11-11. *In this confirmation dialog, you can click the Back button and update information provided on previous dialogs.*

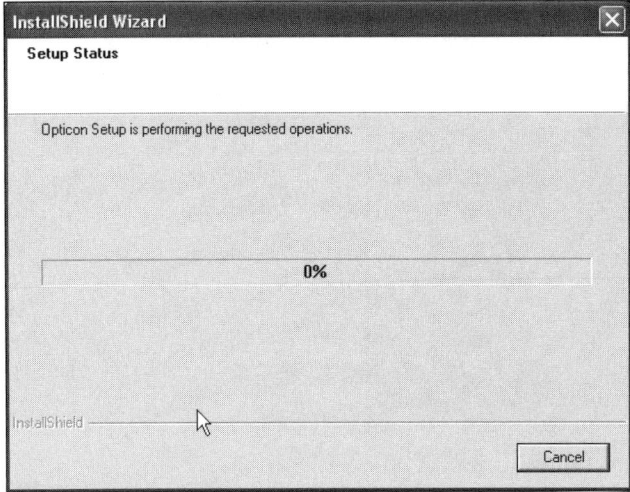

Figure 11-12. *A progress bar displays the status of the installation.*

Figure 11-13. *The final dialog of the Workstation Installation Wizard*

When the Workstation Installation Wizard is completed, the client PC will have a new folder accessible from the Windows Start button, using the All Programs option. The new folder will be labeled Dataflight, and it will contain an Opticon icon that maps to the networked executable used to launch Opticon. Despite this shortcut, the method used to launch Opticon so that it synchronizes with a Concordance database is to open the program using Concordance's camera button.

Summary

Opticon is optional software that can link to Concordance databases. You use it to view graphical representations of document records. Recall that individual document records in Concordance can be comprised of multiple pages. When document records are linked to an image viewer, each page of each document record is converted to an image file. End users use Concordance to search for and retrieve records, then use Opticon to view associated graphical renditions of the records.

Opticon supports a variety of graphical formats, including the popular JPEG and GIF formats that have found wide use on the Web. In most circumstances, though, the Tagged Image File (TIFF) format with Group 4 compression is used. This method of storing image data is a good trade-off between image quality and file size, particularly with images that have been converted to a black-and-white color scheme.

Vendors often provide images and additional metadata that describes file names and paths with Concordance load files. You copy images to appropriate network locations, and metadata about images is loaded into a database's imagebase. To avoid processing errors, you should give vendors specifications regarding image formats and naming conventions.

The remaining chapters of this book pertain specifically to the use and function of Opticon.

CHAPTER 12

Using Opticon

This chapter will cover how end users and administrators can use Opticon to view, navigate, annotate, search, and print images. Opticon is standalone software that can be used in conjunction with Concordance, or launched as a standalone program. In this chapter, it's assumed that Opticon will be used in conjunction with Concordance.

In addition to using Opticon to navigate through images, you can also use the software to work with a range of useful drawing tools. End users can use these tools to "mark up" images with basic shapes (to draw attention to a section of an image), redactions (to hide a section of an image), and text labels. Opticon exploits Concordance's searching power by saving information about markups in a separate Concordance database. End users interact with this database via a search interface embedded in Opticon. Creating and searching through annotations are described in detail in the sections "Redlines Toolbar" and "Searching Redlines."

Of course, end users will want to print hard copies of the images they view in Opticon. Because Opticon can link to a Concordance database containing many records, and because each record might be comprised of many images, Opticon's printing suite has many options that allow a user to identify easily just those images of just those documents they wish to print. The section "Printing Images" describes these techniques.

Setting Opticon As the Default Viewer

The first step to associating Opticon as the viewer that Concordance uses is to configure it from within Concordance itself. You must set Opticon as the default viewer in Concordance before it can be synchronized with a database. You make this setting from Concordance on the Viewer tab of the Preferences dialog (see Figure 12-1). You open this tool from Concordance's Tool ➤ Preferences menu.

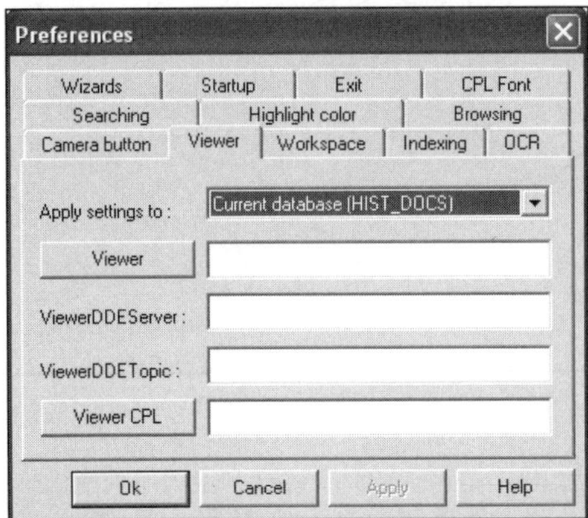

Figure 12-1. *The Viewer tab of Concordance's Preferences dialog. Opticon is configured to be the default image viewer for all databases. You enter the file path and name in the Viewer text field. The ViewerDDEServer setting is Opticon.*

- *Apply settings to*: The setting in this drop-down box determines which databases will use the image viewer defined in other areas of the Viewer tab. There are two choices: "All databases" and the currently active database, which is listed by name. "All databases" is a global setting, and defines viewer settings for all Concordance databases; selecting the name of the currently active database defines viewer settings for that database alone.

- *Viewer*: Clicking the Viewer button opens a Viewer dialog. This dialog behaves like the standard Windows Open dialog (though it has a Viewer label), in that you can use it to navigate to the folder containing the program used to launch a database's image viewer. Double-clicking a file name, or highlighting it and clicking the Open button on the Viewer dialog, enters the full path and file name of the selected file in the open text field adjacent to the Viewer button on the Viewer dialog. If Opticon is to be used as the image viewer for a database, the executable is Opticon.exe.

- *ViewerDDEServer*: Windows *Dynamic Data Exchange* (DDE) is a method used by some Windows programs to communicate with other Windows programs. The entry in the open text field labeled ViewerDDEServer references the name of the image software that Concordance will launch. For Opticon, this value is Opticon. Other image viewers might use a different setting here, as defined by that image viewer's software manufacturer.

- *ViewerDDETopic*: When software programs use DDE, the calling program sends a DDE *topic*, a way of categorizing the kind of data that programs will share. Concordance is configured so that if no value is entered into this field, it will transmit the calling database's file path and name (sans the .DCB extension). When using Opticon as the default viewer for a Concordance database, this setting is left blank.

- *Viewer CPL:* A CPL is a program written using the Concordance Programming Language. The name of a valid CPL file entered into this field will be attached to Concordance's camera button, and that CPL will be triggered instead of an image viewer. The Viewer CPL text field should contain the full path and file name of a valid .CPL or .CPT program. The Viewer CPL button behaves like the Viewer button, in that it opens an Open dialog (with a Viewer CPL label) that you can use to navigate and select the desired CPL program.

An example of a CPL used in this way is the EDocView.cpl program. This CPL is created by Concordance when a database shell is created using the E-Docs database template, and is placed in the same directory as other database files. This CPL launches external files in their native applications, if the appropriate application is installed on the end user's workstation. If a database record is associated with a series of attachments, and full file paths and file names of the attachments are stored in a database's PARAGRAPH field, an end user can highlight the file path and name, right-click, and send this information to the CPL. The file is opened in its native application.

Opticon's Layout

Button bars appear on the top, bottom, and left edges of the Opticon screen. Figures 12-2 through 12-4 display each button bar.

Figure 12-2. *Opticon's Standard toolbar*

Figure 12-3. *Opticon's Image toolbar*

Figure 12-4. *Opticon's Redlines toolbar*

By default, the toolbars are *dockable*, which means that they can be detached from Opticon and moved to a different screen location, if desired (see Figure 12-5).

To detach a toolbar, you must double-click the raised border that appears at the edge of a button bar, displayed in Figure 12-6. With the mouse key depressed, you can then drag the button bar to the desired location.

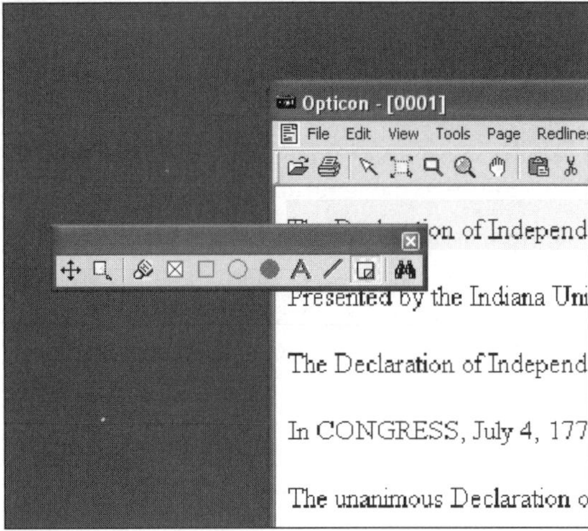

Figure 12-5. *The Redlines toolbar, attached to the left edge of the Opticon screen by default, has been detached from Opticon and moved outside the program. The options on the toolbar continue to function within Opticon, despite the placement outside the Opticon screen.*

Figure 12-6. *The raised border of a toolbar used to detach a button bar*

To reattach a button bar to the top, bottom, left, or right edge of Opticon, double-click a button bar's border, and with the mouse key depressed, drag the button bar to the desired location. When a floating button bar is dragged to a position in Opticon where it can dock (reattach), the button bar will resize slightly—a visual cue to the user.

You can hide toolbars using the View ➤ Toolbars menu. This menu item has three submenu items—Standard, Image, and Redline—and can be toggled. When a submenu item has a check mark, that toolbar is visible. When a submenu item is toggled so that no check box appears, that toolbar is hidden.

■**Note** Unlike in Concordance, menu items in Opticon are fixed, and cannot be customized.

The central body of Opticon is devoted to the image itself. Any redlines (annotations added by end users) appear over the image, and can be moved within the image using the "Move redline" button ✥ located on the Redlines button bar. The use and placement of redlines is described in detail later in this chapter in the section "Using Redlines." You can modify the scale and orientation of images in a variety of ways, described in detail in the section "Viewing Images."

The page number of the currently active image and the total number of pages that combine to form the database record that called the image is displayed in the lower right-hand corner of the screen, in the status bar. It appears in the following form, where n is the current page and m is the total number of pages in the document:

`Page n of m`

When the mouse pointer is inside an image displayed by Opticon, the pointers for the X:Y coordinates within the image are displayed on the status bar as well.

Figure 12-7 shows a cut-away of the bottom right-hand corner of the Opticon screen where page numbers and cursor positions are displayed.

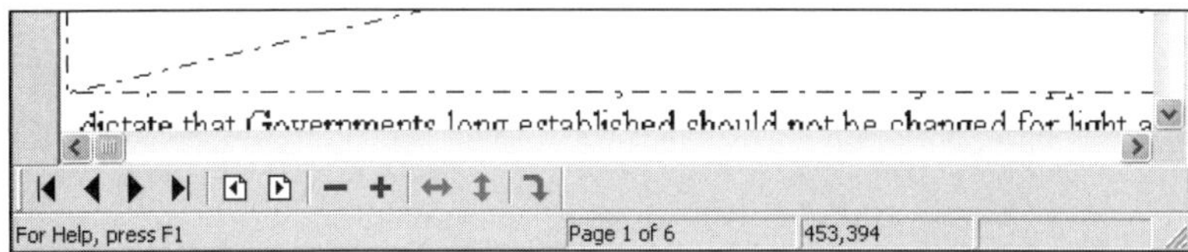

Figure 12-7. *Page numbers and cursor positions displayed on the Opticon screen*

You can hide the status bar by selecting View ➤ Status bar. When the menu item has a check mark, the status bar is visible; when the menu item is toggled so there's no check mark, the status bar is hidden.

Opening Images

You can use Opticon as a standalone program to view images. The File ➤ Open Image menu or the Ctrl+O keystroke combination opens an Open dialog. Double-clicking a file name, or highlighting it and clicking the Open button, opens the image.

■**Note** You can use Opticon as a standalone program to manage imagebases. Chapter 13 explores this capability.

For end users working with Concordance databases, a much more common method of opening Opticon is to launch it from Concordance using the Camera button located on the button bar at the bottom of the Concordance screen when any one of the Browse, Edit, or Table views are active. Opticon launches and displays the first image associated with a document record if the following conditions are met:

- Opticon is configured as the database's image viewer.

  The Concordance database has one field that's set as an image key. If no field is set, the error message displayed in Figure 12-8 is displayed.

- The Opticon imagebase associated with the Concordance database has an entry that matches the image key field value of the currently active record.

  If no match is found, the error message shown in Figure 12-9 is displayed.

Figure 12-8. *If a database has no image key, this error message is displayed when you click the Camera button.*

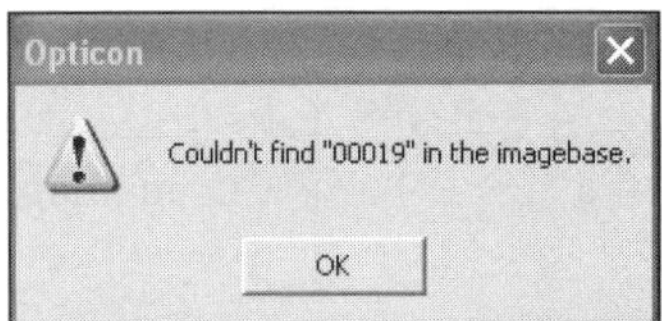

Figure 12-9. *The error message displayed when Opticon cannot locate a matching entry in its imagebase from the image key value passed to it from Concordance*

- The image key referenced in Opticon's imagebase is associated with a valid file path and file name accessible form the end user's workstation. If Opticon attempts to open a file referenced in its imagebase that doesn't exist, the error shown in Figure 12-10 is displayed.

  When Opticon opens the image, you can customize the program's title bar to display the image's alias and complete file path and name.

Figure 12-10. *The error message displayed when Opticon attempts to open a file that doesn't exist*

Note You can modify the message displayed in the title bar of Opticon from the "Title bar" tab of the Imagebase Management dialog. You open this tool by selecting Tools ➤ Imagebase Management; it's covered in Chapter 13.

Viewing Images

Several options exist within Opticon to modify the magnification, orientation, and overall appearance of an image. Most of these options are accessible from Opticon's View menu. Several buttons also modify the appearance of an image.

View Menu

Relevant menu items on the View menu are explained below. Several menu items have sub-menu selections, and those options are listed below the parent menu item. Some menu items have keyboard shortcuts, which are displayed next the menu item in square brackets.

- *Anti-alias*: This menu item is enabled for monochrome images. The term *anti-alias* refers to altering the grayscale hue of pixels along borders and edges in an image. Instead of a stark black and white pixel between lines and shapes, shades of gray are used to blend transitions more smoothly. The effect is to make borders and edges appear less jagged. This menu item has three submenu selections:

    - *None*: No anti-aliasing is used.

    - *Fast (4 shades of gray)*: Uses shades of gray. Borders and edges are made more smooth than if the None option is selected.

    - *Partial (16 shades of gray)*: Uses 16 shades of gray. Borders and edges are made more smooth than if the "Fast (4 shades of gray)" option is selected.

- *Image Type*: Opticon can optimize scaling if it's informed of the type of image being displayed. This menu item has three submenu selections:

    - *Textual [Ctrl+T]*: Used when an image consists primarily of text.

    - *Line Image [Ctrl+L]*: Used for line art.

    - *Photograph [Ctrl+H]*: Used if an image is a monochrome photograph.

- *Invert Color [I]*: Produces a negative effect on monochrome images: blacks are rendered as whites; whites are rendered as blacks.

- *Zoom in 50% [+]*: Magnifies an image by +50 percent, effectively "zooming" in. Depending on the current magnification of an image when this option is selected, some portions of an image might exceed the boundaries of the Opticon window and not be visible. You can resize an image at any time to fit entirely within the Opticon window.

- *Zoom out 50% [-]*: Magnifies an image by -50 percent, effectively "zooming" out. Depending on the current magnification of an image when this option is selected, the image might be smaller than the boundaries of the Opticon window. You can resize an image at any time to fit entirely within the Opticon window.

- *Zoom on Selection [Alt+Z]*: Used in conjunction with the Mark button ⬚ (located on the Standard toolbar), which highlights a rectangular region of an image. When a section of an image is highlighted in this way, the Zoom on Selection menu item centers and magnifies so that it fills the Opticon window.

- *Zoom in a Little [Ctrl +]*: Magnifies the image by small amount.

- *Zoom out a Little [Ctrl -]*: Reduces magnification by a small amount.

- *Fit to Width [W]*: Forces an image to fit into the width defined by the borders of the Opticon window.

- *Fit to Height [H]*: Forces an image to fit into the height defined by the borders of the Opticon window.

- *Full Screen [Ctrl+F]*: This menu item maximizes the Opticon window so that it fills the workstation's monitor. This is known as *full-screen mode*. If Opticon is already in full-screen mode, toggling this option returns the Opticon window size to the last setting before full-screen mode was activated.

- *Rotate from Original Orientation*: This menu item has three submenu selections, which you can use to rotate an image. Any orientation selected from this submenu is applied to the image's initial orientation:

  - *Left [<]*: Rotates the image by 90 degrees counter-clockwise from its original orientation.

  - *Right [>]*: Rotates the image by 90 degrees clockwise from its original orientation.

  - *Flip [/]*: Rotates the image a full 180 degrees from its original orientation.

- *Rotate from Current Orientation*: This menu item has three submenu selections, which are similar to the options described for the menu item Rotate from Original Orientation. However, these settings are applied to an image's orientation as it currently appears in Opticon.

  - *Left [Left Arrow]*: Rotates the image by 90 degrees counter-clockwise from its current orientation.

  - *Right [Right Arrow]*: Rotates the image by 90 degrees clockwise from its current orientation.

  - *Flip [Down Arrow]*: Rotates the image a full 180 degrees from its current orientation.

- *Reset Rotation to Original*: Returns the image orientation to its original state when the image was first opened by Opticon.

- *Mirror Horizontally*: Mirrors an image horizontally.

- *Mirror Vertically*: Mirrors an image vertically.

- *Mirror Both*: Mirrors an image both horizontally and vertically.

- *Reset Mirror*: Removes any mirroring, and returns an image's orientation to its original state when the image was first opened by Opticon.

Tools Menu

By default, any magnification and orientation settings for a given image are lost when a new image is rendered in Opticon. Unless otherwise specified, Opticon presents each image with its original orientation, and sizes the image so that it fits within the Opticon window. Two menu items under the Tools menu affect how Opticon handles the magnification and orientation for successive images:

- *Sticky zoom*: When toggled on, a check mark will appear next to this menu item, indicating that Sticky zoom is active. Magnification settings applied to the current image are carried over to any new images rendered in Opticon.

- *Sticky rotate*: When toggled on, a check mark will appear next to this menu item, indicating that Sticky rotate is active. Orientation settings applied to the current image are carried over to any new images rendered in Opticon.

Standard Button Bar

By default, the Standard button bar is docked to the upper edge of the Opticon screen, just below menu items.

Table 12-1 explains the functions of buttons on the Standard toolbar that pertain to image appearance. These buttons can complement the View and Tools menu options described earlier.

Table 12-1. *Buttons on the Standard Toolbar*

Name	Button	Description
Mark		Highlights a rectangular section in an image. To mark a section, you must click the button first, then click and hold in the image. Moving the mouse resizes the selection until you release the mouse button.
Mark Zoom		When you click this button, you can magnify a specific selection of an image by left-clicking inside the image, then dragging to create a region. Opticon initially displays a hollow rectangle as a visual cue to the boundaries of the image. Releasing the left mouse button magnifies the contents of the image bounded by the hollow rectangle.
Rectangle Magnifier		Creates a permanent magnifier to zoom in on a fixed region of an image until the button is clicked again. You can set the magnifier's size and amount of magnification on the Rectangular Magnifier tab of the Preferences dialog.
Window Zoom		Clicking this button and then clicking anywhere in an image creates a Magnify popup dialog that magnifies a fixed region of the image, as shown in Figure 12-11. The Magnify popup dialog remains open, and updates by magnifying any section of the image that's clicked. You can update the amount of magnification from the popup dialog. Clicking the Close button closes the Magnify popup dialog.
Pan		If an image has been magnified so that portions of it are no longer visible in Opticon, clicking this button will drag the image around the Opticon screen so that hidden areas can be seen. To drag the image, you must press the left mouse button, and keep it depressed while dragging.

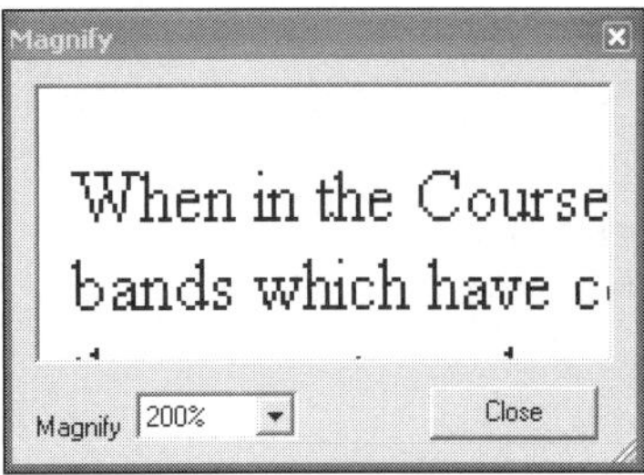

Figure 12-11. *The Magnify popup dialog opens when you click the Window Zoom button. Clicking a different area in an image causes the popup dialog to magnify that region of the image.*

Image Button Bar

The Image button bar contains the icons shown in Table 12-2.

Table 12-2. *Buttons on the Image Toolbar*

Name	Button	Description
Zoom Out	−	Reduces magnification by a small amount.
Zoom In	+	Magnifies the image by small amount.
Fit to Width	↔	Forces an image to fit into the width defined by the borders of the Opticon window.
Fit to Height	↕	Forces an image to fit into the height defined by the borders of the Opticon window.
Rotate Right	↱	Rotates the image by 90 degrees clockwise. The setting is applied to an image's current orientation, so clicking this button four times rotates an image by a full 360 degrees.

Navigating Through Images

A Concordance database record can represent a document that's comprised of several pages. A properly designed Concordance database tracks each document's beginning and ending pages. When used in this way, a Concordance database is said to *unitize* on a document level.

Opticon primarily unitizes at a page level. It can also unitize on document and folder levels. Document, folder, and even box breaks are stored in a database's imagebase, which a Concordance administrator loads. These boundaries aren't required in a database's imagebase, but are necessary for navigation to work smoothly.

■**Note** You can set document, folder, and box breaks from the Edit tab of the Imagebase Management dialog. You open this dialog by selecting Tools ➤ Imagebase Management; it's described in Chapter 13. You can also specify breaks in an imagebase load file, covered in Chapter 13.

While you use a Concordance database to navigate quickly through document records, you can use Opticon to navigate quickly within the pages that define a document. Opticon can also navigate through document records, and if configured properly, can navigate through entire folders containing documents as well. However, at any given time, the contents of the Opticon window correspond to a single image representing a single page.

When Opticon is set as Concordance's default viewer, and is launched from Concordance, administrators and end users should be aware that Concordance and Opticon synchronize. Only those images represented by database records accessible in the last active query in Concordance are accessible to Opticon.

Several options exist within Opticon to assist you when navigating through pages, documents, and folders. All these options are accessible from Opticon's Page menu. Several buttons on the Image toolbar also assist you in navigation.

Page Menu

The following bulleted list explains navigation menu items. These menu items have keyboard shortcuts, which are displayed next to the menu item in square brackets.

- *First [Ctrl+Home]*: Retreats to the first image in a set of images that define a document. If the current image is the first image, selecting this menu item will have no effect.

- *Next [PgDn]*: Advances to the next image in a set of images that define a document. If the current image is the last image of a document record, Opticon will advance to the first image of the next document (if any). When this menu item causes Opticon to cross document boundaries, the Concordance database that launched Opticon will update. The document record corresponding to the next image is made current and active if you enable the "Synchronize paging with Concordance" check box on the General tab of the Preferences dialog.

  If the current image is the last image of all images accessible to Opticon, clicking this button will have no effect.

- *Previous [PgUp]*: Retreats to the previous image in a set of images that define a document. If the current image is the first image of a document record, Opticon will retreat to the last image of the previous document (if any). When this menu item causes Opticon to cross document boundaries, the Concordance database that launched Opticon will update so that the document record corresponding to the previous image is made current and active.

  If the current image is the first image of all images accessible to Opticon, clicking this button will have no effect.

- *Last [Ctrl+End]*: Advances to the last image in a set of images that define a document. If the current image is the last image, selecting this menu item will have no effect.

- *Go to page [G]*: This option opens a "Go to page" popup dialog (see Figure 12-12). Opticon goes directly to the image represented by the number entered into the open text field in the popup dialog. The number entered into the field isn't the image's file name, but represents the *n*th image within a set of images that define a database record. For example, say a database record is represented by five images, and the second image is the current image displayed in Opticon. Entering the number **5** in the field and clicking the OK button causes the fifth (and last) image of the document record to be displayed in Opticon.

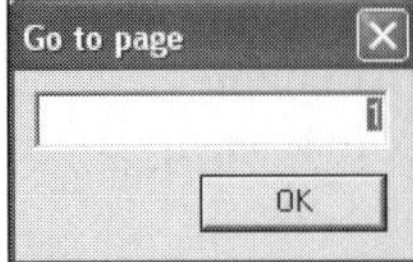

Figure 12-12. *The "Go to page" popup dialog*

Entering a negative number in the field causes Opticon to display the last image of a document record. Entering a number that's greater than the total number of images in a document record also causes Opticon to display the last image.

- *Go to image [Ctrl+G]*: This option opens a "Goto image key" popup dialog (see Figure 12-13). This popup dialog displays all image keys stored in a database's imagebase in a list box. You can scroll through a list of image keys. Entering the first few characters of an image key name in the open text field causes the list box to locate and highlight a best match. Double-clicking a highlighted image key or clicking the "Go to" button closes the popup dialog and causes the highlighted image to be displayed in Opticon.

  Clicking the Cancel button closes the popup dialog.

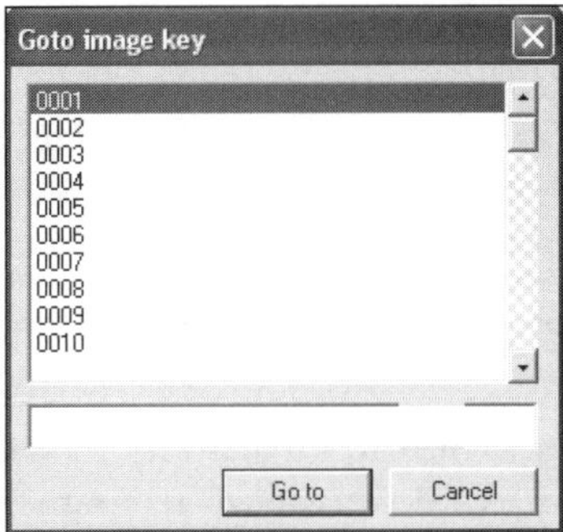

Figure 12-13. *The "Go to image key" popup dialog*

- *Next document [Ctrl+PgDn]*: Advances to the first image of the next document. If there's no document record after the current one, clicking this button will have no effect.

- *Previous document [Ctrl+PgUp]*: Retreats to the first image of the previous document. If there's no document record before the current one, clicking this button will have no effect.

- *Next Folder [Shift+PgDn]*: Advances to the first image of the first document in the next folder, if folder breaks have been loaded into a database's imagebase.

- *Previous Folder [Shift+PgUp]*: Retreats to the first image of the first document in the previous folder, if folder breaks have been loaded into a database's imagebase.

Image Toolbar

By default, the Image button bar is docked to the lower edge of the Opticon screen, just above the status bar (if displayed). Table 12-3 explains the function of buttons on the Image toolbar that affect image and document navigation. In all cases, these buttons perform the same function as the corresponding menu items described earlier.

Table 12-3. *Buttons on the Image Toolbar*

Name	Button	Description
First	◄	Retreats to the first image in a set of images that define a document. If the current image is the first image, selecting this menu item will have no effect.
Previous	◄	Retreats to the previous image in a set of images that define a document. If the current image is the first image of a document record, Opticon will retreat to the last image of the previous document (if any). When this menu item causes Opticon to cross document boundaries, the Concordance database that launched Opticon will update, so that the document record corresponding to the previous image will be made current and active. If the current image is the first image of all images accessible to Opticon, clicking this button will have no effect.
Next	►	Advances to the next image in a set of images that define a document. If the current image is the last image of a document record, Opticon will advance to the first image of the next document (if any). When this menu item causes Opticon to cross document boundaries, the Concordance database that launched Opticon will update so that the document record corresponding to the next image will be made current and active. If the current image is the last image of all images accessible to Opticon, clicking this button will have no effect.
Last	►	Advances to the last image in a set of images that define a document. If the current image is the last image, selecting this menu item will have no effect.
Previous Document		Retreats to the first image of the previous document. If there's no document record before the current one, clicking this button will have no effect.
Next Document		Advances to the first image of the next document. If there's no document record after the current one, clicking this button will have no effect.

Using Redlines

Redlines are text, shapes, and other visual artifacts created by end users using drawing tools accessible from the Redlines toolbar. Information about redlines—such as text, size, and horizontal and vertical position—is stored in a Concordance database that exists in the same directory as primary database files. Opticon creates and manages this database, and users don't interact with it directly. Opticon creates this database the first time a user creates a new redline, and it's named after the Concordance database that was used to launch Opticon. Redlines databases have a -REDLINES suffix. Other files that work together to define a redline database also have a -REDLINES suffix. For example, say the primary Concordance database is named DOCREVIEW.DCB. A user launches Opticon from this database, views an image, then creates a redline using the drawing tools described in the section "Redlines Toolbar." A DOCREVIEW-REDLINES.DCB file is created. Other files that are created are named DOCREVIEW-REDLINES.DCT (the redlines dictionary file) and DOCREVIEW-REDLINES.IVT (the redlines inverted text file).

Because Opticon and Concordance store metadata about the visual artifacts that appear on an image, the redlines aren't a permanent part of an image file unless the end user or an administrator specifically instructs Opticon to *burn* redlines onto an image by saving an image from the File menu (described in the section "File Menu") or during a document production (described in Chapter 14). Until redlines are burned onto an image, they can be thought of as hovering over an image. At any time, you can toggle redline visibility from the Tools menu (described in the section "Tools Menu") to reveal hidden sections of an image.

Another benefit of saving metadata about redlines in a valid Concordance database is that any textual comments are indexed and accessible through a search interface native to Opticon. This interface communicates with the Concordance redlines files described in the previous paragraph. For this feature to work, end users and the administrator should be aware that a redlines database must be indexed, reindexed, or packed accordingly as users update redlines. Indexing and reindexing creates index files that facilitate efficient and speedy search retrieval. The section "Searching Redlines" describes methods used to search through redline comments.

Global Preferences

You set options controlling the global behavior of redlines from the Redline tab of Opticon's Preferences dialog (see Figure 12-14).

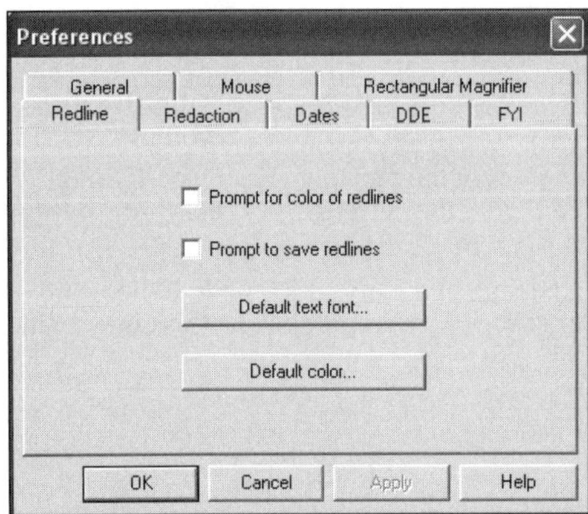

Figure 12-14. *The Redline tab of Opticon's Preferences dialog. Options selected from this tab affect the global behavior of redactions.*

You can set the following global options from this tab of Opticon's Preferences dialog:

- *Prompt for color of redlines*: If this check box is enabled, Opticon will prompt the user to define the color of each new redline as it is created, using the Color dialog (see Figure 12-15). When enabled, the Color dialog will open immediately after a redline is created. You should select this option if you intend to create a series of redlines, each with its own custom color.

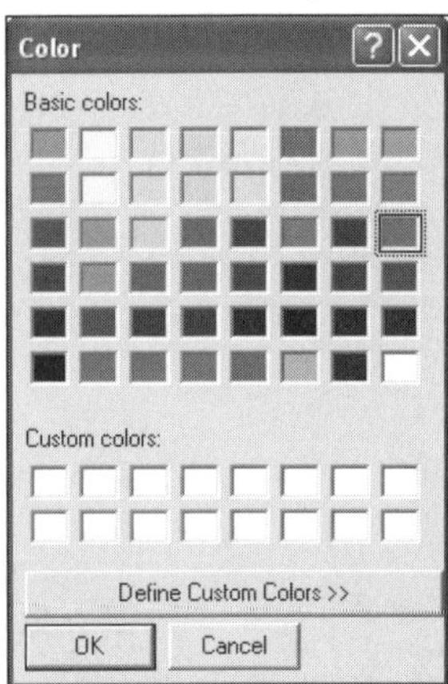

Figure 12-15. *The Color dialog. You can select a predefined color from the "Basic colors" palette, or define a new color using the Define Custom Colors button.*

At any time, you can reopen this same dialog by right-clicking over a specific redline. This causes a shortcut menu to pop up, with a "Change color" option. A color selected in this way overrides any previous color sections, and are applied only to the selected redline.

- *Prompt to save redlines*: If this check box is enabled, Opticon will prompt you to save the redline image for an image when it's closed or when you navigate to a new image (see Figure 12-16). By default, Opticon automatically saves redline information.

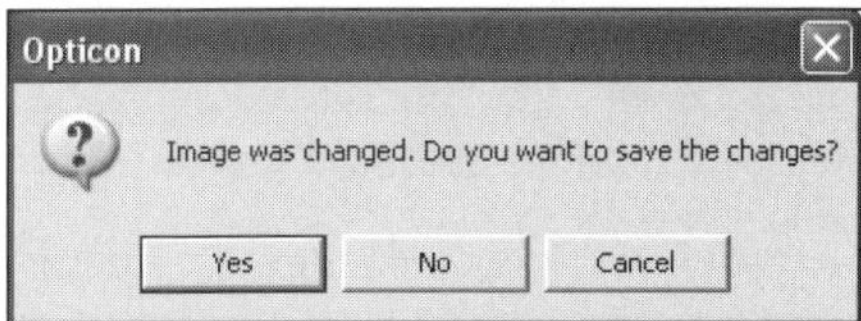

Figure 12-16. *The message box displayed when the "Prompt to save redlines" option is enabled*

- *Default text font*: Clicking this button opens the Font dialog (see Figure 12-17). This dialog is used to set the default font face, style, size, and other formatting options applied to text for those redlines that contain text.

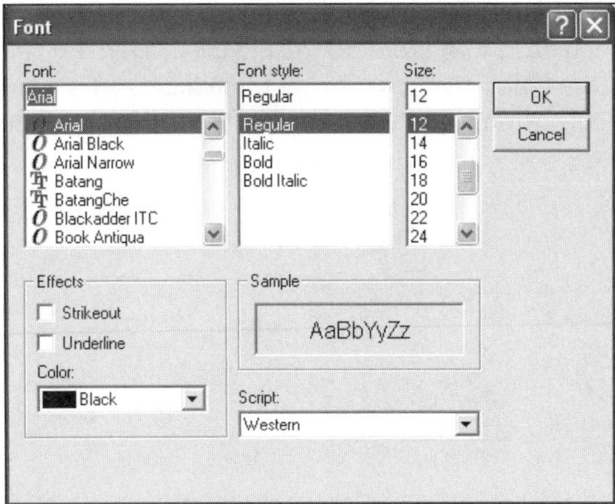

Figure 12-17. *In the Font dialog, you can select font styles that will be applied to all annotation text by default.*

At any time, you can reopen this same dialog by right-clicking over a specific redline, if the redline contains text. This causes a shortcut menu to pop up, with a "Change font" option. Font styles selected in this way override any previous font selections and are applied only to the selected redline.

- *Default color:* Clicking this button opens the Color dialog displayed in Figure 12-15. The color selected from this dialog is applied by default to any new redlines. When first installed, this color is yellow. At any time, you can reopen this same dialog by right-clicking over a specific redline. This causes a shortcut menu to pop up, with a "Change color" option. A color selected in this way overrides any previous color selections and is applied only to the selected redline.

Redlines Menu

The following menu items from the Redlines menu control how Opticon manages a database's redlines database, if one exists:

- *Index:* Performs an initial index of a redlines database. Indexing is necessary when a new redlines database is initially created. Thereafter, a redlines database must be reindexed.

- *Reindex:* Reindexing is required to update a redlines database's index, a necessary step to keep searches up to date and accurate. A database's index must be updated when end users add, modify, or otherwise edit redlines. A check mark next to this menu item indicates that a redlines database must be reindexed.

- *Pack*: When a redline is deleted, only the visual representation of the redline is removed. Metadata about the redline still exists in the redlines database. You use the Pack menu item to truncate the redlines database and remove any references to deleted redlines. Depending on Concordance and Opticon usage, packing might not be necessary every day, but should be scheduled in a regular maintenance cycle to keep Opticon searches efficient.

- *Search*: Opens an Opticon search window. This feature is described in the section "Searching Redlines."

Tools Menu

The Tools menu has an important feature that you can use to affect the appearance of redlines: Toggle Redlines [Ctrl+R] (this menu item's keyboard shortcut appears in square brackets). Each time Opticon opens a new image, any redlines associated with the image are visible by default. You can make redlines over the current image in Opticon temporarily invisible by selecting this menu item. Reselecting the menu item makes invisible redlines visible again. You can determine the state of redline visibility by the check mark that might appear next to the menu item: a check mark means that redlines are visible.

File Menu

The File menu has important features that you can use to make redlines a permanent artifact of an image or to force redlines to appear over an image when it's printed:

- *Save as*: This menu item opens a "Save as" dialog, displayed in Figure 12-18.

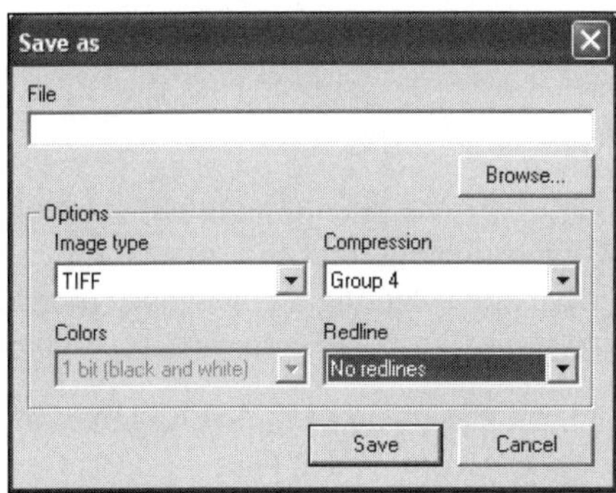

Figure 12-18. *The "Save as" dialog. Note the Redline drop-down box.*

The Redline drop-down box has two selections:

- *No redlines*: Redlines aren't saved with the image.

- *Burn redlines onto image*: Redlines are burned permanently onto the image. This option only works with monochrome images. Color redlines are converted to black and white.

- *Print [Ctrl+P]*: This menu item opens the Print dialog and is described in detail in the section "The Options Tab," under the section heading "Printing Images." The Options tab of this dialog controls how redlines appear on an image when it's printed from Opticon.

Redlines Toolbar

By default, the Redlines button bar is docked to the left edge of the Opticon screen. You use buttons on this toolbar to resize, move, and create redlines. In addition, the Search button opens a search interface that's used to search for text contained in the text of redlines.

The following bulleted list explains the function of each button on the Redlines toolbar. You use most of these buttons to draw redlines over an image. To create a redline, you must click the appropriate button first. To draw the actual redline, you must drag the mouse pointer over the area on which the redline should appear. Depending on the type of redline, you might be prompted for additional information needed to define the redline fully.

Right-clicking over a redline opens a shortcut menu with options that vary according to the type of redline. The shortcut menu always has Move and Delete options.

- *Move redline* ⊕ : Used to move the position of a redline. To move a specific redline, you hover the move icon over the redline, click and hold, and then drag the redline to the desired location. You should click the "Move redline" button again to return Opticon to normal viewing mode.

  An alternative method used to move a redline is to right-click over the redline and then select the Move option. When you use this method, you drag the redline to the desired location and then left-click to release it.

- *Resize redline* ⌐ : Used to resize a redline. To resize a redline, click the "Resize redline" button first, then click and hold over the appropriate redline. Dragging the mouse pointer to a new position causes the redline to resize. You should click the "Resize redline" button again to return Opticon to normal viewing mode.

- *Highlight* ✎ : Highlights a section of an image with the default highlight color defined from the Redline tab of the Opticon's Preferences dialog. You can also change a highlight's color by right-clicking over the highlight and selecting the "Change color" option, which opens a Color dialog (see Figure 12-15).

  The visual effect of this type of redline is the same as using a highlighting marker on a printed page. An example of a Highlight redline is displayed in Figure 12-19.

Figure 12-19. *A section of an image highlighted using the Highlight redline*

When the Highlight button is clicked and the mouse hovered over any area in an image, the standard mouse arrow changes to a highlight pen. You create a Highlight redline by dragging the pen icon over the section to be highlighted.

To delete a highlight, right-click over the highlight, then select the "Delete box" option.

- *Redaction* ⊠ : You use a *redaction* to hide portions of an image. Redactions are often used when images containing sensitive information are released to outside agencies. Redactions in Opticon take the form of a rectangular box. Figure 12-20 displays an example of a Redaction redline.

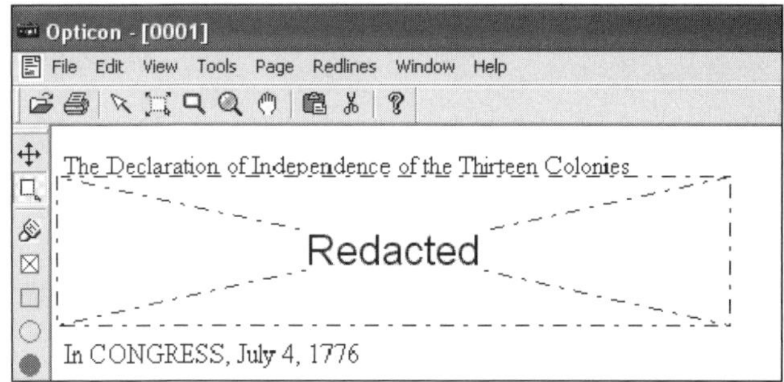

Figure 12-20. *An example of a Redaction redline. You can edit or remove the word "Redacted," which appears inside the redaction, using the "Change redaction text" option from the shortcut menu opened by right-clicking over the redaction.*

When you click the Redaction button and hover the mouse over any area in an image, the standard mouse arrow changes to a redaction icon. To create the Redaction redline, click and drag the icon over the desired section.

To delete a redaction, right-click over the Redaction redline, then select the "Delete redaction" option.

To change the redaction's fill color, right-click over the redaction, then select the "Change color" option, which opens the same Color dialog.

To change the text that's embedded in the redaction box, right-click over the redaction and select one of the options that appear under the "Change redaction text" shortcut menu item. By default, there are three options, though you can modify these selections:

- *<none>*: No text is embedded in the redaction box. This term is included by default in the shortcut menu options under the "Change redaction text" shortcut menu item.

- *Redacted*: The word "Redacted" appears in the redaction box. This term is included by default in the shortcut menu options under the "Change redaction text" shortcut menu item. You can display other terms here using the methods described in the upcoming bulleted list.

- *Edit redaction text*: Opens the Redaction tab of Opticon's Preferences dialog (see Figure 12-21). You can also open this tool from Opticon's Tools ➤ Preferences menu.

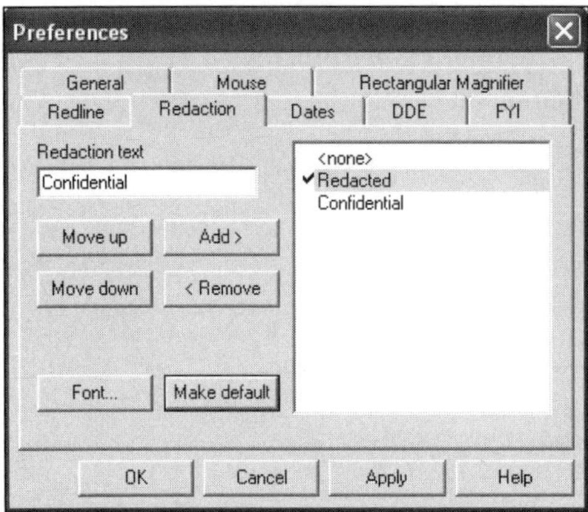

Figure 12-21. *The Redaction tab of Opticon's Preferences dialog. Options on this tab affect how redlines appear over an image.*

The list box on the right displays redaction terms. By default, this consists of <none> and Redacted. The term that has a check box next to it is considered the default redaction term, and is embedded in any new Redaction redline. The following list describes other features on this tab:

- *Redaction text*: To add a new redaction term, enter the text of the term into this empty field.

- *Move up*: Highlighting a redaction term in the list box and clicking this button causes it to move up the list. This list order defines the order in which terms appear in the shortcut menu.

- *Move down*: Highlighting a redaction term in the list box and clicking this button causes it to move down the list. This list order defines the order in which terms appear in the shortcut menu.

- *Add*: Adds the redaction term entered in the "Redaction text" field to the list box. The term appears in the redaction shortcut menu.

- *Remove*: Removes a redaction term from the list. You must first select and highlight the term to be removed in the list. The term will no longer appear in the redaction shortcut menu.

- *Font*: Opens the same Font dialog shown previously in Figure 12-17. Options selected from this dialog affect the font style, color, size, and other properties of redaction terms alone, not any text associated with other redlines.

- *Make default*: Makes the highlighted redaction term the default term when new redactions are created. The default redaction term is denoted by a check mark.

The following sections describe other options on the Redlines toolbar.

Hollow Box

Another type of redline is the "Hollow box" option 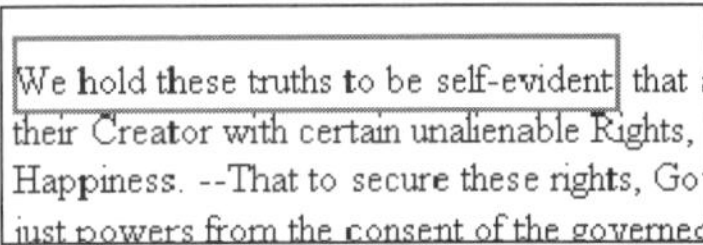, which creates a hollow rectangular box. This type of redline doesn't mask portions of an image, but outlines them. Figure 12-22 displays an example of a hollow rectangular box.

Figure 12-22. *An example of a hollow rectangular box redline*

To delete a hollow box redline, right-click over the box, then select the "Delete box" option.

The border color of the hollow box is, by default, the same color defined as the default color from the Redline tab of Opticon's Preferences dialog. To change the box's border color, right-click over the box, then select the "Change color" option, which opens the same Color dialog shown previously in Figure 12-15. However, color options selected for a specific "Hollow box" redline affect that specific instance only, and don't override default color settings for other redlines.

Hollow Ellipse

The "Hollow ellipse" option 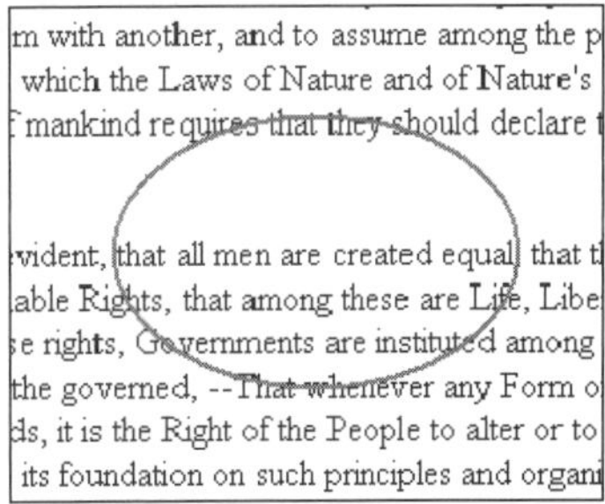 creates a hollow ellipse. This type of redline doesn't mask portions of an image, but outlines them. Figure 12-23 displays an example of a hollow ellipse.

Figure 12-23. *An example of a hollow ellipse redline*

To delete a hollow ellipse redline, right-click over the ellipse, then select the "Delete ellipse" option.

The border color of the hollow ellipse is, by default, the same color defined as the default color from the Redline tab of Opticon's Preferences dialog. To change the ellipse's border color, right-click over the ellipse, then select the "Change color" option, which opens the same Color dialog shown previously in Figure 12-15. However, color options selected for a specific "Hollow ellipse" redline affect that specific instance only, and don't override default color settings for other redlines.

Solid Ellipse

"Solid ellipse" ● creates an ellipse similar to a hollow ellipse, though the shape is filled with color. Figure 12-24 displays an example of a solid ellipse.

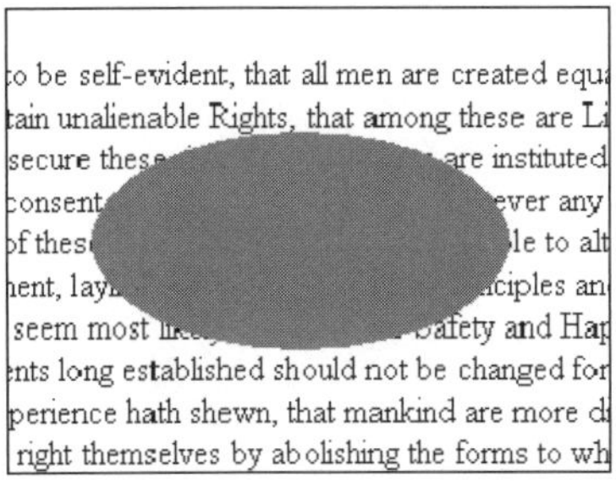

Figure 12-24. *An example of a solid ellipse redline*

To delete a solid ellipse redline, right-click over the ellipse, then select the "Delete ellipse" option.

The fill color of a solid ellipse is, by default, the same color defined as the default color from the Redline tab of Opticon's Preferences dialog. To change the ellipse's fill color, right-click over the ellipse, then select the "Change color" option, which opens the same Color dialog previously shown in Figure 12-15. However, color options selected for a specific "Solid ellipse" redline affect that specific instance only, and don't override default color settings for other redlines.

Text

The Text option A allows you to enter custom text directly over an image. An example of a text redline appears in Figure 12-25.

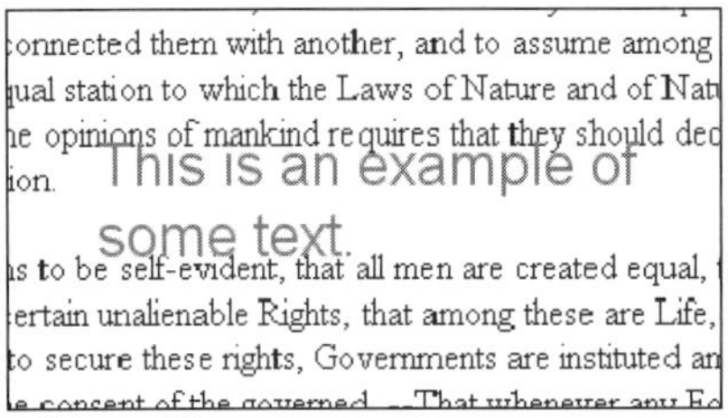

Figure 12-25. *An example of a text redline*

To create a text redline, click the Text button, then drag the cross-hair pointer over a section of an image. When you release the mouse button, Opticon opens a Text dialog (see Figure 12-26).

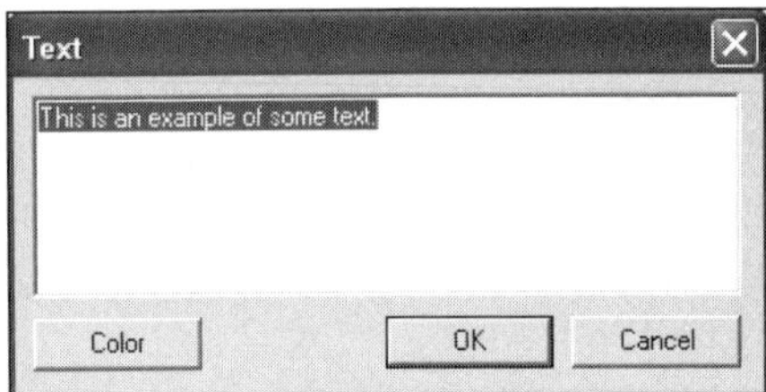

Figure 12-26. *The Text dialog that's used to modify the text associated with the Text redline.*

Text entered in the open text field appears in the redline. You can modify the color of the text by clicking the Color button, which opens the Color dialog previously shown in Figure 12-15. By default, the text color is black. Once you enter the desired text, clicking the OK button closes the dialog and creates the Text redline.

To modify the text in a Text redline, right-click over the redline and select the "Edit annotation" option, or double-click the redline. Either method opens the Text dialog.

To delete a text annotation, right-click over the text annotation and select the "Delete text" option.

To change the color of the text in a text redline, right-click over the redline and select the "Change color" option. This opens the Color dialog shown previously in Figure 12-15. This changes the color of the currently selected text annotation only.

To modify the font style of the text in a text redline, right-click over the Text redline and select the "Change font" option. This opens the Font dialog. Font face and size selected from this dialog alter the appearance of the text in the currently selected Text annotation only.

Line

The Line option ╱ creates a Line redline. An example of a Line redline appears in Figure 12-27.

> When in the Course of human events, it becomes necessary for one people to
> bands which have connected them with another, and to assume among the pow
> the separate and equal station to which the Laws of Nature and of Nature's Go

Figure 12-27. *An example of a Line redline*

To create a Line redline, click the Line button first. The default mouse pointer changes to a cross-hair. Lines may be horizontal, vertical, or diagonal. To start the line, click and hold the mouse button. To terminate the Line redline, move the mouse cross-hair to the desired endpoint, then release the mouse button. The thickness of line redlines is fixed by Opticon and cannot be modified.

To change the color of a Line redline, right-click over the Line redline and select the "Change color" option. This opens the Color dialog previously shown in Figure 12-15. This changes the color of the current Line redline only.

To delete a Line redline, right-click over the Line redline, then select the "Delete line" option.

Note

A Note redline 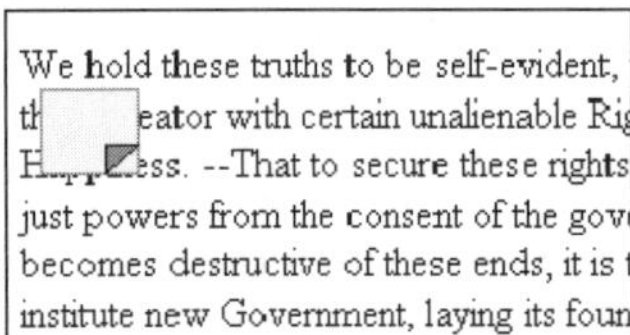 has the appearance of an empty Post-it Note. It can contain a lengthy amount of text (see Figure 12-28). The text of the Note redline isn't immediately visible from the redline itself, regardless of its size. Methods used to display text embedded in a Note redline are described later in this section. The Note redline's fill color is, by default, the same color defined as the default color from the Redline tab of Opticon's Preferences dialog.

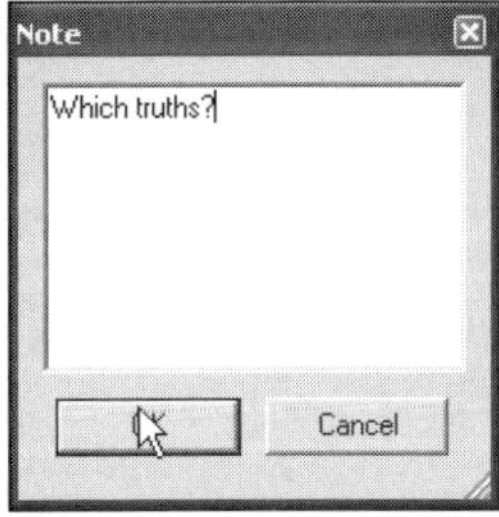

Figure 12-28. *An example of a Note redline*

To create a Note redline, click the Note button first. The default mouse pointer changes to a Note pointer. Click in the image window over the section of text to be described by the note, and drag until the Note redline is the appropriate size. Releasing the mouse button opens a Note dialog (see Figure 12-29).

Figure 12-29. *Text added from the Note dialog is associated with the Note redline.*

The function of this dialog is similar to that of the Text dialog that opens when a user creates a Text redline. Text entered into the open text field is associated with the Note redline. Clicking the OK button closes the Note dialog and returns control to Opticon.

To view or edit the text in a Note redline, right-click over an instance of a Note redline and select the "Edit annotation" option, or double-click inside the Note. The Note dialog is reopened.

To change the fill color of a Note, right-click over the Note and select the "Change color" option. This opens the Color dialog previously shown in Figure 12-15. This changes the color of the current Note only.

To delete a Note redline, right-click over the Note, then select the Delete Note option.

Search

The Search button 🔍 opens an Opticon search window. The following section describes this feature.

Searching Redlines

Clicking the Search button on the Redlines toolbar, or selecting Redlines ➤ Search, opens a Search window in Opticon. Figure 12-30 displays this interface.

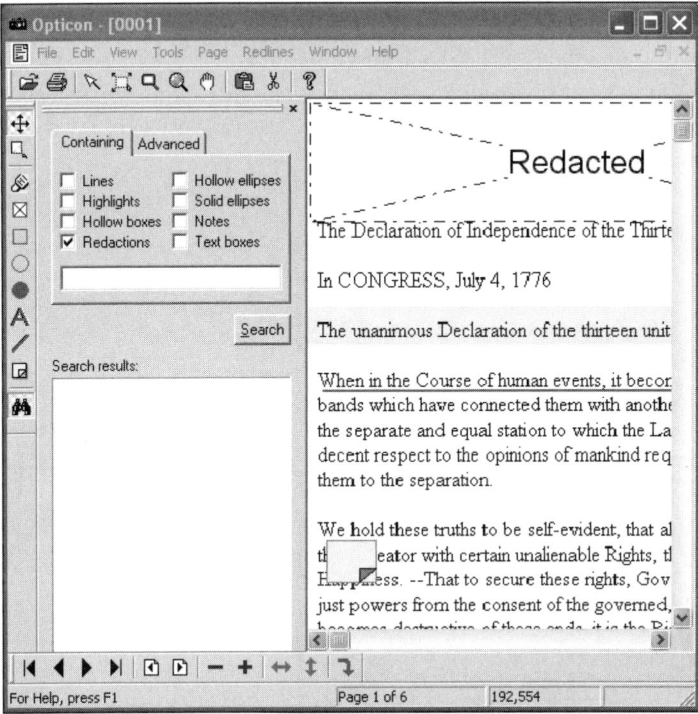

Figure 12-30. *Using the Search window, end users can search for the existence of redlines, and for any text associated with Redactions, Notes, and Text redlines.*

By default, when the Search window is opened, it occupies a section of the Opticon window, as in Figure 12-30. However, the Search window is dockable. Clicking and holding in an open area in the Search window, dragging to another section inside or outside the Opticon screen, and releasing the mouse button detaches the Search window from Opticon (if docked).

The interface provided by Opticon allows users to search through redlines associated with images. Searches can be of redline types, or of text contained within redlines that support text annotations (Text, Notes, and Redactions). Furthermore, you can narrow searches by selecting only those redlines created by specific users. Unlike Concordance, Opticon doesn't maintain a search history. This means that each new search is applied to all images.

Search results are displayed in the "Search results" treeview. A treeview is a special type of list box in which entries (often referred to as *nodes*) can contain subordinate items. You can expand or collapse a specific node by clicking a + (to expand) or – (to collapse) symbol that appears in the node.

In the "Search results" treeview, individual images retrieved from a search are represented by top-level nodes and are associated with a folder icon: 🗀 .

The image's *alias* and *image key* are displayed on top-level nodes. Redlines contained in an image are represented by subordinate nodes and associated with the same symbol used to represent a redline on the buttons on the Redlines toolbar. Clicking a folder icon causes Opticon to navigate to the corresponding image. Clicking a redline's subordinate icon causes Opticon to navigate to the parent image, and causes the specific redline to be made active. When navigating to images in this way, Concordance won't synchronize with Opticon, so that the active record displayed in Concordance isn't changed.

Figure 12-31 shows the "Search results" treeview, with an image node expanded to reveal redline icons. This particular image's alias is 0010, its image key is 0010.TIF, and it contains each type of redline accessible via Opticon.

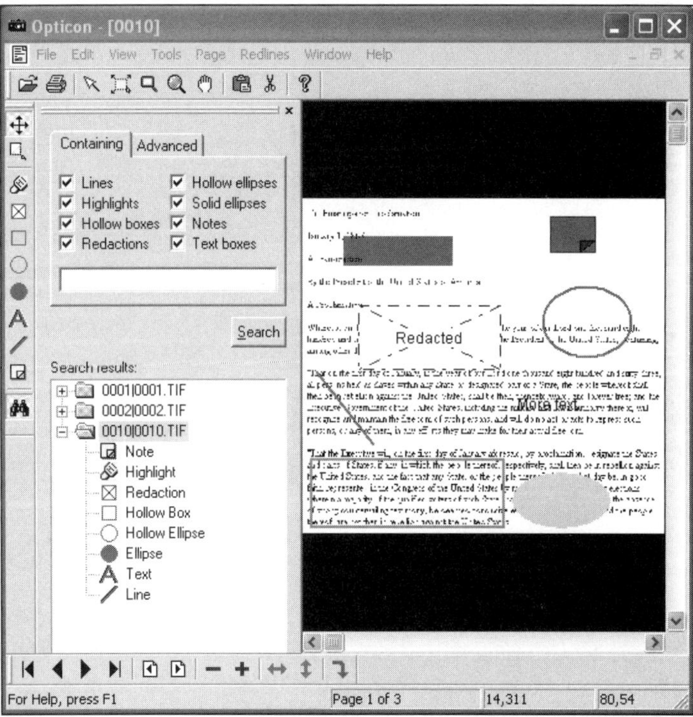

Figure 12-31. *The Search window with the image 0010 expanded to show every type of redaction*

In addition to the "Search results" treeview, the Search window contains two tabs: Containing and Advanced. The following sections explain each tab in detail.

The Containing Tab

You use the Containing tab to specify the types of redlines that will be searches, and any text associated with redlines. It's displayed in Figure 12-32.

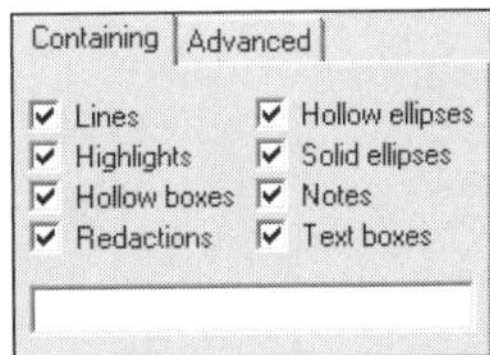

Figure 12-32. *In the Containing tab of the Search window, enabling a check box next to a redline type indicates to Opticon that the redline should be searched.*

Searching by Type of Redline

You can search images according to the types of redlines that have been created on them. To search for a specific type of redline, enable the check box next to the redline's label. Clicking the Search button activates the search and locates images. When used in this way, retrieved images that are displayed in the "Search results" treeview display only those redline types that have been enabled. For example, if you elect to search for "Hollow ellipses" alone, an image that contains two Hollow Ellipse redlines is retrieved and appears as a top-level node in the "Search results" treeview. Expanding the node reveals two separate subordinate nodes representing "Hollow ellipses." The image might contain other redlines types, but because you elected to search "Hollow ellipses" alone, only this type of redline is displayed (see Figure 12-33).

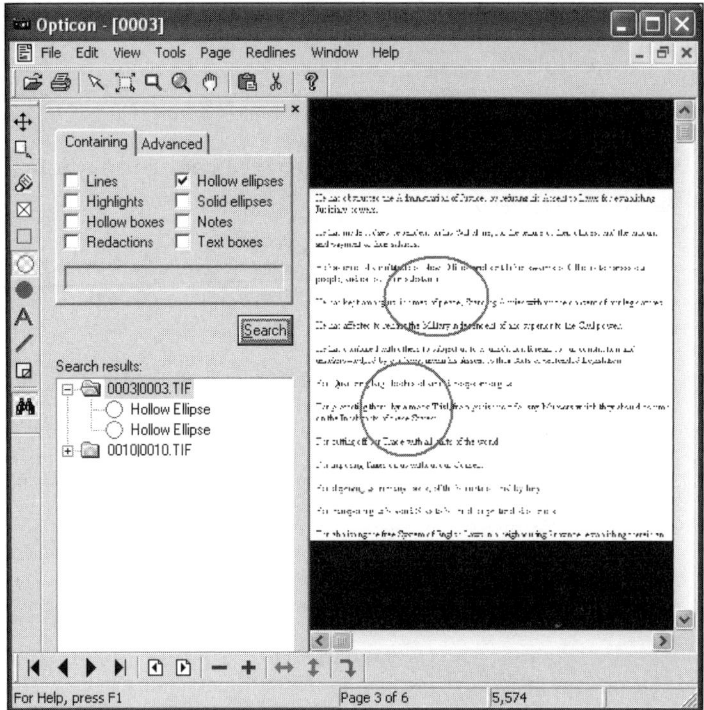

Figure 12-33. *The Search results treeview after a search that located an image that contains two Hollow Ellipse redlines. The image might contain other types of redlines, but they aren't displayed in the treeview because the search was only of hollow ellipses.*

Searching for Text

The empty text field under redline types is unlocked when you enable the Notes, Redactions, and Text boxes redline types. Clicking the Search button retrieves images with redactions that contain text entered in this field. The text associated with redactions is stored in a database's redlines database in a PARAGRAPH field. This means that you can use the methods described in Chapter 9 to search PARAGRAPH fields to locate keywords and phrases in redlines. The same operators described in that chapter apply to a database's redlines database as well. Take the following search:

```
APPLES ORANGES
```

It's equivalent to this one:

```
APPLES adj0 ORANGES
```

Only those redlines containing the text APPLES ORANGES will be retrieved. The following search locates only those redlines in which the term ORANGES appears within five or less words after the term APPLES:

```
APPLES adj5 ORANGES
```

Retrieved images are displayed in the "Search results" treeview as top-level nodes, and those redactions matching specified search criteria appear as subordinate nodes.

When you click a Notes redline's icon in the "Search results" treeview, the image containing the redline will be displayed in Opticon, and the Notes popup dialog will appear, displaying the text embedded in the note. When you click a Text redline's icon, the image and redline will activate in Opticon, and search terms in the Text redline will be highlighted. When you click a Redaction redline's icon, the image containing the redline will be displayed in Opticon, and that redaction made active.

When searching for text within redlines, you should be aware that the redline icons that appear under retrieved image nodes are only displayed if the redline text conforms to the search logic. A search for a Redaction redline containing the redaction term "Redacted" may locate redactions within an image, but any redaction on an image with a different term won't be displayed in the "Search results" treeview.

The Advanced Tab

The Advanced tab displays a list of users who have created redlines. Clicking a user name retrieves only those images that contain redlines created by that user (see Figure 12-34).

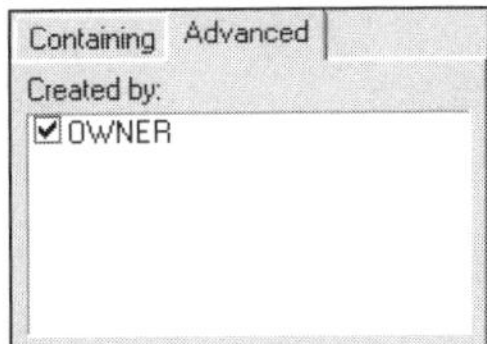

Figure 12-34. *The Advanced tab of the Search window*

Printing Images

You print images from Opticon using the Print dialog. You can activate this dialog from the File ➤ Print menu, by pressing the Ctrl+P keyboard combination, or by clicking the Printer button 🖨 on the Standard toolbar.

This dialog has four tabs that control the appearance and number of images to print: Print, Header & Footer, Options, and Setup. The following sections describe each tab of the dialog in detail.

The Print Tab

Selections from this tab control the range of images to be printed, the number of copies, and if a print profile containing selections from a print session should be opened or saved. It's displayed in Figure 12-35.

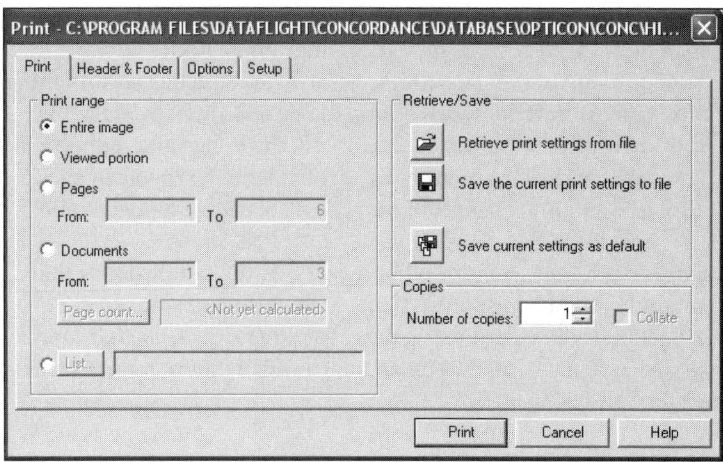

Figure 12-35. *A variety of options are accessible from the Print tab of the Print dialog, from specifying a document range, to calculating a page count, to saving settings to an external print profile.*

Print Range

The "Print range" options control which images are printed. To enable a particular option, you must select the radio button adjacent to the option:

- *Entire image*: Prints the current image only. The entire image is printed.

- *Viewed portion*: Prints only that part of an image that's currently viewed in Opticon. Recall that magnifying sections of an image might cause portions of the image to spill off the viewable Opticon screen. If you select this option, unviewed portions of an image aren't printed.

- *Pages*: The From and To text fields display the total number of images that define the current document record. Changing the From and To values causes some subset of the total number of pages to print. For example, say a document record is defined by ten separate images. When the Print dialog is initially opened, the From field contains 1 and the To field contains 10. Entering **5** in the From field and **7** in the To field prints the fifth, sixth, and seventh images only.

- *Documents*: The From and To text fields display the total number of document records accessible from the last active query in Concordance. If Opticon is opened as a stand-alone application, this option will be disabled. Changing the From and To values causes some subset of the total number of documents to print. For example, say the Concordance query represents ten separate documents. When the Print dialog is initially opened, the From field contains 1 and the To field contains 10. Entering **5** in the From field and **7** in the To field prints images from the fifth, sixth, and seventh document records only.

- *Page count*: Sometimes, it isn't known just how many individual images are represented by a document range defined by a Concordance query. Opticon can calculate the total number of pages contained in a document range. Clicking the Page Count button causes Opticon to add up the total number of pages in each document and to display a sum in the text field.

- *List*: The List button launches an Open dialog. You use the dialog to select a valid Opticon print file. You use this option to print specific images listed in a properly structured, comma-delimited ASCII digital file. The format of the print file is as follows:

```
db,ik,pages,redlines,reserved,upper_left,upper_right,
lower_left,lower_right,paper_source,extra_text
```

Each entry is defined as follows:

- db *(database)*: The full path to the imagebase, including any drive letter or Universal Naming Convention (UNC) mapping, excluding extension.

- ik *(image key)*: The image key as it appears in the Concordance imagebase.

- pages: The number of pages to print, including this image. Normally you can set this value to 1 if you remember to specify each page in the list file.

- reserved: Don't specify anything for this value.

- upper_left: Specifies the text to insert in the upper left corner of the image.

- upper_right: Specifies the text to insert in the upper right corner of the image.

- lower_left: Specifies the text to insert in the lower left corner of the image.

- lower_right: Specifies the text to insert in the lower right corner of the image.

- paper_source: Specifies the driver-dependent paper tray.

- extra text: The text to be included on the extra sheet.

Retrieve/Save

You can save options selected during a print session for later use in a separate file that has an .OPF file extension (see Table 12-4).

Table 12-4. *Buttons Associated with the Retrieve/Save Section of the Print Tab*

Option	Button	Result
Retrieve print settings from file		Opens an Open dialog that you can use to navigate to and open a print profile.
Save the current print settings to file		Opens a "Save as" dialog that you can use to navigate to a folder and save current settings to a Opticon print file.
Save the current print settings as default		Current selections from the print session are saved so that they appear every time the Print dialog is opened in new print sessions.

Copies

Selections in this group of options control the number of copies of each image that will print:

- *Number of copies*: You can use the text field's up and down arrows to specify the number of copies that will print.

- *Collate*: If the destination printer supports collation, this check box will force printed output to be collated. The first set of pages (or documents) will print, then the second set, and so on. If this option isn't selected, the first image will print *n* (as set in the "Number of copies" field) times, then the second image, and so on.

The Header & Footer Tab

Options on the Header & Footer tab control what information, if any, is printed on the header and footer of images. An image's header and footer are each divided into two zones, for a total of four sections: upper left, upper right, lower left, and lower right. Each section is represented by a drop-down box (see Figure 12-36).

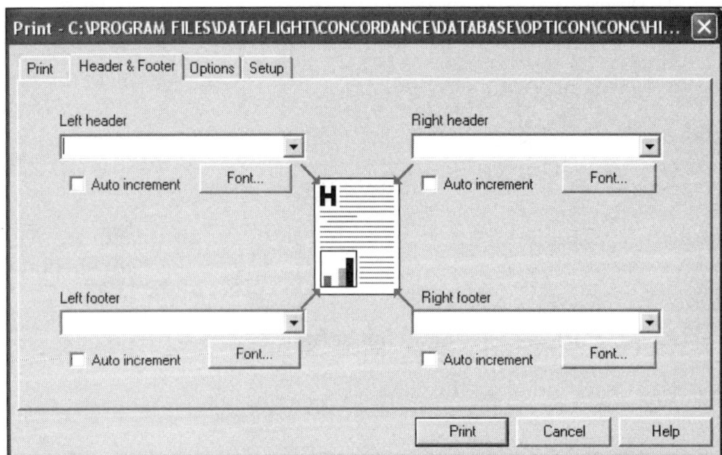

Figure 12-36. *The Header & Footer tab of the Print dialog*

You can customize font styles using the Font buttons adjacent to each drop-down box. Clicking a Font button opens a Font dialog.

The list associated with each drop-down box contains two types of items: database field names and calculated values. Database field names appear in upper case, while calculated values are bracketed by angle brackets (see Table 12-5). Additionally, you can manually key data into these fields.

Table 12-5. *Calculated Value Options, Descriptions and Examples*

Value Name	Description	Example
`<Date & Time>`	The date and time that an image is printed	05/09/2006 08:57 PM
`<Date>`	The date an image is produced	05/09/2006
`<Document number>`	The sequential number of the document being produced	Document 1 of 2
`<Page number>`	The page number of the image within a document	Page 1 of 6
`<Production number>`	Production number values defined from the Numbering dialog	PROD0001
`<Time>`	The time an image is produced	08:57 pm

Note You can configure the format of dates and times from Opticon's Preferences dialog on the Dates tab. You open this dialog from Opticon's Tools ➤ Preferences menu.

Entering or selecting a value from the drop-down box stamps data on an image's header or footer as it's printed. In practice, this tab functions like the Header & Footer dialog of the Production Wizard described in Chapter 14. The only difference is the output: document productions create electronic files, while printing produces paper copies.

The Options Tab

Selections from the Options tab control how redlines appear on images, if a separator sheet should be used, and if printing errors should halt production or be written to a separate file (see Figure 12-37).

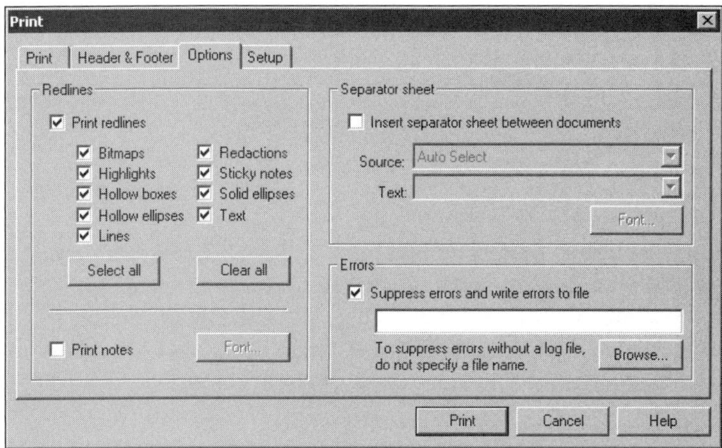

Figure 12-37. *Options on the Options tab of the Print dialog affect how redlines will appear on the printed page. The end user can also specify if a separator sheet will be inserted between each set of pages that represent a document record.*

Redlines

If the "Print redlines" check box is enabled, redlines can be printed directly onto images. Once enabled, check boxes corresponding to different types of redlines are unlocked. Enabling a redline's check box causes it to be printed. You can use the "Select all" and "Clear all" buttons to enable or disable all check boxes, respectively.

The "Print notes" check box determines if the text embedded within Notes redlines should be printed. If enabled, Notes text will print pages after the image is printed. You can use the Font button to specify how this text should be displayed.

Separator Sheet

If you enable the "Insert separator sheet between documents" check box, Opticon will print an additional sheet between each set of images that define a document record.

Source

You use the Source option to select the printer's paper feed source of the separator page.

Text

You use the Text option to specify any text that will be printed on each separator sheet. Text appears in the center of the separator sheet. You can manually key data into this field or select options from the drop-down box, which includes fields from the Concordance database that launched Opticon, or calculated fields displayed in Table 12-6.

Table 12-6. *Calculated Value Options, Descriptions, and Examples Used on a Separator Sheet*

Value Name	Description	Example
<Date & Time>	The date and time that an image is printed	05/09/2006 08:57 pm
<Date>	The date an image is produced	05/09/2006
<Document number>	The sequential number of the document being produced	Document 1 of 2
<Time>	The time an image is produced	08:57 pm

You can use the Font button to specify the font style of separator sheet text.

Errors

If Opticon attempts to produce an image for which there is no original file, an error occurs. Processing halts, and as the administrator, you must provide feedback to the program before it can continue. For a large document production, this can be tedious. Selecting this option causes Opticon to record any errors in an ASCII file that can be opened with a text editor post-production. You can analyze the file, then repair any fault conditions that spawned errors.

Concordance creates the error log when processing begins. You can manually key the file path and log name into the open text field, or use the Browse button to navigate to the desired folder.

If the check box is enabled but no file name is provided, Option will suppress errors and continue processing. Errors won't be logged.

The Setup Tab

Options from the Setup tab control the printer selected for the print session:

- *Name*: The name of the printer that will print the images. You can use the Setup button to select a specific printer. Note that other options, such as available trays, are printer specific, so changing printers might require you to reconfigure other print options.

- *Paper*: You can specify size and source options from the drop-down boxes.

- *Size*: Selections in this drop-down box correspond to paper sizes, such as Letter and Legal.

- *Source*: Selections in this drop-down box correspond to a printer's paper feed source, such as a specific page tray, or a manual paper feed.

- *Orientation*: You can select Portrait or Landscape by enabling the corresponding radio button.

- *Print Quality*: The print quality of an image is defined by the Dots Per Inch (DPI) setting selected from this drop-down box. The default setting depends on the capabilities of the selected printer. In terms of image quality, a setting of 300 dpi is usually sufficient.

Summary

When used in conjunction with a Concordance database, Opticon synchronizes with Concordance, and displays only those images represented by a database's last active query.

You use several menu items and three toolbars to navigate, annotate, and search images. The Standard toolbar has buttons that perform a variety of functions, from opening images to magnifying sections of an image. The Redlines toolbar contains buttons that are used to create various redlines, such as redactions and highlights. You use the Image toolbar to navigate through images, and to magnify and reorient them.

You can search redlines from Opticon when it's synchronized with Concordance. Searches can retrieve images on the basis of redline type, and by the text contained in redlines that supports embedded text. Information about redlines is stored in a supporting Concordance database associated with the primary Concordance database used to launch Opticon. Because information about redlines is contained in a valid Concordance database, many of the familiar search functions accessible via Concordance are exposed to Opticon.

You can print images from Opticon and stamp redlines and fielded data from Concordance on the header or footer of images. You can save settings made in the Print dialog for use in a later print session.

This chapter has detailed features in Opticon that are likely to be used by end users. The next chapter will describe how to load and modify a database's imagebase using Opticon's Imagebase Management dialog, a purely administrative function.

CHAPTER 13

Imagebase Management

The imagebase associated with a Concordance database is a file that contains metadata about images. A Concordance database that isn't associated with images doesn't have to have an imagebase. If it does, the imagebase will have the same name of the primary Concordance .DCB file, and will consist of two important files that have a .DIR and .VOL file extension. For example, the imagebase for HIST_DOCS.DCB consists of files named HIST_DOCS.DIR and HIST_DOCS.VOL.

Imagebase .DIR files store information about the location of images. Opticon communicates with an imagebase seamlessly, so that when a user launches the program from Concordance, Opticon will automatically find and display an image. Imagebases also store information that determines how Opticon behaves as a user navigates through images: if a particular image is the last of a set of images that combine to define a document record, Opticon uses the imagebase to know that the next sequential image represents the first image of a new document record, and will update the page numbers and page counts.

An imagebase .DIR file isn't an ASCII file and isn't properly viewed or modified using a text editor. Imagebase .DIR files are optimized into a series of coded instructions that Opticon can use directly. You interact with a database's .DIR file using methods described throughout this chapter.

Using Log Files

The contents of an imagebase can be represented as an ASCII comma-delimited file. ASCII files that track image path information are often referred to as *log* or *cross-reference files*. Administrators frequently give these files .TXT, .OPT, LOG, or .XRF file extensions. You can use log files to load (*register*) images in an imagebase. Log files are often included with document productions when images are provided to an outside agency. These log files give meaning to a set of images. The log file contains a separate line for each image file, and each line contains data corresponding to, among other things, an image's name, its path, the total number of images that combine to define a document, and if a particular image represents a document break.

Log File Structure

The structure of a log file is fixed. Unlike delimited files that can be exported from Concordance and that can contain a series of entries representing fielded data defined in any order by a Concordance administrator, Opticon log files always have the same number of columns, and those entries appear in the same order. If a log file is missing an entry, or if entries aren't in the following order, the log file is malformed, and cannot be used by Opticon.

Log files often won't use the first row of data to define field names. If individual entries between commas don't use white space, log files don't require the use of double-quote text qualifiers. You must use commas to delimit individual entries, and a new line to separate rows of data.

The entries in a log file must be in the following order:

```
ALIAS,VOLUME,PATH,DOC_BREAK,FOLDER_BREAK,BOX_BREAK,PAGES
```

These entries are defined as follows:

- ALIAS: The matching information that's used to synchronize Concordance and Opticon. If an image's file name is 00001.TIF, its alias is IMG00001. If the image represents the first image in a set of images, the exact value, IMG00001, must be in the key field of a Concordance database for Opticon to find the image path and name in an imagebase. Only one field in Concordance can be designated as a key field, by selecting File ➤ Modify in Concordance.

- VOLUME: Often, the name of the media on which images are stored: the CD, DVD, or storage media itself.

- PATH: The file path and file name of an image.

- DOC_BREAK: The first image (page) of a set of images that combine to define a document is considered to be a *document break*. The letter Y is used to denote a document break. The letter N or an empty entry indicate that an image doesn't represent a document break.

- FOLDER_BREAK: The first image (page) in a folder of documents is considered to be a *folder break*. The letter Y is used to denote a folder break. The letter N or an empty entry indicate that an image doesn't represent a folder break. An image that is a folder break should also be a document break.

- BOX_BREAK: The first image (page) in a box is considered to be a box break. The letter Y is used to denote a folder break. The letter N or an empty entry indicate that an image doesn't represent a box break. An image that is a box break should also be a document break.

- PAGES: The total number of pages in a document. This should be a pure number, and appears as lines in a log file that represent the first image of a set of images that define a document.

Figure 13-1 displays a sample log file.

```
0001,DVD1001,\DVD001\001\0001.tif,Y,,,6
0002,DVD1001,\DVD001\001\0002.tif,,,,
0003,DVD1001,\DVD001\001\0003.tif,,,,
0004,DVD1001,\DVD001\001\0004.tif,,,,
0005,DVD1001,\DVD001\001\0005.tif,,,,
0006,DVD1001,\DVD001\001\0006.tif,,,,
0007,DVD1001,\DVD001\001\0007.tif,Y,,,3
0008,DVD1001,\DVD001\001\0008.tif,,,,
0009,DVD1001,\DVD001\001\0009.tif,,,,
0010,DVD1001,\DVD001\001\0010.tif,Y,,,3
0011,DVD1001,\DVD001\001\0011.tif,,,,
0012,DVD1001,\DVD001\001\0012.tif,,,,
```

Figure 13-1. *A sample Opticon log file*

Examples of Log Files

The appearance of a log file depends on the use of single- vs. multi-page images. If single-page images are used, images can be in any of the supported image formats listed in Chapter 11. If multi-page images are used, images must be in a TIF format; other image formats cannot combine multiple images into a single file.

Single-Page TIFFs

Say two documents are represented by five individual pages each, and say images are single-page TIFFs. The images for the first document are named 0001.TIF through 0005.TIF and have aliases PX0001 through PX0005. The images for the first document are named 0006.TIF through 0010.TIF and have aliases PX0006 through PX0010. Finally, the media volume is DVD001. The structure of the log file describing these images could be as follows:

```
PX0001,DVD001,C:\IMAGES\DVD001\001\0001.TIF,Y,,,5
PX0002,DVD001,C:\IMAGES\DVD001\001\0002.TIF,,,,
PX0003,DVD001,C:\IMAGES\DVD001\001\0003.TIF,,,,
PX0004,DVD001,C:\IMAGES\DVD001\001\0004.TIF,,,,
PX0005,DVD001,C:\IMAGES\DVD001\001\0005.TIF,,,,
PX0006,DVD001,C:\IMAGES\DVD001\001\0006.TIF,Y,,,5
PX0007,DVD001,C:\IMAGES\DVD001\001\0007.TIF,,,,
PX0008,DVD001,C:\IMAGES\DVD001\001\0008.TIF,,,,
PX0009,DVD001,C:\IMAGES\DVD001\001\0009.TIF,,,,
PX0010,DVD001,C:\IMAGES\DVD001\001\0010.TIF,,,,
```

When documents are represented by single-page images, the log file will contain a separate and unique entry for each page. The first image corresponding to the first page of the first document contains the letter Y in the DOC_BREAK position of the file. Successive pages contain the letter N, to indicate that they're part of the same document. The sixth line of the file representing 0006.TIF represents the first page of a new document. The DOC_BREAK position of that record contains the letter Y.

Multi-Page TIFFs

Say two documents are represented by five individual pages each, and say images are multi-page TIFFs. The images for the first document are named 0001.TIF through 0005.TIF and have aliases PX0001 through PX0005. The images for the second document are named 0006.TIF through 0010.TIF and have aliases PX0006 through PX0010. Finally, the media volume is DVD001. The structure of the log file describing these images could be as follows:

```
PX0001,DVD001,C:\IMAGES\DVD001\001\0001.TIF,Y,,,5
PX0006,DVD001,C:\IMAGES\DVD001\001\0006.TIF,Y,,,5
```

When documents are represented by multi-page images, the log file will contain a separate and unique entry for the combined set of images. The first line corresponding to the first document (associated with images 0001.TIF through 0005.TIF) contains the letter Y in the DOC_BREAK position of the file. The second line of the file representing the second document (associated with images 0006.TIF through 0010.TIF) represents the first page of a new document. The DOC_BREAK position of that record also contains the letter Y.

Note The maximum number of pages that can be contained in a multi-page TIFF is 4,096. If single-page images are used, the maximum number of files that can be contained in a single directory is also 4,096.

Exporting an Imagebase to a Log File

You can export an imagebase to an ASCII file from Opticon's Tools ➤ Export imagebase to log file menu. Selecting this menu item opens the Export Imagebase dialog, displayed in Figure 13-2.

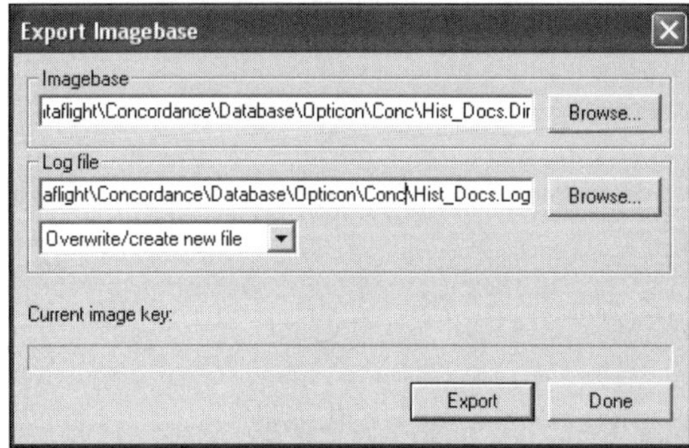

Figure 13-2. *The Export Imagebase dialog allows you to select an imagebase to export; to specify the name of the exported file; and to create a new log file, or append to an existing one.*

- *Imagebase*: The file path and name of the imagebase to be exported. You can manually key this information into the text field, or use the Browse button to open an Open dialog that you can use to select an imagebase.

- *Log file*: The name of the log file to be created or appended. You can manually key this information into the text field, or use the Browse button to open an Open dialog that you can use to specify the log file's name and location. If you select "Overwrite/create new file" from the adjacent drop-down box, a new log file will be created, or an existing log file will be completely overwritten. If you select "Append to file," data from an imagebase will be appended to an existing log file.

- *Export*: You use the Export button to trigger the export. While an imagebase is being exported, each image's alias and key is displayed under the "Current image key" label.

- *Done/Cancel*: When an imagebase is exporting, this button is labeled Cancel. Clicking the Cancel button during an export halts the procedure. Between exports, the label on the button is Done. Clicking Done closes the Export Imagebase dialog.

Working with the Imagebase Management Dialog

You can accomplish most administrative functions involving an imagebase from the Imagebase Management dialog. You open this dialog in Opticon by selecting Tools ➤ Imagebase Management. When you select this menu item, Opticon opens an Open dialog. You can use this dialog to navigate to the folder containing the desired imagebase.

The following sections display and describe each tab of the dialog in detail.

Path

You use the Path tab of the Imagebase Management dialog to set file paths that will be applied globally to an imagebase (see Figure 13-3). These settings are useful when file paths in an imagebase don't use a Universal Naming Convention (UNC) or drive mappings. Settings can be applied to all users, or configured uniquely for specific users.

An imagebase contains file path and file name information for images. The file path can be complete and explicitly refer to the server on which an image resides. This is known as the *UNC path* for a file. UNC paths use two backslashes to introduce a server name, and single backslashes when referring to subordinate folders. For example, say the server name is IMAGE_SERVER, the foldering structure containing an image is \IMAGES\CD001\001\, and an image name is 00001.TIF. The UNC path and name of this image is \\IMAGE_SERVER\IMAGES\CD001\001\00001.TIF.

As long as a user has network permissions to access the server and subordinate folders that contain this image, he or she will be able to view the image successfully using Opticon.

Instead of using a UNC path, an imagebase might refer to a drive letter. The drive letter might refer to a user's workstation, or to a networked server. A drive letter used in this way is known as a *drive mapping*. In Windows operating systems, you can configure drive mappings by selecting Tools ➤ Map Network Drive in Windows Explorer. Selecting this menu item opens a Map Network Drive dialog (see Figure 13-4).

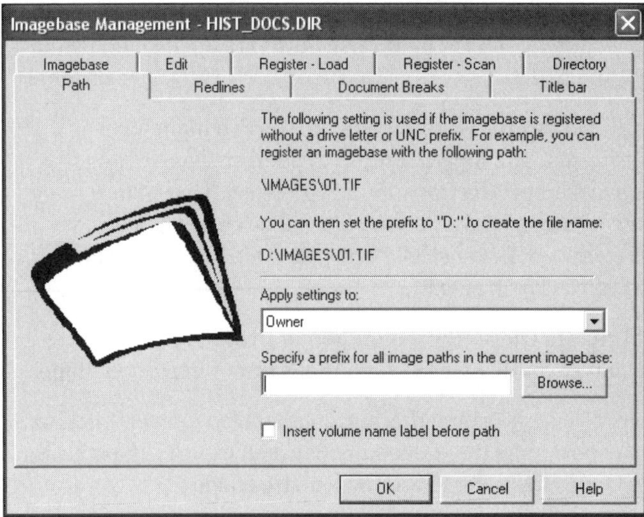

Figure 13-3. *You use the Path tab of the Imagebase Management dialog to set path information for an imagebase. Settings can be applied globally, or configured separately for individual users.*

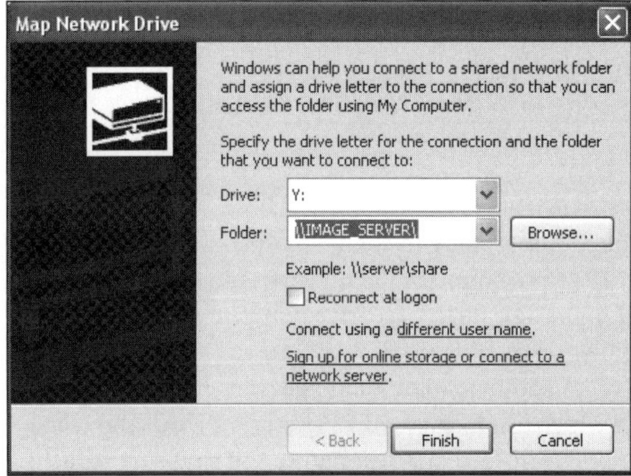

Figure 13-4. *You open the Map Network Drive dialog by selecting Tools ➤ Map Network Drive in Windows. This particular dialog was opened using a Windows XP operating system; the appearance of this dialog will vary slightly in other versions of Windows.*

■Note You should enable the "Reconnect at logon" check box if the drive mapping should be persistent. If you don't select this check box, the drive mapping won't exist when a user logs off when a workstation is rebooted.

Most workstations have some drive mappings preconfigured. Common settings might be an A:\ drive that refers to a floppy disk, a C:\ drive that refers to the workstation's hard drive, and a D:\ drive that refers to the workstation's CD/DVD drive. Other drives might be installed on the workstation, and use other letters as drive mappings.

Drive letters can be also associated with networked servers. For example, the server name \\IMAGE_SERVER might be referenced on a user's workstation as a V:\ drive. Given the file paths and file name used in the preceding example, you can reference the path and name in an imagebase like this: V:\IMAGES\CD001\001\00001.TIF, where V:\ is used as a substitute for the server name \\IMAGE_SERVER. As long as a user has network permissions to access the server and subordinate folders that contain this image, he or she can view the image successfully using Opticon.

Another method of referencing image paths exists in Opticon. Instead of a UNC path or a drive mapping, the imagebase might contain just the subordinate folders of images. In the previous examples, this is \CD001\001\00001.TIF.

Opticon can open the image if you configure parent path information from the Path tab of the Imagebase Management dialog. Following are the individual settings on this tab:

- *Apply settings to*: You can apply settings to just the current user, to all users, or both. This means that file path stem information set for <All users> can be different from those set for the current user.

- *Specify a prefix for all image paths in the current imagebase*: You enter the parent file path stem to be used throughout an imagebase in this text field.

- *Insert volume name label before path*: This option appends an image's volume information after the file path stem defined earlier. This setting is commonly used when images are stored in a CD/DVD jukebox, a storage device that holds two or more individual CDs or DVDs. Given the file paths and file name used in the preceding examples, the CD volume of image 00001.TIF is CD001. If you enable the "Insert volume name label before path" check box, and the parent path information entered in the "Specify a path" text field is \\IMAGES_SERVER\, Opticon will resolve the image path as \IMAGE_SERVER\IMAGES\CD001\001\00001.TIF.

You can modify volume information for sets of images registered in an imagebase from the Directory tab of the Imagebase Management dialog. The section "Directory" describes settings from this tab.

Redlines

You use the Redlines tab of the Imagebase Management dialog to import and export redlines data in a delimited format (see Figure 13-5). Given that redlines data is stored in an underlying Concordance database, this is the equivalent of opening the -redlines.dcb database and exporting all fields to a delimited text file.

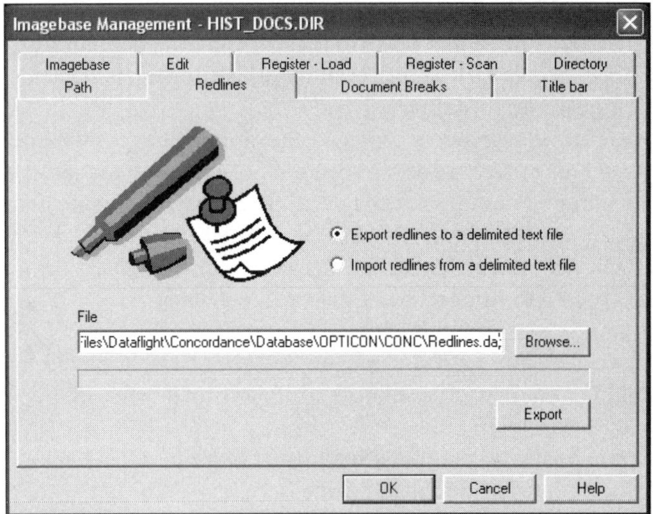

Figure 13-5. *You use the Redlines tab of the Imagebase Management dialog to export redlines data to a delimited text file, or to import redlines data from a delimited text file.*

- *Export redlines to a delimited text file:* Select this option if redlines data should be exported from the current imagebase.

- *Import redlines from a delimited text file:* Select this option if redlines data should be imported to the current imagebase from an external file.

- *File:* This is the file path and name of the redlines data file to be imported from or exported to. You can manually key this information into the text field, or use the Browse button to open an Open dialog that can be used to select a file.

- *Export/Import:* The label on this button depends on which option is selected: "Export redlines" or "Import redlines." Clicking the button triggers the procedure. A status bar under this button displays the procedure's progress.

Document Breaks

You use the Document Breaks tab of the Imagebase Management dialog to set and reset document breaks in an imagebase according to the beginning image key values contained in a Concordance database (see Figure 13-6). Document page breaks are affected for only those images associated with the last active query in the Concordance database used to launch Opticon. If Opticon isn't synchronized with any Concordance database—if the software is run as a standalone program—the Set button on this tab is disabled.

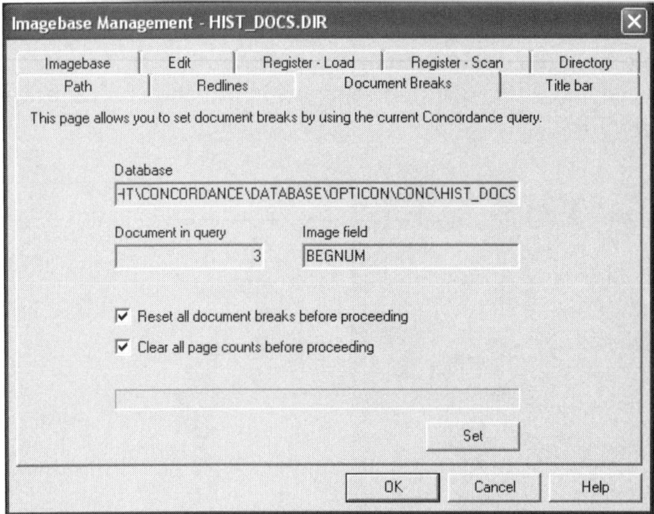

Figure 13-6. *The Document Breaks tab of the Imagebase Management dialog. You can reset document breaks in an Opticon imagebase according to the image key values contained in a linked Concordance database.*

The current imagebase determines entries in the Database, Document in query, and Image field text fields. This might be the imagebase that was selected when the Imagebase Management dialog was initially activated, or it could be an imagebase opened from the Imagebase tab. The Imagebase Management dialog prepopulates these fields when an imagebase is first opened. Following are the meanings and usages of these and other fields on the Document Breaks tab:

- *Database*: Displays the path and name of the Concordance database that will be used to guide the tool through setting document breaks.

- *Document in query*: Displays the total number of documents used in the last active query in the Concordance database displayed in the Database field described earlier.

- *Image field*: Displays the field name of the image key from the Concordance database referenced in the Database field.

- *Reset all document breaks before proceeding*: If this check box is enabled, the tool will clear any existing document break information before processing.

- *Clear all page counts before proceeding*: If this check box is enabled, the tool will clear all document page counts to zero before setting document breaks.

- *Set*: You use the Set button to trigger the process. A status bar under this button displays the procedure's progress.

Title Bar

By default, Opticon displays the text "Opticon -" and an image's alias in the title bar. You use the "Title bar" tab of the Imagebase Management dialog to configure information that appears in the title bar of Opticon (see Figure 13-7).

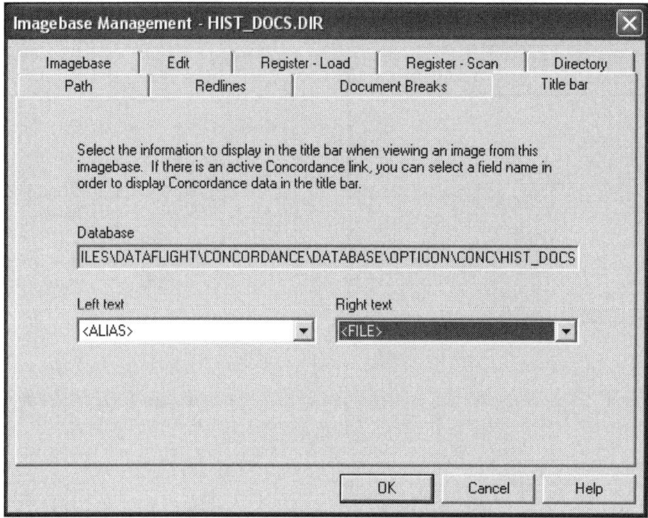

Figure 13-7. *The options on the "Title bar" tab of the Imagebase Management dialog control what type of text appears in the title bar of Opticon when an image is opened.*

- *Database*: Displays the path and name of the Concordance database currently linked to Opticon.

- *Left text/Right text*: Selecting an option from the "Left text" or "Right text" drop-down boxes modifies the information that appears in the left or right section of Opticon's title bar. The following selections are in each drop-down box:

  - *<Default>*: If both the "Left text" and "Right text" drop-down boxes are set to <Default>, Opticon will display the image's alias on the left side of the title bar.

  - *<ALIAS>*: Displays an image's alias. This might or might not be the same as an image's file name.

  - *<FILE>*: Displays the full file path and name of an image.

  - *FIELD NAMES*: Shows all field names from a linked Concordance database. If you select a field name, the appropriate value from the corresponding database record will be displayed in the title bar.

Figure 13-8 shows the Opticon title bar when <ALIAS> and <FILE> are selected in the "Left text" and "Right text" drop-down boxes, respectively.

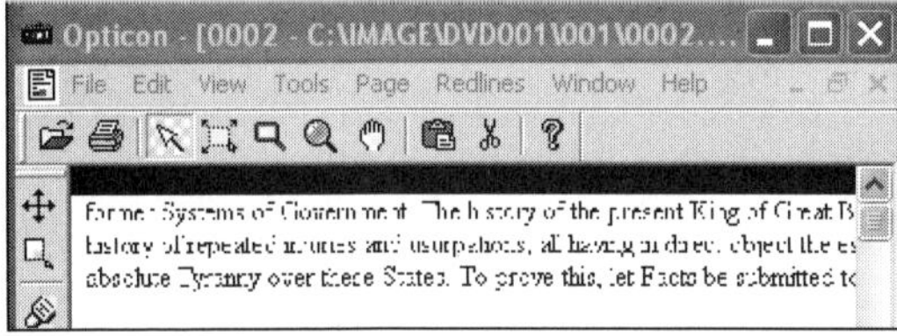

Figure 13-8. *The title bar of Opticon with an image's alias, file path, and name displayed*

Imagebase

You use the Imagebase tab of the Imagebase Management dialog to open an existing imagebase, to create a new one, or to merge the contents of a different imagebase with the current one (see Figure 13-9).

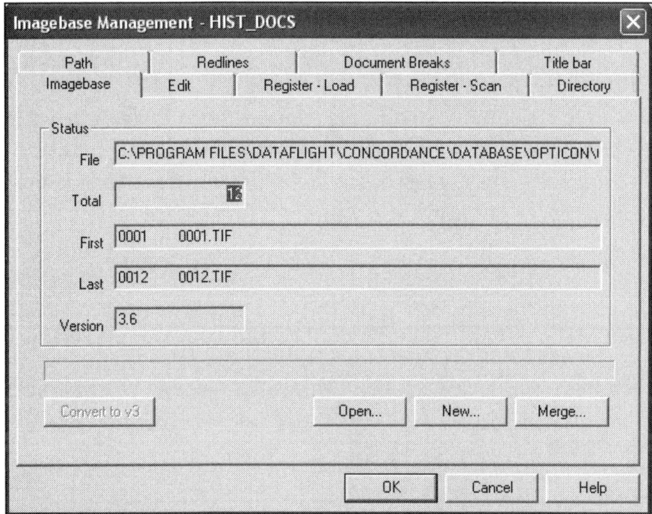

Figure 13-9. *The Imagebase tab of the Imagebase Management dialog*

The current imagebase determines entries in the File, Total, First, Last, and Version text fields. This might be the imagebase that was selected when the Imagebase Management dialog was initially activated, or it could be an imagebase opened from the Imagebase tab. The Imagebase Management dialog prepopulates these fields when an imagebase is first opened. Following are the meanings and usages of these and other fields on the Imagebase tab:

- *File*: Displays the full path to the folder that contains the currently active imagebase.

- *Total*: Displays the total number of images contained in the currently active imagebase.

- *First*: Displays the alias and image name of the first entry in the currently active imagebase.

- *Last*: Displays the alias and image name of the last entry in the currently active imagebase.

- *Version*: Displays the version number of Opticon.

- *Convert to v3*: Version 2.0 of Opticon stored redlines data in a separate .RED file. Beginning with version 3.0, redlines data is stored in a -redlines.dcb database, as described earlier in this chapter. You can use the "Convert to v3" button to convert redlines stored in an earlier version of Opticon into a format compatible with a version 3 or higher instance of Opticon.

- *Open*: Opens an Open dialog that you can use to select another imagebase. When you open a new imagebase, settings for the previous imagebase are saved, and fields on the various tabs of the Imagebase Management dialog are prepopulated with information from the selected imagebase.

- *New*: Opens an Open dialog that you can use to create a new imagebase. You can use the Open dialog to navigate to the desired folder. When you provide a new imagebase name and click the Open button in the Open dialog, Opticon will create a new, empty imagebase.

- *Merge*: You use the Merge button to combine the contents of an external imagebase with the current one. Clicking this button opens an Open dialog, which you can use to select the source imagebase. When imagebases are merged, any matching entries (duplicates) in the source imagebase will overwrite entries in the destination imagebase.

Edit

You use the Edit tab of the Imagebase Management dialog to modify individual image settings in an imagebase (see Figure 13-10).

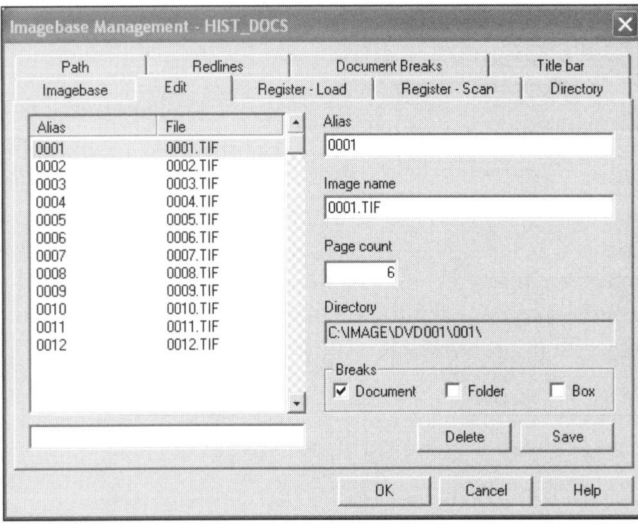

Figure 13-10. *The Edit tab of the Imagebase Management dialog*

Each image is listed by its alias and file name. You can use an open text field to jump to an image. Entering characters in this field triggers the list box to jump to the first best match by comparing image aliases with text in the field. For an imagebase with thousands or millions of images, this is the most convenient method of locating a specific entry in the list.

You can modify the settings for an image using the following text fields and check boxes:

- *Alias*: Displays an image's alias. This might or might not be the same as an image's file name (without the file extension). An image's alias should match the data contained in a Concordance database's image key field; Opticon uses this information to synchronize to a Concordance database.

- *Image name*: The actual file name of the image highlighted in the list box.

- *Page count*: When a page is marked as the first page of a document, the total number of pages (images) in the document is displayed here. As long as document breaks are set, this value isn't required for Opticon to function smoothly. However, page count information is helpful, in that it's used to calculate page counts from the Print dialog. If at all possible, you should endeavor to determine and load page count information for each document. Scanning and coding vendors that process documents and electronic files are able to provide this data in an Opticon load file.

- *Directory*: The full file path to an image.

- *Breaks*: The term *break* is used to denote those images that represent the first image of a document, a folder, or a box.

  - *Document*: You should enable this check box for the image that corresponds to the first page of a document. Although document breaks aren't a requirement for Opticon to open images, they're needed when using the Previous Document ◁ and Next Document ▷ buttons on Opticon's Image toolbar. If at all possible, you should endeavor to determine and document break information for each document. Scanning and coding vendors that process documents and electronic files can provide this data in an Opticon load file.

  - *Folder*: You should enable this check box for the image that corresponds to the first page of a set of documents contained in a folder. Folder break information isn't as essential as document break and page count data, though it's necessary for the Page ➤ Next Folder and Page ➤ Previous Folder menu items to function properly. Scanning and coding vendors that process documents and electronic files can provide this data in an Opticon load file.

  - *Box*: You should enable this check box for the image that corresponds to the first page of a set of folders contained in a box. Scanning and coding vendors that process documents and electronic files can provide this data in an Opticon load file.

- *Delete*: Deletes the reference to the image from the imagebase. Image references cannot be restored from the tool once they've been deleted. In fact, there's no method in Opticon to create a reference to an image, other than loading data from a valid Opticon log file.

- *Save*: Saves settings for the currently highlighted image. You must click this button each time an image's data is to be written to the imagebase. Updating an image's settings and then highlighting another image in the list without saving causes updated values to be lost. When updating several images, you must save each image's settings individually.

Register - Load

You use the Register - Load tab of the Imagebase Management dialog to load an imagebase with data from an external log file (see Figure 13-11).

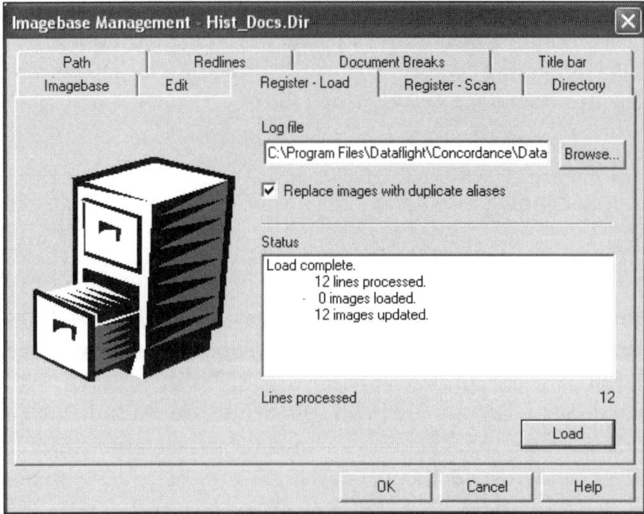

Figure 13-11. *The Register - Load tab of the Imagebase Management dialog*

This tool assumes the log file is properly structured. The section "Exporting an Imagebase to a Log File" discusses the structure of a log file.

The "Log file" text field displays the full file path and file name of the log file to be loaded. You can manually key this information into the field, or use the Browse button to open an Open dialog, which you can use to navigate to and select the desired log file.

Once you select the log, the Load button triggers the load. As each line of the log file is loaded, if Opticon finds a matching row in the imagebase, data for an image is updated to match data from the log file. If no match is found, new image entries are appended to the imagebase. The Status field displays feedback to you about the load's progress and tallies final results (see Figure 13-12).

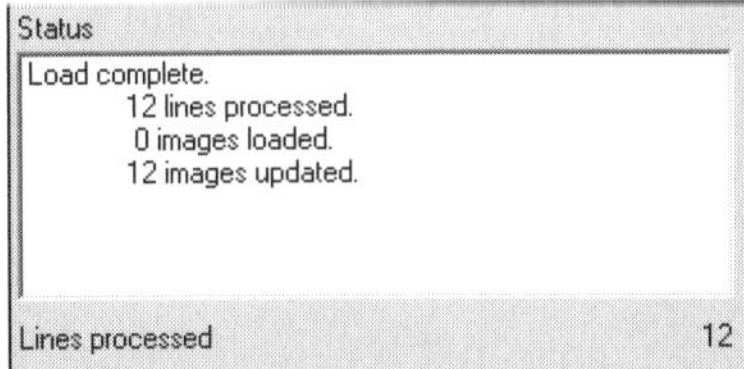

Figure 13-12. *Feedback provided by the Register - Load tab*

Register - Scan

You can use the Register - Scan tab of the Imagebase Management dialog to create an imagebase from a directory (see Figure 13-13).

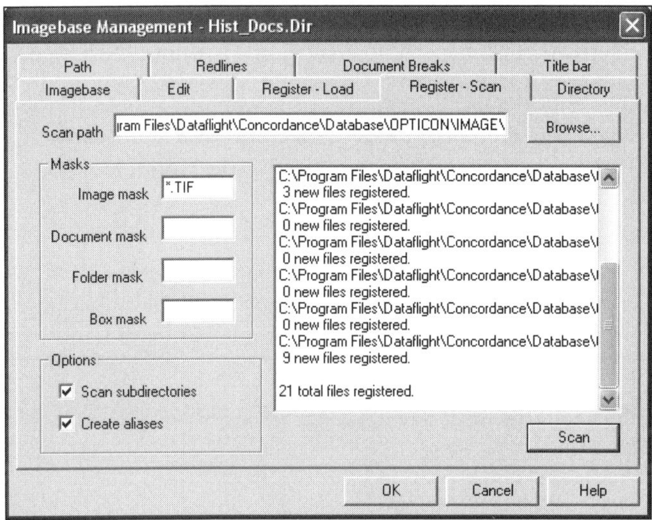

Figure 13-13. *The Register - Scan tab of the Imagebase Management dialog*

- *Scan path*: The top-level folder that should be scanned. You can scan subfolders using the "Scan subdirectories" option. You can manually key this information into the text field, or use the Browse button to open an Open dialog that you can use to select the root folder.

- *Masks*: Masks support the use of the * (asterisk) wildcard. You use masks to match patterns in file names. The mask *.TIFF represents only those files that are TIFFs. The mask *.* represents all files. The mask DX*.JPG represents only those files that have a DX prefix and are JPEGS.

  - *Image mask*: Files that match the pattern defined by the mask in this field are registered in the imagebase. Files that don't match the pattern aren't registered.

- *Document mask*: Files that match the pattern defined by the mask in this field are registered as document breaks.

- *Folder mask*: Files that match the pattern defined by the mask in this field are registered as folder breaks.

- *Box mask*: Files that match the pattern defined by the mask in this field are registered as box breaks.

- *Options*: These options control the behavior of a scan.

  - *Scan subdirectories*: If you enable this check box, subordinate folders under the root folder entered in the "Scan path" text field will be included in the scan. Masking options defined earlier for the root folder are applied to subordinate folders as well.

  - *Create aliases*: If you enable this check box, the scan tool will create aliases for images using sequential numbers, starting at zero. If you don't enable this check box, an image's alias will be the same as the image's file name (without the image's file extension).

- *Scan*: Clicking this button triggers the scanning procedure. The Status field displays feedback to you about the load's progress and tallies final results (see Figure 13-14).

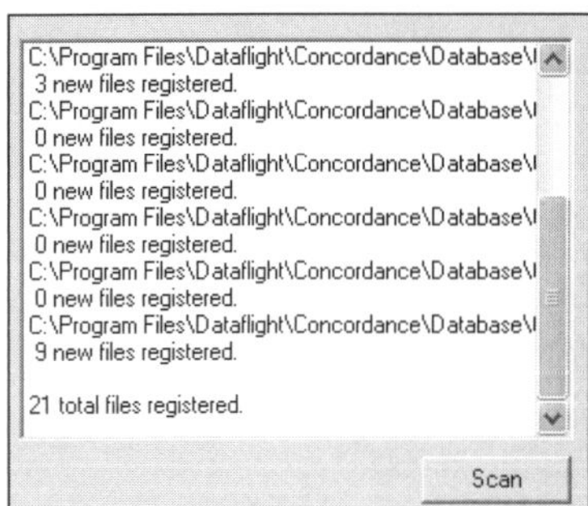

Figure 13-14. *Feedback provided by the Register - Scan tab*

Directory

You use the Directory tab of the Imagebase Management dialog to view and modify the individual directories and volumes that are contained in an imagebase (see Figure 13-15).

The list box displays the key, volume, and directory information of folders that appear in an imagebase. Note that, in this list, the *key* value refers to a volume's key, not that of images. Opticon itself configures a volume's key information, and you cannot edit or otherwise modify these values.

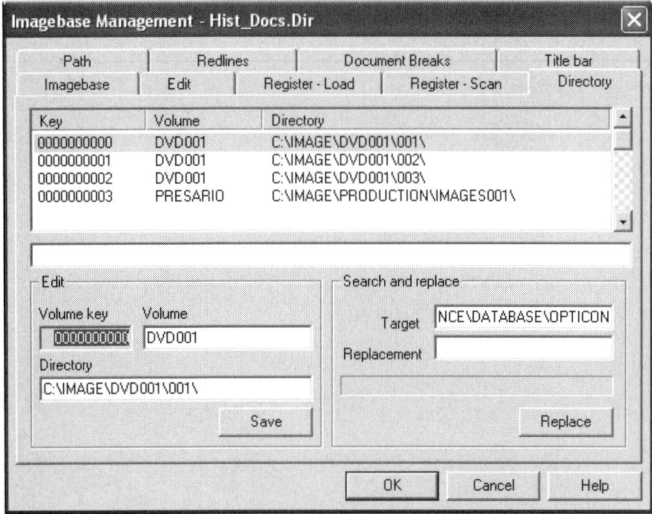

Figure 13-15. *The Directory tab of the Imagebase Management dialog*

You can scroll through the list, or use the empty text field to look up entries. Entering characters in this field triggers the list box to jump to the first best match by comparing volumes with text in the field.

- *Edit*: Entries in the Volume key, Volume, and Directory text fields are determined by the directory selected from the list box. These fields are populated when you highlight a directory.

  - *Volume key*: Opticon assigns a numeric value to each directory. This value is a system field, and you can't edit it directly. Therefore, this text field is locked.

  - *Volume*: The volume associated with a directory. Recall that a volume refers to the media on which images were stored when provided to a Concordance administrator. As a result, many directories can share the same volume. In the example displayed in Figure 13-16, three directories share the same volume: DVD001.

  - *Directory*: The directory associated with a set of images. Data in this field is associated with the current directory highlighted in the list. Note that entries under the Directory label in the list represent the lowest subordinate folders in which images are stored. For example, say a volume contains a root folder—DVD001—and three subordinate folders—001, 002, and 003. Images are contained in folders DVD001\001\, DVD001\002\, and DVD001\003\. The list will contain three separate images (see Figure 13-16).

- *Save*: When you update an entry for a directory, you must click the Save button before selecting another item in the list. Unsaved data is lost when you select a new directory.

Key	Volume	Directory
0000000000	DVD001	C:\IMAGE\DVD001\001\
0000000001	DVD001	C:\IMAGE\DVD001\002\
0000000002	DVD001	C:\IMAGE\DVD001\003\
0000000003	PRESARIO	C:\IMAGE\PRODUCTION\IMAGES001\

Figure 13-16. *An example of volume and directory entries in the Directory tab's list*

- *Search and replace:* You can globally update directory information. This feature is useful when a server name or drive mapping changes. Changes made to directory information using this feature are permanent, and cannot be undone.

  - *Target:* The text that will be replaced.

  - *Replacement:* The text used to overwrite text specified in the Target field.

- *Replace:* Clicking the Replace button triggers the search and replace procedure. A status bar under this button displays the procedure's progress.

Summary

This chapter has covered the methods you use to interact with a database's imagebase. Often, you'll export data from an imagebase to an external, delimited log file. Unlike delimited files used with Concordance, the structure of an Opticon log file is fixed, with the same number of elements appearing in the same sequence in every log file. You can use log files—sometimes referred to as cross-reference files—to load image data into an imagebase.

You accomplish the bulk of administrative tasks in Opticon from the Imagebase Management dialog. This dialog has several tabs, each pertaining to a specific administrative function. This chapter has discussed the features accessible from each of these tabs in detail.

However, a common administrative task not referenced in this chapter remains: exporting image data during document productions. This particular method of exporting data from Opticon is so important that the next chapter is wholly devoted to this procedure.

CHAPTER 14

Producing Documents in Opticon

Opticon can export images in a variety of supported formats, export ASCII files describing image file names and paths, or export both ASCII files and image files. Exporting image files and metadata about those files enables Concordance administrators to transfer data to other organizations.

Concordance administrators often use the term *produce* in this context. To produce in Opticon means to export images and metadata. A *document production* refers to the act of exporting data using Opticon, and the term is sometimes used to refer to the actual files themselves.

Although it's possible to transfer image data by simply copying image files from one location to another, in most circumstances, as the administrator, you'll prefer to use the tools available in Opticon to enable productions. These tools enable powerful export options that allow you, among other things, to change the export image format, to endorse annotations permanently onto exported images (often referred to as *burning redlines*), and to create a new numbering scheme for image names. Furthermore, because Opticon links only to those document records visible from the last active search applied to a Concordance database, you can use Concordance to filter database records, then export image data for those records alone.

Note Opticon only exports image data. To export fielded data from Concordance, you must use the methods described in Chapter 6.

This chapter fully explains the methods used to complete a document production in Opticon. First, however, you'll find the discussion of some preliminary and key concepts in the following section helpful.

Production Numbers

In many Concordance databases, particularly those that describe documents and files, an arbitrary numbering system is used to identify uniquely every page of every document of a *document universe*. This numbering system can be alphanumeric, with an alphabetic prefix or suffix, but it's normally comprised of a sequential numeric stem. To identify each page usefully, no two pages from any documents will share the same identifier.

These values don't only serve to identify documents. They can also identify individual document boundaries, if a Concordance database has been designed so that each database record has at least two fields: one for the identifier corresponding to the first page of a document, and one corresponding to the last page of a document. Many Concordance administrators name these fields something descriptive, such as BEGDOCNO and ENDDOCNO, or BEGID and ENDID.

Note Although it's possible to calculate document boundaries with a BEGDOCNO value alone in a series of sequential document records, it's suggested in Concordance database design to include an ENDDOC field to explicitly define the end of a document boundary.

Concordance administrators sometimes refer to this identifier as a *document control number*. An equivalent term for this value might be *image control number*, particularly if the Concordance database containing the data is linked to an image viewer. If a linked viewer is used, it's necessary to denote one field in a Concordance database as an *image key field*. You set this attribute from the Modify dialog, opened from Concordance's File ➤ Modify menu. An external viewer uses the image key to locate the file paths of associated images corresponding to a document record.

During a document production, you might wish to export image key data about images to a metadata file. However, a facility exists within Opticon to create a new numbering scheme to identify images that have been produced. The values that refer to images as they're exported are called *production numbers*. If you use Opticon to create a new numbering scheme, document records in Concordance corresponding to produced images will have *two* sets of identifiers: the original set used in initial BEGDOC and ENDDOC fields, and the new production set. A complete Concordance database will have two fields to record the new production numbers, perhaps named PRODBEG and PRODEND. (The methods used to capture production number data and to write those values back into Concordance from Opticon are described in the section "Numbering Dialog.")

Redlines

Redlines is a term used to describe annotations added over an image. Redlines include textual comments, highlights, hollow geometric shapes, and solid geometric shapes used to hide a section of an image (otherwise known as a *redaction*). End users add redlines from within Opticon. Information about redlines, such as the vertical and horizontal placement, the text (if any), and type of geometric shape (if used) is stored in the same directory as the database to which the images are associated. This file is, itself, a Concordance database, though a user will never open it as such in normal practice. The file's name is a derivative of the main database's name, with a -redlines.dcb suffix.

When Opticon opens an image, it checks to see if there's redline data about the image in a supplementary -redlines.dcb database. If there is, Opticon will paint a graphical representation of the redlines over the image. Redlines aren't a permanent artifact of the image file. They're edited, removed, or augmented without modifying the underlying image file. Despite the appearance of what might be numerous redlines on an image viewed from Opticon, the same image opened in a different application compatible with the image type appears unmarked.

During a document production, you can elect to ignore redline data, to export redline data as metadata, or to copy redlines as permanent artifacts of the exported images. This last option creates images that differ from the originals in that text, highlights, and shapes become part of the file. Litigators find this to be useful when sharing image data with opposing counsel. Some portions of pages might contain confidential information, which can be hidden by permanently signing redactions (solid geometric shapes) onto images.

Producing Documents

The following discussion will demonstrate, step by step, how to complete a document production. For the purposes of this example, a database has been created named HIST_DOCS.DCB. Table 14-1 outlines this database's structure.

Table 14-1. *HIST_DOCS.DCB Database Structure*

Field	Type	Description
BEGNUM	TEXT (10)	Beginning document control number
ENDNUM	TEXT (10)	Ending document control number
DOCDATE	DATE (MMDDYYYY)	Date the document was created
FOOTER	TEXT (60)	Statement to be copied onto the footer of produced images
DOCTEXT	PARAGRAPH	Full text of the document
PRODBEG	TEXT (10)	Beginning production number
PRODEND	TEXT (10)	Ending production number
CDATE	DATE (MMDDYYYY)	Date the document record was loaded into the database
EDATE	PARAGRAPH	Audit field to track the date and user name of edits to database records
AUTOID	NUMERIC	Accession ID field

This database has been preloaded with three document records that represent the text of the Declaration of Independence, the Bill of Rights, and the Emancipation Proclamation. Single-page TIFFs have been created to complement the database. The database record corresponding to the Declaration of Independence is associated with six TIFF images, named 0001.TIF through 0006.TIF. The BEGNUM and ENDNUM values of that record are 0001 and 0006, respectively. These images are stored in the folder C:\Program Files\Dataflight\Concordance\Database\OPTICON\IMAGE\DVD001\001\.

The database record corresponding to the Bill of Rights is associated with three TIFF images. The file names of these images, which correspond to that record, are 0007.TIF through 0009.TIF, respectively. These images are stored in the folder C:\Program Files\Dataflight\Concordance\Database\OPTICON\IMAGE\DVD001\002\.

The database record corresponding to the Emancipation Proclamation is associated with three TIFF images. The file names of these images, which correspond to that record, are 0010.TIF through 0012.TIF, respectively. These images are stored in the folder C:\Program Files\Dataflight\Concordance\Database\OPTICON\IMAGE\DVD001\003\.

Figure 14-1 displays the first record in the database, corresponding to the Declaration of Independence.

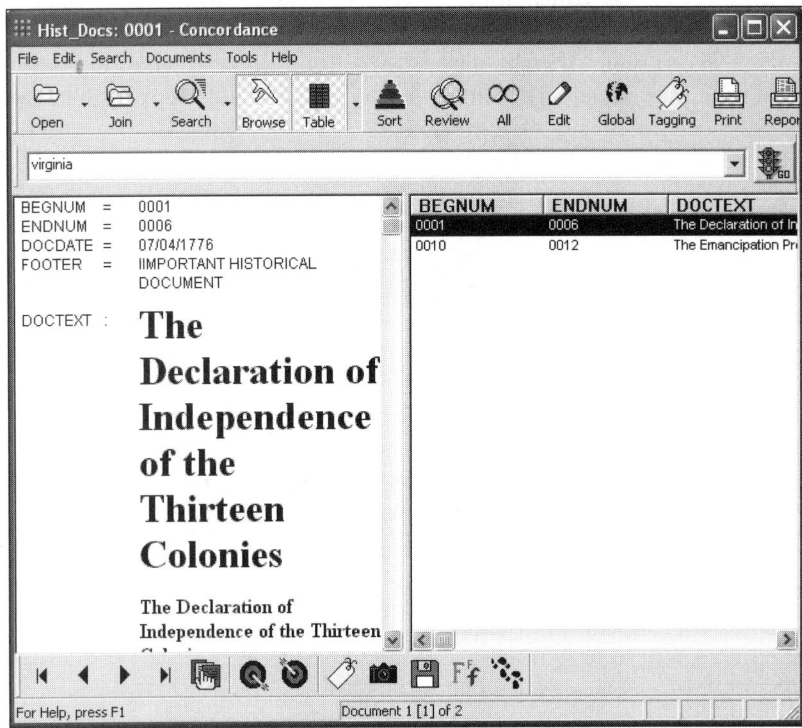

Figure 14-1. *Split screen view of the database record corresponding to the Declaration of Indepen-dence. This is the first record in the database.*

Figure 14-2 displays the first TIFF image, 0001.TIF, associated with the Declaration of Independence database record, and viewed with Opticon. This image has three annotations: the title of the document, The Declaration of Independence of the Thirteen Colonies, is high-lighted; a note appears in the upper right-hand corner of the image; and a redaction covers the first few sentences of the second paragraph.

Finally, Figure 14-3 displays the folder structure of the images representing the three data-base records. TIFF files associated with the Declaration of Independence are stored in folder 001. TIFF files associated with the Bill of Rights are stored in folder 002. TIFF files associated with the Emancipation Proclamation are stored in folder 003. These folders are stored under a parent folder, DVD001, which is assumed to be the media volume containing the data when it was delivered to an administrator.

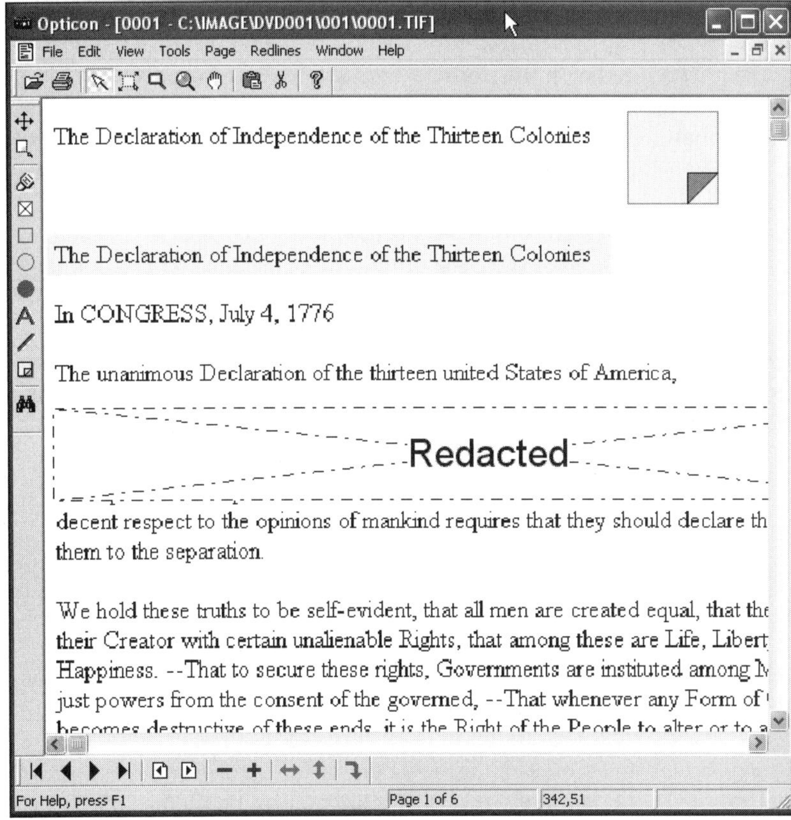

Figure 14-2. *The first image of the Declaration of Independence database record, 0001.TIF, viewed in Opticon*

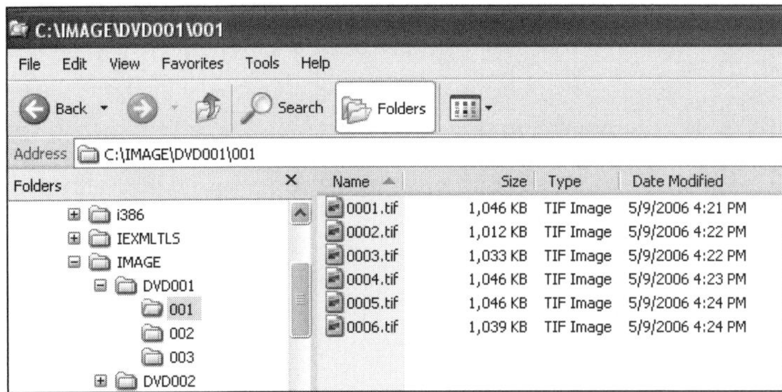

Figure 14-3. *The folder structure containing TIFF images for the sample database, HIST_DOCS.DCB*

In this example, new TIFF images will be created and assigned unique production numbers. Production numbers represent a new numbering scheme, and can be written back to the Concordance database associated with the production, for reference purposes. In this example, PRODBEG and PRODEND fields will store the beginning and ending production numbers assigned to each document record. This new numbering scheme doesn't supersede the original numbering scheme used to identify document records and corresponding images; it complements the original numbering scheme by uniquely identifying exported images. Opticon calculates production numbers automatically as the production processes each image, and the production numbers are written back into the Concordance database only if you elect to do so. In this example, production numbers are endorsed directly onto each image so they appear in an image's footer.

A statement is written directly onto the footer of each produced image. Unlike production numbers, this data isn't calculated automatically, but is stored in the FOOTER field of the HIST_DOCS.DCB database. The exact statement is IMPORTANT HISTORICAL DOCUMENT. The FOOTER field of each database record to be produced has been prepopulated with this value.

Selecting Records from Concordance

Opticon produces only those images associated with the last active query in a Concordance database. The first step of a production doesn't involve the use of Opticon. You must first select only those records in Concordance that are to be produced. Furthermore, Opticon processes document records in the order in which they appear in Concordance. If the order in which documents are processed as the production progresses is important, you must sort database records first.

In this example, the production involves images associated with the database records representing the Declaration of Independence and the Emancipation Proclamation. The Bill of Rights record is excluded. The two documents are processed in chronological order, so the earlier one is produced first. Both these document records contain the word Virginia. Figure 14-4 displays the HIST_DOCS.DCB database after the keyword search VIRGINIA. The document records have been sorted by the field DOCDATE to ensure that the records appear in the correct chronological order.

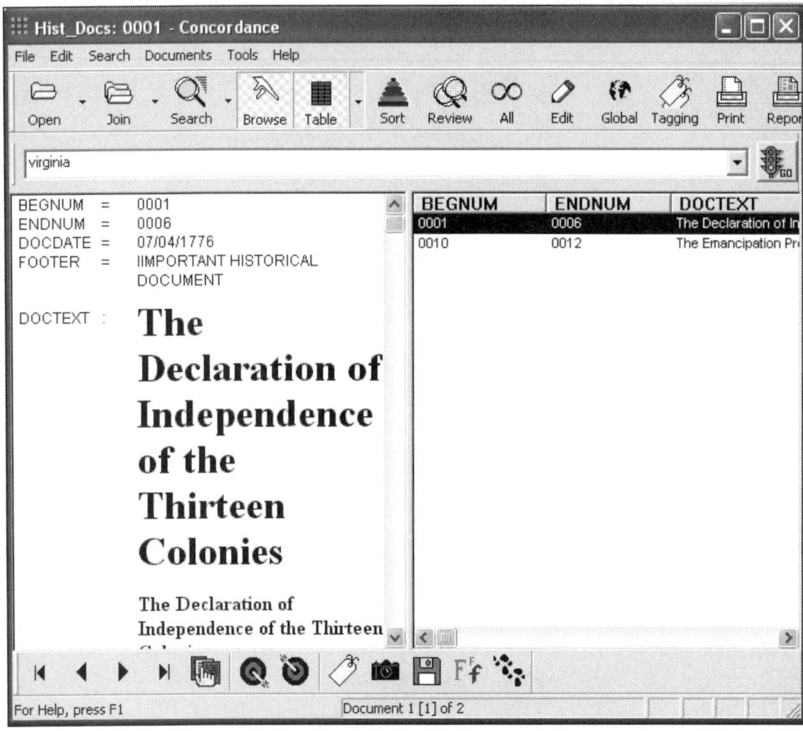

Figure 14-4. *The HIST_DOCS.DCB database after the keyword search for VIRGINIA. Document records have been sorted so that the earlier of the two documents appears first.*

Producing Documents with the Production Wizard

You initiate document productions using Opticon. Once you've selected and sorted records in Concordance, click the Camera button located on the lower tool bar of Concordance when either Browse view or Table view is active. The Tools ➤ Produce menu item in Opticon opens the first dialog of the Production Wizard (see Figure 14-5). You're prompted to create a new production, or to open a previous production's saved profile. Production profiles are saved as separate files and have a .PSF file extension. In this example, a new production is initiated from the "Select this option to start the Production Wizard" button.

From this point on, you can use the Next and Back buttons to navigate within the various dialogs that comprise the Production Wizard. The following sections discuss each dialog.

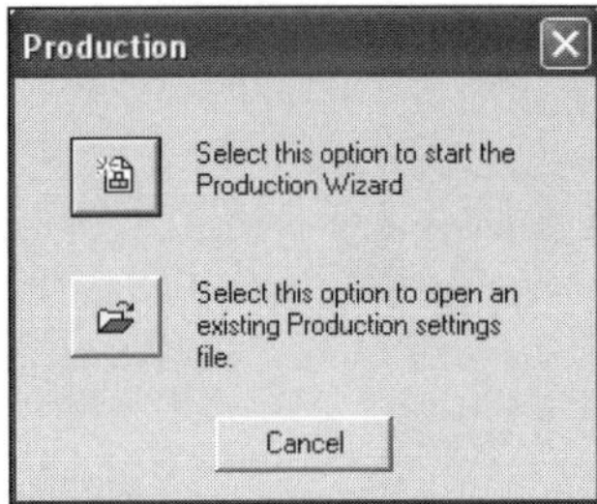

Figure 14-5. *You can open a new document production or a previously saved production profile from this dialog.*

Range Dialog

For a new document production, you use the Range dialog to select some subset of the records displayed in the last active query in Concordance (see Figure 14-6). The First and Last text fields correspond to the ordinal position of records in Concordance. In this example, both the first and second document records will be produced, and the default values on this dialog are accepted.

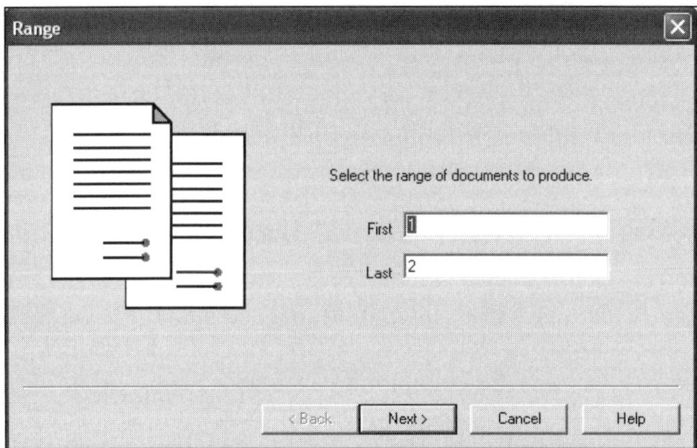

Figure 14-6. *In the Range dialog of the Production Wizard, by default, the First and Last values correspond to the beginning and ending documents in the last active Concordance query.*

Images Dialog

Figure 14-7 displays the next dialog, Images. The onscreen descriptions that appear when you hover your mouse over each option fully describe each possible selection, and are included in italics in the following bulleted list. Additional comments are in normal font.

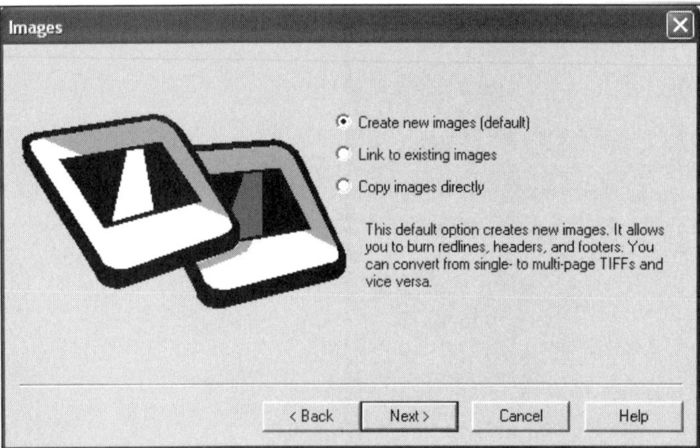

Figure 14-7. *In the Images dialog of the Production Wizard, you can copy images directly from an original location on a workstation or network. You can also create new images, a useful option when the images are to be endorsed with production numbers, field values, or header and footer values.*

- *Create new images (default)*: This default option creates new images. It allows you to burn redlines, headers, and footers. You can convert from single- to multi-page TIFFs, and vice versa. This is the option chosen for this example, as new images will be created and endorsed with production numbers and the statement contained in the database's FOOTER field.

- *Link to existing images*: Select this option to link to existing images. This is useful in creating subset imagebases. You cannot change the format of the original image or burn redlines or other text information onto the image. This option doesn't export images. Rather, it creates a valid Opticon cross-reference file or an imagebase that links to existing images.

- *Copy images directly*: This option directly copies the images from the source directory to the destination directory. You cannot burn redlines or add text information to the images. You also cannot change the format of the original image. This option exports images and creates a valid Opticon cross-reference file or an imagebase. Exported images aren't modified in any way.

Directory Dialog

With the "Create new images (default)" option selected, clicking the Next button opens the next dialog, Directory (see Figure 14-8). You can use the Browse button to open an Open dialog, and navigate to the folder in which exported images will be saved. For the purpose of this example, the output folder is C:\IMAGE\PRODUCTION\.

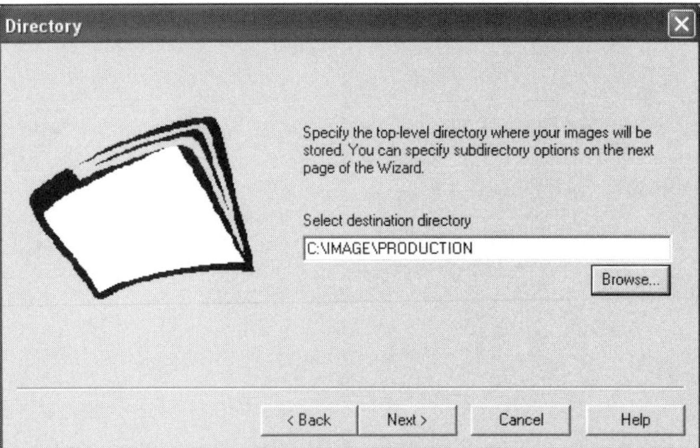

Figure 14-8. *In the Directory dialog of the Production Wizard, the text field labeled "Select destination directory" represents the output destination of exported images.*

Subdirectory Dialog

The next dialog of the wizard, Subdirectory, appears (see Figure 14-9). The options available on this screen allow you to specify separate volume and subfoldering information.

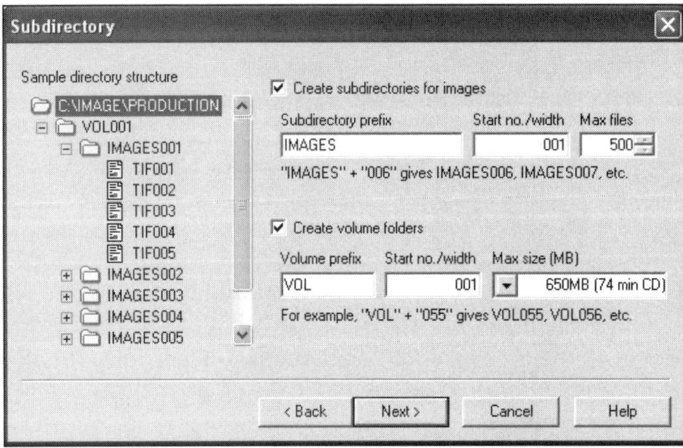

Figure 14-9. *The options in the Subdirectory dialog of the Production Wizard control the foldering structure in which produced images are created.*

- *Create subdirectories for images*: This option is enabled when you select the "Create subdirectories for images" check box. You can use the text fields located here to create a subfoldering structure for produced images, and to specify how many images will be stored in each subfolder. Options under "Create subdirectories for images" are as follows:

- *Subdirectory prefix*: Subfolder names will contain this value as a prefix. The default value is IMAGES. Assuming the value specified in the "Start no./width" field is 001, folder names will be IMAGES001, IMAGES002, and so on.

- *Start no./width*: Subfolder names will be based on this value as a suffix. It should be a numeric value (the starting number) with leading zeros (the width). For example, say this value is 001. Assuming the value specified in the "Subdirectory prefix" field is IMAGES and the value specified in the field "Max files" is 500, the first 500 produced images will be stored in a folder named IMAGES001, the next 500 images will be stored in a folder named IMAGES002, and so on.

- *Max files*: The numeric value entered here controls how many images will be contained in each subfolder. The default setting is 500.

- *Create volume folders*: This option is enabled when you select the "Create volume folders" check box. Recall that, in the context of Concordance data, the term *volume* is often used to refer to the media on which data is received from an outside agency, such as a vendor, and then subsequently copied to a network and loaded into Concordance and Opticon. CDs, DVDs, or external hard drives are examples of common media types. A media's volume is also its name. Options under "Create volume folders" are as follows:

  - *Volume prefix*: Volume names will contain this value as a prefix. The default value is VOL. Assuming the value specified in the "Start no./width" field is 001, volume names will be VOL001, VOL002, and so on.

  - *Start no./width*: Volume names will be based on this value as a suffix. It should be a numeric value (the starting number) with leading zeros (the width). For example, say this value is 001. Assuming the value specified in the "Volume prefix" field is VOL, the first volume will be named VOL001, the second volume will be named VOL002, and so on. You control the size of each volume using the "Max size (MB)" setting.

  - *Max size (MB)*: If you know that the transmitting media you'll create to transfer data to an outside agency will consist of either CDs or DVDs, the size selected in the "Max size (MB)" drop-down box will force Concordance to keep the size of a volume below a certain threshold. You can use this option to ensure that individual volumes will fit on a CD or DVD. If the export is to an external hard drive and you feel confident that the total size of all produced images will be less than the total available free space on the hard drive, you might not need this option.

Note When document productions are to be copied to CDs, you should select the 650MB option, to ensure image data will completely fit on a CD. The 700MB option can sometimes create errors if the actual allocated space on a given CD is somewhat shy of 700MB because of manufacturing errors.

This production example uses the following default settings:

- *Subdirectory prefix*: IMAGES

- *Start no./width*: 001

- *Max files*: 500

Imagebase Dialog

When you're satisfied with the selections on the Subdirectory dialog, clicking the Next button opens the Imagebase dialog of the wizard (see Figure 14-10). From this screen, you can create a new imagebase, append to an existing imagebase, or create an Opticon cross-reference file, as discussed in the following sections.

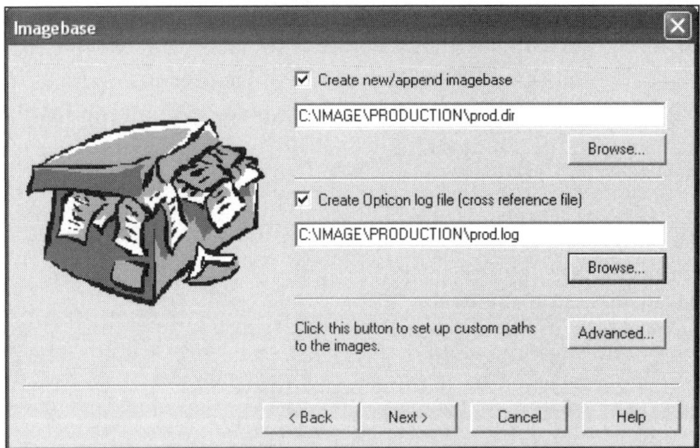

Figure 14-10. *The Imagebase dialog of the Production Wizard*

Create New/Append Imagebase

Selecting the "Create new/append imagebase" check box either appends data to an existing imagebase, or creates a new imagebase entirely. If appending to an existing imagebase, use the Browse button to navigate to the folder containing the appropriate .DIR file.

An existing imagebase chosen in this way is updated with file and path information corresponding to the produced images as the production progresses. If a new imagebase is to be created, enter the full path and imagebase name into the empty text field under the check box.

Alternatively, you can use the Browse button to navigate to the appropriate folder where the new imagebase should be stored. If you use the latter method, you must enter the imagebase name in the "File name" text field of the "Save as" dialog that's opened when you click the Browse button. When a new imagebase is created, two files are created, one with a .DIR file extension (containing image name and path data), and one with a .VOL file extension (containing volume data). This example won't create or update an imagebase, and this check box is not enabled (although it's enabled in Figure 14-10, for easier viewing).

Create Opticon Log File

Selecting the "Create Opticon log file (cross reference file)" check box creates an ASCII text file that you can use to load image paths to a database's imagebase. The file has a .LOG extension. Because the file is clear text, you can edit it to update file paths. This is often necessary when produced images will be stored on a network or workstation different from the original images. In this example, produced images are stored in the location C: IMAGE\PRODUCTION\.

Every row of the cross-reference file created by the production includes this file path. If the produced images are to be stored in a different location, you can use a text editor to perform a global find and replace to update this file path to a different value. Often, produced images are provided to an outside agency, and it's customary for the administrator to provide a cross-reference file. However, you might not know the network architecture on which exported images will be stored. In such a scenario, you might elect to remove the file path stem from the cross-reference file, leaving only the subfolder paths in each row. This practice assumes that the recipients of the data will update paths in the cross-reference file to reflect valid file paths on their network.

In this example, the cross-reference file is named prod.log.

Advanced

The Advanced button opens a dialog that allows you to specify custom image paths for each image. The Opticon cross-reference file created during the production will reference file paths entered in this dialog, perhaps as they would appear on another person's network. If you provide no file path information using this tool, the cross-reference file will reference valid file paths on your network.

Numbering Dialog

The next dialog of the wizard, Numbering, is where you specify the format of production numbers, if they are to be created (see Figure 14-11). Options on this dialog are locked by default, and are opened when you enable the "Create production numbers" check box.

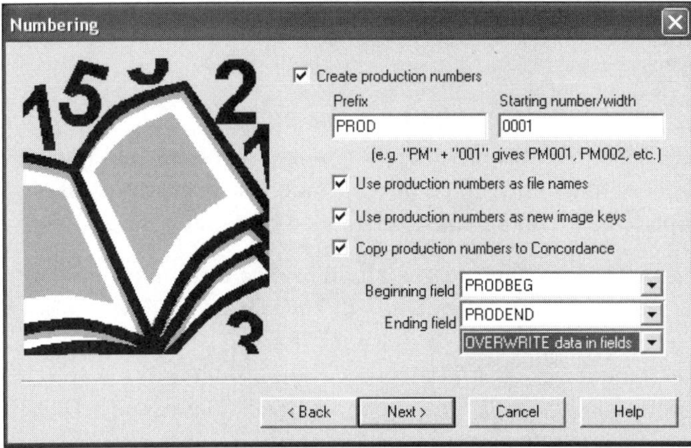

Figure 14-11. *The options in the Numbering dialog of the Production Wizard control how production numbers are formatted.*

- *Prefix*: Production numbers will contain the value entered in this field as a prefix. For example, if the value entered in this field is PROD and the "Starting number/width" value is 0001, the first production number corresponding to the first produced image will be PROD0001, the second production number corresponding to the second image will be PROD0002, and so on. This value advances sequentially by one for each image processed. Using the previous values specified, a production set containing a thousand images will be assigned a production range from PROD0001 to PROD1000.

- *Starting number/width*: Production numbers are based on this value as a suffix. It should be a numeric value (the starting number) with leading zeros (the width). For example, say this value is 0001. Assuming the value specified in the Prefix field is PROD, the first image will be named PROD0001, the second image will be named PROD0002, and so on. The width setting is defined by the number of digits entered into this field. You should ensure that the width of production numbers should accommodate the total number of produced images. If the produced set consists of a 10,000 images, a value of 0001 doesn't provide for enough individual numbers to encompass all production numbers, and the 10,001st production number won't be properly named. You should use some care—if you're aware of future document productions that might exceed 100,000 images, you're advised to select the width of production numbers for *any* production in a database's lifecycle so that they're six characters long.

Note You can access the total number of images in a production from the File ➤ Print menu of Opticon. The "Page count" button on the Print dialog calculates the total number of images corresponding to the documents accessible from the last active query in Concordance.

- *Use production numbers as file names*: Selecting this option forces the names of produced images to be production numbers. The structure of file names follows those guidelines described earlier. The original image name is abandoned in favor of the production number. For example, say the "Prefix value" is PROD and the "Starting number/width" value is 0001. If the original file name of the first image to be produced is 00245.TIF, the exported image will be named PROD0001.TIF.

- *Use production numbers as new image keys*: Recall that when Opticon is synchronized with Concordance, an image key field contains data that informs Opticon of the value of the first page of a set of pages that define a document. Opticon accepts the value, and uses it to look up the full file path of the image referenced by the image key value.

During a document production, if you've elected to append or create an imagebase, or if you've elected to create a cross-reference file, this option will force Opticon to write production number data as image keys. In this production example, the BEGNUM field is the image key for the HIST_DOCS.DCB database. If the "Use production numbers as new image keys" option isn't selected, the production set will continue to use the values in the BEGNUM field as image keys. If the option is selected, the output imagebase or cross-reference file will make no reference to original image key values, but will instead write production number data to export files.

This concept is most easily conveyed by an example. Assume the production numbers are to be assigned to a document production, but the "Use production numbers as new image keys" option is enabled. If the format of production numbers is PX001, the exported Opticon log file might look like the following:

```
PX0001,,C:\CONCORDANCE\PRODUCTION\PX0001.TIF,Y,,,6
PX0002,,C:\CONCORDANCE\PRODUCTION\PX0002.TIF,Y,,,1
PX0003,,C:\CONCORDANCE\PRODUCTION\PX0003.TIF,Y,,,1
```

Note that PX001, PX002, and PX003 appear in the first column of the log file, the alias (image key) column.

If the option isn't enabled, the exported Opticon log file might look like the following:

```
0001,,C:\CONCORDANCE\PRODUCTION\PX0001.TIF,Y,,,6
0002,,C:\CONCORDANCE\PRODUCTION\PX0002.TIF,Y,,,1
0003,,C:\CONCORDANCE\PRODUCTION\PX0003.TIF,Y,,,1
```

Note that the alias column contains the original image key values used in the HIST_DOCS.DCB example database. However, exported TIFFs are named using the production number scheme: PX0001, PX0002, and PX0003.

The Numbering dialog has several more options:

- *Copy production numbers to Concordance*: Selecting this option unlocks the "Beginning field," "Ending field," and "APPEND/OVERWRITE data to field" options. These values are used to write production numbers back into Concordance, and assume that appropriate fields have been predefined to contain this information. You track document boundaries using original image key data in the HIST_DOCS.DCB database in the BEGNUM and ENDNUM fields. The fields PRODBEG and PRODEND serve the same purpose, but contain production number values.

- *Beginning field*: Production numbers corresponding to the first page of a document are written to this field.

- *Ending field*: Production numbers corresponding to the last page of a document are written to this field.

- *APPEND/OVERWRITE data to/in fields*: This option controls how Opticon writes production number data back into Concordance. If the "APPEND data to fields" option is selected, production number values will be tacked on to the end of existing data, on a new line. This is useful if some documents might be produced more than once, and multiple production numbers should be tracked. For this option to work effectively, the production number field in Concordance should have a PARAGRAPH data type, as PARAGRAPH fields can contain line breaks. If you select the "OVERWRITE data in fields" option, data in the production number field is erased and overwritten with production number values calculated during the production.

In this example, the following options have been selected:

- *Prefix*: PROD

- *Starting number/width*: 0001

- *Use production numbers as file names*: Enabled

- *Use production numbers as new image keys*: Enabled

- *Copy production numbers to Concordance*: Enabled

- *Beginning field*: PRODBEG

- *Ending field*: PRODEND

- Data will be overwritten in fields

Header & Footer Dialog

The next dialog, Header & Footer, controls how Opticon treats the header and footer of each image (see Figure 14-12). Selections from this dialog are copied directly onto images during the production and become a permanent artifact of the files.

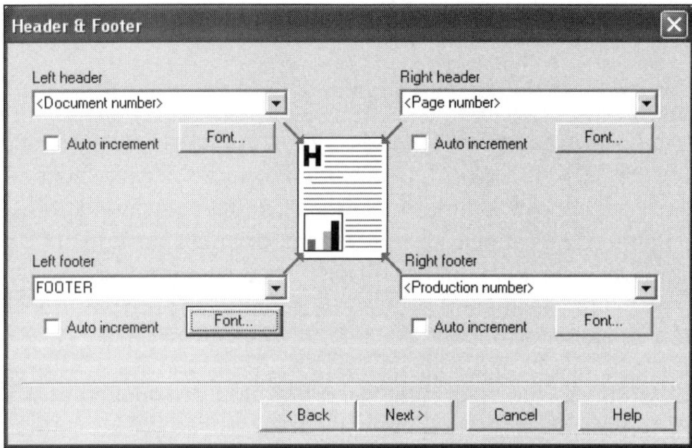

Figure 14-12. *The Header & Footer dialog of the Production Wizard*

This dialog is divided into four sections, corresponding to the left- and right-hand portions of an image's header and footer. Each section contains a drop-down box containing field names from the Concordance database that was active when Opticon was initially launched, and other selections that can calculate information on the fly as the production progresses. If you leave a drop-down box's selection blank, no data is stamped in that region on the image.

You can customize font styles using the Font buttons adjacent to each drop-down box. Clicking a Font button opens a Font dialog (see Figure 14-13). You can configure font face, style, size, and other options.

The list associated with each drop-down box contains two types of items: database field names and calculated values. Database field names appear in upper case, while calculated values are bracketed by angle brackets. Additionally, you can manually key data into these fields.

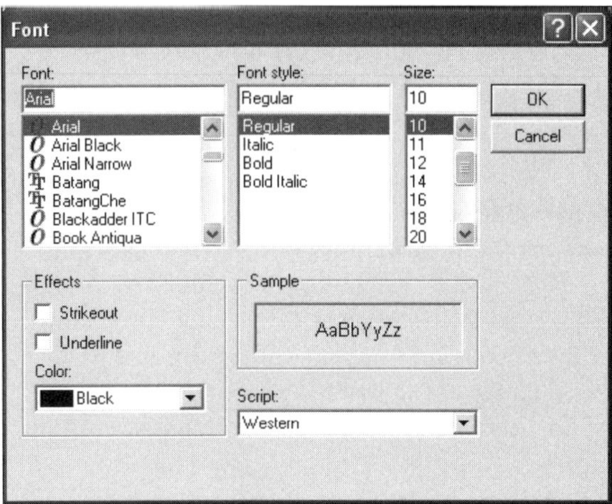

Figure 14-13. *The Font dialog of the Production Wizard*

Selecting a database field name causes data contained in that field to be stamped directly onto the produced image. Because Concordance synchronizes with Opticon, only data from the database record that corresponds to an image is written. In the HIST_DOCS.DCB database, the DOCDATE field contains the date that a document was created. For example, if you select the DOCDATE field from the top left drop-down box, produced images corresponding to the Declaration of Independence will have the value 07/04/1776 stamped on the upper left-hand corner. Images corresponding to the Emancipation Proclamation will be stamped with the value 01/01/1863.

The FOOTER field in the HIST_DOCS.DCB database was prepopulated with the same value for all records, IMPORTANT HISTORICAL DOCUMENT. In this example, this value will be stamped on the lower right-hand corner.

Unlike database fields, which stamp like data on groups of images corresponding to the same document, calculated values endorse images with data that's calculated at the moment that an individual image is produced. For the purposes of this example, the <Production Number> values created by Opticon, based on the formatting decisions selected in the Numbering dialog, will be stamped on the lower left-hand corner of the image. Table 14-2 offers a complete description of how each selection calculates data.

Table 14-2. *Calculated Value Options, Descriptions, and Examples*

Value Name	Description	Example
<Date & Time>	The date and time that an image is produced	05/09/2006 08:57 PM
<Date>	The date an image is produced	05/09/2006
<Document number>	The sequential number of the document being produced	Document 1 of 2
<Page number>	The page number of the image within a document	Page 1 of 6
<Production number>	Production number values defined from the Numbering dialog	PROD0001
<Time>	The time an image is produced	08:57 PM

Note You can configure the format of dates and times from the Dates tab on Opticon's Preferences dialog. You open this dialog from Opticon's Tools ➤ Preferences menu.

You can use the "Auto increment" check box adjacent to each drop-down box to create a sequential numbering system, in addition to any production numbering schema already defined from the Numbering screen in the dialog. If you manually key the value EXPORT0001 into a field, and the "Auto increment" check box is enabled, the images will have the values stamped on them in the form of EXPORT0001, EXPORT0002, and so on. For the purposes of this example, production number values are used in lieu of any auto-incrementing value.

In this example, the default font settings are used, and the following options are chosen:

- *Upper left*: <Document number>

- *Upper right*: <Page number>

- *Lower left*: FOOTER

- *Lower right*: <Production number>

Options Dialog

The next dialog of the wizard, Options, serves two purposes: to define the output image format, and to create an optional error log (see Figure 14-14).

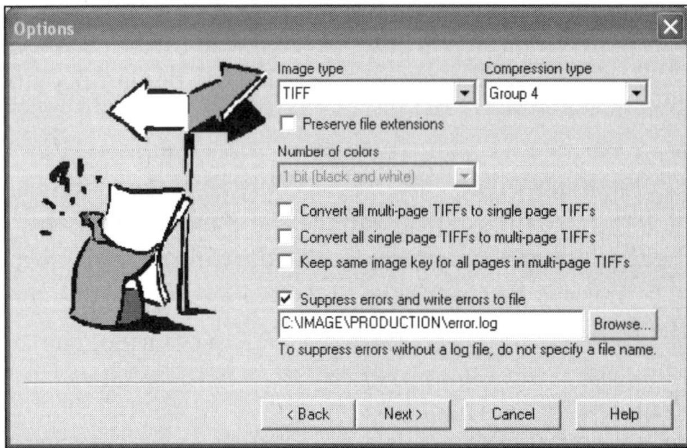

Figure 14-14. *The Options dialog of the Production Wizard*

- *Image type*: This option controls the output image format. Chapter 11 discusses these and other image formats in detail. Supported file types are TIFF, PCX, CALS, and JPEG.

- *Compression type*: Compression types are predefined for the PCX, CALS, and JPEG image formats. However, the TIFF output format has several possible values. The default setting is Group 4, and is suitable for most purposes. Table 14-3 lists supported export image formats and compression types.

- *Preserve file extensions*: This option forces Opticon to assign file extensions to produced images based on the original file extension.

- *Number of colors*: The number of colors that can be retained in exported images depends on the image format and selected compression. Table 14-3 lists supported export image formats and associated color options.

  In high volume environments, where a full-text information retrieval system might contain hundreds of thousands of documents and be linked to millions of images, monochrome images are usually preferred. The addition of color information in images can cause file sizes to expand, an accumulated effect that can strain network resources.

Table 14-3. *Supported Image Formats and Associated Compressions*

File Type	Compression Type	Number of Colors
TIFF	None	Monochrome, 16, 256, True color
	Group 3	Monochrome
	Group 3 2D	Monochrome
	Group 3 TIFF	Monochrome
	Group 4	Monochrome
	Pack Bits	Monochrome, 16, 256, True color
PCX	PCX	Monochrome, 16, 256
CALS	Group 4	Monochrome
JPEG	JPEG	True color

Note The term *monochrome* refers to black and white images (two colors). The term *true color* refers to 16,777,126 possible colors. Most video adapters used in modern workstations are capable of displaying true color images.

Other options in the Options dialog are as follows:

- *Convert all multi-page TIFFS to single page TIFFs*: If original images are multi-page TIFFs, produced images are converted to single-page TIFFs as they are exported. This option is exclusive of the option "Convert all single page TIFFs to multi-page TIFFs."

Note If you don't know if original images are single-page, multi-page, or some combination of the two file types, selecting this option will ensure that all images are exported as single-page TIFFs, thus creating a uniform export format.

- *Convert all single page TIFFs to multi-page TIFFs*: If original images are single-page TIFFs, produced images are converted to multi-page TIFFs as they are exported. This option is exclusive of the option "Convert all multi-page TIFFs to single page TIFFs."

- *Keep same image key for all pages in multi-page TIFFs*: If a document production involves the export of images as multi-page TIFFs, there's a one-to-one correspondence between database records and TIFF images. If the production involves the creation of production numbers, and if those production numbers are to be endorsed in the header or footer of each image, every image will display a unique production value. If you select this option, Opticon will stamp the beginning production number key value onto every image. If you don't select the option, each production number created for each image will be endorsed.

- *Suppress errors and write errors to file*: If Opticon attempts to produce an image for which there is no original file, an error occurs. Processing halts, and you must provide feedback to the program before it can continue. For a large document production, this can be tedious. Selecting this option causes Opticon to record any errors in an ASCII file that can be opened with a text editor, post-production. You can analyze the file and then repair any fault conditions that spawned errors.

  Concordance creates the error log when processing begins. You can manually key the file path and log name into the open text field, or use the Browse button to navigate to the desired folder. If the check box is enabled, but no file name is provided, Opticon will suppress errors and continue processing. Errors won't be logged. In this example, the following options have been selected:

  - *Image type*: TIFF

  - *Compression type*: Group 4

  - *Suppress errors and write errors to file*: Enabled

  - *Error log path and file name*: C:\IMAGE\PRODUCTION\error.log

Redlines Dialog

The next dialog, Redlines, gives you control over how redlines are handled (see Figure 14-15). *Redlines* is a term that refers to any annotations that have been overlaid onto images by end users with drawing tools in Opticon. Metadata about these annotations is stored in a database's -redlines.dcb file, as outlined in the section "Redlines." The dialog displays a matrix of annotations with check boxes, which you can enable according to which types of redlines should be part of the production. The "Select all" button selects all options; the "Clear all" button clears all options.

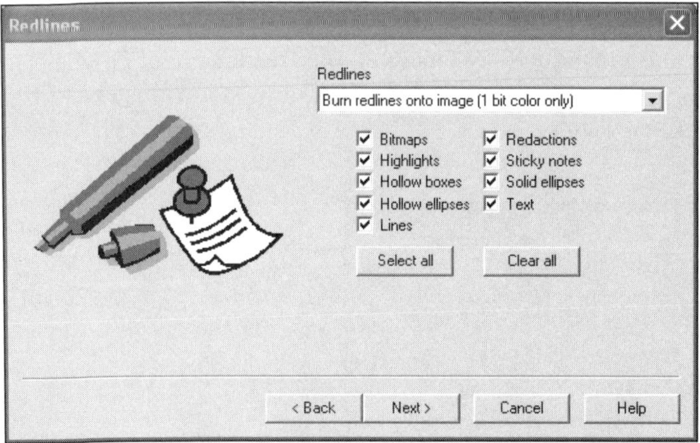

Figure 14-15. *The Redlines dialog of the Production Wizard*

The Redlines drop-down box has three options:

- *No redlines*: Redlines are ignored. Produced images aren't altered from the originals, save for any header and footer endorsements specified from the Header & Footer dialog.

- *Copy redlines to .RED file*: This option copies metadata about redlines to a separate file. Produced images aren't altered from the originals, save for any header and footer endorsements specified from the Header & Footer dialog. This option is only meaningful when you select an imagebase from the Imagebase dialog. Recall that during a production, you can update an existing imagebase with production data or create a new imagebase entirely. When you select the "Copy redlines to .RED file" option, Opticon will create (or update) a series of supporting files that describe the structure and placement of redlines. These files combine to create a valid Concordance database, though the .DCB file name will be the name of the imagebase with a -redlines.dcb extension. For example, say you elect to create a new imagebase named PROD. The -redlines.dcb file created by the production will be named PROD-REDLINES.DCB. Support files will carry the same PROD-REDLINES name, but will have different file extensions.

- *Burn redlines onto image*: This option only works if the file type and compression types selected from the Options dialog support a monochrome color scheme. Redlines are stamped directly onto produced images and become a permanent artifact of the files. No metadata files, such as those described earlier, are created.

In this example, all redline types have been selected, and the Redlines option is "Burn redlines onto image."

Produce Dialog

The final dialog of the wizard is labeled Produce (see Figure 14-16). The document range is displayed, as well as the file paths of the source imagebase and the destination imagebase, if one was selected from the Imagebase dialog.

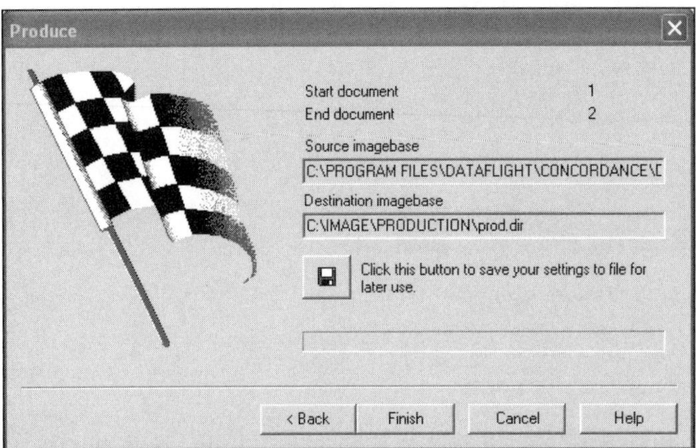

Figure 14-16. *The Produce dialog of the Production Wizard*

You can save the options set in all the dialogs of the wizard by clicking the Save button. Clicking this button opens a "Save as" dialog. You can navigate to the folder in which the production profile should be saved, then name it accordingly. The production profile is saved in a separate file and has a .PSF file extension. As a matter of practice, you should save a document production's profile, in case the production must be repeated at a later date.

Production Output

Given the options that have been selected for this example, the production exported images and saved them in a subfolder named IMAGES001. If there had been more than 500 images in the production, images 501 through 1,000 would have been saved in a folder named IMAGES002.

This production comprised nine individual TIFFs that define two database records. The produced images are named PROD0001.TIF through PROD0009.TIF. The first six images correspond to the Declaration of Independence database record, while the last three images correspond to the Emancipation Proclamation. Figure 14-17 shows the folder structure and files as created by the production.

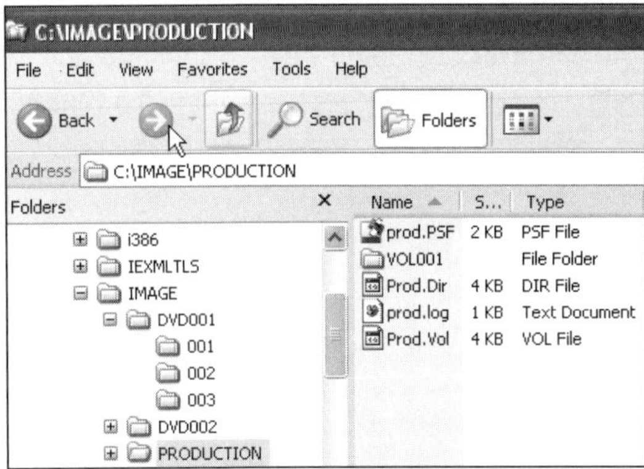

Figure 14-17. *Folder structure and images created by the example production*

Using the Production Wizard, options were selected from the Header & Footer dialog to stamp document numbers (*Document n of m*), page numbers (*Page n of m*), production numbers (PROD0001, PROD0002, and so on), and a statement (IMPORTANT HISTORICAL DOCUMENT) onto images. Other options from the Redlines dialog were selected to burn redlines directly onto images. As the production progressed, Opticon calculated this data or retrieved it from Concordance accordingly, and permanently wrote this data onto each image. The first image exported by the production, PROD0001.TIF, is displayed in Figure 14-18, and is compared with the original image.

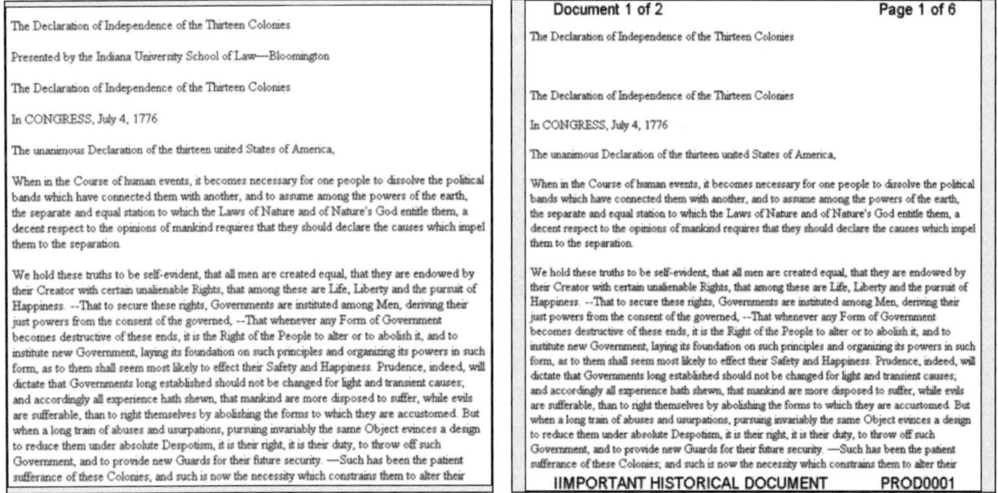

Figure 14-18. *A comparison of the original image and produced image corresponding to the first page of the first database record. The original image is on the left. The produced image is on the right.*

Opticon created a cross-reference file based on the options selected from the Imagebase dialog. This file is displayed in Figure 14-19. Note that use of the letter Y on the first and seventh lines, to denote the beginning of a new document. The first and seventh lines also contain the total number of pages per document: 6 and 3, respectively.

```
PROD0001,VOL001,C:\IMAGE\PRODUCTION\VOL001\IMAGES001\PROD0001.TIF,Y,,,6
PROD0002,VOL001,C:\IMAGE\PRODUCTION\VOL001\IMAGES001\PROD0002.TIF,,,,
PROD0003,VOL001,C:\IMAGE\PRODUCTION\VOL001\IMAGES001\PROD0003.TIF,,,,
PROD0004,VOL001,C:\IMAGE\PRODUCTION\VOL001\IMAGES001\PROD0004.TIF,,,,
PROD0005,VOL001,C:\IMAGE\PRODUCTION\VOL001\IMAGES001\PROD0005.TIF,,,,
PROD0006,VOL001,C:\IMAGE\PRODUCTION\VOL001\IMAGES001\PROD0006.TIF,,,,
PROD0007,VOL001,C:\IMAGE\PRODUCTION\VOL001\IMAGES001\PROD0007.TIF,Y,,,3
PROD0008,VOL001,C:\IMAGE\PRODUCTION\VOL001\IMAGES001\PROD0008.TIF,,,,
PROD0009,VOL001,C:\IMAGE\PRODUCTION\VOL001\IMAGES001\PROD0009.TIF,,,,
```

Figure 14-19. *The cross-reference file created by the example production*

In a valid cross-reference file, the characters on each row of data from the beginning of a line to the first comma represent an image's key, or *alias*. The option "Use production numbers as new image keys" was enabled on the Numbering dialog of the wizard. This caused the first eight characters of each line in the file Opticon.log to be the same as the production numbers created during processing. If this option had not been selected, the characters occupying this position in the file would be based on the BEGDOC values in the HIST_DOCS.DCB database. Rerunning the production using the exact same options, but with the "Use production numbers as new image keys" option disabled, would create the cross-reference file displayed in Figure 14-20.

```
0001,VOL001,C:\IMAGE\PRODUCTION\VOL001\IMAGES001\PROD0001.TIF,Y,,,6
0002,VOL001,C:\IMAGE\PRODUCTION\VOL001\IMAGES001\PROD0002.TIF,,,,
0003,VOL001,C:\IMAGE\PRODUCTION\VOL001\IMAGES001\PROD0003.TIF,,,,
0004,VOL001,C:\IMAGE\PRODUCTION\VOL001\IMAGES001\PROD0004.TIF,,,,
0005,VOL001,C:\IMAGE\PRODUCTION\VOL001\IMAGES001\PROD0005.TIF,,,,
0006,VOL001,C:\IMAGE\PRODUCTION\VOL001\IMAGES001\PROD0006.TIF,,,,
0007,VOL001,C:\IMAGE\PRODUCTION\VOL001\IMAGES001\PROD0007.TIF,Y,,,3
0008,VOL001,C:\IMAGE\PRODUCTION\VOL001\IMAGES001\PROD0008.TIF,,,,
0009,VOL001,C:\IMAGE\PRODUCTION\VOL001\IMAGES001\PROD0009.TIF,,,,
```

Figure 14-20. *A cross-reference file created by the example production, but with the "Use production numbers as new image keys" option not enabled*

In a valid cross-reference file, the characters on each row of data between the second and third commas represent the full file path and file name of the produced images. In this example, the option "Use production numbers as file names" was selected from the Numbering dialog. The result is that exported images were renamed according to the production numbering scheme specified in the Prefix and "Starting number/width" options on that same dialog. If this option hadn't been selected, original file names would be retained, and Figure 14-21 displays the cross-reference file that would have been created.

```
PROD0001,VOL001,C:\IMAGE\PRODUCTION\VOL001\IMAGES001\0001.TIF,Y,,,6
PROD0002,VOL001,C:\IMAGE\PRODUCTION\VOL001\IMAGES001\0002.TIF,,,,
PROD0003,VOL001,C:\IMAGE\PRODUCTION\VOL001\IMAGES001\0003.TIF,,,,
PROD0004,VOL001,C:\IMAGE\PRODUCTION\VOL001\IMAGES001\0004.TIF,,,,
PROD0005,VOL001,C:\IMAGE\PRODUCTION\VOL001\IMAGES001\0005.TIF,,,,
PROD0006,VOL001,C:\IMAGE\PRODUCTION\VOL001\IMAGES001\0006.TIF,,,,
PROD0007,VOL001,C:\IMAGE\PRODUCTION\VOL001\IMAGES001\0007.TIF,Y,,,3
PROD0008,VOL001,C:\IMAGE\PRODUCTION\VOL001\IMAGES001\0008.TIF,,,,
PROD0009,VOL001,C:\IMAGE\PRODUCTION\VOL001\IMAGES001\0009.TIF,,,,
```

Figure 14-21. *A cross-reference file created by the example production, but with the "Use production numbers as file names" option not enabled*

Final Steps

Data created in the example outlined in this chapter represents a fully qualified and valid production set. Image data and file path metadata represented by a cross-reference file might be all that's needed for a particular project. However, you can take additional post-production steps to refine production data.

Modifying Relative File Paths

If production data is to be transferred to an outside agency, the file structure of that agency's network might not be known. File paths created in the cross-reference file won't be valid unless the recipient of the production copies images to an identical location on his or her own workstation. In the example outlined in this chapter, the file stem of the export path is C:\Program Files\Dataflight\Concordance\Database\OPTICON\IMAGE\ PRODUCTION\. Any subfoldering under this parent folder was created by Opticon during the production itself. The recipient most likely won't modify the subfoldering, and it can be considered to be absolute. Though it's not a requirement, you might wish to remove any relative file stem from the cross-reference file using a text editor and a global find and replace function. In this example, a blank argument would replace all references to C:\Program Files\Dataflight\Concordance\Database\OPTICON\IMAGE\PRODUCTION\. Figure 14-22 displays the updated cross-reference file.

```
PROD0001,VOL001,\VOL001\IMAGES001\0001.TIF,Y,,,6
PROD0002,VOL001,\VOL001\IMAGES001\0002.TIF,,,,
PROD0003,VOL001,\VOL001\IMAGES001\0003.TIF,,,,
PROD0004,VOL001,\VOL001\IMAGES001\0004.TIF,,,,
PROD0005,VOL001,\VOL001\IMAGES001\0005.TIF,,,,
PROD0006,VOL001,\VOL001\IMAGES001\0006.TIF,,,,
PROD0007,VOL001,\VOL001\IMAGES001\0007.TIF,Y,,,1
```

Figure 14-22. *A cross-reference file with relative file paths removed*

Exporting Concordance Data

Images produced from Opticon are often used to complement a Concordance database that represents documents corresponding to the production. If production numbers are used as image keys, the original Concordance database used to spawn the production won't synchronize with production images. In the HIST_DOCS.DCB database, the field BEGDOC is used as the image key, and is used to synchronize with Opticon to open the preproduction images. To have this database synchronize with post-production images where the production numbers are used as image keys, you could modify the original database and set the PRODBEG field to be the image key. However, this causes database records that weren't part of the production set (and that don't have a production number) to cease synchronizing with their original, unproduced images.

The solution is to export data corresponding to produced records from the original Concordance database to a new database. The PRODBEG field in a new production database is then set to be the image key. This practice serves to keep distinctions between produced and unproduced document records clear. The original database is known to contain the entire document universe and is linked to preproduced, unmarked images. The production database, a subset of the document universe, is known to contain only those records that have been transmitted to an outside agency, and is linked to post-production images on which redactions, production numbers, and footer statements have been permanently endorsed.

Summary

This chapter has detailed an important administrative function: document productions. Document productions are often a standard part of an administrator's workflow when annotated images are to be provided to an outside agency. A document production is, in essence, an export of images. During a production, you can elect to create a new numbering scheme, to copy (burn) redlines directly onto images, and to create an ASCII file containing metadata about the production or to update an existing imagebase. Post-production, many administrators will create an entirely new Concordance database consisting only of produced documents, to easily manage those documents that have been reviewed (the original document universe) and a subset of documents that have been exported (the production).

Glossary

Accession field

A field attribute. When applied to a field that has a NUMERIC data type, this field will advance by one with each new record that's appended to a database.

Active Workspace

When no view (Browse, Table, or Edit) is selected, Concordance defaults to a screen that displays the name of the currently active database, and a history of previously opened databases (if this option has been configured).

Annotation

A term that collectively refers to notes, issues, or attachments associated with a section of text in Browse view.

Anti-alias

Altering the grayscale hue of pixels along borders and edges in an image so that borders and edges in the image appear smooth.

ASCII

A standard for mapping characters on a keyboard, and some nonprintable characters, to numbers. ASCII stands for the American Standard Code for Information Interchange.

Attachment

An external file linked to a section of text in Browse view.

Authority list

A means of restricting values in a field. An authority list is a set of presaved values that's associated with a given field. When users enter data in this field, they can choose one of the values.

Beginning control number

The value assigned to the first page of a document. When an optional image viewer is used, such as Opticon, this number can guide the viewer to the correct graphical images corresponding to the database record.

Boolean operator

You can use Boolean operators such as AND, NOT, and OR to include or exclude documents by comparing them against conditions. APPLES OR ORANGES locates documents that contain either the term APPLES or the term ORANGES.

Box break

A phrase used to describe the boundaries defined by a box, a common way of storing folders of documents. In an ASCII Opticon log file, the letter Y in the *box break* position means that the image file corresponds to the first page in a box.

Browse view

A screen in Concordance that's used to view the contents of a single database record.

Clear text

Data that isn't encrypted or compiled, and that can be interpreted by a human. Also, plain text.

Coded data

Fields that pertain to document records that might or might not be contained in full text, but that have been placed in unique fields to streamline the organization (and eventual retrieval) of document data. Sometimes referred to as *fielded data.*

Coded field

A field that results from the intervention of a human during scanning, in which metadata about a document is manually keyed into a load file.

Coding

The act of recording information about a document that cannot be extracted through an automated process.

Command line interface

A text-based interface that accepts user input and displays output.

Compression

A computer algorithm that's applied to a computer file to reduce its overall size.

Concatenation

A method of combining several databases so that they appear as a single virtual database.

Concordance Programming Language (CPL)

A programming language associated with Concordance, which can be used to open, query, and modify databases. CPLs can also launch external programs.

Context operator

Context operators SAME and NOTSAME and search limiters locate documents that include or exclude combinations of keywords.

Creation date

A field attribute. When applied to a field that has a DATE data type, this field will contain the date on which a database record was appended to a database.

Data typing

A characteristic of a field that describes the type of data to be contained in the field. In Concordance, there are four data types: TEXT, NUMERIC, DATE, and PARAGRAPH.

Database

An organized body of related information.

Database management system (DBMS)

Software used to formally structure a collection of related data.

Deduplication

The act of identifying electronic files that, given predetermined parameters, contain identical data.

Delimited file

A digital file that has a *text qualifier*, a *delimiter*, and a *line separator* to structure data uniformly.

Delimiter

Used to clearly designate the distinction between data elements.

Deposition

The memorialized minutes of an interview between a member of the legal profession and a litigant or witness.

Dictionary cache

RAM allocated for the management of list files, security files, and other Concordance-specific features.

Dictionary file

A file created when a database is indexed, which facilitates searches. A database's dictionary file contains entries that record the existence of words in fields that have a PARAGRAPH data type, or fields for which the indexed attribute has been set to True.

Dockable

Toolbars in Opticon can be detached from the border in Opticon to which they are fixed, and moved to another border. They can also float freely outside the program. Toolbars that can be moved in this way are said to be dockable.

Document

In Concordance, a document record is a record associated with a logical combination of pages. With paper, this term refers to collections of pages. With electronic files, this term refers to a digital file.

Document boundary

The distinction that separates the end of one document, and the beginning of another.

Document break

A phrase used to describe the boundaries defined by a document, or collection of pages. In an ASCII Opticon log file, the letter Y in the *document break* position means that the image file corresponds to the first page of a document.

Document control number

A value assigned to each page in a series of documents.

Document-level tag

A marker applied to a database record.

Dots per inch (dpi)

The number of picture elements (or pixels) that fit in a square inch of an image. The higher the density of dots per square inch, the more detailed an image appears to the human eye.

Edit date

A field attribute. When applied to a field that has a PARAGRAPH data type, this field will update each time a database record is edited. The information recorded is the date of the edit, the name of the user who made the edit, and an alphanumeric string of characters to identify the edit. New edits are appended to the file on new lines. When the field assigned as an edit date field has a TEXT data type, only the most recent edit is memorialized.

Edit view

A screen in Concordance that's used to edit the contents of a single database record.

Electronic data discovery (EDD)

The process of collecting electronic files.

E-mail client

A program used to send and receive e-mail messages.

E-mail server

A dedicated server that's used to store and route e-mail messages.

Ending control number

The value assigned to the last page of a document.

Entry function

The main function that's first processed when a CPL program is activated.

Exploded sort report

A report that structures and sorts data in fields that contain multiple values, separated by a delimiter.

Extended ASCII

One of several possible variants that extends the 128 characters codified by basic ASCII.

Field

The smallest unit of data in a Concordance database.

Fielded data

Fields that pertain to document records that might or might not be contained in full text, but that have been placed in unique fields to streamline the organization (and eventual retrieval) of document data. Sometimes referred to as *coded data*.

File extension

A two- to four-character designation that's appended to the file name. File extensions serve to identify the type of a computer file.

File Transfer Protocol (FTP)

A way for a user to connect to a server, via the Internet, for the purpose of uploading or downloading files.

Folder break

A phrase used to describe the boundaries defined by a folder, a common way of storing documents. In an ASCII Opticon log file, the letter Y in the *folder break* position means that the image file corresponds to the first page in a folder.

Full-text data

Full text refers to the words, sentences, and paragraphs contained on the pages of documents.

Full-text information retrieval system

Software used to manage and retrieve document records that contain large amounts of text.

Function

A series of CPL program lines that work together to perform calculations, modify data in a database, or initiate some programmatic action.

Fuzzy terms

Concordance maintains a list of words that are similar in spelling to words contained in a database's dictionary file. This list is unique to each database and is built during indexing.

Hash value

A unique alphanumeric value that's assigned to an electronic file.

Heavy litigation

Documents that are relatively difficult to organize and convert into a digital format, which can be loaded into a full-text information retrieval system.

Hit

Keyword(s) located in document records. Hits are highlighted in red (by default) in Concordance's Browse view.

Image format

The specific way in which image data is organized in a file. For many Concordance applications, the Tagged Image File Format (TIFF) is a common method of storing image data.

Image key

A field attribute. If Concordance is associated with an optional image viewer, a field designated as an image key will link with the viewer, providing lookup information about where an associated image is located.

Image viewer

A tool used to view images associated with a document record.

Imagebase

Just as a collection of Concordance files defines a database, the .DIR and .VOL files combine to form an imagebase, or a set of data that describes the locations and names of image files.

Inbox

A virtual repository for the storage of a user's incoming and outgoing e-mail messages and associated attachments.

Index

When used as a verb ("to index a database"), this term refers to the process in which Concordance builds files that integrate with the program and that facilitate searches. When used as a noun ("the database's index"), this term refers to the files that are created. It's also a field attribute. Fields that are designated as indexed fields have their contents scanned and added to the files that Concordance creates to facilitate searches.

Indexing cache

RAM allocated by Concordance and used during indexing.

Indexing

A procedure in which Concordance creates supporting files that contain information about the existence and placement of words in a database. Two important files that are created during indexing are the dictionary and inverted text files. Indexing is a prerequisite to accurate full-text searches.

Inverted text file

A file created when a database is indexed that facilitates searches. A database's inverted text file contains entries that record the placement of words in fields that have a PARAGRAPH data type, or fields for which the indexed attribute has been set to True.

Issue

A tag that's used to categorize a section of text within a document.

Key

A field attribute. Key fields have their contents scanned and added to special key files that integrate with Concordance and that facilitate searches on the field.

Keywords in Context (KWIC)

A way to make otherwise lengthy reports more manageable and concise by displaying just those sections of indexed fields that contain selected keywords.

Light litigation

Documents that are relatively easy to organize and convert into a digital format, which can be loaded into a full-text information retrieval system.

Line separator

Used in delimited files, a character that denotes the end of a row of data.

Log file

An ASCII-delimited file that describes the locations and names of image files. A log file can be used to load an imagebase.

Lossless

A form of compression in which no information about a file is lost.

Lossless compression

A method of digitizing images that creates an exact rendition of the original object.

Lossy

A form of compression in which information about a file is lost. Ideally, information that's lost isn't essential to the overall quality of the file.

Lossy compression

A method of digitizing images that creates an accurate rendition of the original object, but that loses some detail so that the result is not exact.

Mapped drive

A drive letter used as a shortcut by an operating system to refer to a network server, or a shared folder on a network server.

Marginalia

Handwritten notes, usually written in the margins of a document.

Masking

The use of a wildcard to locate patterns of keywords.

MD5

An abbreviation for Message Digest 5, an algorithm used to assign alphanumeric values to electronic files.

Metadata

Properties associated with a document that might or might not be contained within the body of the document.

Multi-page TIFF

A specific type of Tagged Image File Format (TIFF) image file in which many pages are combined into a single file.

Native application

The software used to activate, run, or otherwise view a digital file.

Native format

A computer file that exists in the form in which it was created, prior to any conversion.

Non-persistent tag

A tag that's deleted unless it's applied to at least one database record, or at least one section of text in Browse view.

Note

Subjective comments created by a user and assigned to a selection of text within a document.

Operator

A reserved word or symbol that Concordance interprets to be part of search query syntax.

Optical Character Recognition (OCR)

An electronic process where the text in paper documents or digital files is extracted and prepared for eventual loading into a full-text information retrieval system.

Pack

The act of removing records from a database that have been marked for deletion. Packing a dictionary file removes references to textual units identified by indexing or reindexing that are no longer in a database.

Persistent tag

A tag that exists between sessions, even if it hasn't been applied to any database record, or any section of text in Browse view.

Pixel

Picture element. Used in conjunction with raster images, in which visual details are distilled into a matrix of dots (pixels).Visually, a pixel is the smallest building block of an image.

Plain text

Data that isn't encrypted or compiled, and that can be interpreted by a human. Also, clear text.

Proximity operator

The proximity operators `ADJ` and `NEAR` are used to locate words within a specified distance from each other. These operators can use optional numerical arguments. The search `APPLES ADJ5 ORANGES` locates documents where `ORANGES` appears within five words after the word `APPLES`.

Q&A pair

Used in a transcript or deposition, a coupling of a question posed to an individual, and his or her reply.

Query 00000 (query zero)

An alias for all records in a database.

Random Access Memory (RAM)

A type of computer storage.

Raster graphics

Digital representations of images in which visual details are distilled into a matrix of dots.

Read-only attribute

One of a series of individual file characteristics. An end user can't modify a file for which the read-only attribute is set to TRUE. Files copied from fixed media such as CDs or DVDs to a workstation or network location will have their read-only attribute automatically set to TRUE.

Records

Individual objects in a full-text information retrieval system. Usually, these objects represent documents.

Redaction

A blocked section of text intended to prevent others from viewing sensitive information in a document.

Redlines

Subjective text, notes, or symbols placed on a graphical image by an end user, which represent subjective information about the image.

Reindexing

A procedure that's functionally similar to indexing. Reindexing updates the files created during a database's initial indexing, and is required when data changes in a database through user input, or when database records are imported or updated.

Relational operator

Relational operators, such as less than (LT) and greater than (GT), can be used to test data against specific values.

Render

The process of interpreting formatting tags so that the font style, font face, and font weight of text displays as intended.

Replication

A method of comparing changes in two otherwise similar databases to create a single database that reflects the latest modifications in both dependent databases.

Rich text

A way of formatting the font style, font face, and font weight of text.

Scanning

An automated process that converts paper or electronic documents into a Concordance-ready format.

Search limiter

Search limiters are used to include or exclude field names, and are considered to be context operators. The use of a single period includes a field: `memo.DOCTYPE.` locates records where the `DOCTYPE` field includes the value `memo`. The use of two periods excludes a field: `(apples)..FRUIT.` locates all documents that contain `apples` in any field other than the field `FRUIT`.

Single-page TIFF

A specific type of Tagged Image File Format (TIFF) image file in which many individual pages are separated into individual files. For example, a 40-page document could be represented as 40 individual TIFF files.

Snapshot

A snapshot is used to retain the results of one or more searches, and is a static picture of a database.

Specification sheet

Also known as a spec sheet. A document that outlines the basic design of a database, and can be used to instruct a vendor as to the structure and format of expected deliverables.

Stop word

Words that are so common that they are of no use in the intent of a search. Examples of stop words that are included by default by Concordance in a new database are the words `and`, `for`, and `the`.

Switch

An argument used when issuing a command line directive. Switches modify the behavior of a command.

Table view

A screen in Concordance that's used to view several database records.

Tag

A marker in Concordance that can be used to categorize a document or a section of text within a document (*Issues*).

Tally

A method of counting the number of unique values that appear in a field across all records in a query.

Template

A preformed database shell that can be used to build a database quickly. Templates contain no records, but have predefined field names, field types, and other field attributes.

Text qualifier

Used in delimited files, a character that's used to bracket an element of data.

Transcript

The memorialized minutes of a legal proceeding.

Universal Naming Convention (UNC)

A UNC path explicitly refers to the server and directory on which a file resides. It follows the form \\SERVER_NAME\FOLDER_NAME.

Vector graphics

A method of displaying image data such that visual details are translated into simple geometric shapes, such as lines, points, and curves. A vector file contains data about the shapes that combine to produce a visual approximation of the source object.

Vendor

A third-party corporate entity that specializes in processing and converting paper and electronic documents into a Concordance-ready format.

Volume

A term sometimes used to identify the media from which a set of records was loaded. When this information is populated in an appropriate field, this data can assist you in locating the source of a set of database records.

Wildcard

One of two characters used in pattern matching. The ? character is used to match single characters. The search WOM?N locates WOMEN and WOMAN. The * character is used to match two or more characters. The search STA* locates any word where the first three letters are STA.

Windows dialog

An interactive screen that requests information from a user.

Zap

An action that deletes all records from a database.

Index

S

FIND IT FAST
with the Apress *SuperIndex*™

Quickly Find Out What the Experts Know

Leading by innovation, Apress now offers you its *SuperIndex*™, a turbocharged companion to the fine index in this book. The Apress *SuperIndex*™ is a keyword and phrase-enabled search tool that lets you search through the entire Apress library. Powered by dtSearch™, it delivers results instantly.

Instead of paging through a book or a PDF, you can electronically access the topic of your choice from a vast array of Apress titles. The Apress *SuperIndex*™ is the perfect tool to find critical snippets of code or an obscure reference. The Apress *SuperIndex*™ enables all users to harness essential information and data from the best minds in technology.

No registration is required, and the Apress *SuperIndex*™ is free to use.

1. Thorough and comprehensive searches of over 300 titles

2. No registration required

3. Instantaneous results

4. A single destination to find what you need

5. Engineered for speed and accuracy

6. Will spare your time, application, and anxiety level

Search now: ***http://superindex.apress.com***

You Need the Companion eBook